The Future of Sociology

Edited by
Edgar F. Borgatta
& Karen S. Cook

Published in cooperation with the
Pacific Sociological Association

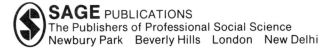
SAGE PUBLICATIONS
The Publishers of Professional Social Science
Newbury Park   Beverly Hills   London   New Delhi

For information address:

SAGE Publications, Inc.
2111 West Hillcrest Drive
Newbury Park, California 91320

SAGE Publications Inc.
275 South Beverly Drive
Beverly Hills
California 90212

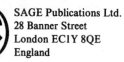

SAGE Publications Ltd.
28 Banner Street
London EC1Y 8QE
England

SAGE PUBLICATIONS India Pvt. Ltd.
M-32 Market
Greater Kailash I
New Delhi 110 048 India

Printed in the United States of America

Library of Congress Cataloging-in-Publication Data

Main entry under title:

The Future of sociology / [edited by] Edgar F. Borgatta, Karen S.
   Cook.
      p.   cm.
   Bibliography: p.
   ISBN 0-8039-3024-0
      1. Sociology—Congresses. 2. Sociology—United States—
Congresses. I. Borgatta, Edgar F., 1924- . II. Cook, Karen S.
HM13.F88 1988
301—dc19   88-10898
                                                           CIP

FIRST PRINTING

The
Future
of
Sociology

Contents

Preface   7

PART I: THE FIELD OF SOCIOLOGY   9

1. Sociology and Its Future
   Edgar F. Borgatta and Karen S. Cook   11
2. Sociological Theory
   Herman Turk   18
3. Research Methodology in Sociology
   Herbert L. Costner   42
4. How Applied Sociology Can Save Basic Sociology
   Richard A. Berk   57

PART II: INSTITUTIONAL AREAS IN SOCIOLOGY   73

5. Medical Sociology
   Howard E. Freeman   76
6. Sociology of Education
   Leonard Gordon   86
7. Family Sociology
   Rhonda J.V. Montgomery   105
8. Sociology of Religion
   Anson Shupe and Jeffrey K. Hadden   120
9. Organizational Sociology
   Lee Clarke   138
10. Political Sociology
    Paul Burstein   160

PART III: APPROACHES TO SOCIAL PHENOMENA   179

11. History in Sociology
    Gary G. Hamilton and John Walton   181
12. Urban Sociology
    Barrett A. Lee   200
13. Demography
    Thomas W. Pullum   224
14. Social Psychology: Models of Action,
    Reaction, and Interaction
    Karen S. Cook and Kenneth C. Pike   236

**PART IV: SOCIAL CONTROL, COMMUNICATION,
AND CHANGE** **255**

15. Deviance and Social Control:
Revisiting Our Intellectual Heritage
Lois B. DeFleur and Robert F. Meier 257
16. Sociology of Law
H. Laurence Ross and Lee E. Teitelbaum 274
17. Criminology
Kyle Kercher 294
18. Media Systems and Mass Communication
S. J. Ball-Rokeach 317
19. Social Change
Wilbert E. Moore 333

PART V: SOCIAL STRATIFICATION **345**

20. Social Stratification
Edgar F. Borgatta and Laurie Russell Hatch 347
21. Sociology of Race Relations
in the United States
Edna Bonacich 355
22. Sociology of Gender
Margaret Mooney Marini 374
23. Age, Aging, and the Aged:
The Three Sociologies
Judith Treas and Patricia M. Passuth 394

About the Authors 418

Preface

Any book with a title like *The Future of Sociology* has to be more ambitious than what can actually be delivered. Still, if we do not aspire, we also do not achieve. The origin of this book is associated with the design of the 1985 program for the Pacific Sociological Association annual meetings, which had the theme: The Future of Sociology. It was clear that if effort was to be put into sessions so designed, we could assemble an array of scholars representing different subspecialties and different experiences and persuasions to give special thought to where the discipline is likely to go, and where they felt it should go, and to write these thoughts down so that we could prepare a volume on this theme.

We were gratified to get the cooperation of many of our colleagues who would participate in the meetings, but we invited participants more broadly than the region. We proposed some standardization for the essays, with a brief review of the origins or history of the subspecialty, a nod to some of the notable scholarly work, and then a presentation by the author of what could be anticipated in the future.

As can be imagined, interpretations of the task were quite different, but we were extremely fortunate. Virtually all who promised to participate did so and delivered papers, but then we had to deal with the common problems of editors. There were many delays, and predictably, many of the essays were too long. We owe a special thanks to the authors for their patience in the delays of publication but also for their good-spirited cooperation in shortening papers. In general, this proved a virtue for the book, as authors became careful to retain the most essential parts of their essays, and the essays were sharpened as they were shortened. We hope this will be appreciated by the readers.

Although we have a broad coverage, the book does not cover all of the field of sociology. We do hope, however, that for the reader there will be a sense of breadth and the communication that there are many points of view represented in sociology. We have in no way attempted to edit the content of the authors.

PART I

THE FIELD OF SOCIOLOGY

The first part of this volume includes basic essays for the field of sociology. In the first chapter, the editors remind the readers of some global trends and suggest in a broad sense where the field may be going. The themes in the first chapter will be encountered several times in the book, but the broad coverage of the book also provides other views of the history of sociology and other prospects anticipated for the future. Borgatta and Cook note that sociology may have been bypassed in some aspects, particularly in the development of research and theory in areas that are viewed as applied. Other professions have grown or developed to fill gaps that could have been opportunities for sociologists. Opportunities obviously still remain, and some, such a positive thrust in the application of sociological knowledge may flourish in the future.

According to Turk's analysis of journal publications, sociological theory as a special interest in sociology has declined. He examines why this has occurred in terms of competing interests, and then suggests particular activities of theorists who are likely to influence sociology. Turk does not anticipate further polarization "between philosophy, speculation, and criticism, on the one hand, and quantitative empiricism on the other."

Costner sees John Stuart Mill as setting an agenda in the middle of the nineteenth century for research methodology that has been that of sociology in large part. He gives particular attention to the problem of nonadditive effects and that of designing variables. The complexity of interpretation of data, and indeed of appropriate examination of data, is illustrated in several examples. Costner sees the future of methodology optimistically, but not without problems that are both technical and a matter of how sociologists address their research.

Berk's point of departure in considering the place of applied sociology in the discipline is based on the types of challenges and criticisms that have been directed to the profession, even by those who have been constructive supporters of sociology. Forecasting is introduced through an example, and then forecasting models are considered in the context of how values are involved in the process. The avenue of applied social research is seen as less than easy, but necessary for the progress of sociology.

Readers will find that although they do not overlap directly, the papers in this section touch each other in many ways. This will be seen many times in the coverage in this and the other parts of the volume, and if sociology has coherence this should happen when scholars independently make assessments of the current status and future prospects of the discipline.

1

SOCIOLOGY AND ITS FUTURE

Edgar F. Borgatta
Karen S. Cook
University of Washington

Sociology as a recognized discipline has existed for at least a century, and as it has developed it has progressed through a number of stages. In the early writings of scholars such as Auguste Comte, Herbert Spencer, and Emile Durkheim there were insights and considerations that still attract attention. The early scholars examined social phenomena with a motivation to establish a science, and they accomplished the objective reasonably. Positivism was prominent in the formative period, as was a self-conscious concern for some of the values associated with science, particularly a call for objectivity.

Except possibly for studies that depended largely on enumeration and registration data, however, sociology tended to be dependent on informal observation. The development of more systematic observation and data collection in sociological research, with minor exceptions, does not begin until much later in the history of the discipline. Field studies of varying degrees of inclusiveness occur in the beginning of this century, but the empirical thrusts of the science do not really occur until the 1920s. In fair part, the expansion of sociology in this century is associated with the growth in numbers of departments of sociology and of rural sociology and, correspondingly, of doctorates in sociology in the United States. The current (modern) period of sociology is probably reasonably associated with the 1930s, and with such developments as the support of community research by the Works Progress Administration (WPA) during the depression years. In addition, during this period the development of systematic field studies was beginning, including the commercial versions of polling.

The social sciences generally began a flourishing period in the 1930s, and during the 1940s, with the period of World War II, some aspects were particularly reinforced. One of the products emanating after World War II, the *American Soldier* series edited and written by Samuel A. Stouffer and his associates, in some ways reflected the state of the art for a substantial portion of empirically based sociology. But, of course, other notable studies were present, such as the Lynds's *Middletown*, which influenced the development of sociology. As suggested, however, the expansion of the base for sociology did not occur in a vacuum, and other social sciences grew as well, including closely related areas in anthropology, economics, political science, and psychology, the latter sharing with sociology the field of social psychology. Social psychology involved an enormous growth in field studies and experimental research as well as development of middle range theory. While there were a number of volumes that attempted to assess sociology in the post-World War II period, one that essentially provided a broad summary prior to the new thrusts was *Twentieth Century Sociology* (1945) edited by Georges Gurvitch and Wilbert E. Moore.

The purpose of *Twentieth Century Sociology* was not grossly dissimilar from the task authors were asked to address here. "Each author was asked (1) to set forth the major trends in the special field discussed, (2) to discuss these trends critically, and (3) to summarize the present position of the field with particular emphasis on problems requiring further research" (p. 2). The first essay in the volume by Huntington Cairns was on "Sociology and the Social Sciences," and it is interesting that at that point questions about what sociology should encompass and how it should relate to other social sciences required explicit attention. It is a bit of *deja vu* that those who taught in the period will experience, as every introductory class in sociology seemed to require some justification of sociology as a science. Cairns's essay was not a staking out of the field as the queen of the social sciences, but a raising of questions about the nature of the discipline that are in many cases relevant today. In comparing sociology to natural science, for example, he stated: "in such cases [as in the transformation of geometry in the nineteenth century] the continuity of the investigation is usually uninterrupted. This means that the later investigation which may be directed towards a subject matter which has been fundamentally revised, builds for the most part upon data already accumulated. Sociology does not exhibit a comparable continuity. In both its theory and its subject matter it displays a mutative quality that forcibly indicates a relatively rudimentary stage of development" (p. 4.).

Cairns's characterization of sociology was made in a direct and possibly oversimplified way, but it corresponds to the kind of self-searching questions that serious sociologists continue to ask. Why does sociology not appear to be a coherent and cumulative science? It is this type of concern that motivates asking what the future of sociology will be.

It is a useful exercise to review history, and *Twentieth Century Sociology* is highly recommended as a reference point. In this volume it will be seen that although there have been shifts in sociological interest since then, the basic field has not changed greatly. However, what may be most instructive to the reader is that fully one-third of that volume was devoted to sociology by national or regional areas (e.g., German sociology, Italian sociology), and a cursory inspection of the chapters can remind the reader of the selective perception that can occur in any ivory tower.

In the post-World War II period there was a massive growth of higher education in the United States, and with it of sociology. With regard to methodological status, as just noted in passing, one aspect of change was the growing acceptance of the systematic use of the interview or questionnaire in data collection for field studies. With regard to analytic techniques in the handling of data, attention was being given to Guttman scaling, and secondarily by the few who had the technical qualifications to read the material, to Lazarsfeld's latent structure analysis. Not many sociologists were well trained in mathematics or statistics, so analyses tended to be simple, often presented in tabular form, and rarely of a multivariate nature.

The 1950s was a period of vital growth, with many supportive new bases becoming available for sociology. The Russell Sage Foundation, with the leadership of Donald R. Young and Leonard S. Cottrell, Jr. initiated a program to stimulate sociological research in the professions, interdisciplinary research, and research on social indicators. The Social Science Research Council sponsored a program for the training of sociologists and other social scientists in mathematics. And, the technological underpinnings of the social sciences began to change with the diffusion of use of IBM accounting machines and the 80-column reading sorter/printer. The availability of this computing technology continued to accelerate, attracting some sociologists, with the availability of the accessible "modern" resources beginning in the late 1950s, but not diffusing generally until the mid- to late-1960s. Emphasis is placed here on this development because it did two important things. It made multivariate procedures available to a broader spectrum of researchers, and it freed the research enterprise from the labor-intensive use of clerks, which escalated the cost of research beyond the reach of many.

In substantive areas, new developments were visible, such as the thrust known as "small groups research." In sociology this development placed much emphasis on systematic observation and was accompanied by a growth of interest in experimental research. The importance of support from research branches of the armed forces in this historical development should not be missed. In the short period since World War II, it is of interest that an area like small groups research could appear as such an important development, only to recede in prominence in the 1970s and 1980s.

Other new areas appeared in sociology, such as the predictable concern with "mathematical models." In large part in response to the stimulus from the Russell Sage Foundation, applied research was stimulated and a new name, "evaluation research," was added to the lexicon. In some fields there were substantial new developments or elaborations that essentially changed the scale of work. For example, with the investment of the government in studies of the labor force, there was an increase in the number of studies investigating the social factors associated with economic well-being, including studies of intergenerational stability and change in social stratification. Demographic studies took on a new perspective with the development of public access samples. Additional new perspectives of quite a different nature also must be noted. "Critical sociology" developed a following in the 1960s, and there were more restricted developments, such as ethnomethodology, that challenged the fundamental tenets of the existing research methodologies in sociology.

Touching on these historical developments also requires turning a little attention to what did not happen in sociology as a discipline. Some of these omissions may suggest areas in which sociology can develop in the future. For example, in the development of applied research and evaluation research in particular, sociologists have not been particularly prominent. In the major studies of the impact of income maintenance on social status and mobility, sociologists have at best been consultants. In the myriad studies on family and welfare, similarly, sociologists have tended to be marginal. During this period schools of social work often expanded to become schools of social welfare, and with this they developed research investments that took over research enterprises in which sociologists could have been the primary investigators. It is appropriate to ask why sociologists are not more directly involved in research on social phenomena and the examination of the consequences of social policy. An answer is not provided for this question, but it is suggested here that if sociology is to have a future, it has to be able to do work—useful work. In this sense, unless the discipline wishes to express suicidal tendencies, a substantial thrust of sociology in the future will need to be in applied research. (The reader will please forgive the anthropomorphism.)

Some aspects of sociology have had substantial investments in applied areas. For example, sociologists have been able to maintain substantial contact with the growing areas associated with social control, particularly in the administration of justice, probation and parole, criminology and juvenile delinquency, and the study of the legal system. While special schools of criminology have arisen, sociologists have been involved substantially in their development. However, within departments of sociology, often such areas are defined as less than central in comparison to, say, theory or macrosociology, and thus are often less nurtured.

One point that needs to be emphasized is that, for whatever reasons, sociology as a discipline has lost much of its claim to many areas that have been taken over by other disciplines and professions. An area such as systems analysis could have involved sociologists in a major way. The field of marriage and the family in sociology has been eclipsed by the National Council on Family Relations. Although the field of psychology had virtually no interest in the family after World War II, it is a massive area now. Indeed, psychology now has a section on Population Psychology that might make sociologists concerned about their own images. Industrial psychology, personnel psychology, and consulting psychology have virtually taken over the fields that sociologists used to occupy under the title industrial sociology, a title that is virtually forgotten. Psychology has been imperialistically successful, particularly in the field of social psychology where it dominated the experimental field and moved into the more social areas of inquiry, such as studies of social issues, of attitudes and behavior, of discrimination, and of environmental psychology. The growth of other fields is not to be denied or decried, but it is reasonable to ask whether sociology as a discipline has missed major opportunities for development, and raise questions about why. A detailed answer to such questions is not provided here, but at minimum it can be remarked that the values and reward systems have not nurtured such development.

The process of fostering development of sociological areas is not, of course, entirely controlled by sociologists. Funding agencies allocate most of the resources that support research, and these often target funds with specific expectations. Because a problem is likely to involve issues that should be within the domain of sociology does not mean that the funding agencies will look for sociologists. Rather, given other factors, they look for prestigious and successful performers, and sociologists may not have the credentials. In the evaluation of research proposals, major criteria are the completeness and detail of the proposal, down to finished forms and procedures that have gone through pretests. Often professional schools, research institutes, or beltline research organizations can fund such investments before the fact, but individual researchers cannot in the absence of strong research support organizations in their universities. So, research on a topic that may involve social factors that are critical to knowledge may be funded in a major organization, rather than with persons who, on the basis of interest and training, may be well or even better qualified to conduct the research. Proposals for research no longer are judged as *proposal* but on the basis of accomplished investments in the research that warrant support to completion. The notion that proposals can be viable because they incorporate important new research by a competent scholar has at minimum lost some of its potency. In addition, as intimated in the National Institutes of Health, for example, research on health matters is associated with things medical and personnel that is medical. "Epidemics" of AIDS and other sexually transmitted diseases are seen as requiring medical research, not research on the social processes that underlay the necessary contacts for transmission. In a global sense, sociology will need to adapt to the structural demands of funding agencies if it is to remain viable in some major aspects of the research enterprise. The era of the individual scholar as the research entrepreneur has more of an element of romanticism attached to it than is appropriate in the real world of research. Sociology has to become more responsive to these changes if it is to expand its empirical base, rather than lose more parts of the discipline.

In the last few decades some changes have occurred in the conceptualization of some of the central concerns in sociology. It is our impression, for example, that the field of "theory" has moved in several directions. First, the emphasis on history has become a more explicit and distinct notion, and is less often meant to cover the area of theory. In addition, there appears to be less interest in the notion of a "grand" theory. What has been called theory in the past two decades is associated more with specific substantive (or "middle-range" theories). Recently, more of what is called theory is also associated with what has come to be called macrosociology. Currently, there is a revival of interest in the development of theory in sociology, but the new efforts are aimed at synthesis and integration as is evident in new volumes on "theoretical sociology" and the "micro-macro link." Though it is not clear in what direction the field of sociology will move, if it moves in the direction in which other (natural) sciences have moved in the past, then the importance of the notion of "grand" theory will diminish and there will be a greater emphasis on specific theories and their elaboration based on empirical observations. That is, theory and empirical research will become more tightly integrated.

The concern with methodology of research, presumably including statistics and other tools, is likely to be prominent in the future of sociology, as has been true in the past. There has been a major shift in sociology to the expectation that those actively involved in scholarship and research will have at least enough technical training to be able to critically read the literature. It is likely that in the future this will continue to be emphasized, but not without a continued division of labor in which methodologists and statisticians provide staff support. With the development of technical support in the form of user friendly statistical and other programs, the recurrent theme has become acknowledged more generally that "garbage in" results in "garbage out," but this has always been true. Some caution is still required: refinements in statistical analytic procedures may provide some types of improvement, but they cannot provide a substitute for the basic observations on which they are applied. A thrust in which sociologists need to be more involved in the future is concern with the development of better data bases and more complete knowledge of the limits of their data sets.

One thrust that sociology may develop is to become more concerned with the application of knowledge. In other words, we might ask that if our knowledge of social behavior and social structure has worth, then how can it be applied? The purpose of evaluation research and decriptive research in general is to represent properly the social phenomena of interest in summary form. Hypotheses, usually globally stated, may be tested in terms of policy implementations. However, these are hypotheses based on the specific policies that have been developed. At some point, sociologists should begin to become concerned with a more proactive stance with regard to policy. This stance could be phrased as follows: Given that a set of values or goals have been stated to be implemented, what alternative policies could be formulated? Of course, this is only the first question, since the development of models of social structures have many ramifications, and these would need to be considered. It is an ambitious agenda. But, in addition to this, it may be that the time is approaching when microanalytic models can be reasonably developed, and although there have been some thrusts in this direction in the past, this task is probably one that is most relevant for sociologists to tackle.

Our coverage of the field has been both general and segmented. No chapter and no modest sized book can encompass all of sociology or project complete information about the full range of the future based on current and past experience. However, the variety of points of view and the breadth of the topics included in this volume should make a significant contribution to what is a constant task for sociologists, asking where it will be productive to invest resources in the future to advance knowledge.

REFERENCE

Gurvitch, Georges and Wilbert E. Moore (1945) *Twentieth Century Sociology*. New York: Philosophical Library.

2

SOCIOLOGICAL THEORY

Herman Turk

University of Southern California

The popularity of sociological theory has declined in the United States. Articles about theory and concepts had been appearing at a steady rate of about 13%-19% since the beginning of the *American Sociological Review* (ASR, REL). Now their frequency is only half of that.[1] And the second most prestigious, widely cited general sociological journals, the *American Journal of Sociology* (AJS) and *Social Forces* (SF)[2] show the same low rate (see the top half of Figure 2.1).[3] Further, the frequency of empirical articles *not* based on deductions from theory—no matter how vague the deduction or how specialized the theory—has risen from an estimated low of 24% in 1965-78 to 40% in the *American Sociological Review* and even higher in the other two journals (bottom half of Figure 2.1).[4] This approaches an earlier peak during 1936-1949 at the end of the social problems era. Reasons for these declines in theory may be found, I believe, in outside incentives to make sociologists immediately useful within the United States and in the strong position that quantitative methods hold within sociology. (My setting national limits, an expedient, presumes that we still help shape world sociology and that the discipline's experiences in various countries are likely to converge.)

INFLUENCES OUTSIDE SOCIOLOGY

Societal differentiation, bureaucratization, pragmatism, and consumerism in the service sector are important forces toward making sociologists useful to specialized organizations and service providers, including publishers and other entertainers. Unlike clinical practice and other applica-

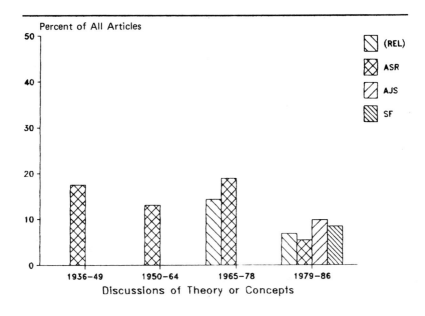

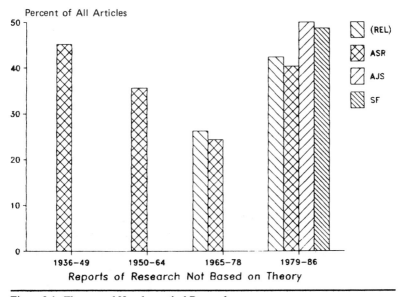

Figure 2.1 Theory and Nontheoretical Research

tions, theory is abstract. Therefore, it seldom meets the immediate demands
for concrete activities made by bureaucracies and practitioners. Nor is it
likely to be so entertaining that even the *New York Times* book reviews will
give it much space. Yet the American Sociological Association's main
medium for the profession's affairs (*Footnotes*) has recently legitimated
such use-value by instituting a column featuring coverage of sociologists by
the news media. Theorists will probably not be mentioned by it very often.
For they are unlikely to contribute to the newsworthy image of rebellious
muckraking that "sociology" has conveyed in popular books (Friedrichs,
1970: 57-58) or to make dramatic pronouncements about modern life. Not
being cast in this image might protect theorists from distrust by established
elites, but the price they will pay is to be ignored.

Quantification

Differentiated, bureaucratic, and pragmatic society—one might also
speculate—has reinforced but redirected sociology's posture as a natural
science.[5] Reinforcement is by the steady increase of surveys as the main
data source—not experiments, anecdotes, interpretive descriptions, or
artistic portrayals. In the *American Sociological Review,* survey reports
rose steadily from estimates of 30% of all articles in 1936-1949 to 89% in
1979-1985, a rate approximated by current ones in the *American Journal of
Sociology* and *Social Forces* (top half of Figure 2.2). Use of episodic or
interpretive data has steadily decreased from about 32% to about 5%
(about 10% and 8% in the *American Journal of Sociology* and *Social
Forces*); and at no time have estimated rates of experimental reports—the
mark of a laboratory science—exceeded 5%. Domination of our main
journal by natural sciences rather than by the humanities, since the Second
World War at least, can further be seen in the statistical treatment of these
empirical articles. Percentages that reported distributional, bivariate, or
multivariate rather than nonquantitative analyses were 36 in 1936-1949, 53
in 1950-74, 71 in 1965-1978, and 80-91 among the three journals in 1979-
1985. Moreover, incorporations of multivariate techniques have risen from
none or almost none to an estimated 75%-89% of all articles currently in the
three journals (bottom half of Figure 2.2).[6]

It is unlikely that this trend will be reversed in a pragmatic, differentiated,
and bureaucratic world. Numbers are high technology. They are relatively
universal. And they are consumed voraciously by formal organizations.[7]
Boudon's observation that the state originated statistics— the word as well
as the thing—is cogent. Often governmental and other large organizations

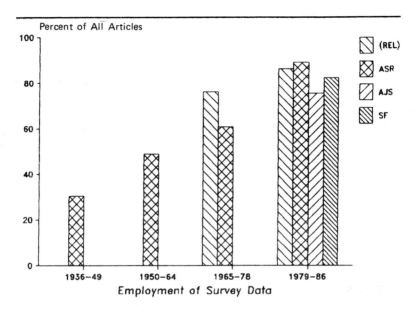

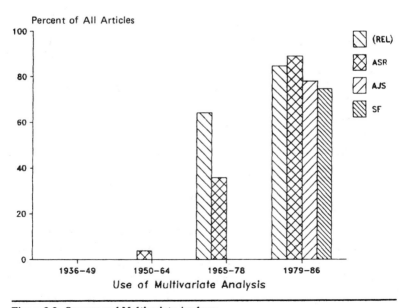

Figure 2.2 Surveys and Multivariate Analyses

even provide the costly data, or see to its collection, in the form of censuses, personnel records, and budget information, upon which research sociologists depend. This creates a situation that would be like that of astronomers if they had to rely on data from observatories over which they had no control (Boudon, 1980: 33). Moreover, articles in sociology journals that reported research funded by organizations, mainly by foundations and government agencies, incorporated statistics more frequently than did unsupported research during 1955-1964 (McCartney, 1970).[8] It is not unreasonable to presume that external forces rival the discipline's theories, or other internal content, in shaping its methods.

Application

The modern institutions that have reinforced sociology's posture as a natural science have also weakened that posture by favoring social technology directed toward the aforementioned end of everyday utility. They have done this through incentive and pressure to demonstrate value to the diversified practical concerns of bureaucratized power-elites, insurgents, reformers, and visionaries alike.[9] Major reductions of federal funds for basic research, the demise of UNESCO, the excess of sociologists over academic vacancies, private foundation focus on world problems, National Science Foundation emphases on social indicators and on applied research, and the increasing number of social movement organizations all provide anecdotal evidence. This has moved sociology toward social reporting and social engineering, as implied by Figure 2.1.[10]

The same external forces have also favored those forms of client-oriented research that lack the methodological[11] rigor or theoretical sophistication required for inclusion in the general sociology journals (Freeman and Rossi, 1984). And much of what is called "applied sociology" by its nonacademic practitioners is actually "applied research methodology" (Costner, 1983). Yet the American Sociological Association has legitimated the term during the 1980s in various ways. One of its leading exponents became president; both he and another president of the 1980s featured, in their presidential addresses, external applications of the discipline. The association also sponsored a separate national conference on applied sociology followed by an edited volume (Freeman et al., 1983). Moreover, applied sociology is the theme of the only article (Freeman and Rossi, 1984) that appeared in the *American Sociological Review*'s section called "The Profession" after that journal was given a mandate to assume some of the functions of the defunct *American Sociologist*.

Prestige/Stigma, Autonomy/Captivity

Quantitative methodology has been able to both gain external prestige—by being useful in producing censuses, social indicators, consumer profiles, land-use projections, and the like—and retain autonomy from the day-to-day world through its esoteric language and procedures, without hearing the word "gobbledygook." Sociological theory does not have this opportunity. Its choice is *between* being accepted *and* retaining a private language or set of procedures. This means that theory has to defend itself against either public scorn or rebuttal in terms of the "common wisdom" of the laity.

Statements made about theory in the U.S. Congress (Rossi, 1980) illustrate the pressures for immediate utility. They have also stigmatized the trivia that we sometimes have to use as indicators of abstract concepts, even including a "Golden Fleece Award" as the booby prize for such endeavors. This suggests in yet another way a drop in the external prestige of abstract theory. In contrast, one of the main rationales provided for keeping the ASA annual, *Sociological Methodology,* during the American Sociological Association's periodic review was the acceptance it was said to provide for the discipline. This publication, be it noted, has had only quantitative methodologists as its editors.

The result of all this is that general social theory is considered neither relevant nor profound outside of the discipline, but quantification is considered to be both.

Specialization

Society's differentiation into diverse bureaucracies, each with its specialized practical concerns, has supported specialized sociologies that develop specialized theories to address these concerns: fertility expectations, being old, deinstitutionalization of offenders, and practitioner-client relations are just a few examples of what "mission-oriented" outside support has encouraged. But even here, theory, unlike method, does not produce results directly, nor is its jargon safe from attack. About 50% of the 1979-1986 articles reporting support by mission-oriented organizations were among those characterized (Figure 2.1) as not having been based on theory, not even specialized theory, compared to only 27% of ones reporting support by organizations less likely to exclude basic research and 17% of those not reporting any support.[12]

Sociological theory has simply become a *means*—often kept hidden from the outside world—to the production of results, whereas methodology is viewed as a producer per se.[13] Theory no longer provides—if it ever did—a basis for differentiating the subject matter of sociology that has been deemed necessary for coherence as a scholarly profession (Gouldner, 1970: 445; Boudon, 1980: 2-5; Stinchcombe, 1984). Sociology's current differentiation follows, in part, the current differentiation of society. This may be seen in the numerous problem-oriented multidisciplinary associations to which sociologists belong, and in the mission-oriented sections of the American Sociological Association as well as in its mission-oriented publications.[14] Concern with the resulting fragmentation led to considerable debate among the association's leaders in the early 1980s as to whether to reduce the number of special publications. So far there has been little effect.

INFLUENCES WITHIN SOCIOLOGY

On the whole, sociologists tolerate theorists and nonquantitative investigators. Both continue to be elected to high office in sociological societies. This exemplifies norms of scholarship that cause diverse elements to be accommodated whether or not they are currently prestigious or powerful. The American Sociological Association has done so by establishing special publications and special sections. Theory and methodology each has its own publication and its own section. And not all of the remaining sections and publications are based on externally demanded contents. Some of them are determined by theoretical content, such as Marxism, or by special method, such as comparative historical.

Isolation

Yet there does appear to be a split between the theory written by theorists, who I believe to be dismissed by the external world, and the theory employed by empirical investigators, who I believe to be subject to it (Warshay, 1975: 169-178; Menzies, 1982). Sampling articles from the three journals considered here and from the main Canadian and the three main British journals, Menzies (1982: especially 175-190) reported marked discrepancies between theory articles and research articles as to the frequencies with which various types of theories appeared. Moreover, his examination of citations in six theory books showed theoretical materials to account for 61% and modern research for only 12% (another 8% referred to old research). Theorists mainly cite other theorists. On the other hand, it was Menzies's impression (as it is mine) that the references in a typical research paper are to other research papers dealing with a very narrowly defined substantive area. Also cited in this context is Chase's (1970) report that only 26% of American social scientists surveyed considered theoretical significance an essential feature of scientific writing, 36% considering it only somewhat or not very important.

Sociological theorists have considered themselves slighted or disparaged by their profession. Over the past few years, several of the newsletters (*Perspectives*) of the American Sociological Association's Theory Section discussed the difficulty that theorists have in being published by that association's periodicals. According to a newsletter statement by its current chair, theory might appear to be a luxury or esoteric to many younger sociologists who find applied sociology attractive, and there might be pressures to reduce the theory requirement in some graduate programs (Tiryakian, 1985). Unlike *Sociological Methodology*, the American Sociological Association's *Sociological Theory*, first an annual book, now a semiannual journal, has been on almost continuous probation (see Abrahamson, 1984).

The pride with which quantitative sociologists speak of their "mathematical revolution" has been mentioned by another leading spokesperson for the Theory Section (Collins, 1986), who added that they sometimes dismiss the rest of the field—presumably including work by theorists—as a nonquantitative minority. Yet he supported the position of sociology as a science, tacitly attesting to the power of that position by mentioning its contradiction of prevailing beliefs in current philosophy and metatheory. Indeed, endorsement of quantitative methodology by the American Sociological Association is symbolized by retention of *Sociological Methodology* as one of its publications, in spite of very small circulation. Prestige among other disciplines—another source of power—was one of the reasons given for that decision.

The author of what I consider one of the best short surveys of social theory (Turner, 1986: 30) believes that the natural science advocates in social theorizing have lost ground to those who do not feel that the theoretical procedures of the other sciences are relevant to human beings. This could possibly be so among persons doing basic research and within the inner circle of those calling themselves "theorists." But the dominance of latter-day application and quantification within the discipline's main journal, within its methodology annual, and in tasks supported by its main funding sources suggests that use of *any* theory will rest more and more upon its relevance to societal and world affairs and upon its implementation by the dominant methodologies, which *are* those of the natural sciences.

Nonaccommodation

Certain symbolic interactionists, phenomenologists, dramaturgists, ethnomethodologists, and persons favoring related theoretical frameworks are among the metatheoretical critics of surveys and quantification; they have failed to accommodate. Taken together because of their infrequency, the approaches of such theorists have appeared in only about 4%-9% of all *American Sociological Review* articles, continually, from 1936 to the present. Current rates are about the same (nonsignificantly lower) in the *American Journal of Sociology* and *Social Forces*. Among the three journals, only one of the empirical articles within these frameworks relied on the expected episodic/interpretive data during 1979-1986, the remaining ones dividing themselves between survey and experiment. Except in the one interpretive article, the method of analysis is multivariate. Such frequency is not likely to represent the thrust of research within these frameworks, only the small portion that has accommodated to prevailing criteria for publication.

Indeed, these frequencies of survey methods, experiments, and multivariate analyses resemble ones reported in articles that draw upon behavioral psychology, which is, historically, scientific in these respects. Such articles are being published at rates of about 10% in the *American Sociological Review* and 9% and 21% in the *American Journal of Sociology* and *Social Forces*.

Publication of *Social Psychology Quarterly* by the American Sociological Association cannot account for the relative infrequency of *both* kinds of microsociology in the journals. For in spite of this outlet, the most frequently reported level of analysis, in all three general journals, is that of role or individual person.[15] The two kinds of microsociology appear less often than, say, person in social structure, which also operates at this level of analysis. What does distinguish the articles employing either sociological microframework from articles having other social psychological content is that they consistently yield the highest rates of theory-based and experimental research over the 1979-1986 interval. I take this to mean that abstractions, sometimes considered only in the laboratory, simply do not accommodate to emphases on application. Evidently other microsociological theory has proven more popular, even in providing post hoc accounts of research.

Criticism

Impact on the discipline by microsociological or other theorists will not only depend upon value to applied research but also upon convincing currently powerful methodologists. Successful critical influence on the content of quantitative methodology will require greater sophistication on the parts of the critics. For example, unqualified critiques of statistics have lumped the question (1) of whether numbers can adequately portray social phenomena with the question (2) of whether probability can be employed to assess the generality or typicality of, say, one of the types of everyday drama that Goffman has described. It will also be necessary to explore systematic alternatives to numerical analysis, for "mathematics" subsumes more than just numbers. Indeed, such nonnumerical systems as topology might gain wider recognition as alternatives to quantification than will the more intuitive methodologies.

Method over Substance

Failure of many theories to explicate their implementation seems to have turned even the task of *generating propositions* over to more empirically oriented and methodologically sophisticated colleagues. Indeed, several main figures coming to mind under the term *theory construction* had either earned their reputations in methods, statistics, or the philosophy of science or had been sophisticated in such skills but earned their reputations in one or two specialties. One illustration of how prestigious methodology has filled theoretical vacuums lies in the use of the term *mathematical model* rather than *sociological model.* Whatever else the term might mean, scientific models are representations of nature, whereas pure mathematics need not have any empirical referents. "A path model of . . . " is, sociologically, no more informative than is "A numerical description of population size."

Negative outcome. My samples do suggest, without a formal count, that path analysis was a ubiquitous method of the 1970s (also see Turner, 1986: 19, and, by implication, Menzies, 1982: 144-169, 186). It did what the simple "axiomatic theory" criticized by Costner and Leik (1964) could not do: show, within a single design, deductions of both the same and opposite theorems from alternative sets of premises. The version of axiomatic theory that this dominant method implemented was, however, quite limited. It emphasized the *additivity* of independent effects implied by logically independent "or" rather than the *joint operation* of influences implied by logically contingent "and."

This one-sidedness is curious, even if one fails to accept theorist Stuart Dodd's claim (Dodd and Christopher, 1966) that "Products Predict [Social] Interaction Where Sums Do Not." It may account for some of the distrust that *typologists* have had of quantitative sociology. But there is nothing in the logic of path analysis that precludes multiplying discrete properties by one another to constitute complex types, whose effects upon one another can then be assessed. It simply had not been done very much. Failing to recognize this possibility, Weber (1946) just had to avoid quantification when he described the necessity of *both* peer organization of labor *and* worldly asceticism for capitalist endeavor (p. 322). More generally, any social action may be characterized as the product of capacity *and* incentive *and* opportunity; if any one of the three is zero, the product will be zero, and action simply will not occur (Turk, 1970, 1985).

Emphasis on applied sociology is not likely to explain why so few joint effects like this one were implemented by what we call statistical interaction, because applied sociology often has goals of full prediction of concrete outcomes. And at least one of the most widely used statistical software packages makes it very easy to consider every possible main effect of *and* interaction among variables in attempts to maximize R-square. Rather, I believe, this lack occurred because interaction effects were less easy to deal with technically than were the effects of variables taken individually (see, for example, Pedhazur, 1982: 385-387). In the absence of theoretical guidance, the methodological tail has been allowed to wag the dog. How many of us have been enjoined to assess main effects first and then the interactions, no matter what the theory. Are we compelled as often to demonstrate robustness in our main effects independently of the influences of their interactions?[16]

Positive outcome. There are cases, however, where methodologies have *more* to say about the subject matter of sociology than do its theories. If society is composed of relationships among specified collective or individual actors, sociometric analysis and graph theory—recently revived as network analysis—constitute appropriate tools. Network analysis has been called theoretically barren. This claim is exaggerated. Consider, for example, the microsocial exchange theories of Emerson (see Turner, 1986: 287-305), Cook with Emerson and others (Cook et al., 1983: 275-305), and Willer (1981); also consider Mizruchi's (1982) application of pluralist and neo-Marxist perspectives to the study of corporate interlocks.[17]

Any lack of substance that remains in network analysis very likely results in part from the current state of sociological theory, which has very little to say about the structure of relationships, except in the gross sense of structural shapes implied by such terms as *value homophily, propinquity, common stratum, coalition, hierarchy, differentiation,* and *pluralism.* Here we have method that is likely to be a forerunner of theory, which, in turn, may very likely lead to the method's modification. One such possibility is that some structural theories may require greater attention to network methodologies that are not based on summing numerous dyads or aggregating actors in equivalent positions.

IMPLICATIONS FOR INFLUENTIAL THEORIZING

I do not anticipate any major break with current trends. These suggest that theorists likely to influence sociology are ones who (1) accommodate to external demands for application, (2) provide formal propositions or codify empirical results, or (3) employ formal language in addressing the process through which theory is developed. Examples follow.

Accommodation to Application

In its recent newsletters the Theory Section's chair (Tiryakian, 1985, 1986) proposed attention by theorists to such empirical transformations in the world as the biophysical effects of robotics and biomedical engineering, the sexual revolution, and emergent modernity in East Asia—organizing sessions around some of these topics at the section's annual meetings. It is likely that such accommodation by theorists to popular or prestigious empirical concerns will increase the attention they receive both within sociology and as *priests* or *prophets* (terms from Friedrichs, 1970) outside it. One might expect excesses in any such accommodation to be countered by the reactions of other theorists.[18]

Some of these accommodations may make almost direct contributions to theory. It could be, for example, that scholarly attention to gender— partly attributable to such social-movement elements of the sexual revolution as Sociologists for Women in Society—will continue to prompt reexamination of such middle-range theories as ones of status attainment, minority relations, multiple economies, role relations, and the social self. This is because the classes of phenomena considered are near-universal, and their empirical descriptors tend to coincide with conceptual categories (e.g., "gender"). However, undue attention to "modernity" and "development" might well continue to be called culture-bound by other theorists (Eisenstadt with Curelaru, 1976: 2-4, 18) or continue to be regarded by them as "specialism" (Boudon, 1980: 10-11).

Failure by theorists to be selective regarding the empirical issues they address could add to the current proliferation of special theories of limited scope, which—contrary to some uses of the term—are not what was originally meant by theories of the middle range. It appears that the sociology of gender has the potential for its own middle-range theories but that the sociology of modernization does not.

Formalization and Codification

It is my impression from the 1965-1986 samples just cited—not as the result of specific coding—that an increasing proportion of the theory articles are employing mathematical forms of expression. Boudon (1980: especially 205-226) has made a compelling case for mathematical formalization, providing several exemplary illustrations. Using the word in its broadest sense, formalization is another accommodation that is increasingly likely to be required of theory. The profession will look kindly on formal theories that are quantifiable and empirically testable, like Peter Blau's (1977) recent work (discussed by Sampson, 1984). It will also favor ones based on propositional inventory—especially the codification of empirical works, such as those by Homans (1950, 1961) on groups and social behavior. Indeed, like others (Bates and Cloyd, 1971), both of these sociologists were granted the label "theorist" after their specialized empirical works or their codifications of the empirical works of others became more widely known.

Already known as a theorist, Merton, with Kitt-Rossi (1950), provided an exemplar of codified *quantitative* findings in his first demonstration of theory of the middle range. Based on cross-tabulations of data provided by World War II soldiers for other purposes, it is an extension of the theory of reference groups to subsume such lower level concepts as relative deprivation and anticipatory socialization. That theory was well-received by applied empiricists as well as methodologists.

Marxism. Theories that both demonstrate their applicability and are formalized in terms of the dominant methodologies receive attention, even when they challenge or modify existing formulations. For challenge is a scientific norm. One example is the recent burst of empirical macrosociology that incorporated Marxian or neo-Marxian perspectives. The percentage of articles addressing such frameworks jumped from an estimated 0-2 in the *American Sociological Review* during 1965-1978 and before to 30 in 1979-1986 (24 in the *American Journal of Sociology* and 13 in *Social Forces*). This does confirm predictions made by Gouldner (1970) and Friedrichs (1970) concerning modifications of and radical challenges to structural-functional theory.[19] But also note that application is built into Marxist theory with the concept of *Praxis*.[20] Moreover, a preponderance of these articles accommodated to dominant methodology by reporting multivariate analyses of survey data.[21]

The substantive shift could further mean that neo-Marxists have recently had more to say formally about society in general than have microsociologists or functionalists. Indeed, during 1979-1986 the 30% of all articles in the *American Sociological Review* that included neo-Marxist frameworks accounted for an estimated 63% of all the articles that employed the societal or institutional level of analysis. Articles in the *American Journal of Sociology* and *Social Forces* show this same pattern. And since analyses at that level apply to current pragmatic issues of Third-World relations, fiscal strain, urban decay, insurgency, revolutions, and international tensions, they have become fundable by all manner of organizational client. Given their empirical thrust, it is quite possible that the coming years will see further challenges to, or revisions of, these newly influential formulations. Though not employing quantitative method-ologies, Habermas has, for example, incorporated intersubjectivity into Marxist theory in seeking an empirical account of why the proletarian revolution has not shown signs of occurring in industrial societies.[22]

Qualitative formalization. Letting methodological custom define socio-logical inquiry has led to trenchant criticism of quantitative research. Qualitative investigators properly say that the most frequent kinds of quantitative sociology miss the very totality, complexity, or uniqueness of that which is observed. However, such lacks need no longer be considered consequents of quantification in general. Dummy (i.e., binary) variables— as many as needed—are now being used, both jointly and additively, to describe types, syndromes, and processual sequences as these appear in the notes of the artist, ethnographer, or *verstehende* sociologist. Indeed, the computer software now available for qualitative data is designed to do just this. After all, digital computers can even store poetry, music, color paintings, or sculpture as combinations of dummy variables. The introduc-tion of qualitative sociologists to some of the discrete multivariate techniques that have been developed, let alone to computer packages specifically designed for ethnographers, is, paradoxically, likely to increase the dominance of quantification even more.

In general. The more suitable they are shown to be to all manner of theory, the more influential will the dominant methodologies become. This makes it even more likely that theorists will have to convince methodologists by explicating method in order to have any effect. There is work (e.g., Freese, 1980) that shows ways of doing this. Even the processes of theory development require the theorist to use quantitative language in order to reach beyond other theorists. Some examples follow along these lines.

Quantification and Processes of Theory Development

Mathematical or other formal explication of the very processes of formulating, refining, modifying, combining, contrasting, and challenging theories is likely to benefit theory and increase its influence on the content and conduct of research. The following illustrates a very small part of what this means.

It is often the history of grand theory that it purports to account for more of the everyday world than later proves to be the case. Returning to a previous example, Marxian conflict theory seems to apply better in nonindustrial than in industrial nations (see, for example, Skocpol, 1979, Skocpol and Trimberger, 1986). Provisos like this one imply various strategies for specifying or modifying theory. Included among them are stating empirical applicability more precisely and introducing new theoretical properties as alternatives, add-ons, or multipliers.

These strategies may be illuminated by drawing upon and adding to the illustrations provided by an important article on theory construction, which is likely to have considerable influence on both method and application. Walker and Cohen (1985) recently demonstrated that falsification of a theory requires statement of its scope—that is, the empirical conditions under which it is expected to hold. They provide several well known relational structures in illustrating both the strategy they favor for falsification and certain inductive strategies that have been used to elaborate or generate theory.

Generalizable to relations among continuous variables, their hypothetical data on Table 2.1, which I have recaptioned and slightly reorganized, show the association between defendant's social status X and severity of sanctions Y in each of three southern states. Note that association is negative in State A, zero in State B, and positive in State C. The authors correctly point out that considering the data from all three states would have led to the conclusion that there is no consistent relationship between X and Y. They are also correct in saying that if only A had satisfied their

TABLE 2.1

Relationship Between Defendant's Social Status
and Severity of Sanctions by Variable Z

Condition Variable Z	Defendant's Social Status (X)	Severity of Sanctions (Y)		Chi-Square	p
		Low	High		
A	high	30	20		
	low	20	30	4.00	< .05
B	high	25	25		
	low	25	25	0.00	n.s.
C	high	20	30		
	low	30	20	4.00	< .05

NOTE: Hypothetical data from Walker and Cohen (1985), tabular format and captions modified slightly.

restrictions of scope, then they would have ignored B and C. In that case the familiar relationship of necessity and sufficiency, $-X \rightarrow Y$, is suggested once the tabled values of dummy (dichotomous 0, 1) variables X and Y are substituted into the usual bivariate expression:[23]

$$\text{logit}(\hat{Y}) = \text{intercept} - b_{YX}X$$
(where b_{YX} is a constant)

They contrast this with the result of a different strategy, elsewhere found effective, in which State A might have differed from the other two states (B + C combined) in terms of a third dummy variable called Z. Collapsing the data, first, over both values of X and then over their two values of Z, shows that neither variable affects Y. Here no part of the multicausal relationship $\pm X$ *or* $\pm Z \rightarrow Y$ is satisfied by substituting the given values of the three dummy variables into the usual additive expression that results (X and Z scored in either direction):

$$\text{logit}(\hat{Y}) = \text{intercept} \pm b_{YX}X \pm b_{YZ}Z$$
(where b_{YX} and b_{YZ} are constants)

Using still another strategy, the authors reject the possibility, given these data, that X and Z affect Y jointly—a possibility I have urged investigators not to ignore. The relationship $\pm X$ *and* $\pm Z \rightarrow Y$, also fails to be satisfied by substituting values supplied for the dummy variables into the appropriate multiplicative expression (X and Z again scored in either direction):

$$\text{logit}(\hat{Y}) = \text{intercept} \pm b_{YXZ}XZ$$
(where b_{YXZ} is a constant)

Other strategies also fail with these data when, like the preceding, they are based on collapsing parts of Table 2.1. But I propose an additional strategy for making sense out of the frequencies tabled by Walker and Cohen, drawing upon substantive theory developed for smaller social settings.

It illustrates how niches can be found for special theories: in this case, through formal specification of conditions under which association between variables is, respectively, negative, zero, or positive. Sherif and Sherif (1964: 93, 178-180, 265-266) found that the higher the status within a group the *less* severe were the sanctions for minor infractions but the *more* severe were the sanctions for major infractions. This is because the higher the status of the offender the more severe are the consequences of major infractions believed to be by members of the group or society. (Not being a foot soldier, Benedict Arnold might have been allowed to miss a parade; but—unlike the foot soldiers who changed sides—he became a lasting symbol of infamy when he defected.) Then, to the extent that only minor crimes were reported by State A, equal numbers of major and minor crimes by State B, and only major ones by State C, one can expect the value of Z—severity of infraction—to affect how positive the association will be between X and Y. The relationship $Z \rightarrow$ covariation$_{YX}$ may be expressed as follows by depicting the Z trichotomy with two dummy variables, Z_A, only minor crime and Z_C, only major crime:[24]

$$\text{logit}(\hat{Y}) = \text{intercept} - b_{YXZ_a}XZ_A + b_{YXZ_c}XZ_C$$
(where b_{YXZ_a} and b_{YXZ_c} are constants)

Taking direction into account and combining the (exact) probabilities of the two nonzero degrees of association by Fisher's method (Fisher, 1970: 99-101) yields overall significance at the .005 level. Expressing X and Y as continuous variables would permit the same expression but predicting Y rather than logit(Y) through ordinary least squares regression. This also holds for the three preceding expressions.

As theorists like Walker and Cohen concern themselves more and more with the relationships between theory, on the one hand, and operations, on the other, quantitative investigators are likely to produce fewer specification errors, such as ignoring interaction among variables. Both theorists and methodologists will be given the means of examining the fit between deductions from (or inductions to) theory and properly organized data, which is—after all—what the discipline of sociology is about. And, whatever their dominance, quantitative methodologists are scholars, thus likely to assimilate any criticism by theorists that results, especially because it will be in their own language. Whether my illustrations have been in that language remains to be seen.

SPECULATION ABOUT THE NEAR FUTURE

Whether they explicitly refer to theory or not, the articles have become predominantly empirical and quantitative. It seems that the emphasis on quantity over quality is, as Marx suggested, associated with the substitution of (external-applied) exchange value for (internal-theoretical) use-value in sociology. But then again Marx simply may not have seen how easy it might become to describe qualities with the quantities zero and one and how this might blur the distinction.

Fragmentation Versus Polarization

Be that as it may, it is unlikely that sociological theory will be caught between philosophy, speculation, and criticism, on the one hand, and quantitative empiricism, on the other, as it was in Germany and France (see, for example, Boudon, 1980: 172; Eisenstadt with Curelaru, 1976: 157-158). Application is too important to the sociological establishment and quantitative methodology too influential. Sociology may continue to be fragmented, but it is not likely to become polarized. If anything, quantitative methodology might provide integration in terms of the "mathematical models" that it sanctions. And the effect that sociological theory will have upon the discipline might become more indirect, in terms of its influences upon such sanctioning.

Theoretical Intersections

It is possible that tendencies toward fragmentation among special theories that arise to meet external demands for information will be blunted by the very purpose of such theory. In responding to these same demands, it will often prove necessary to consider intersections among several formulations in order to maximize the prediction of concrete events. Thus some potentials for providing theoretical syntheses are nontheoretical in their origins. Intersubjective formulations in microsociology have been found useful, for example, in such macrosociological pursuits as explaining similarities among administrative hierarchies, expanding theories of mass communication, and accounting for large-scale fiscal processes. Further examples of intersections are recent combinations of ecological with neo-Marxian perspectives in urban and world systems research, combinations of organizational theory with theories of collective behavior in studies of insurgency and social movements, demographic theories of social organization, and inquiries (by family counselors and criminologists) that join conflict and social control. Formal attention to any potential contrasts or syntheses that might ensue and to any theoretical convergences (as, for example, by Wallace, 1983; Wagner and Berger, 1985), could serve to intensify these antifragmenting tendencies in applied sociological theory. Formal inventories, taken together with their origins in survey research and multivariate analysis, can only serve to assure attention to the theoretical outcomes.

Other intersections occur because of the multidisciplinary character of applied social science. Cross-fertilization has accompanied research on industry, aging, poverty, and health practices, to give only a few examples. This aside, I have also suggested that quantitative methodology confers prestige on sociology through its acceptance by other disciplines and that such acceptance seems to be deemed important by the sociological establishment. It should follow that, given fragmentation of the discipline, those fragments that are "at the boundary" such as sociobiology, political economy, and behavioral social psychology will also receive disproportionate attention by theorists as well as by other sociologists. Any theoretical syntheses that result could either strengthen sociological theory in the ways I have considered or divide its contents among other disciplines. This might depend in large measure upon the extent to which sociology is retained as a reference group by sociologists whom the other disciplines accept. Could quantitative methodologists be especially susceptible to extra-sociological identification?

Substantive Integration

Concern has been expressed that centrifugal tendencies like these will endanger the discipline's claims to its own unique core of knowledge (for its quantitative methods are hardly unique). Sociology has become so highly organized professionally, I believe, that if any such identity crisis were to erupt, the profession would be successful in commissioning the consequent tasks of inventory, codification, and general description. The most likely choices for those assignments would be sociological theorists, for who else makes a career out of bringing coherence to diversity? It might be the theorists after all who will define the core of sociological knowledge, for methodologists to legitimate and for others to apply on the outside.

NOTES

1. This cannot be explained by the appearance of the American Sociological Association's new annual, *Sociological Theory* in 1983, because the rate had already dropped as early as 1974.

2. These are the three journals generally taken as prestigious or influential (see, for example, Crawford and Biderman, 1970; McCartney, 1970; Glenn, 1971; Lin, 1974; Snizek, 1975). They are cited most frequently according to the *Social Science Citation Index* (1980: 3-13; 1984: 3-14). Menzies (1982: 5-8, 191) has even argued that the three provide the major important component of published sociology, adding that, barring this, they are still viewed as highest in prestige. Please note throughout this chapter how similar I found these journals' contents to be.

3. Data from 1936 through 1978 are slightly reorganized versions of Wells and Picou's (1981) tabulations of articles in the *American Sociological Review* (ASR in the figures). I have extended the tabulations through June 1986 (also ASR) after assessing my reliability with a recoded 5% sample (stratified by volume and month) that covers their latest period, 1965-1978 (REL). They have my gratitude for the coding instructions and other materials they sent me. Using their 27% sampling fraction, I sampled every issue appearing in 1979-1986. The same was done with the *American Journal of Sociology* (AJS) and *Social Forces* (SF). Reliability for this period was assessed by comparison to all articles in a sample of six issues of the *American Sociological Review*—each from a different year and month—that had been analyzed three months earlier (also REL). The following total numbers of articles (including research notes but not commentary) apply to all of the bar graphs and other statements of frequency; they are provided here just once in order to avoid clutter: 1936-1949: ASR, 217; 1950-1964: ASR, 289; 1965-1978: ASR, 201 / (REL), 42; 1979-1986: ASR, 129 / (REL), 59 / AJS, 82 / SF, 119.

Unless explicitly stated otherwise, the ASR rates "fit" rates in (REL), AJS, and SF at two-tailed probabilities above .20. Any unqualified reference in this chapter to change or to difference means significant at at least the two-tailed .05 level. Qualification by any variant of "tend" or "tendency" means significant at the two-tailed .10 level. Needless to say, my impressions will outreach the systematically assembled data; I hope that it will be apparent when they do.

4. Even higher rates resulted from a senior colleague's independent recoding of 20 empirical articles that constituted a random subset of those sampled from all three journals during 1979-1985. The recoding not only confirmed that seven of these were not based on

deductions from theory but also added six of the remaining 13 to that category. The two-tailed probability of the direction of disagreement is .032.

5. Gouldner (1970: especially 500-502) and Friedrichs (1970: especially 310-312) correctly predicted this continuation of a close link they saw between sociology's posture and that of the natural sciences, despite strong criticism of that posture from within the discipline.

6. My discrepant 1965-1978 recoding—the only one occurring—probably results from a strict definition of "multivariate," which also included all nonzero order tables. However, even my recoded rate is significantly lower than the rate for 1979-1986.

7. See Crawford and Biderman (1970) for the increasing funding levels of sociology and the other social sciences over 1950-1968 and increasing acknowledgment of funding in the three journals considered here. See Useem (1976a, 1976b) concerning government applications of social research.

8. This has not been the case in 1979-1986. I found identically high rates regardless of whether the article (1) reported support by (mission-oriented) organizations that reputedly sponsor only applied research, (2) reported support by ones not likely to exclude basic (i.e., theoretically prompted) research, or (3) did not report any source of support. During much of this period, the National Science Foundation or its foreign equivalents provided the bulk of what federal support there was for basic research. Even the National Institute of Mental Health increased its emphasis on specific health problems, eventually abandoning any support for basic research by act of Congress. University grants to faculty, also reported in the sample (REL only, owing to time constraints), were likely to have favored basic research. Failure to reproduce the earlier findings might simply mean that organizational sponsorship had contributed in the past to what is the institutionalized use of statistics in the present and near future.

9. This is an expansion of what Gouldner (1970) had referred to more feistily as "conceptually uncommitted and empty methodological empiricism . . . to service the research needs of the Welfare State" (p. 445) and administrative / managerial sociology in the service of societal elites and the status quo (pp. 473-475). I view sociology's clientele as far more diversified than this, but all of them press sociology to be pragmatic.

10. Drawing on Parsons's theory of stratification, Boudon (1980: 171-172) suggested that a major societal shift from instrumental-achievement orientation would be necessary in the United States in order for the dominance of application over science to lessen. Such dominance can become worldwide to the extent that these orientations are also appearing elsewhere.

11. I shall use "methodology," "methodological" and "methodologist" in the restricted sense of "research methods and statistics," as this phrase appears, say, in brochures for sociology graduate students.

12. See Note 8 for details on the types of support.

13. Sociology is not unique in this respect. Hajjar et al. (1977) found articles on methodology to be the most frequent (34%) in the *American Political Science Review* during 1970-1975. Articles specific to the United States and its political affairs were next most frequent (27%). And political theory ranked only fourth in a seven-category scheme (12%). A survey of social scientists in anthropology, economics, political science, and psychology asking about their research during 1968-1973 (Useem, 1976a) showed both quantification and policy relevance to be closely associated with federal funding.

14. Collins (1986) views the proliferation of sections as the end product of the dramatic growth in numbers of sociologists and accompanying needs to become visible in milieus smaller than the entire profession.

15. Boudon (1980: 10, 25) and others have observed that the bulk of American empirical work is microsociological, and Hinkle (1980: 324) has suggested that the assumptions of

voluntaristic nominalism might well have pervaded American sociological theory through the time of his writing.

16. In this and other respects, Costner (ch. 3 of this volume) expresses remarkably similar thoughts about statistical interaction, although we developed them completely independently of one another.

17. For other applications of network approaches see Cook (1977) and Turk (1985).

18. See, for example, a critique of the chair's statement in that same section newsletter (Engelmann, 1986).

19. Increased attention to Marxism was anticipated by Gouldner (1970: 443-444) but incorrectly attributed to a radical break from science-oriented, "methodologically empiricist" work (1970: 473-477). Friedrichs (1970: especially 286-287, 326) also foresaw this development but incorrectly expected it to characterize the 1970s rather than later (Wells and Picou, 1981: 161-162).

20. Wallerstein (1986) even has raised the interesting question of whether Marxists of the nineteenth and twentieth centuries had not, as had the state structures and the universities, taken the Baconian-Newtonian version of science as the only rational worldview conceivable.

21. Through 1964, *American Sociological Review* articles at the societal/institutional level of analysis—very few of these Marxist or neo-Marxist—showed significantly greater reliance on sample quotes and typical statements than those at any of the lower levels (Wells and Picou, 1981: 139). Since then the estimated rate of such use has dropped from 60% to 5. (The *American Journal of Sociology* and *Social Forces* currently tend to show somewhat higher rates of about 23 and 41 respectively.) In all three journals, the use of multivariate analysis at this level now either equals or is close to its high rates of use at the other levels.

22. See Turner's (1986: 189-212) summary of Habermas's thought.

23. To attribute necessity and sufficiency to the top third of Table 2.1 one must consider the nonzero frequencies in the smaller diagonal to have been generated by measurement error. Walker and Cohen are not responsible for any of my statements of logic, arrow diagrams, or equations. "$\hat{Y}$" is always the predicted value of Y. In the case of a continuous dependent variable, the left side of each expression simplifies to $\hat{Y}$ alone, the expression becomes an ordinary least squares regression equation, and the b's become the familiar slope coefficients.

24. When one of the two is 1, the other will be 0, and Y will vary either positively or negatively with X; when both are 0 (midvalue of the Z trichotomy), Y will simply equal the constant intercept.

REFERENCES

Abrahamson, Mark (1984) "The survivability of an annual theory volume." Contemporary Sociology 13: 27-29.

Bates, Alan P. and Jerry S. Cloyd (1971) "Homans' transactional theory in footnotes: the fate of ideas in scholarly communications," pp. 93-101 in Herman Turk and Richard L. Simpson (eds.) Institutions and Social Exchange: The Sociologies of Talcott Parsons and George C. Homans. Indianapolis: Bobbs Merrill.

Blau, Peter M. (1977) Inequality and Heterogeneity. New York: Free Press.

Boudon, Raymond (1980) The Crisis in Sociology (Howard H. Davis, trans.; original work published 1971). New York: Columbia University Press.

Chase, Janet M. (1970) "Normative criteria for scientific publication." American Sociologist 5: 262-65.

Collins, Randall (1986) "Is 1980s sociology in the doldrums?" American Journal of Sociology 91: 1336-55.

Cook, Karen S. (1977) "Exchange and power in networks of interorganizational relations." Sociological Quarterly 18: 62-82.

Cook, Karen S., Richard M. Emerson, Mary R. Gillmore, and Toshio Yamagishi (1983) "The distribution of power in exchange networks: theory and experimental results." American Journal of Sociology 89: 275-305.

Costner, Herbert L. (1983) "[Introduction to] sociologists in diverse settings," pp. 65-76 in Howard E. Freeman, William F. Whyte, Peter H. Rossi, and Russel R. Dynes (eds.) Applied Sociology. San Francisco: Jossey-Bass.

Costner, Herbert L. and Robert K. Leik (1964) "Deductions from axiomatic theory." American Sociological Review 29: 819-35.

Crawford, Elisabeth T. and Albert D. Biderman (1970) "Paper money: trends of research sponsorship in American sociology journals." Social Science Information 9: 51-77.

Dodd, Stuart C. and Stephen C. Christopher (1966) "Products predict interaction where sums do not." Sociological Inquiry 36: 48-60.

Eisenstadt, S.N. with M. Curelaru (1976) The Form of Sociology—Paradigms and Crises. New York: John Wiley.

Engelmann, Hugo O. (1986) "Commentary on chair's first message." Perspectives 6 (3): 3-4.

Fisher, Ronald A. (1970) Statistical Methods for Research Workers (14th ed.). Darien, CT: Hafner.

Freeman, Howard E. and Peter H. Rossi (1984) "Furthering the applied side of sociology." American Sociological Review 49: 571-80.

Freeman, Howard E., William F. Whyte, Peter H. Rossi, and Russel R. Dynes [eds.] (1983) Applied Sociology. San Francisco: Jossey-Bass.

Freese, Lee [ed.] (1980) Theoretical Methods in Sociology: Seven Essays. Pittsburgh: University of Pittsburgh Press.

Friedrichs, Robert W. (1970) A Sociology of Sociology. New York: Free Press.

Glenn, Norval D. (1971) "American sociologists' evaluations of sixty-three journals." American Sociologist 6: 298-303.

Gouldner, Alvin W. (1970) The Coming Crisis of Western Sociology. New York: Basic Books.

Hajjar, Sami G., James S. Bowman, and Steven J. Brzezinski (1977) "The literature of political science: professional journals in four nations." International Social Science Journal 29: 327-32.

Hinkle, Roscoe C. (1980) Founding Theory of American Sociology 1881-1915. London: Routledge & Kegan Paul.

Homans, George C. (1950) The Human Group. New York: Harcourt Brace and World.

Homans, George C. (1961) Social Behavior: Its Elementary Forms. New York: Harcourt, Brace and World.

Lin, Nan (1974) "Stratification and the formal communications system in American sociology." American Sociologist 9: 199-206.

McCartney, James L. (1970) "On being scientific: changing styles of presentation of sociological research." American Sociologist 5: 30-35.

Menzies, Ken (1982) Sociological Theory in Use. London: Routledge & Kegan Paul.

Merton, Robert K. and Alice S. Kitt-Rossi (1950) "Contributions to the theory of reference group behavior," pp. 40-105 in R. K. Merton and P. F. Lazarsfeld (eds.) Continuities in Social Research: Studies in the Scope and Method of 'The American Soldier.' New York: Free Press.

Mizruchi, Mark S. (1982) The American Corporate Network 1904-1974. Beverly Hills, CA: Sage.

Pedhazur, Elazar J. (1982) Multiple Regression in Behavioral Research. New York: Holt, Rinehart & Winston.

Rossi, Peter H. (1980) "The presidential address: the challenge and opportunities of applied social research." American Sociological Review 45: 889-904.

Sampson, Robert J. (1984) "Group size, heterogeneity, and intergoup conflict: a test of Blau's 'Inequality and Heterogeneity.'" Social Forces 62: 618-39.

Sherif, Muzafer and Carolyn W. Sherif (1964) Reference Groups: Exploration into Conformity and Deviation among Adolescents. New York: Harper & Row.

Skocpol, Theda (1979) States and Social Revolutions: A Comparative Analysis of France, Russia, and China. New York: Cambridge University Press.

Skocpol, Theda and Ellen Kay Trimberger (1986) "Revolutions: a structural analysis," pp. 59-65 in J. A. Goldstone (ed.) Revolutions: Theoretical, Comparative, and Historical Studies. New York: Harcourt Brace Jovanovich.

Snizek, William E. (1975) "The relationship between theory and research: a study in the sociology of sociology." Sociological Quarterly 16: 415-28.

Social Science Citation Index, Volume 7: Journal Citation Reports (1980, 1984). Philadelphia: Institute for Scientific Information.

Stinchcombe, Arthur L. (1984) "The origins of sociology as a discipline." Acta Sociologica 27: 51-60.

Tiryakian, Edward T. (1985) "Chair's message." Perspectives 6 (2): 1-3.

Tiryakian, Edward T. (1986) "Chair's message." Perspectives 6 (3): 1.

Turk, Herman (1970) "Interorganizational networks in urban society: initial perspectives and comparative research." American Sociological Review 35: 1-19.

Turk, Herman (1985) "Macrosociology and interorganizational relations: theory, strategies, and bibliography." Sociology and Social Research 69: 487-500. (Please overlook the unavoidable disaster in typography and proofreading.)

Turner, Jonathan H. (1986) The Structure of Sociological Theory. Chicago: Dorsey.

Useem, Michael (1976a) "Government influence on the social science paradigm." Sociological Quarterly 17: 146-61.

Useem, Michael (1976b) "State production of social knowledge: patterns in government financing of academic social research." American Sociological Review 41: 613-29.

Wagner, David G. and Joseph Berger (1985) "Do sociological theories grow?" American Journal of Sociology 90: 697-728.

Walker, Henry A. and Bernard P. Cohen (1985) "Scope statements: imperatives for evaluating theory." American Sociological Review 50: 288-301.

Wallace, Walter L. (1983) Principles of Scientific Sociology. New York: Aldine.

Wallerstein, Immanuel (1986) "Marxisms as utopias: evolving ideologies." American Journal of Sociology 91: 1295-1308.

Warshay, Leon H. (1975) The Current State of Sociological Theory: A Critical Interpretation. New York: David McKay.

Weber, Max (1946) From Max Weber (H. H. Gerth and C. W. Mills, trans. and eds.; original work published 1922). New York: Oxford University Press.

Wells, Richard H. and J. Steven Picou (1981) American Sociology: Theoretical and Methodological Structure. Washington, DC: University Press of America.

Willer, David (1981) "The basic concepts of the elementary theory," pp. 25-53 in D. Willer and B. Anderson (eds.) Networks, Exchange, and Coercion: The Elementary Theory and Its Applications. New York: Elsevier (distributed by Greenwood Press).

3

RESEARCH METHODOLOGY
IN SOCIOLOGY

Herbert L. Costner

University of Washington

An invitation to speculate about the future is an invitation to play a game with very few rules. The "futurist" is usually expected to give a rationale for all prognostications and to make them interesting, but even these minimal rules seem often to be violated. Thus the role of "futurist" gives maximum play to individual biases and predilections. And so it is that scholars, in the role of "futurists," typically see their own interests as predicting the wave of the future, their own ideas as destined to emerge as the dominant ethos of a newly enlightened age, and their own preferred solutions to current problems as likely to be victorious as soon as a few more people see the light. Do not be surprised, therefore, to find in these comments on the future of research methodology in sociology, ideas that are already familiar. The "futurist" can do little more than entice others to see some familiar ideas in a new light, and to appreciate in new ways their implications for what lies ahead.

The most plausible projections of the future are those that are clearly built on the present with roots in the past, so that the projection is a continued unfolding of developments originally set in motion long ago. Your attention is therefore directed to the root source of our research methodology, a truly remarkable document that has set the agenda for methodology for more than a century: John Stuart Mill's *A System of Logic,* first published in 1843 (see edited and abridged version in Nagel, 1950). As suggested in the prologue to *Sociological Methodology 1971* (Costner, 1971: ix-xvi), Mill's treatise has set the agenda for research methodology from his time to ours. Although Mill did not always foresee exactly what form the answers would take, important developments in research methodology since the mid-nineteenth century can be seen as answers to questions and problems posed by Mill in his attempt to describe a "larger logic, which embraces all the general conditions of the ascertainment of truth" (Mill, *An Examination of Sir William Hamilton's Philosophy,* 1867: 461; quoted in Nagel, 1950: xxxi-ii). Thus, for example, what we now know as the problem of internal validity was one of the principal themes of Mill's work, and he had, for his time, an exceptionally sophisticated conception of multiple causation. Long before bivariate regression had been developed, Mill saw the need for the technique that we now know as multiple regression. And when he considered the potential development of social science—which was then barely conceived—he suggested the necessity for building what we would now call models of complex social phenomena and for the assessment of such models by exploring the correspondence between their implications and the results of empirical observation. Additional comments on Mill's anticipation of the future of research methodology as he saw it almost a century and a half ago, will be found in the prologue of *Sociological Methodology 1971* (Costner, 1971, pp. ix-xvi). But it is even more informative to read Mill's own commentary on what was for him the future, which was foreseen by a surprisingly prescient enthusiast for empirical research and theoretical reasoning.

One can reasonably foresee the future of research methodology in sociology as a further unfolding of the agenda suggested by Mill in 1843. This implies, among other things, that the continuing refinement of what is now called the "quasi-experimental method" will continue to occupy an important place in the attention of specialists in research methodology. It also suggests that sociologists will be increasingly involved with the development and testing of models of complex social phenomena. Such models may take various forms, including the kinds of causal models now familiar to most sociologists. But they will probably also include models that seem closer to what Mill himself had in mind in his discussion of the future of social science, namely, what we would now call decision-making or rational choice models.

No detailed inventory of the methodological developments suggested by the further unfolding of Mill's agenda for research methodology will be attempted here. Instead, these remarks will concentrate on a few selected methodological problems that Mill seems to have seen very dimly, if at all, even though they are clearly relevant to the central problems that he emphasized. The general assumption underlying these remarks is that our best clues to the near-term future in research methodology are the problems to which we are now sensitive but for which we are still groping for a solution—that "necessity is the mother of methodological invention," if you prefer that statement. Hence we will examine current problems, confidently hopeful that they will soon be resolved. For all of his insights, Mill did not perceive all of the problems that seem more evident to us now. Hence Mill's 1843 treatise cannot serve as an unerring guide to the research methodology of the twenty-first century. It is amazing enough that Mill could foresee methodological needs for a century and a half, and we should not expect his work to continue to constitute the agenda for research methodology forever!

In the pages to follow, two important and interesting problems in current sociological research methodology will be examined: (1) the problem of nonadditive effects and (2) the problem of designing variables.

The problem of nonadditive effects. At least since the time of John Stuart Mill, there has been a pervasive, if not always explicit, assumption in data analysis that additive effects are properly the major focus of attention. Mill was unequivocal in stating his assumption that additive effects dominate in the social world, as illustrated in the following quotation: "the effect produced, in social phenomena, by any complex set of circumstances amounts precisely to the sum of the effects of the circumstances taken singly" (quoted in Nagel, 1950: 332). One cannot get any more explicit about the assumption of additivity than that; in fact, Mill's statement reads almost like a definition of additivity. Few other social scientists have been quite so explicit as Mill, but they have typically indicated indirectly their preference for considering only additive effects in that they have ordinarily not bothered to consider nonadditive effects. There are exceptions, of course; one exception among sociologists is the explicit attention by Paul Lazarsfeld to what he called the "specification" of an effect.

There are, of course, familiar ways of discerning nonadditive effects. In the analysis of variance and of covariance, one considers the possibility of interaction effects before proceeding to the consideration of "main" effects. But one sometimes gets the impression from textbook treatments of these analysis techniques, and from their applications, that the interaction test is viewed as a kind of nuisance that has to be completed as a ritualistic preliminary to the truly interesting analysis of additive effects. And even in these techniques in which the exploration for interaction is quite explicitly included, the outcomes are attributed to nonadditivity only if the additive hypothesis leaves a residue of variation that is too large to attribute to random sources, rather than proceeding in the reverse order, that is, attributing the outcomes to additivity only if a specific nonadditive hypothesis leaves a residue of variation that is too large to be dismissed as random noise. There is no a priori reason why we should not assume a nonadditive effect as the initial hypothesis and then include additive effects only if the residuals seem to require it. That is not the established practice, of course, although it should be if substantive theory suggests it. As for the exploration of interaction effects by including product terms in a multiple regression equation, our current procedures seem to be in a confusing state of disarray, despite the cavalier way that product terms seem to be thrown into such equations. It should be evident that the use of products presumes ratio variables, and it can be readily shown that the pattern of variation among products, that is, the very ordering of cases with regard to the magnitude of the product of two variables, can be greatly changed by shifting the zero point on one or both variables. This point is illustrated in Table 3.1.

Although it seems counterintuitive, Allison (1977) has shown that such striking changes in the pattern of variation of the products do *not* invalidate the conventional test for the significance of interaction. But such changes do affect the pattern of correlation between the product term and the other predictors in the same equation and as a consequence these changes render invalid the test of significance for at least some of the additive terms when one or more of the product term factors has an arbitrary zero point. The implication is that "when one or more of the variables in the product term are measured on interval scales, it is useless to attempt to substantively interpret or test hypotheses about the coefficients for the other variables entered singly" (Allison, 1977: 148). Furthermore, again quoting from Allison, "it is an exercise in futility to attempt to determine the relative importance of main effects and interaction by examining the standardized coefficients" (p. 149). It is worth noting also that even with ratio variables the conclusions drawn from product term tests for interaction in regression equations may be misleading. We almost invariably take the products of variates to the first power; but there is no a priori reason to suppose that first power products fit best in the least squares sense or that they come reasonably close to the kind of interactions that prevail in social phenomena.

Ironically, the lack of attention to nonadditive effects in our data analysis and the awkward implications of our attempts to include an exploration for such effects stand in sharp contrast to the frequency with which nonadditivity is implicitly assumed or explicitly stated in substantive discussions of social science. A social psychologist may tell us that the response to an event depends on the context, or that the reaction to failure depends, in part, on how the performance dimension in question fits into the subject's self-image. A specialist in complex organizations may tell us that the way organizations adapt to a change in their environment will

TABLE 3.1
Patterns of Variation in the Products of Two Variables with an Arbitrary Zero

		The Products					
		The zero points are left unchanged		The zero point for X_1 is lowered by 10 points		The zero point for X_2 is lowered by 10 points	
X_1	X_2	$X_1 X_2$	Rank order of the products	$(X_1 + 10)X_2$	Rank order of the products	$X_1(X_2 + 10)$	Rank order of the products
1	2	2	1	22	2	12	1
2	4	8	3	48	4	28	2
3	1	3	2	13	1	33	3
4	5	20	5	70	5	60	4
5	3	15	4	45	3	65	5

depend, in part, on the internal structure of the organization. Specialists in the family may suggest that the reaction of a couple to a crisis in their lives depends on the strength of the bond between them. A world system theorist may tell us that the impact of a change in exports on the internal stratification of a nation will depend on whether that nation is in the core of the world capitalist system or on its periphery. Such statements do not simply propose the effect of one variable on another. On the contrary, these are all statements of nonadditivity, that is, claims that the effect of one variable on another depends on the level of a third. I have made no attempt to inventory substantive claims that are of this general form, but I suspect that there are thousands of such claims in contemporary social science, although the language in which they are expressed sometimes makes them difficult to identify. One wonders how nonadditivity could be so pervasive in substantive discussions about sociological topics and so infrequently included in data analysis procedures.

There are several possible reasons for this discrepancy between substantive claims and methodological procedures. Some might propose that it would be premature to explore more complex effects until the simpler additive effects have been established. That proposition seems to ignore the fact that it may be difficult to establish the simple effects if we ignore the nonadditive effects; we will be plagued repeatedly by contradictory findings as we explore the results of different studies. Others might suggest that the discrepancy occurs because of the division of labor in social science between methodologists, who prefer additive effects and assume that they suffice, and the substantive specialists, who may not realize that their ideas are inaccurately represented in data anlaysis. This position seems to exaggerate the separation of the roles of methodologist and substantive specialist—and to assume that each is blind to the insights of the other. Still others may point to the difficulty of incorporating appropriate explorations for interaction effects in many of our commonly employed data analysis procedures. This is, perhaps, something of an illusion since nonadditive or interaction effects can always be explored by examining the relationship between two variables within subcategories of a third variable. This is, admittedly, not always a highly satisfactory way of exploring for interaction for a variety of reasons, not least of which is the implied need for a very substantial sample size if the subcategories of the control variable are to represent anything other than crude groupings. But, whatever the reason, the discrepancy between assumptions of nonadditivity in substantive claims and assumptions of additivity in data analysis strikes a jarring note in contemporary social science methodology. We need more satisfactory ways of exploring for nonadditivity in conjunction with our most commonly used data analysis procedures. While not a solution to this need, I call attention to the work of Charles Ragin (Ragin, 1987) on techniques for discerning the various configurations of predictors that seem to influence a given outcome, a technique quite explicitly based on the supposition that interaction effects, not additive effects, predominate in many of the phenomena of interest to social scientists.

The problem of designing variables. No deep knowledge of the history of research methodology is required to see that methodologists have lavished most of their systematic attention on the analysis of data rather than on the development of the data to be analyzed. Again quoting from the prologue to *Sociological Methodology 1971*:

> The major thrust of methodological effort in sociology has remained concentrated on Mill's basic concern, that is, how to draw valid conclusions from data, while the problem of how to produce the data to be thus utilized has remained a neglected stepchild in sociological methodology. This is not to disparage efforts to improve the quality of sociological data, but simply to note that the problem of data production has always been less systematically treated than has the problem of drawing conclusions from data.... Although we know something of observer bias, Hawthorne effects, measurement and classification errors, although we have some rather highly developed models for scaling and sampling, and although we have a considerable body of accumulated wisdom in regard to observation, interviewing, and question- naire construction, our methodological knowledge in regard to data production remains to be systematized [Costner, 1971: x-xi].

This statement, from approximately 17 years ago, still seems true today, except that we have developed new insights into measurement problems and new leads that may be useful in developing a more systematic treatment of data production in social research since that statement was written. These insights and leads have emerged from the development and application of what we now commonly call *multiple indicator models,* and while this term refers to what is fundamentally a data analysis technique, this type of data analysis and the models underlying it suggest new insights into problems of data production.

Multiple indicator models in measurement theory are not at all new. Psychometricians have been using multiple indicators—usually called test items—for decades. But measurement theory as developed by psychometri- cians earlier in this century was dominated by the clinical and administrative concerns that motivated the development of psychological tests and measurements; psychometrics has been rather little influenced until very recently by concerns for drawing theoretically relevant research conclusions—although, in all fairness, I should add that it was not originally evident that the two might lead in different directions. Given their clinical and administrative concerns, early psychometricians—whose work has continued to influence the prevailing conception of measurement in all the social and behavioral sciences except economics—developed multiple indicator models for assessing their measures, but those models represented each dimension and its multiple indicators (or "test items") as an isolated and independent system of variables. Thus, for example, traditional reliability theory is clearly based on the assumption that one has several indicators for the same underlying dimension, and reliability is estimated from the correlation among those indicators. Such an estimate is based on the assumptions—always there but not always explicit—that the indicators are what we would now call "reflector indicators"[1] and that the only reason for the lack of perfect correspondence between the dimension and each of its several indicators is random measurement error. The development of exploratory factor analysis entailed the recognition that a given indicator or "item" might be "loaded" on more than one dimension or "factor." This is clearly a recognition that something other than random measurement error might be entailed in the lack of perfect correspondence between a dimension and its indicators. But this recognition did not seem to shake the prevailing presumption that the adequacy of a measure based on multiple indicators should and could be assessed independently of the research context in which that measure is to be used, in which context some of the other factors on which the indicator "loads" might also be included. More recent developments suggested by the new kind of multiple indicator models—perhaps best represented by referring to "causal models with multiple indicators"—clearly suggest that measures need to be assessed within a specified research context. These newer multiple indicator models shift attention from the assumption that data production should be designed to minimize random measurement error to the somewhat more complex assumption that, while random measurement error is bothersome, data production should be designed primarily to minimize correlated measurement error, which has the far greater potential for leading us astray in our conclusions.

A substantive illustration may assist in highlighting the potential impact of correlated measurement error on our conclusions, and in suggesting how sensitivity to correlated measurement error may assist in the design of indicators and in the correct specification of multiple indicator models. We consider an investigator who proposes that variation in the "divorce rate" among the 50 states of the United States is explained, in part, by variation in the "status of women." To explore this possibility, the investigator suggests that a reflector indicator of the "status of women" (i.e., the degree to which men and women are status equals) is the level of female employment (i.e., the proportion of women, 20 to 65 years of age, in the paid labor force at least half-time). The investigator also proposes that a reflector indicator of the "divorce rate" (i.e., the propensity of marriages to be terminated by divorce) might be the ratio of divorces to marriages at risk (i.e., the ratio of divorces during a given year to the number of marriages at the beginning of that year). The investigator's reasoning about the dimensions and their indicators is represented in Figure 3.1A.

We now consider factors other than the dimensions indicated that seem likely to influence the indicators. For simplicity in this illustration, we focus only on the level of female employment, which, we reasonably argue, will be influenced by the level of household prosperity (i.e., many poor families will lead to a higher rate of female employment) and by the number of female-headed households in the population. These additional hypothesized influences on the indicator are represented in Figure 3.1B.

As a third step, we consider possible connections between the factors influencing the indicator in question and the other variables included in the system being analyzed. If no such connections seem likely, we might proceed to treat the "extraneous" influences on the indicator as if they behaved like random measurement error. But if there is a plausible connection between these "extraneous" influences and other variables in the model, we will have correlated measurement error, which should lead either to our dropping the indicator or specifying the correlated error as a part of the model. We reason that the proportion of female-headed households in a given year will be influenced by the divorce rates of prior years and that there will be an autocorrelation between the divorce rates of succeeding years. Hence, we posit a correlation between the "propensity of marriages to be terminated by divorce" and the measurement errors in "female employment" as an indicator of the "status of women." Note that this does *not* imply that "female employment" has correlated measurement error when used as an indicator of some other dimension or in a model that does not include the "propensity of marriages to be terminated by divorce" as one of the dimensions. It is in this sense that the adequacy of the indicator is specific to the research context in which it is employed. We assume further that the level of household prosperity will influence not only the level of female employment but also the propensity of marriages to be terminated by divorce. And so we have identified a second reason for a correlation between the "propensity of marriages to be terminated by divorce" and the measurement errors in "female employment" as an indicator of the "status of women." We translate this into the hypothesis of

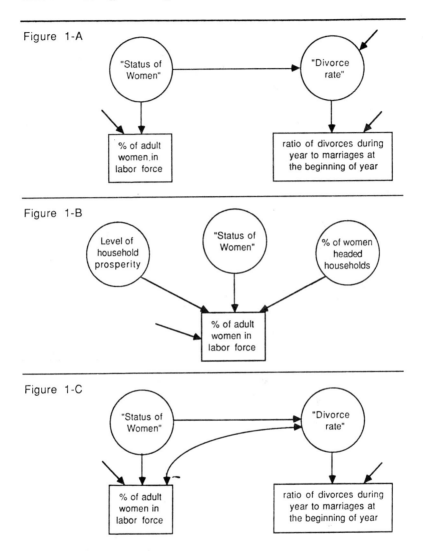

Figure 3.1 Steps in the Specification of Correlated Measurement Error

a "loading" of the indicator on the second dimension in the system being analyzed. The respecified model, incorporating these assumptions about correlated measurement error, is shown in Figure 3.1C.

This illustration should help clarify the following points: (a) Without a recognition of the possibility of correlated error, as illustrated in Figure

3.1C, we might have drawn a misleading conclusion. Otherwise stated, we might mistake the correlated error for an effect of the "status of women" on the "divorce rate." (b) We can specify plausible correlated errors by considering the factors that may influence an indicator and then considering the connections between those factors and other variables in the system being analyzed. These steps are illustrated in Figures 3.1B and 3.1C. (c) We would ordinarily prefer indicators that are not contaminated by correlated measurement error and hence would attempt to design indicators that lack this complication or to select from several possible indicators those that lack this complication. (d) If we cannot design or select indicators that are reasonably assumed to be free of correlated measurement error, the alternatve strategy is to incorporate suspected correlated measurement errors into the specification of the measurement model. Such a specification is illustrated in Figure 3.1C, although to keep the illustration simple we have, of course, specified a model that is underidentified. But a model that includes correlated measurement error may be identified, given a sufficient number of indicators.

In still another respect, the increased attention to causal models with multiple indicators has shifted our attention in ways that seem likely to be productive. At first glance, the shift may seem to be a minor one, but it is a shift that will probably be important. I refer here to the fact that "causal models with multiple indicators" encourage one to think, not simply of a set of potential "predictor variables" for a given "criterion variable" (to adopt the traditional language of multiple regression), but of a set of dimensions that play a role in an explanatory formulation and of potential indicators for those dimensions. This mode of thinking seems likely to encourage us, first, to think more carefully about "how the world works," instead of thinking about a set of variables that happen to be convenient for us to measure. Second, because we are constrained to think of measures that reflect dimensions that play a role in a specific explanatory formulation, this mode of thinking also seems likely to encourage us to recognize that measures need to be designed to correspond to the specific dimensions and explanatory formulation that are to be explored with the data.

This point may be clarified by the following substantive illustration. We consider an investigation of the perceived level of equity prevailing in a series of partnerships. The measure of equity is not our primary concern here, but we assume that it is measured by responses to a series of questions about whether the respondent feels that he or his partner realizes a better "deal" from the partnership. Our focus is on understanding variation in such equity judgments, for example, what factors help explain why partner A in the A-B partnership feels that he gets a very good deal, while partner C in the C-D partnership feels that he doesn't do so well. Our explanatory variables might be conceived as describing both the "investments" and the "rewards" of the partners. Thus in the A-B and C-D partnerships just mentioned, we seek to determine how much A puts into the A-B partnership and how much he receives from it, and similarly, how much C puts into the C-D partnership and how much he receives from that input. We anticipate that these variables will be predictors of the "equity judgments" of A and C respectively. We proceed to devise a set of questions to determine "investments" and "rewards," enter them as predictors in a multiple regression equation, and see which "investments" and which "rewards" are the best predictors, and how well the set collectively predicts variation in equity judgments. This might sound like a very reasonable way to proceed, and a way that is warranted on the basis of an accumulated literature emphasizing the roles of "investments" and "rewards" in judgments of equity. But the use of the predictor variables as described makes an implicit assumption that does not correspond well to the literature on the contribution of "investments" and "rewards" to "equity judgments." In the procedure described, we are implicitly assuming that the comparison reference group of our respondents is composed of other persons in other partnerships, whereas the literature on equity suggests that the comparison reference group should be the other member(s) of each respondent's partnership.

If we wish our measures to correspond to the prevailing perspective in the literature on equity, i.e., to serve as a measure of the "investments" and "rewards" of each partner relative to the other member of that partnership, the variables just described are not well designed to do so. To have measures that correspond to the prevailing theoretical assumption, we must devise a measure of "investments" (to narrow our attention to investments only, dropping rewards from the further discussion of this illustration for the purpose of simplicity) relative to the other investments in each partnership. This point is illustrated in Table 3.2 for the oversimplified condition of only two partnerships, each with two members. To emphasize the difference, the hypothetical illustrations in Table 3.2 have been contrived to yield contradictory predictions about the relative level of the "equity judgments" of A and C, one partner in each of the two partnerships.

To give a substantive interpretation of the first outcome (i.e., assuming the relevant reference group for each respondent is the set of other respondents in other partnerships), we might suppose that A takes note of the fact that his investment in the A-B partnership is high when compared to the investment of C in the C-D partnership. Hence A, comparing himself to C, concludes that his own A-B partnership is relatively costly to him and

TABLE 3.2

Alternative Theoretical Assumptions, the Corresponding
Variables for "Investments" as Predictors of "Equity Judgments,"
and the Implied Predictions

Assume: Two partnerships: (A, B) and (C, D)

"Equity judgments" about these partnerships by A and C, i.e., E_a and E_c respectively

Measures of the "investments" into their respective partnerships of all partners,
i.e., I_i, where i = a, b, c or d

Theoretical assumption	Corresponding "investment" variables	Hypothetical illustration	Implied prediction
		Assume $I_a = 30$	Assume a higher "investment" implies a lower "equity judgment"
		$I_b = 40$	
		$I_c = 20$	
		$I_d = 10$	
The relevant reference group for A and C is each other	$I'_a = I_a - \overline{I}_{ac}$ $= I_a - \dfrac{I_a + I_c}{2}$ $I'_c = I_c - \overline{I}_{ac}$	$I'_a = 30 - 25 = 5$ $I'_c = 20 - 25 = -5$	$E_a < E_c$
The relevant reference group for A is B and the relevant reference group for C is D	$I''_a = I_a - \overline{I}_{ab}$ $= I_a - \dfrac{I_a + I_b}{2}$ $I''_c = I_c - \overline{I}_{cd}$ $= I_c - \dfrac{I_c + I_d}{2}$	$I''_a = 30 - 35 = -5$ $I''_c = 20 - 15 = 5$	$E_a > E_c$

so judges that he is getting a bad bargain, that is, his "equity judgment" is relatively low. In contrast, C perceives that he is advantaged as compared to A and hence his "equity judgment" is relatively high.

We now consider a substantive interpretation of the second outcome (i.e., assuming the relevant reference group for each respondent to be the other member of his own partnership). We thus suppose that A takes note of the fact that his investment in the A-B partnership is low relative to that of his partner, B, and so concludes that he, A, is getting a good deal. On the other hand, C notes that his investment in the C-D partnership is high relative to that of his partner, D, and hence concludes that he, C, is not getting a fair shake in this partnership.

But what does all this have to say about the design of variables? The illustration serves to point to a kind of "reference group" assumption that is implicit in our usual statistical procedures. For example, when we regress earnings on education among a broadly based sample of adults, our procedure will measure variation in education around the mean for the total sample. Thus implicit in this procedure is the assumption that the effect of education on earnings depends, not on the educational level of each person relative to other educational levels in that person's employing firm, for example, but on the educational level of each person relative to the educational levels of all persons in all firms. Insofar as reference groups other than the total sample seem relevant to our substantive interests and to the theoretical formulation at issue in the research, we will need to design a variable that will reflect those concerns. But more generally, the illustration is intended to highlight how crucial it is that the variables operationalized in research correspond to the underlying theoretical reasoning at issue in the research. One is reminded of an often quoted definition of measurement that refers simply to the assignment of numbers to objects. That is a terribly misleading conception of measurement because it makes no reference to the fact that measurement is always measurement *of* something, that is, of a dimension of interest. Hence, measurement is more adequately conceived as the assignment of numbers to "objects" (cases) so as to represent the relative positions of those "objects" along some dimension of interest. Attention to "causal models with multiple indicators" has served to highlight, not only the fact that measures are attempts to represent positions on some dimension, but that these dimensions derive their meaning and importance from their role in a theoretical formulation. Thus we would do well to remember that our variables are not "given" but must be designed to measure the dimensions conceived in our theoretical arguments. The implied movement away from an extreme form of "operationalism" toward a conception of research methodology that entails a closer integration of theoretical reasoning and research operation is one of the major trends in sociological research over the past 30 years. In accord with the common practice in "futurist" projections of turning biases into prognostications, we can reasonably anticipate that this trend will continue.

The optimistic futurist. If "necessity is the mother of methodological invention," we can anticipate that the problems just outlined will be resolved so that sociological research will become more informative. In this rosy scenario, the "quasi-experimental method," originated by John Stuart Mill a century and a half ago, will continue to be refined in its social research applications. We will also devise more adequate ways of exploring for the nonadditive effects that sociological theorists suggest are ubiquitous, and do so with scales that have arbitrary zero points and by methods that do not entail the loss of information about additive effects in the process. And we will develop a more systematic conception of the process of data production as we recognize that variables are not "given" but have to be designed to serve in the empirical exploration of specific theoretical formulations.

There will, of course, be those who insist that they have no time to wait for such finicky refinements in methodology, or even no inclination to use them when they have been developed. They will insist, with some justification, that sociologists of the future will—and should—"muddle through," much as those of the past have done. But the optimists among us, at the risk of going to the very pinnacle of optimistic futurism, can foresee the emergence of a corps of sociologists who see their role to consist, not simply of engaging in an ongoing activity commonly called "doing research," but as engaging in that activity in ways that are likely to yield enduring sociological knowledge. We haven't made striking progress toward that goal in the century and a half since John Stuart Mill charted the course, but we do seem to be getting better at it all the time.

NOTE

1. If the causal arrow goes from the underlying dimension to the indicator, that indicator is a "reflector indicator." This contrasts to a "producer indicator," which is presumed to have an effect on the underlying dimension (as when an experimental manipulation serves as an indicator) and to a "correlate indicator," in which case indicator and dimension are correlated because both have common sources of variation rather than being linked by cause and effect.

REFERENCES

Allison, Paul D. (1977) "Testing for interaction in multiple regression." American Journal of Sociology 83: 144-153.
Costner, Herbert L. [ed.] (1971) Sociological Methodology, 1971. San Francisco: Jossey-Bass.
Nagel, Ernest [ed.] (1950) John Stuart Mill's Philosophy of Scientific Method. New York: Hafner.
Ragin, Charles C. (1987) The Comparative Method: Moving Beyond Qualitative and Quantitative Strategies. University of California Press.

4

HOW APPLIED SOCIOLOGY CAN SAVE BASIC SOCIOLOGY

Richard A. Berk

University of California, Los Angeles

There have always been sociologists critical of their discipline. Over the past generation, for example, mainstream sociology has been taken to task from a variety of perspectives. Glaser and Strauss (1967) used "theoretical sampling" to attack conventional survey (probability) sampling, Gouldner (1970) challenged through "reflexive sociology" an alleged functionalist hegemony, and Cicourel (1964) employed ethnomethodology to inveigh against the ubiquitous questionnaire.

It is my sense, however, that these sorts of challenges have, by and large, come from the margins of profession; fundamental criticism of conventional sociology has not been part of conventional sociology itself. While there has certainly been lots of petty bickering, none of the enterprise's foundations have been seriously questioned by the profession's insiders. None, that is, until quite recently.

In Peter H. Rossi's 1980 presidential address, we were told that the discipline suffered from a debilitating "ambivalence" toward applied work. In a similar vein, the following year found William Foote Whyte's presidential address (1981) calling for a basic "reorientation" toward greater "practical relevance." In other words, two ASA presidents had apparently abandoned important tenets underlying basic sociological research.

Taking a very different cut, Lieberson (1985) more recently has argued that the mainstream's quantitative tradition is foundering on causal modeling based on "the experimental traditions of the natural sciences."[1] Duncan's (1984) new effort is perhaps even more unsettling. He effectively

Author's Note: Thanks go to Otis Dudley Duncan, Michael Sobel, and Thomas Pullum for comments on an earlier draft of this chapter.

dispatches with virtually all quantitative sociological research relying on measures of subjective states. In short, whether the target is sociology's stance toward the empirical world or its quantitative apparatus, some of the discipline's major figures are now suggesting that as currently undertaken, the enterprise is probably bankrupt.

One can draw a number of lessons from such criticism. For purposes of this chapter, three stand out. First, a prima facie case exists that mainstream sociology is in serious, and perhaps unprecedented, trouble. Second, virtually no part of the field is immune, certainly not the flagship of basic quantitative research. Third, none of the critics are nihilistic. For example, neither Leiberson nor Duncan argue for abandoning quantitative social research. Rather, all propose alternatives to current practice that in time may significantly improve matters.

In the pages that follow, I plan to draw on these three lessons while focusing on an aspect of the "current crisis" that previous critics have overlooked. I will argue that values *necessarily* figure in all quantitative social research in ways far more subtle than earlier sociological observers have apparently understood. These values, in turn, can affect one's empirical findings. Whether *distortions* result depends upon the fit between the values implicit in one's statistical procedures and the values one holds. I will then propose that the inconclusiveness that characterizes all sociological literatures (or at least those with which I am familiar) derives significantly, but certainly not exclusively, from haphazard relationships between the values held by researchers and the statistical procedures they employ. Finally, I will suggest that in *applied* social research there is the prospect of a solution.

AN EXAMPLE

Perhaps the best way initially to approach material is through a concrete application. I hope to introduce all of my major points through a real problem facing applied social researchers. The problem is "career criminals," the proposed solution is "selective incapacitation," and the engine powering the solution is predictions of "future dangerousness."

The Policy Question

Over the past five years, there has been a growing realization that a relatively small proportion of offenders commit the vast majority of property crimes (e.g., Chaiken and Chaiken, 1982). Most property felons dabble in crime, but a few seem to do little else. It follows, then, that on grounds of cost-effectiveness at least, criminal justice resources should be directed toward arresting, convicting, and sanctioning the criminal over-achievers. *If* high rate offenders could be found before a significant number of their future crimes were committed, and *if* their prison sentences could be lengthened to include their especially active years, the aggregate property crime rate should be dramatically reduced. Moreover, costly prison resources (about $15,000 per year per prisoner) would be more efficiently allocated.

The case for this sort of "selective incapacitation" has been made by a number of policy analysts (e.g., Wilson, 1983) and while the jurisprudential issues are difficult, they do not seem to preclude sentencing with selective incapacitation as one of the considerations (Morris and Miller, 1985). Yet, whatever the practical merits, everything depends on an ability to predict accurately future criminal behavior.

There is now a sizable and respectable applied research community believing that, at least in principle, "future dangerousness" can be predicted in a useful manner (Monahan, 1981; Greenwood, 1982; Blumstein, 1983; Cohen, 1983; Blumstein et al., 1985). It is known, for example, that high risk offenders tend to begin their illegal activities at a relatively early age, are typically incarcerated one or more times while still juveniles, rarely finish school, have intermittent employment histories, and often develop various kinds of drug dependencies. These and other characteristics lead naturally to forecasting models with some a priori rationale.

It may seem that once one has decided to work on the problem of forecasting future dangerousness, value-free research procedures take over. In other words, although the policy arguments and the jurisprudential debates necessarily mix value with fact, the development of forecasting models becomes a routine undertaking for quantitative social science. Put still another way, we leave to science the job of constructing the model, and we leave to politics the job of how the model will be used. To decide, however, whether this neat division of labor is realistic, we need to consider briefly how statistical techniques may be employed to predict future dangerousness.

A Primer on Statistical Forecasting

The process of forecasting can be distilled into the following framework (see Granger, 1980, for an accessible introduction to the issues and Berk and Cooley, 1987, for a more abstract treatment). Suppose one has a set of observations based on either a cross-sectional or time series design and wants to make predictions about a future set of observations (or in the case of cross-sectional data, alternative observations). It is typically assumed that the observations in hand and the observations that one cannot observe are realizations (i.e., random samples) from the same underlying probability density (or equivalently, of the same underlying stochastic process), indexed by the same parameters. In other words, the future will be like the past except for chance variation and in some cases, changes in the values of the density's parameters.

It should be apparent that the ideal information to have would be the underlying probability density with its future parameter values. With this information, one could select any point estimate of interest. For example, if the exact future density were known, one might pick the mean (i.e., expected value) or the median of that density as one's point forecast. One could also employ region forecasts using confidence intervals (i.e., for forecasts of a range of outcomes in which a given case is likely to appear).

While there is some very recent work showing how in principle whole densities may be forecast (Cooley and Parke, 1985),[2] virtually all forecasting efforts to date have had to settle for less (Granger and Newbold, 1977: 112). One problem, for instance, is that predictors themselves often have to be predicted. Thus if employed individuals are less crime prone, and if employment status is a predictor in a forecasting model, predictions of future dangerousness also require predictions of future employment. The uncertainty introduced by predicted predictors leads to virtually intractable problems when attempts are made to generate future densities.

Rather than produce the entire density, therefore, researchers typically have "skipped" to point estimates of interest. For example, the relationship between an outcome to be forecast and a set of explanatory variables is initially specified. The parameters of this relationship are then estimated with data on hand. Finally, the data and the parameter estimates are used to produce one or more numbers (sometimes coupled with confidence intervals) to be used as forecasts. For example, when multiple regression is used to produce forecasts, the conditional mean of the dependent variable is usually taken as the point forecast.

Forecasting models can take a wide variety of forms and capitalize on many different statistical technologies. For example, as examined in some depth in Cooley and Berk (1985), forecasting models may be structural or astructural. An astructural model includes explanatory variables that can account for variation in the outcome (and are not consequences of the outcome variable), even if there is no causal relationship in the usual sense (e.g., the definition of Granger Causality in Granger and Newbold, 1977: 224-226). That is, a change in one of the explanatory variables need not lead to a change in the outcome variable. Race, for instance, may be a useful predictor of criminal activity, but it is not usually conceptualized as a cause of criminal activity. A structural models may be estimated in many ways, but Box-Jenkins time series techniques are popular, in part because no causal structure need be imposed (Box and Jenkins, 1976).

Structural models, in contrast, purport to represent the *mechanisms* by which the explanatory variables affect the outcome variable. That is, it is assumed that changes in each of the explanatory variables lead to changes in the outcome variable. In fact, explanatory variables that account for substantial portions of the variation in the outcome variable, but are not causal, are excluded. Structural models too may be estimated in a variety of ways, but regression techniques are common.

Whether one's model is structural or astructural, the aim is typically to produce (at least) point forecasts. These may be properly conceptualized as *central tendency measures* of (typically) unspecified future densities that depend, in turn, upon predictor variables. Thus the value of such central tendency measures will vary depending on whether the individual is, for instance, male or female, employed or unemployed, and/or a first offender.

How Values Necessarily Enter

An absolutely critical question, therefore, is which central tendency measure to use. If large forecasting errors are to be given special relative weight compared to small forecasting errors, the conditional mean might well be preferred. This leads in turn to the usual multiple regression approach based on the least squares (LS) principle. Under multiple regression, the predicted values from the regression equation (which are nothing more than conditional means) are the forecasts that minimize the sum of the squared forecasting errors (Pindyck and Rubinfeld 1981: 206-207). The same conclusion holds for the Box-Jenkins time series procedures (Granger and Newbold, 1977: 111-126). Put another way, the predicted values from the regression equations are the numbers that will minimize one's aggregate *squared* forecasting errors. This implies that if the mean of the underlying probability density is one's most sensible forecast, multiple regression or Box-Jenkins time series procedures are appropriate.

However, if large forecasting errors are not to be given special relative weight, least squares approaches (even if estimated by maximum likelihood techniques) are incorrect. Rather, one must employ multivariate techniques that minimize the sum of the absolute values of the forecasting errors and in the process, produce the conditional median, not conditional mean, as the forecast. Least absolute residual regression (LAR) accomplishes this end. In other words, least absolute residual regression will minimize the aggregate forecast error, when errors are defined by their absolute values, not their square. Just as when the unconditional mean and median are compared, one's forecasts can be dramatically affected by the choice between the conditional mean and median. In other words, the forecasts from least squares regression can differ substantially from the least absolute residual regression forecasts.

Consider Table 4.1, which shows a random draw from each of two different lognormal distributions. The lognormal is chosen partly for computational convenience and partly because it reflects the kinds of highly skewed distributions one often finds for criminal justice outcome variables (Cohen, 1983; Schmidt and Witte, 1984).[3] Note that the first distribution has a smaller mean and median than the second (i.e., 3.07 versus 4.32 and 1.24 versus 1.32).

Suppose that for purposes of exposition (and no loss in generality) the two distributions represent the number of crimes committed in the past month for two different groups of convicted felons and that there is a single, binary variable that distinguishes meaningfully between them (e.g., black versus white). That is, the two groups (i.e., I and II) are on the average identical on all other variables that might influence the number of crimes committed in the past month.

One might explore the relationship between the binary explanatory variable and the outcome variable by regressing the outcome on the binary variable. Should a least squares procedure be employed, the regression coefficient is 1.25 (4.32-3.07). Should a least absolute residual procedure be employed, the regression coefficient is .08 (1.32-1.24). The former is statistically significant at the .05 level, while the latter is not.[4] In other words, under least squares, one expects on the average about 1.25 more crimes from group II than from group I, while under least absolute residuals, the groups are effectively indistinguishable. Thus LS leads to using the binary variable as a predictor, while LAR does not.

In addition, should these regression results be used as the basis for forecasts, the two procedures generate very different predictions. With LS, about three crimes are predicted for group I and about four crimes for group II. With LAR, a little more than one crime is predicted for both groups I and II. In short, under LS, the expected danger is three to four times greater than under LAR.

It cannot be overemphasized that both the least squares results and the least absolute residual results are technically correct. Which one chooses to

TABLE 4.1
Two Lognormal Distributions
$(N_1 = N_2 = 500)$

I. mean = 3.07   standard deviation = 5.16   median = 1.24

No. of crimes	Proportion
1	.45
2	.18
3	.09
4	.07
5	.04
6	.04
7	.02
8	.03
9	.01
10	.01
11	.01
12	.01
13+	.04

II. mean = 4.32   standard deviation = 9.44   median = 1.32

No. of crimes	Proportion
1	.42
2	.18
3	.09
4	.07
5	.05
6	.02
7	.03
8	.03
9	.01
10	.01
11	.01
12	.01
13+	.07

Regression Results
(standard errors in parentheses)

LS: No. of crimes = 3.07 + 1.25 (binary variable)
           (.23)   (.48)

LAR: No. of crimes = 1.23 + 0.08 (binary variable)
           (.28)   (.60)

use depends on how the forecasting errors should be weighted relative to one another. And that choice is necessarily value laden.

To illustrate, consider the following two forecasting errors: (1) one crime is forecast and three are committed, and (2) one crime is forecast and five are committed. Under LAR the forecasting errors are weighted 1:2, while under LS the forecasting errors are weighted 1:4. Is the second forecasting error twice as bad or four times as bad as the first forecasting error? It depends on the *consequences* of the forecasting errors. The value of the errors cannot be determined until their consequences have been specified and evaluated. In this instance, consequences would depend upon what *action* was taken as a result of the forecasts.

To continue with the example, suppose a convicted felon's prison sentence is pegged to a forecast of one crime and as a result, a sentence of 18 months is served. After release from the 18-month sentence, the felon quickly commits five crimes that at least in theory would have been prevented had an accurate forecast been made and proper prison sentence been attached. The sentence served was far too short; had five crimes been predicted, the felon would have served, say, 60 months, and the five crimes would have been prevented. Now consider a second felon for whom one crime is predicted and three crimes are committed after an 18-month sentence. Is the first error four times or two times worse than the second? If four times, the forecast should have been based on LS procedures. If two times, the forecast should have been based on LAR procedures. In practice, such issues have been to my knowledge universally overlooked. Forecasting techniques are chosen on other grounds, and the value decisions are made implicitly.

One might well worry about whether the results in Table 4.1 represent atypical patterns. However, when the outcome variable is substantially skewed, ordinary least squares regression results and least absolute residual regression results will differ dramatically. Recall that the purpose of recent selective incapacitation proposal is to separate the bulk of offenders with low crime rates from the few offenders with high crime rates. Data sets that include both kinds of offenders will have highly skewed outcome variables and be vulnerable to just the kinds of difficulties shown in Table 4.1.

More Realism and More Complications

The discussion so far has contrasted two different weighting schemes for forecasting errors and examined what those schemes imply about appropriate forecasting techniques. In fact, forecasts of future dangerousness almost certainly require far more complicated weighting procedures and far more complicated conceptions of cost.

A bit more formally, the quadratic and linear weighting procedures we have discussed may be represented respectively as

$$(1) \ \text{Cost}(e_f) = A(e_f)^2 \text{ or } \text{Cost}(e_f) = A|e_f|,$$

where "Cost(e_f)" stands for the cost (or loss) function of the forecasting errors, and "A" is a constant measure of value (e.g., in dollars) by which the weighted forecasting errors (i.e., e_f) are multiplied. With the weighting schemes we have considered, the constant A has no impact on which forecasting procedure one chooses, and so it has not been discussed. It would have a critical impact, however, on the policy implications of any forecasts, such as whether selective incapacitation were cost-effective.

The first and probably most important complication is that the forecasting errors associated with future dangerousness probably should not be treated symmetrically. For example, a prison term that is inappropriately too long by three years probably should not be weighted the same as a prison term that is inappropriately too short by three years. That is, false positives should not be treated the same as false negatives.

Second, the precise nature of appropriate asymmetric weighting will depend on a number of particulars. For example, a sentence that is three years too short for a burglar may have quite different consequences from a sentence that is three years too short for a rapist. Likewise, a sentence that is three years too long will have one set of consequences for a felon who has a family to support and another set of consequences for a felon who will, upon release, move in with his parents.

Third, the assignment of costs has to allow for substantial asymmetries and discontinuities. For example, in *Barefoot v. Estelle* [103 S. Ct. 3383 (1983)], the U.S. Supreme Court determined that in death penalty cases, predictions of future dangerousness could be used in sentencing decisions. Clearly, false positives should not be weighted the same as false negatives, but in addition, the costs of false positives are probably discontinuous. The costs of prison sentences for homicide that are inappropriately too long probably increase in a reasonably smooth fashion with sentence length. But costs (for most observers) increase suddenly and enormously when the death penalty threshold is incorrectly passed. Similar discontinuities are likely to be associated with all binary decisions in criminal justice processing such as decisions on whether to release on bail, whether to indict, and whether to "divert" before trial.

Unfortunately, the moment one confronts asymmetric and/or discontinuous cost (or loss) functions, existing forecasting technology is left behind. With a very few and simple exceptions, *there are no forecasting techniques yet developed that are able to respond appropriately* (Granger and Newbold, 1977: 155-119). In other words, there are no forecasting techniques that are likely to correspond to the required cost function, and if some other technique is used instead, an incorrect cost function will be automatically imposed. The results may well be forecasts that are some distance from the forecast that would have been produced with appropriate procedures.

In summary, the moment one moves beyond very simple and often unrealistic cost functions, there exists *no* appropriate forecasting technology. The use of an alternative and available procedure will impose a cost function that may be very different from the cost function desired. Hence, the forecasts produced will be some distance from the forecasts that, in principle, are being sought. As a result, decisions made on the basis of those forecasts will often be different from the decisions that would have been made if the forecasting technology were consistent with the cost function. Simply put, there will be bad decisions.

Some Implications

Forecasts of future dangerousness used to affect the lives of people being processed by the criminal justice system necessarily *depend* on the costs associated with forecasting errors. The dependency affects which statistical procedures are appropriate (when they have been developed) and, therefore, the actual forecasts produced; different costs may well lead to different numbers. And the costs are necessarily premised on values. I see no way to purge values from the "technical" process of producing forecasts of future dangerousness, or any other outcome of policy interest; built into the justification for any statistical forecasting procedure are values preferences.

It follows, therefore, that these values need to be articulated before an informed choice of forecasting technique can be made. It also follows that in the absence of such disclosures, important values are implicitly built into what are typically advertised as value-free predictions. Moreover, forecasts may be produced that are inconsistent with the values of researchers and/or policy makers. Finally, it follows that when the underlying values do not inform the applied researcher's choice of forecasting technique, statistical techniques are being selected in somewhat haphazard fashion that, not surprisingly, may generate a haphazard applied literature.

STATISTICAL GENERALIZATIONS

The necessary link between values and forecasting in policy settings is easily generalized to a number of other statistical decisions in applied research. First, it is widely recognized that the choice of the critical level in significance tests and/or the production of confidence intervals implies value trade-offs between Type I and Type II errors. For example, significance tests for estimates of impact of some social programs should rest on a judgment of the relative costs of falsely concluding that the program works, compared to falsely concluding that the program does not work. This requires, in turn, an assessment of the likely consequences of actions based on the significance tests. In fact, the entire significance tests framework can, under the rubric of statistical decision theory, be expanded and altered formally to take the costs of various actions into account (e.g., DeGroot, 1970).

Less widely recognized, perhaps, is that the choice of one's estimator also rests on value premises. For example, virtually all estimators are evaluated with respect to bias (among other things). But the concept of bias makes no distinction between underestimates and overestimates of population parameters. That is, an estimator of program impact that on the average inflates the program's importance is treated the same as an estimator that on the average deflates the program's importance. Consequently, average estimation errors are treated symmetrically, which is clearly a value judgment. Even more fundamentally, under an asymmetric cost function, an equivalence between the sampling distribution's expected value and the value of the population parameter may *not* be desirable.

Estimators are also often justified with respect to the variance of their sampling distributions (essentially, efficiency). The definition of variance clearly implies a quadratic cost function (as does the mean square error criterion), whose limitations we have addressed in the forecasting context.

In short, the entire estimation apparatus applied researchers employ rests on cost functions that may well be different from the cost functions desired. Moreover, the justification for these or other cost functions are *not* statistical problems. As Barnett (1982: 19) has observed, there are no "truly objective grounds for assessing the merits of internal criteria, such as, for example, the *unbiasedness* of point estimators" (emphasis in the original).

Third, the rationales for procedures used to construct estimators are equally value laden. As I have already noted several times, the least squares criterion implies a quadratic cost function. The same holds for minimum Chi-squared methods. And why under maximum likelihood estimation should we feel good when estimators are chosen at the mode of the likelihood function? Drawing once again on Barnett (1982: 147), "it is difficult to formally justify 'maximizing the likelihood.'"

To summarize, it is difficult to imagine a statistical procedure whose use does not invoke an implicit cost function. If some procedures are better than others, a value-based yardstick must be operating. Then applied researchers can be seriously misled when the values they hold (or their audience holds) are inconsistent with the cost functions inherent in the statistical procedures employed.

IS BASIC RESEARCH IMMUNE?

In the section headed: An Example, I demonstrated how forecasts of future dangerousness are necessarily related to values. The statistical tool selected to produce a forecast has clear implications for how one is weighing positive and negative forecasting errors. Ideally, therefore, one should specify a cost function and then select an appropriate forecasting technique (assuming that appropriate statistical procedures exist). It cannot be overemphasized that different statistical procedures can generate different forecasts. It also cannot be overemphasized that a cost function is necessarily implied by one's forecasting procedures, even if that cost function is unacknowledged.

In the section headed: Statistical Generalizations, I drew on well-known statistical concepts to show that for applied problems, cost functions affect far more than one's forecasting tools. For example, the estimator one chooses necessarily implies a cost function; indeed, the very criteria developed more generally to justify particular estimators rest on specific cost functions. Again, values affect how one decides to analyze data.

But, are cost functions relevant only to applied work? I think not. When, for example, one chooses the OLS estimator for a basic research problem, a quadratic cost function is necessarily implied. The same holds for any estimator; the inferential statistics used can be justified *only* with respect to one or more cost functions that, in turn, *must* be value-laden. And these values are involved even when they are unacknowledged. Calling our research "value-free" only obfuscates.[5]

But, does it matter? I think so, although the issues rapidly become very complicated. There is, it seems to me, no argument that when any estimator is used, a value position is necessarily being taken. Likewise, there should be no argument that different values imply different cost functions and that, in turn, different estimators will typically be implied.

However, whether different estimators produce *substantively* different estimates depends in part on the data. To take a simple example, since for a symmetric distribution the mean is the same as the median, a quadratic cost function and an absolute-value cost function produce equivalent results. And although realized distributions found in data will never be exactly symmetric, many will be symmetric for all practical purposes. Put another way, the distortions that may result from choosing the wrong estimator will be the least of one's problems. Yet, many empirical distributions are a very long way from symmetric, and symmetry in the empirical distribution buys very little when one's cost function is not symmetric as well.

In short, whether values will make a difference depends on (a) whether the (typically) implicit cost function is appropriate for the analysis, (b) the distribution of the variable(s) in question, and (c) the form of one's cost function. Empirical literatures in sociology will be in disarray to the degree that inappropriate cost functions are implied in the context of asymmetric data distribution(s) and cost functions.

Is it possible for basic researchers to avoid these problems by claiming to have no cost function? I do not see how. The moment one chooses an estimator, a value position is at least implicitly taken. Is it possible for basic researchers to argue that popular cost functions are analogous to "prior ignorance" in Bayesian statistics (e.g., Barnett, 1982: 206-209)? Again, I do not see how. It is one thing to proceed as if all possible parameters values are equally probable a priori, and quite another to give all errors equal weight. Finally, is it possible for basic researchers to claim that their research has *no* consequences and, therefore, that cost functions are irrelevant? Once again, I am not persuaded. When an estimator is chosen, the researcher is behaving as if the research really mattered. I do not see how the basic researcher can have it both ways.

APPLIED RESEARCH AS A SOLUTION

I have argued that the cost functions associated with particular estimators can affect one's empirical results in practice as well as principle. It follows, therefore, that estimators should be selected based on a particular cost function and its inherent values. But the values operating in a cost function can be determined only from the *uses* to which the empirical results will be put; the importance attached to a given error (e.g., a sampling error) depends on the *consequences* of that error. And the moment researchers begin to take the consequences of their work into account, they have entered the applied arena. In other words, the proper use of statistical procedures in basic research may well require that basic researchers be dragged (kicking and screaming?) into applied social research.

To make this more concrete, suppose that one wanted to estimate the impact of schooling on future earnings. Clearly, an estimator must be chosen. The use of ordinary least squares could be justified by the minimum variance criterion (among the set of linear, unbiased estimators), if, on the average, underestimates of the impact of schooling were as troubling as overestimates, and if, on the average, large errors in either direction were especially troubling. But how could such a determination be made without considering the *consequences* of one's findings?

Although I believe that it is only through applied considerations that statistical procedures can be used properly, there are at least four major obstacles. First, the introduction of cost functions that take the consequences of one's research into account almost certainly moves one from classical inference to Bayesian inference. This is no small leap either in technology or philosophy. In other words, if the role of values is to be taken seriously and rigorously in sociology, major methodological retooling is required.

Second, it is no easy matter to specify a cost function, even in settings that are explicitly applied. For example, in order to specify a cost function, all consequences must be placed on the same metric (e.g., dollars). And that assumes that all of the consequences can be designated. In addition, it is not apparent how to proceed when a given study is linked to several different cost functions (e.g., for different audiences). Aggregating cost functions requires a whole new set of value-laden premises. Perhaps the best one can do is report one's results conditional upon particular cost functions. That is, there would be different empirical results depending on the assumed cost function. Analogous procedures are common in applied research (e.g., "alternative futures" in long range forecasting), and could be easily transported to basic research enterprise. Returning to our earlier illustration, one might report both LS and LAR results for an analysis of recidivism.

Third, there is considerable debate among statisticians about the validity of introducing cost functions into statistical inference, and even among those who acknowledge a role for cost functions, disagreement exists over significant practical details (Barnett, 1982). The same holds of Bayesian procedures more generally. In other words, even if a cost function can be specified, it may not be clear how to use it.

Finally, there remain a number of unsolved technical problems. For example, there will often be cost functions for which no estimator has yet been developed. Recall that in the forecasting case, statistical procedures were not available for all but the simplest kinds of asymmetric cost functions.

Yet, to say that the road will be difficult is not to say that the road should not be taken. Indeed, there seems to be no alternative. Current practice will not do, and basic researchers may have no choice but to begin thinking about the consequences of their work.

NOTES

1. Lieberson's instincts are basically sound, although most of his technical arguments are nonsense.

2. Even for predictive likelihood methods, however, the kinds of cost functions we discuss later are operating. The argument is too lengthy to present here, but would not materially alter the general points to be made.

3. Both lognormal distributions were generated by first selecting two random samples of 500 numbers from two normal distributions. Both had a variance of 1.5, but the first had a mean of .20, while the second had a mean of .25. The difference in the means, plus chance patterns, led to rather different lognormal distributions after exponentiation. Other draws with the same parameters for the two parent normal distributions produced on the average very similar results. That is, Table 4.1 does not reflect an unusual pattern.

4. Heteroskedasticity was taken into account in the significance tests. Among other things, this implies that we are capitalizing on the asymptotic properties of our estimators. With a sample of 1,000, all should be well.

5. In all fairness, the issues are not quite that simple, and among statisticians there is lively debate about "objectivity." Even the advocates of "classical inference" sometimes disagree among themselves about how far scientists should go in acting on their findings (and hence, compromising objectivity). For example, Barnett (1982: 129-132) reports that R. A. Fisher was associated with the "pure significance test" that assesses the probabilities associated with particular hypotheses, but does not go the next step of rejecting or failing to reject a given hypothesis. Neyman and Pearson are linked to "hypothesis tests," in which decisions about the hypothesis are formally made. More generally, there remains a large group of statisticians who separate inference, which is supposed to be objective, from decision making, which is not. In my view, the objectivists are kidding themselves.

REFERENCES

Barnett, V. (1982) Comparative Statistics Inference. New York: John Wiley.

Berk, R. A. and T. F. Cooley (1987) "Errors in forecasting social phenomena." Climatic Change 11: 247-65.

Blumstein, A. (1983) "Prisons: population, capacity, and alternatives," in J. Q. Wilson (ed.) Crime and Public Policy. San Francisco: ICS.

Blumstein, A., Farrington, D. and Morita, N. (1985) "Delinquency careers: innocents, desisters and persisters,"in M. Tonry and N. Morris (eds.) Crime and Justice: An Annual Review of Research. Chicago: University of Chicago Press.

Box, G.E.P. and G. M. Jenkins (1976) Time Series Analysis: Forecasting and Control. San Francisco: Holden-Day.

Chaiken, J. M. and M. R. Chaiken (1982) Varieties of Criminal Behavior (Series R-2814-NIJ). Santa Monica, CA: Rand.

Cicourel, A. V. (1964) Method and Measurement in Sociology. New York: Free Press.

Cohen, J. (1983) "Incapacitation as a strategy for crime control: possibilities and pitfalls," in M. Tonry and N. Morris (eds.) Crime and Justice: An Annual Review of Research. Chicago: University of Chicago Press.

Cooley, T. F. and W. R. Parke (1985) "Asymptotic predictive likelihood." University of California—Santa Barbara, Department of Economics. (working paper)

Cox, D. R. and D. V. Hinkley (1974) Theoretical Statistics. New York: Chapman and Hall.

DeGroot, M. H. (1970) Optimal Statistical Decisions. New York: McGraw-Hill.

Duncan, O. D. (1984) Note on Social Measurement. New York: Russell Sage.

Glaser, B. G. and A. L. Strauss (1967) The Discovery of Grounded Theory. Chicago: Aldine.

Gouldner, A. W. (1970) The Coming Crisis of Western Sociology. New York: Basic Books.

Granger, C.W.J. (1980) Forecasting in Business and Economics. New York: Academic Press.

Granger, C.W.J. and P. Newbold (1977) Forecasting Economic Time Series. New York: Academic Press.

Greenwood, P. W. (1982) Selective Incapacitation (Series R-2815-NIJ). Santa Monica, CA: Rand.

Greenwood, P. W. (1983) "Controlling the crime rate through imprisonment," in J. Q. Wilson (ed.) Crime and Public Policy. San Francisco: ICS.

Lieberson, S. (1985) Making It Count. Berkeley: University of California Press.

Monahan, J. (1981) Predicting Violent Behavior: An Assessment of Clinical Techniques. Beverly Hills, CA: Sage.

Morris, N. and M. Miller (1985) "Predictions of dangerousness," in M. Tonry and N. Morris (eds.) Crime and Justice: An Annual Review of Research. Chicago: University of Chicago Press.

Pindyck, R. S. and D. L. Rubinfeld (1981) Econometric Models and Economic Forecasts. New York: McGraw-Hill.

Rossi, P. H. (1980) "The presidential address: the challenge and opportunities of applied social research." American Sociological Review 45: 889-904.

Schmidt, P. and A. D. Witte (1984) An Economic Analysis of Crime and Justice. New York: Academic Press.

Whyte, W. F. (1982) "The presidential address: social inventions for solving human problems." American Sociological Review 47: 1-13.

Wilson, J. Q. (1983) Crime and Public Policy. San Francisco: ICS.

PART II

INSTITUTIONAL AREAS IN SOCIOLOGY

The chapters in this section of the book focus on some of the main institutional areas of inquiry in sociology: the family, religious institutions, political institutions, complex organizations, educational institutions, and health services organizations. The authors range from pessimistic (Freeman) to optimistic (Gordon) in their orientations toward the future, but all agree that there are major new trends that have transformed the work in each of these areas of inquiry. These trends are methodological, theoretical, and applied.

Freeman argues that medical sociology has been marginal in the parent discipline and that rapid developments in the field of health care delivery make it imperative that sociologists with interests in this area have ongoing contact with health care specialists. Without this contact it is unlikely that sociologists will retain a "competitive" advantage in this discipline. Thus training programs in medical sociology must be altered to acknowledge this reality. Low status and marginality within the parent discipline are also noted by Gordon in his discussion of the origins of the sociology of education. However, he concludes on a more positive note indicating that with the increase in policy-oriented research in sociology in the past two decades, commencing to some extent in the sociology of education with the publication of Coleman's (1966) influential book on the equality of educational opportunity, and with demographic factors indicating a rise in the school age population in the 1990s, education will emerge as an important area of inquiry. He forecasts increased concern with quality of education and the performance of teachers, as well as with the specific nature of the social process in the classroom. In conjunction with the increase in policy oriented research in this area of inquiry, Gordon predicts the potential for involvement in controversy, but the potential gains in the advancement of basic theoretical and empirical research are commensurate with the risks.

Montgomery makes a similar claim to that made by both Freeman and Gordon regarding the shift toward a greater policy orientation in research on the family. She goes beyond this claim to argue that, in addition, theory and research on the family must move beyond historical

accounts of changes in the institution over time and microanalytic
models of family interaction to a systematic analysis of the link between
the family as a "group" or organization and other institutions in society.
She claims that prior research has treated the family as if it were
somehow isolated from other social structures. The family can be treated
as well, she argues, as the "mediator" between the individual and other
social institutions as it was in some of the early classic sociological
treatments of the family as a social system. A significant role as experts
and informed public policy analysts is projected by Montgomery for
family sociologists of the future.

Shupe and Hadden review the "dismal" state of the sociology of
religion in its early forms arguing that despite the primary role granted
religion in many of the theoretical classics in sociology (e.g., by
Durkheim and Weber), the field went into a significant decline as the
secularization of the society increased. Now, however, they argue that
"all has changed" and that there is a resurgence of interest in religion
accounted for in part by recent trends in the 1980s that they perceive will
continue into the future. These include the rise of fundamentalism and
the resurgence of evangelical Christianity, coupled with an increased
interest in the link between religion and politics.

Organizational sociology and political sociology do not suffer from
ever having been marginal to the field of sociology, but both fields
connect directly to applied topics of inquiry that are not as much the
focus of the reviews by Clarke and Burstein. Rather these authors point
to recent theoretical developments within these fields that are
noteworthy. Clarke lists three in organizational sociology: (1) loose-
coupling decision-making theory, (2) institutional theories of
organizational structure, and (3) population ecology models. A critique
of these developments is offered by Clarke, but the list is selective.
Burstein provides more of a history of the field of political sociology and
a commentary on developments in the field over time, restricting his
attention to five primary topics: government action, public opinion,
formal organizations, culture and ideas, and causality in politics. He
omits consideration of the recent developments in theories of the state
and in the field of political economy, more generally.

What remains to be seen is the exact direction work on institutions
will take within sociology in the future. With the reemergence of
institutional theories and a renewed focus on linkages between
institutions there may be much room for creative synthesis and for cross-
fertilization as between organizations and politics and organizations and

the family, as well as between politics and education and education and the family. Certainly, there are links to be forged between politics and medicine and theories of formal organization and the health care delivery system as a complex and nested set of organizations. The potential for cross-fertilization both theoretically and empirically in large-scale interdisciplinary research efforts may also improve the nature of our policy-oriented research in these areas, which in the past has focused too often on each system or institution in isolation from all others.

5

MEDICAL SOCIOLOGY

Howard E. Freeman

University of California, Los Angeles

Historians have a knack of tracing just about every intellectual idea and body of scientific knowledge back to antiquity. Thus it is hardly surprising that the late George Rosen—medicine's virtually irreplaceable social historian—credits Plato and Hippocrates with first identifying the relations between health problems and political, economic, and social conditions (Rosen, 1979). This sop to the ancients aside, certainly by the mid-eighteenth century the links between medicine and social science were clear. The two principles, still relevant to our work on health and illness today, were well explicated by then, Rosen (1979) credits them to Virchow and Neumann respectively:

— The health of community members is a direct concern and obligation of society.
— Social and economic conditions have an important, often crucial impact on health and disease and that these relations must be subjected to scientific inquiry.

Indeed, before the eighteenth century ended, an American physician had begun to promote the term *medical sociology* (McIntire, 1894) and social science concepts began to sneak into the medical curriculum in lectures on social medicine and classes in preventive medicine. But the truth is that the genealogical exercise of identifying the roots of medical sociology pretty much results in a fabricated heritage of little relevance to the way the field has shaped up. The fact is that medical sociology as we know it today is a post-World War II phenomena.

THE EMERGENCE OF MODERN MEDICAL SOCIOLOGY

Modern medical sociology is a social invention that follows Merton's dictum that most "discoveries" occur numerous times but are accepted and adopted only when there is "structural readiness" for them (Merton, 1965).

In the case of medical sociology, the changes in the diagnosis and treatment of patients, in the financing of health care, and in the selection and education of physicians and other health personnel occurred at the same time that sociology (along with the other social sciences and academia in general in the United States) began a remarkable growth spurt.

The late 1940s and early 1950s was the period in medicine when virtually all identified acute illnesses were brought under control by antibiotics, and when sophisticated technologies for the diagnosis of disease and the extension of life became commonplace. It was also when the idea of national health insurance first was discussed as a realistic possibility (Medicaid and Medicare eventually emerged as a political compromise, much to the disgust of advocates of a single national health care system). So, too, it was the time when the medical establishment's control of the number and social characteristics of persons admitted to medical schools was seriously challenged. Contrast this to the 1930s when TB and pneumonia were often fatal diseases, when physicians could virtually carry all of their "tools" in a small black bag, and when only a limited number of Jewish applicants and practically no Blacks or other minorities were allowed to fill the carefully controlled number of medical school openings.

These changes in medicine resulted in the need for studies on the ways to reshape the educational process within health science schools and for research on the ways persons coped with illness, on the medical care received by individuals of different social and demographic characteristics, on the utilization of health services and preventive practices, and on the appropriate use of medical technology. Perhaps even more important, it brought new sets of players into the smoky back rooms in which politicians—with and without medical degrees—determined health policy, and into the power elite that controlled organized medicine and its institutional settings. Questioning of practices and procedures on the admission and discharge of medical and psychiatric patients, on postgraduate medical training, on the organization and staffing of health care settings, and on the allocation of health care resources provided opportunities for a wide range of social research activities as well.

But medical sociology would not have emerged as a special field of inquiry except for the growth of our parent discipline of sociology during this period. This growth was based in part on the conceptual and methodological advances that resulted from sociologists and persons in their sibling disciples working on military-related research problems. It also was a result of the liberation of many American sociologists from the intellectual dominance of European scholars as a consequence of the destruction of Europe's academy and the fates of many scholars there. Then, too, it was a period in which many sociologists became identified with a "positivist" outlook and a willingness to engage in large-scale data collection and analysis efforts, including studies of the delivery of health services and the outcome of treatment modalities.

It took some time, of course, for medical sociologists to seize on the opportunities that opened up, and it was not until nearly the 1960s that the field was *institutionalized* in the sociological sense of this term. For example, it was possible as late as the mid-1950s, in a comparatively short paper, to examine and cite virtually every article on health written by one or more sociologists and published in sociological journals, as well as a fair sampling of similar papers that had appeared in medical journals (Freeman and Reeder, 1957). But one should not get the impression that the development of medical sociology was accidental or spontaneous.

THE GROWTH OF MEDICAL SOCIOLOGY

The growth of medical sociology that began in the 1950s was not by any means an indigenous social movement instigated by the common folk in sociology. Rather, it was a well thought-out plan (radical sociologists in the 1960s preferred the word plot) whose strategists were people with power. Donald Young, president of the Russell Sage Foundation, figured to make his mark by invading the professional schools with social scientists and, since he was a sociologist, particularly by us. His strategy was to start social science units in "elite" places such as the Harvard School of Public Health.

At more or less the same time, the National Institute of Mental Health began its social science training program, doing it somewhat surreptitiously by using psychiatric training funds (Freeman, Borgatta, and Siegel, 1975). Also, NIMH began during this period to support social science research projects, ones lead by social scientists and using our range of methodologies. That John Clausen and other of our kin had made their way into and up in this establishment is to be noted, and undoubtedly they had much to do with the start-up of NIMH's training and research programs as well. A number of the NIH institutes shortly discovered the social science and the potential of social research, and they started ambitious research and training efforts.

There is no doubt that the very rapid growth of medical sociology was related, to a considerable extent, to the resources provided by various government and foundation groups. It is fair to observe, however, that the generalship of a few sociologists in powerful places was perhaps as important. But it was more than that: There was a national need for more and better trained social scientists to man our then burgeoning graduate and undergraduate departments, and the sponsorship of health-related training and research programs was a means of supporting sociological activities in general. Nevertheless, it did introduce a significant proportion of graduate students, at least to some degree, to the sociology of health and illness.

In any event, the 1960s and early 1970s were golden years for sociology in general, and for medical sociology in particular. Research funds were readily available, our graduate departments attracted bright students in large numbers and the resources were there to support them, and yes, important work really was undertaken.

Parsons's (1951) "sick role" paper had a major theoretical impact in sociology, Robert Merton teamed up with George Reader and Patricia Kendall (1957) to do *The Student Physician,* Becker, Geer, and Hughes (1961) published *Boys in White,* Freidson's (1970) work on the profession of medicine was read widely, and many of us had at least some impact on the field of mental health. "Social epidemiology," a phrase that eventually meant any survey-type medical or social psychiatric study to the discomfort of "real" epidemiologists, were voluminous in number. Hollingshead and Redlich's (1958) investigation of social class and mental illness, for example, was probably the most cited of all empirical investigations in sociology for a number of years.

In actuality, medical sociology has contributed to theory, empirical knowledge, and method across the spectrum of sociological work. Contemporary theoretical work on the social networks draws on studies of the relations between family roles and post-hospital adjustment, understanding of social psychological processes has been considerably enhanced by the literature on stigmatization and on the stress of life events, and theories of organizational behavior have profited from the spate of studies that have been undertaken on hospitals and other health care institutions. National surveys of health care services have documented the relations between social position and access to resources, findings on gender differences in mortality and use of health services have raised important issues regarding the roles of biology and of cultural norms in determining behavioral outcomes, studies of health prevention have illustrated the complexities in and difficulties of modifying routine behaviors, research on health science education has provided important information on the educational process in general, and studies on health and illness among the aged have provided valuable insights about adult socialization and coping behavior. There have been important methodological contributions as well, including studies of mental hospitals and medical education that are exemplars of ethnographic work, longitudinal analyses of addictive and deviant careers that illustrate the power of contemporary quantitative procedures, and the use of innovative network sampling procedures to obtain sufficient numbers of "rare" individuals that have application in a variety of areas. And these are but illustrations of work of relevance to various parts of the sociological enterprise. (Space prohibits citing references for even a representative sampling. Rather, see Freeman and Levine, 1988; Aiken and Mechanic, 1986; Mechanic, 1978.)

Organizationally, medical sociology prospered as well. Medical sociology became the largest section in the American Sociological Association, and the ASA took over an existing journal and changed its name slightly from the *Journal of Health and Human Behavior* to the *Journal of Health and Social Behavior*. A number of other general and "subspecialty journals" are now published, and handbooks, texts, and readers have been spawned in large number. Most graduate departments now offer training in the field, and medical sociology is an allowable "concentration" or "specialty area" or whatever be the designation in many sociology departments. The "American model" of medical sociology has been exported to many industrial and lesser developed countries, and both research and debate now often have an international flavor.

Medical sociology, however, is not entirely a success story. Like the U.S. automobile business, failure to adapt to changing times and tastes, blindness to competition, and stodgy ways have resulted in a precarious future for the field. It faces, as we move to the end of the 1980s, stiff competition from others who do the same work.

COMPETITORS TO MEDICAL SOCIOLOGY

The field was not without controversy during its period of remarkable growth, and debate about its boundaries and what constitutes appropriate work has continued since then. Robert Straus (1957) made himself instantly famous by offering the distinction between the "sociology of medicine" and "sociology in medicine." Whether he meant to do so or not, the field interpreted undertaking the former as virtuous, doing the latter was seen as akin to selling your body for the most perverse purposes.

When medical sociologists tired of discussing Straus's distinction, they would then turn to the problems of working in health science schools. Doing so virtually labeled a person as a "failure," who either could not find a job in a respectable sociology department or had sold out for a few more bucks than sociologists typically received. It was held that sociologists in professional schools suffered from alienation and were deprived of opportunities to communicate with their peers—as if our sociology departments, then and now, are centers of intellectual exchange in which everyone is devoted to the scientific enterprise, and sites in which there is continual collaboration between all faculty members.

It might have happened anyway, but certainly the outlook of medical sociologists during the 1960s and afterwards, their disdain to do applied work, their worry about their "identity," and their aloofness about really involving themselves with health professionals and health care certainly did not impede the development of "the competition." At the same time that medical sociologists were working, *and complaining*, our ideas, concepts, and particularly our technology was transferred, borrowed, stolen—however one wishes to describe it—to persons without hangups about working *in* medicine.

First, in many ways there neither was nor is anything very unique about sociological methodology. True, in the past, in our surveys compared with the way many epidemiologists worked, there was more of a concern with question wording and item order. During this period, sociologically trained field researchers probably were more systematic about observing and recording than, say, psychiatrists doing "clinical" studies. Also, persons out of business schools in which they were trained primarily by economists were less sensitive than we to validity and reliability issues in data collection. But a combination of didactic teaching, informal conversations, and wider dissemination of our literature soon taught others our stock in trade. There is no question today that many social research *in medicine* studies are just as good as, and sometimes better, than our *of medicine* work.

But perhaps more powerful in the development of the competition was the growth of professional "health-related" education. Along with the rapid development of federal programs, Medicare, Medicaid, and community mental health centers, to name a few, there was the need for staff—managers and executives, planners, evaluation specialists, research analysts and the like—and for persons to work for the consulting industry that grew up to service the health care enterprise. Staff for these enterprises certainly were not coming out of sociology or other social science departments (except for some economics departments). Even if all of our graduate students during those years had gone into firing-line jobs in the health care world, it would not have been anywhere enough; but, of course, medical sociologists had and have little interest in encouraging persons to do such "dirty work."

Rather, existing schools in public health, nursing, hospital administration, and the like expanded and added "professional" doctorates, though some are called Ph.D.s. Other programs started *de novo*, for example, in schools of management, social planning, and public administration. I do not know who started the "rule," but at least everyone believes that you cannot give doctoral-level training unless there is a body of knowledge. Since physicians and other persons in health care for a long time, as noted, have said that medicine is a social as well as a biological science, it was easy to support the proposition that professional medical care and health research educational programs must be rooted in the social sciences.

As these professional schools and programs have prospered, they not only have attracted a significant number of ASA card-carrying sociologists but have bred their own social researchers. Increasingly, the faculties of these professional programs have recruited their own students to staff their schools and the proportion of sociology Ph.D.s (and of other social scientists with the possible exception of economists) has substantially declined. And these professionally trained persons have generally done very well in terms of jobs, consulting, and research opportunites. They, along with M.D.s, also dominate the private health foundation world and have a strong representation in federal and state health care agencies, profit-making and nonprofit research organizations, and in the policy sector.

Moreover, a significant number of "real doctors," and other health-care trained professionals, either by formal training or on their own, have learned the social research trade and are not distinguishable from others doing the same work. Even in these times of tight money for social research training, there are serious efforts to increase the numbers of such persons. For example, the Robert Wood Johnson Foundation has "clinical scholars"—physicians who spend two years after their clinical residencies learning about social research and policy studies at selected medical schools that have social research affiliations on and off their campuses. Moreover, despite severe cutbacks in federal training funds, the NIHs and NIMH continue to provide research training for health professionals as well.

Some of this heterogeneous group of social-science trained researchers in the health field have kept their disciplinary identities, others have not. What has occurred, as might be expected, is the development of a new set of labels to describe the work being done—"health service research" is the most common. And the creation of this new profession has been accompanied by the development of national and regional "trade associations," journals, and so on. In brief, what we now have are two types of social researchers, the "of medicine" or perhaps "of health" group is better—medical sociologists in a traditional sense—and the "in health" group. And the boundaries between the two groups have become increasingly firm; the wall between them higher and less scalable.

It is pointless to argue that the work on one side or the other is "better," more lasting, or in other ways of greater social worth. Both types use a range of methods; both may be theoretical or atheoretical, and both may reach wide audiences or be disseminated and examined by only a few. There are differences in emphasis, of course. The "health services crowd" shifts their interest in particular dependent variables more rapidly and markedly. For example, from concern with "access to care" to "cost containment." And as noted in a paper with Rossi (Freeman and Rossi, 1984), there are substantial differences in doing applied and "academic" research. In other words, not only are there two leagues operating in the health research arena, but there is little reason and likelihood that any merger or meaningful integration is possible.

THE FUTURE OF MEDICAL SOCIOLOGY

Given current interests in the medical arena, the priorities among both governmental granting agencies, and the emphasis on operational problems by the leadership of medical care organizations, it is difficult to be optimistic about the future of the sociology *of* medicine, of what many in the field think of as the core of "medical sociology." In order to find employment in and outside of academia, and to obtain research support, sociologically trained health researchers must be able to wear both hats, to function as health services researchers as well as engaging in sociology *of* medicine studies. Unless the current cadre of medical sociologists do so, and teach their students to do so, at least in the short-term future—certainly for the rest of this decade or longer—the "of medicine" crowd are in for hard times. Research funds for such work currently are tight and probably will continue that way; major support is pretty much limited to policy and applied work. For example, it is probably the case that the annual health care research budget of the Rand Corporation is larger than all the research grant funds administered through *sociology departments* throughout the country. The fact is that while many sociologists are doing major studies, in terms of the cost criterion at least, practically none of them is being done out of sociology departments.

Admittedly, there are types of studies that do not require extensive budgets and it is possible to do good work without large amounts of extramural support. But doing so does not solve the other problems that the times have thrust upon us. We must face up to the problems of career mobility and the recruitment of persons into graduate programs in medical sociology. Sociology departments are not going to grow very much, at least most of them. Our pool of students for graduate work in sociology in most places is getting smaller, or is at least in a steady state, and at best many departments have to be less choosy in student selection. Why should it be otherwise? Currently, it is neither generally possible to promise students sufficient support during their graduate studies, nor a wide selection of jobs after their doctorates.

This is an additional matter, one that perhaps should be of most concern. Health care and the health science professions are undergoing rapid and major changes, and are qualitatively different than even a decade ago. It is not possible to do most types of health care research unless the researcher is fully conversant with current activities and has antennae directed at emergent changes. For example, without a fair degree of knowledge about DRGs, with the various types and limitations of different capitation programs, and with the financing of postgraduate medical education, it simply is not possible to undertake sound organizational studies in the health field. Without a full understanding of the supply and oversupply problems of practitioners, of the impact of different types of technology, and of the roles of government and third-party insurance carriers in today's health care market, it is not possible to do any research on the professions. And so on, and so on.

Of course, is it a maxim that one must understand the context to do effective research. But there is reason to question, given the pace of change in the health field, whether it is possible to "keep up" without sustained contact with the health care world; and it is very difficult to believe that the required interaction with physicians and medical care professionals is possible to achieve for those who function solely in a "sociology of health" role. As in most economically oriented professions, the majority of persons in the health world are not altruistic, and unmotivated to continually inform, educate, and update the medical sociologist on the qualitative and quantitative changes that are occurring without some quid pro quo. Unfortunately, perhaps, most of the work of the sociology of medicine genre is neither interesting enough nor sufficiently entertaining to be perceived as enough of a "pay back."

Thus any realistic review of the field of medical sociology must end on a pessimistic note, and to sound a warning about continuing its current trajectory: Given the current times and competition, sociology departments offering training in medical sociology must change their curricula and train their students for health services type research roles—for doing sociology *in* medicine studies—as well as for undertaking the more academically-rooted sociology *of* medicine research activities. Unless this is done, sociologically trained persons increasingly will lose opportunities to undertake both sociology *in* and sociology *of* health work. The issue is not whether to pursue a strategy that encourages both types of work but how to do so.

REFERENCES

Aiken, Linda H. and David Mechanic [eds.] (1986) Applications of Social Science to Clinical Medicine and Health Policy. New Brunswick, NJ: Rutgers University Press.

Becker, Howard S., G. Geer, and H. Hughes (1961) Boys in White: Student Culture in Medical School. Chicago: University of Chicago Press.

Freeman, Howard E., Edgar F. Borgatta, and Nathaniel H. Siegel (1975) "Remarks on the changing relationship between government support and graduate training," in N. J. Demerath III, O. Larsen, and K. F. Schuessler (eds.) Social Policy and Sociology. New York: Academic Press.

Freeman, Howard E. and Sol Levine [eds.] (1988) Handbook of Medical Sociology (4th ed.). Englewood Cliffs, NJ: Prentice-Hall.

Freeman, Howard E. and Leo G. Reeder (1957) "Medical sociology: a review of the literature." American Sociological Review 22: 73-81.

Freeman, Howard E. and Peter H. Rossi (1984) "Furthering the applied side of sociology." American Sociological Review 4: 571-580.

Freidson, Eliot (1970) Profession of Medicine: A Study of the Sociology of Applied Knowledge. New York: Dodd-Mead.

Hollingshead, August B. and Frederick C. Redlich (1958) Social Class and Mental Illness: A Community Study. New York: John Wiley.

McIntire, C. (1894) "The importance of the study of medical sociology." Bulletin of the American Academy of Medicine 1: 425-34.

Mechanic, David (1978) Medical Sociology. New York: Free Press.

Merton, Robert K. (1965) On the Shoulders of Giants. New York: Harcourt Brace and World.

Merton, Robert K., George G. Reader, and Patricia L. Kendall [eds.] (1957) The Student-Physician: Introductory Studies in the Sociology of Medical Education. Cambridge, MA: Harvard University Press.

Parsons, Talcott (1951) "Illness and the role of the physician: a sociological perspective." American Journal of Orthopsychiatry 21: 452-60.

Rosen, George (1979) "The evolution of social medicine," in H. E. Freeman [ed.], The Handbook of Medical Sociology (3rd ed.). Englewood Cliffs, NJ: Prentice-Hall.

Straus, Robert (1957) "The nature and status of medical sociology." American Sociological Review 22: 200-204.

6

SOCIOLOGY OF EDUCATION

Leonard Gordon

Arizona State University

The future prospects for the sociological analysis of education in American society and elsewhere appears stronger than its past development. Until recently this specialization held low appeal and low status within sociology. As Neal Gross (1961) observed over two decades ago in *Sociology Today*: "There are currently only a handful of sociologists who make this field their specialty" and "few courses or seminars at the graduate level are offered in this area" (p. 128).

At about the time Gross was making this desultory assessment of the sociology of education, the distinguished British sociologist John Madge (1962) gave a series of invitational lectures on the major works of empirical sociology from the 1890s to the 1950s. Beginning with Durkheim's study of suicide and anomie, Madge provided an assessment of a number of classic studies. He included Thomas and Znaniecki's work on the Polish peasant adaptation to modern life, the Chicago School urban works of Burgess, Park, Wirth, and others, and Myrdal's *An American Dilemma* (1975) interracial national study analysis, among others. None of the selected studies dealt in any direct way with the sociological analysis of education.

Signs of change are evident. If Madge were now to select major empirical sociological works, it is likely that James Coleman's directed national study, *Equality of Educational Opportunity* (Coleman et al., 1967), would be included. Further, the early philosophical and sociological interest in education by Dewey (1916), Durkheim (1973), Whitehead (1929), and others has been readdressed. By the mid-1950s Brookover (1955) began a trend to develop sociology of education texts that offered a systematic analysis of the American school rather than limited applied education themes (Gross, 1961: 129).

Along with Coleman, other contemporary leading sociologists have addressed the aspects on analysis of education. These include Riesman

(1956) on the problematic nature of education in modern mass society; Parsons (1961) on the diverse functions of education; Becker, Greer, and Hughes (1968) on the nature of collegiate academic life; and Meyer (1977) as a central part of his world-system analytic efforts. Furthermore, most departments listed in the American Sociological Association's *Guide to Graduate Departments of Sociology* now list the sociology of education as one of their specializations.

In the early formation of the United States, Thomas Jefferson, John Adams, and other founders saw the general educational process as critical for the future social, political, and economic development and stability of the society. By the time sociology as a discipline became established early in the twentieth century, mass education had taken root. While most sociologists turned their attention toward large urbanization and industrial social forces or the socialization adaptation of racially and ethnically diverse groups in close interaction, the massively developing school systems were raising critical issues for some analysts.

Durkheim's concerns respecting societal prerequisites for social boundaries and substantial normative consensus in context of rapid social growth drew his attention to moral education as a function of schools beyond technical skills or bases of knowledge (Durkheim, 1973). John Dewey studied how the character of the educational system influences the stability or instability of a democracy. He noted, as a case in point, the undermining of democratic values of students in pre-World War I Germany where the schooling emphasis was on discipline rather than personal development, and on subordination rather than on independent inquiry (Dewey, 1916: 108-110). This perspective was reflected by Lester Ward in the early Chicago School's sociological emphasis on social progress, with education viewed as the primary institutional mechanism for an ameliorative orientation (Ward, 1906).

Yet few sociologists took a research lead in expanding knowledge about education. The low historical status of the sociology of education (Brim, 1958; Gross, 1961) was paralleled by the low status of the teaching profession below the collegiate level (Brookover, 1949; Lieberman, 1956). The early social science research response to growing public interest in education was characterized by aptitude, intelligence, and psychological socialization measures and analyses of G. Stanley Hall, Edward Thorndike, William James, Charles H. Judd, and other psychologists rather than sociologists (Edwards and Richey, 1963: 530-532).

By the 1960s a combination of societal developments moved sociologists increasingly to the sociology of education for empirical research and theoretical interpretations respecting the nature of modern society and social change (Rubinson and Ralph, 1984). Over the past quarter of a century, the American Sociological Association-sponsored journal on the *Sociology of Education* has become a mainline, widely cited source with broad-based sociological journal aims as noted on its masthead: "A Journal of Research in Socialization and Social Structure." Articles on education in basic general sociological sources now regularly appear.

CURRENT STATE OF THE FIELD

The extended formal schooling of higher proportions of the population has resulted in the sociology of education becoming more varied and complex. What Riesman (1956) refers to as the credentials nature of modern mass society has helped transform the field into a mainline venture for sociological research.

In this, American society and American sociology reflect what is occurring globally as education assumes greater consequence on the futures of individuals, groups, and entire societies (Boli et al., 1985; Meyer et al., 1977). Neal Gross's (1961) assessment of a quarter-century ago that "education is a relatively unexplored but potentially rich area for sociological inquiry" (p. 152) does not reflect the current state of theory, empirical research, or the evolvement of specialization.

Research advances in education take up old problems and ones that have been recognized or have emerged in recent years. Gross (1961: 131) identified four problem areas addressed at the turn of the century by Durkheim and Ward, which still have salience. These were (1) the social structure and the functioning of the school, (2) the classroom as a social system, (3) the external environment of the schools, and (4) education as an occupation and career.

Of these, considered here is a synthesis of continuing developments in the first two systemic concerns and on the third, the impact of the external environment. The last concern, respecting education as an occupation and career, received relatively little systematic attention prior to Gross's analysis (1961: 147-152). References are made here to education as an occupation in the context of other issues, while attention is directed at three emergent areas. These areas, along with those of longer interest, are considered in historical sequence of analytic attention: (1) the school as a social system; and (2) the impact of the external environment on the schools; with the additional and more recent research problem areas as: (3) equality and inequality of educational opportunity, (4) the sociology of mass higher education, and (5) mass education in global perspective.

The School as a Social System

It is a recent development that all theoretical orientations are well represented in sociological research on education. When education began to become a major concern of sociological analysis after midcentury, Parsonian functional systems theory was the major analytic mode (Davis, 1959; Merton 1968). This emphasis on the systemic functions of schooling coalesced with the early sociological research agenda for education initially proposed by Durkheim. In his *Education and Society* (1956) Durkheim framed the research areas for the sociological analysis of education as (1) identification of the social facts of education and their functions; (2) identification of the relationship between education and social change; (3) cross-cultural comparative research on educational systems; and (4) empirical studies of the classroom and the school as a social system.

This primary sociological focus on analyzing schools as social systems was reflected as early as Willard Waller's 1932 text on the *Sociology of Teaching*. In Brookover and Gottlieb's (1964) text, the major concerns are with "the school as a social system" and the "relationship of the educational system to other aspects of the society" (p. 12). Within this perspective, attention has been directed toward the socialization functions of education. The socialization literature in education overlaps with structural analyses to the point of considering it here as part of the systemic approach.

Structural and functional aspects of schools. Harriott and Hodgkins (1969: 152) encompass the functional purposive institutional perspective when they observe that "the primary social purpose of the institution of education in modern society is that of transmitting technical skills and an appropriate orientation for their implementation in adult life." While recognizing schools as open social systems in interaction with other powerful, influential social structures, functional analysis predominantly takes up Durkheim's concern with the school as an ongoing social system.

The educational structure forms the analytic framework of schools as social systems. As described in the federal government's *Digest of Educational Statistics* (1981), the approximately 85% of schools that are public and 15% private exhibit the same basic pattern. Separate elementary, secondary, and collegiate schooling exist in every region and state. Community colleges and technical schools supplement this three-tiered institutional structure of schooling.

This broad structural framework has been analytically addressed by Parsons (1966), Parsons and Platt (1973), Meyer (1977) in global perspective, and others in terms of the increasing complexity of modern formal school systems. A major focus is on the changing division of labor and the status and role sets to accomplish the manifest aims of schooling. Inherent structural strains and contradictions have been identified. Merton's (1957, 1968) advancement of status and role set theory has been applied to clarify the empirical testing of complementary and conflicting roles in context of multiple statuses held by school board members, parents, administrators, teachers, students, and others. This approach was related to such efforts as Gordon's (1958) study, *The Social System of the High School,* advancing understanding of youth and adult culture conflicts and Hollingshead's *Elmtown's Youth* (1949), documenting the varying aims of superintendents and school board member relationships on the support base and content of schooling.

This early concern with structure and function in education is still manifested in assessments of the academic performance effects on students in differential organizational formats and programs. A variety of regression test models have been advanced. Examples are Alexander and Eckland's (1977) study of varying school contexts and college selectivity institutional constraints in educational stratification and Hanks and Eckland's (1976) national longitudinal study of the effects of athletic programs for high school student educational attainment.

While no longer the predominant mode of analysis, articles in the *Sociology of Education* indicate that typical issues continue to include structural and functional studies.

Socialization functions of schools. The socialization functions of schooling received sparse attention compared to the socialization functions of the family until past midcentury (Gross, 1961: 133). In his article, "The School Class as a Social System," Parsons (1961) took up this issue. He highlighted the import on values and behaviors of the school environment on children and adolescents beyond the home environment.

More initial socialization attention was given to the manifest aims of schooling than to latent consequences and informal influencing processes. As with early-century interest in psychological testing, much sociological attention was addressed to the correlates of schooling respecting the pragmatic skill and cultural value goal-directed aspects of schooling emphasized by Dewey and Durkheim. The credentials-oriented nature of post-World War II society resulted in attention to socialization processes that lead more students to extend their schooling beyond secondary schools in preparing them to adapt to a rapidly changing high technology postindustrial society (Bell, 1967; Berg, 1978).

Increased attention has been directed at the socialization functions of both school environments and extra-schooling socialization (Gordon,

1978: 73-75). An example is Vander Zanden's (1970: 532) observation that schools perform a custodial function for children, enabling many mothers to develop job and career interests. Other examples are Farber's (1983) and Dornbusch et al.'s (1986) delineation of prior socialization effects of differential family patterns on the interaction orientations of children in school settings. A related line of inquiry is Benin and Johnson's (1984) documentation of the effects of like-sex and cross-sex home sibling relationships on attainment within schools.

Problematical aspects of latent socialization functions, stressed by Merton (1968: 50-84) also have been a concern. Moore and Tumin (1949) present an early example. They addressed the socialization effects of differentiated local school district support for elementary and secondary schools and the consequences of the poorest quality schooling being located in the poorest neighborhoods. They observed that the latent consequence of such a system was to maintain ignorance and reinforce the advantage middle-class children accrue.

This concern of Moore's and Tumin's has been taken up in context of the 1960s civil rights movement toward equality of opportunity. The latent self-fulfilling socialization consequences of rejecting attitudes toward Polish children (Thomas and Znaniecki, 1927) was taken up by Rosenthal and Jacobson (1968). In their *Pygmalian in the Classroom,* they aroused contemporary interest in negative labeling effects on black children's academic and social behavior. Silberman (1970) summarized much such research respecting the particular effects on minority children generally resulting from low teacher expectations and this is a line of continuing research.

It would be of interest and value if the variability results, based on negative findings, gained more attention. Under what school conditions do students respond differently than one would expect, based on students' background characteristics? The complex of issues related to this basic question respecting schooling is being addressed primarily by sociologists attracted to this field of inquiry in context of equality of educational opportunity.

Impact of the External Environment

A variety of issues have been addressed on the impact of the external environment on school. These include the influence of social class background on students and teachers, the composition and role of school boards or regents, and demographic changes in the society or in particular locales. Of these external factors, most attention has been given to social class and its relation to the nature of schooling.

The interest in class and education is related to the general sociological interest in the nature of social stratification and social mobility. Systematic social class analysis begun by Warner and his associates a half-century ago took into account the relationship between educational achievement and social status. This was a major point of analysis in Warner, Havighurst, and Loeb's (1944) study, *Who Shall Be Educated?* This synthesis of earlier studies focused on the salience of social class background on all aspects of schooling and its consequences. This interest has continued (e.g., Gross [1953], Glick and Miller [1956], Riesman [1975], and Alba and Lavin [1981]). A recurring theme is how schools facilitate by program and practice a continuation of inequalities in life opportunities. As Turner (1960) put it, social mobility "is only one of several social functions of the school, and not the most important function" (p. 856).

Brookover and Gottlieb (1964: 190-191), summarizing studies completed in the 1960s, considered the mobility options in American society as: (1) the recognition and acceptance of inequality within the three-tiered school system that he thought unlikely because of the long-held American creed ideal myth on counteracting arbitrary class barriers, (2) the attempt to maintain low class barriers and increase mobility, which he held was unrealistic since there was allegedly little evidence to support the substantial impact of educational training on social mobility, and (3) continuing the policy of verbalizing values of equality and upward mobility while maintaining the educational and noneducational institutionalized policies of a distinct stratification system. All perceived options were upwardly mobile in nature.

Brookover and Gottlieb held that the third alternative was the probable educational policy future. Conditions and events since have drawn some analysts to a more conflict-interest group and change-oriented perspective. Changing conditions and social protest forces resulted in policy pressures to change the upwardly mobile potential of schooling. This was the manifest aim of the civil rights-related 1965 Elementary and Secondary Education Act.

In this context a major emphasis has been on class related reference group behavior that influences the values and attitudes of children. One line of inquiry is in respect to students' orientations toward delayed gratification relating to academic achievement (e.g., Beilin, 1956; Lewis, 1964). More recently, there has been examined a more complex set of linkages with educational attainment and social class in relation to familial backgrounds including parenting styles, sex role socialization, and ethnic identity (e.g., Benin and Johnson, 1984; Dornbusch et al., 1986; Farber, 1983).

Much of the early concern with the school's external environment linked middle- and upper-class influentials to school board membership (Gross, 1961: 146-147). With the varying shift toward federal and state support of local school districts attention has developed in respect to larger external forces on the functioning of schools. Demographic data as that provided by the U.S. Census Bureau's (1985) intercensal reports form the basis of much research on student projections. One common theme is the analysis of the implications of projected low or high growth rates on school attendance at varying levels and locales (Astin, 1982; Trow, 1976).

A number of national longitudinal studies are in progress that correlate changing educational attitudes and attendance of blacks, Hispanics, women, and other selected population groupings. These studies generally show that groups with low past collegiate rates expect to go further in formal educational training than did previous generations (Hansen, 1982; Mare, 1978-1979). Another major monitoring point of demographically related longitudinal research is in respect to the changing age, class, and ethnic support levels for education (Brown and Saks, 1985).

Equality and Inequality of Educational Opportunity

Much of the concerns with external environmental factors on schools has developed out of collective social protests since the 1960s. Education was a major focus of the black-led movement as evidenced by the passage of the 1965 Elementary and Secondary Education Act with its provisions on federal funding for poverty-affected, high-minority concentrated schools. The passage of the Bilingual Education Act of 1967 was reflective of expanding social pressures and recognition of educational needs of the Hispanic and Native American Indian populations.

The federally sponsored Coleman report (Coleman et al., 1967) and Silberman's (1970) Carnegie Foundation-supported national study were further indications of high societal interest that generated a growing body of basic and policy-oriented sociological research on schooling for minority status groups. The literature in this area was advanced by new journal outlets including *Integrated Education*, expanded attention to equality of education issues in the *Sociology of Education* and other long established journals, and widely read books based upon sociological research such as Kozol's (1967) *Death at an Early Age*.

A central issue in this literature is the attempt to evaluate the independent effects of schooling on intergroup attitudes and behaviors and on educational achievement. Coleman et al. (1967) held that the primary effects on student performance were associated with such nonschooling factors as parental educational level and income and that within schools the quality of teachers and material support was less influential than was peer interaction. Evaluating the same data and other data sources, Jencks (1979) concluded that the quality of schooling an individual receives makes little difference.

Although most of this literature weighed the differential social environmental effects on student school achievement (e.g., Coleman et al., 1967; Jencks, 1979; Alexander and Eckland, 1977), some attention has been directed at genetic differences between different racial, ethnic, and gender groups. Arthur Jensen's (1969) *Harvard Educational Review* article on IQ and race generated the most public attention and public policy and research debates. Jensen held that: "Compensatory education has been tried and it apparently has failed" (p. 2).

Goldberg (1975) synthesized the general research rejection of Jensen's thesis. The critique centered on a dubious assumption that compensatory education had been sufficiently implemented to test its effects independent of race or other genetic factors. Still, a number of sociologists have picked up on Harvard biologist E. O. Wilson's sociobiological thesis. Research continues to be directed toward biological factors independent of social environment that influences all forms of behavior, including schooling achievement behavior (e.g., Barash, 1979; Ellis, 1977; Rossi, 1977).

While considerable public attention has been directed toward Jensen's and related genetic assessments, most sociological research in education has been exploring the socioenvironmental question of when schools reinforce structures and socialization processes of inequality and when they promote equality of educational opportunity. The Coleman report led to a variety of efforts to desegregate public schools including forced and voluntary busing and centrally located magnet schools. Situational factors vary and the assessed effects on student achievement and intergroup attitudes has not been consistent (Crain and Weisman, 1972; Hawley, 1981; St. John, 1975).

The varying consequences of school desegregation has led to a series of efforts to assess the particular conditions that result in different student achievement levels, attitudes, and socializing behaviors. Most of this research has focused on the issue of black-student achievement and interracial attitudes (Hawley, 1981; Patchen et al., 1977; Smith and Moore, 1985; St. John, 1975). An increasing amount of attention has been directed at achievement attitudes by and toward women (Benin and Johnson, 1984; Stockard et al., 1980).

Research findings give support to the view that schooling can have more independent attitudinal and achievement effects on students than Coleman, Jencks, and others envisioned when the issue of equality of educational opportunity gained sociological research attention in the 1960s. Coleman (1982) has argued this point in terms of Catholic and other private schools making a difference independent of race and class. While assessments of this research question the confounding effects of private school selectivity compared to more inclusive public schools (Goldberg, 1981), there is increasing evidence that the nature of schooling can make a substantial difference. Employing a national sample, with sex as an independent variable, Miller, Kohn, and Schooler (1985) found that "the 'quality' of the school experience does make a difference" (p. 942).

In terms of race, independent effects have also been found. Sometimes these effects are negative, as when preexisting hostile attitudes are activated more intensively within desegregated schools (Patchen et al., 1977; St. John and Lewis, 1975). In contrast, in court ordered busing and boundary changes to achieve desegregation, parents in these situations have been found to be more accepting of and oriented to change than were adults without children or parents with children in unaffected private schools (Farley, 1978; Gordon, 1969; Jacobson, 1977). Within schools, there is evidence that changes toward interracial friendliness and maximizing student achievement in an integrated process develops most effectively when begun in the earliest schooling years (Singleton and Murray, 1977), whereas much initial school desegregation has begun at the secondary school level (Weinberg, 1968, 1977). Still insufficiently explored are the qualitative schooling factors—teacher training, nature of course assignments, peer influences—which may make significant attitudinal and cognitive differences among minority-status students.

Given continuing inequality of educational opportunity, a concern of future sociology of education research will be that of identifying the conditions leading to more effectively incorporating minority-status students into the schooling process. For all the productive developing research on intraschooling conditions that result in greater educational opportunity independent of race, ethnicity, sex, or class, most black, Hispanic, and Native American Indian students still do not complete secondary school (U.S. Census, 1985). In a society that increasingly calls for more advanced postsecondary schooling for upward mobility, higher collegiate education has become a mass phenomenon for most. Since this is not the case for substantial and growing black, Hispanic, and Native American Indian populations (U.S. Bureau of the Census, 1979, 1980, 1985), research implications are large and important.

The Sociology of Mass Higher Education

The combination of social forces since midcentury—including the Serviceman's Readjustment Act of 1944 (GI Bill of Rights) and a rapidly expanding cybernetic economy calling for advanced technical, managerial, and professional training—resulted in the first mass expansion of enrollment in colleges (Federal Role in Education, 1965). The massive growth of the collegiate population spawned both a growing public and specialized sociological interest in higher education.

There has developed wide societal interest in the quality of higher education as evidenced from such national reports as the Association of American Colleges' *Integrity in the College Curriculum* (1985), and the National Institute on Education's *Involvement in Learning: Realizing the Potential of American Higher Education* (1985). While the desire for a high quality mass higher education system is clear, what is not clear is what the appropriate level of inclusiveness into college education should be. There appears no clear consensus in these reports, as there has long been on elementary and secondary schooling, that college education is important for all and, if not for all, which students should be admitted and under what criteria.

Lang (1984) well states the wide recognition that mass higher education "plays a key role in providing a technically trained work force for a growing industrial society and is linked to broader systems of social stratification, a concern with the accessibility to and mobility within the academic hierarchy has [therefore] become all the more critical and widespread" (p. 1). This concern is evident in generic assessments of the American university system (Barzun, 1968; Sanford, 1962) as well as in analyses of specific aspects of colleges including universities as complex organizations (Parsons and Platt, 1973), student perceptions and experiences (Becker et al., 1968), the role of community colleges in higher education (Alba and Lavin, 1981), admission to and the role of elite public and particularly private universities (Lang, 1984), and minority access to college (Sewell, 1971).

Mass higher education has become so central an avenue for maintenance of high social status and for upward mobility that the conditions of equality and inequality at this level of education is receiving extensive attention. There are generic conflict-vested class interest analyses in which a key issue is the expansion of college student loan aid in the 1960s and its contraction, evident by the mid-1970s. This has been assessed as attempts by those with the greatest economic and political influence to reestablish sharp dichotomized class positions and opportunities (Bowles and Gintis, 1976; Collins, 1979).

In this context Freeman (1976) argued that the infusion of lower-middle- and lower-class students into college in the 1960s and early 1970s overloaded the college graduate occupational opportunity system even as there is documentation of increasing benefits for middle-class minorities and women (Hansen, 1982; Wilson, 1987). A number of studies indicate a new form of unequal higher educational opportunity based upon a web of private expensive schools and parental alumni influence, operating to feed advantaged students into elite private universities and high prestige public universities, with token and decreasing acceptance of low-income minorities (Lang, 1984; Kulis et al., 1987).

Mass higher education has become a critical setting for a complex of larger societal issues. The questions of individual economic prospects, group position, social and political influence, and American societal economic and even military competitive capability are now clearly linked to the viable nature of the mass higher educational system. As such, a large proportion of future sociology of education research will focus on this educational arena.

Mass Education in Global Perspective

Beyond the United States and other modern societies, the expansion of education in most nations began at a minimal minority midcentury level. By 1980 over two-thirds of the children of primary age in developing countries were in formally constituted schools (UNESCO, 1983). In commenting on the growing universality of mass education, Boli, Ramirez, and Meyer (1985) observe: "For most people [today] education is the most important element of their social status, and their educational background will have a greater impact on their life chances than any other element but their nationality" (1).

Mass education, globally, is a major interest respecting the growing economic, political, and social interdependence of societies in the works of Thomas and Meyer (1984), Tilly (1975), and other modern world analysts. Mass education has emerged as a key variable in assessing the dynamics of state expansion and social change in developing societies, as it has long been in technologically advanced societies (Altbach, 1978; Boli et al., 1985; Meyer et al., 1977). While mass education has rapidly become a universalistic feature of the modern state system, there are considerable divergent perspectives on its causation and meaning. Sometimes overlapping functional, conflict, and interactionist perspectives diverge on interpretations of the same data sets.

Functionalists tend to argue that a Durkheimian division of labor has evolved to meet the need for generalized internalizing of values about a rationalized economic system for generalized societal stability (Inkeles and Smith, 1974). Conflict theorists have argued that with mass education in every society there remains substantial differentiation that operates in such a fashion as to enhance the status and power of prevailing dominant groups (Collins, 1979). A global interactionist perspective has advanced the argument that mass education is a product of nation-state competition in which there has emerged common values of achieving national social progress that cut across class lines (Boli et al., 1985).

Many unresolved research issues have been identified. Among the more consequential are attempts to explain why in many societies mass education has occurred prior to substantial technological expansion and in some as a consequence of technical change, attempts to assess to what extent educational opportunity has become a major reform issue in social protest movements in modern societies and a revolutionary issue in a number of developing societies, and what dynamics generate an over-production of advanced educational training among the population. These and related issues are influencing not only the assessment of education in the context of world systems analysis, they are becoming a factor in evaluating the nature of social forces affecting the American mass educational system.

EMERGENT DEVELOPMENTS: DEMOGRAPHIC FORCES AND POLICY-ORIENTED RESEARCH

Demographic trends provide one basis of projecting research expansion in the areas of concern. World population has expanded so rapidly that most of the developing societies' population bases are in the early schooling or preschooling age groups (UNESCO, 1983). In the United States, even with lowered per capita birth rates, enough women of the population boom generation of the 1950s and early 1960s are aving children so that a significant rise in elementary school enrollment is expected by the early 1990s (U.S. Bureau of the Census, 1985), with relatively greater growth in the school age populations among blacks and Hispanics (U.S. Bureau of the Census, 1979, 1980).

Given the demands for expanding education across class and national lines, the sociology of education will likely be one of the growing specialties. A resurgence of interest can be expected in elementary, secondary, and collegiate teaching as a profession, a point of some past interest (Barzun, 1968; Brookover, 1955; Gross, 1961). Given the credentials nature of contemporary society, it appears likely that those in the teaching profession may face increased social pressures for both greater status recognition and compensation. There is here a basis for research on a complex of status, economic competitive, social movement, and other issues increasingly involving the educational system.

The interest in education is so broad that no one interpretive theoretical orientation has emerged in any dominant way as did functionalism at the time of Gross's (1961) assessment. While functional systemic analyses continue (Hoffer et al., 1985; Meyer, 1977), there has been a growth in class conflict-based interpretations of the evolving educational system (Bowles and Gintis, 1976; Collins, 1979). As school settings lend themselves to experimental designs not often available, micro-level socialization studies continue to draw sociological attention and can be expected to be a research staple in the future (Miller et al., 1985; Singleton and Murray, 1977).

Whatever the theoretical perspectives, empirical research in the sociology of education will include a heavy emphasis on policy alternatives and debates. Sociology has become a policy-oriented social science, as has economics, political science, and psychology. Consequently, congressional, executive, and judicial decisions have occurred with involvement and citation of sociology of education research as in the 1954 *Brown* desegregation decision and the passage of the 1965 Elementary and Secondary Education Act. Coleman (1976) points out that policy-oriented sociological research "has been carried out in several institutional areas, but the largest part of it has been in education" (p. 304).

Policy-oriented research will invariably bring sociology into social controversy. Periodically, sociologists will be pitted against each other or against other social scientists in their analyses of policy consequences as has occurred on such issues as assessing the schooling and community effects of forced busing to achieve school desegregation (Coleman, 1975; Farley, 1980), interpreting the cause of resolution of interracial conflict in school settings (Weinberg, 1968; 1977), evaluating the effects on student academic and social behavior of major intercollegiate athletics (Edwards, 1970), drug use in school settings (Hardert, 1986), among other issues of wide public interest that coalesce in schools.

There are risks for the field in such policy-oriented researches. Research funds are often dependent on sources of private and public sources bent on their particularized interests and policy perspectives. This can lead to distortions of independent analysis predicated on pleasing policymakers who fund much research, as per Gouldner's (1970) warning. The policy-oriented nature of much sociology of education research also has potential to heighten interest in sociological research and, as Coleman (1976) and Rossi (1981) have argued, still advance basic theoretical and empirical research.

REFERENCES

Alba, R. and D. Lavin (1981) "Community colleges and tracking in higher education." Sociology of Education 54: 223-237.

Alexander, K. and B. Eckland (1977) "High school context and college selectivity: institutional constraints in educational stratification." Social Forces 56: 166-188.

Altbach, P. G. (1978) "The distribution of knowledge in the third world," pp. 301-330 in P. Altbach and G. Kelly (eds.) Education and Colonialism. New York: Longman.

Association of American Colleges (1985) Integrity in the College Curriculum. Washington, DC: Author.

Astin, A. W. (1982) Minorities in Higher Education: Recent Trends, Current Prospects, and Recommendations. San Francisco: Jossey-Bass.

Barash, D. (1979) Sociobiology: The Whisperings Within. New York: Harper & Row.

Barzun, J. (1968) "Notes on the post-industrial society." The Public Interest I (Winter): 24-35, and (Spring): 102-118.

Becker, H., B. Greer, and E. Hughes (1968) Making the Grade: The Academic Side of College Life. New York: John Wiley.

Beilen, H. (1956) "The pattern of postponability and its relation to social class mobility." Journal of Social Psychology 44: 33-48.

Bell, D. (1967) "Notes on the post-industrial society." Public Interest I (Winter): 24-35, and II (Spring): 102-118.

Benin, M. and D. R. Johnson (1984) "Sibling similarities in educational attainment: a comparison of like-sex and cross-sex sibling pairs." Sociology of Education 57: 11-21.

Berg, I. (1970) Education and Jobs: The Great Training Robbery. New York: Praeger.

Boli, J., F. Ramirez, and J. W. Meyer (1985) "Explaining the origins and expansion of mass education." Presented to the 1985 annual meeting of the Pacific Sociological Association, Albuquerque.

Bowles, S. and H. Gintis (1976) Schooling in Capitalist America: Educational Reform and the Contradictions of Economic Life. New York: Basic Books.

Brim, O. (1958) Sociology and the Field of Education. New York: Russell Sage.

Brookover, W. (1949) "Sociology of education: a definition." American Sociological Review 14: 407-415.

Brookover, W. (1955) A Sociology of Education. New York: American.

Brookover, W. and D. Gottlieb (1964) A Sociology of Education. New York: American.

Brown v. (Topeka) Board of Education (1954) Volume 347 of the United States Reports (official reports of the Supreme Court, p. 483). Washington, DC: Government Printing Office.

Brown, B. W. and D. H. Saks (1985) "The revealed influence of class, race, and ethnicity on local public school expenditures." Sociology of Education 58: 181-190.

Bruner, J. (1960) The Process of Education. Cambridge, MA: Harvard University Press.

Carman, H. J. and H. C. Syrett (1954) History of the American People, Vol. I. New York: Knopf.

Coleman, J. (1975) "Racial segregation in the schools: new research with new policy implications." Phi Delta Kappan 57: 75-82.

Coleman, J. (1976) "Policy decisions, social science information, and education." Sociology of Education 49: 304-312.

Coleman, J. S., E. Q. Campbell, C. J. Hobson, J. McPartland, A. M. Mood, F. D. Weinfeld, and R. York (1966) Equality of Educational Opportunity. Washington, DC: Government Printing Office.

Collins, R. (1979) The Credential Society: An Historical Sociology of Education and Stratification. New York: Academic Press.

Crain, R. and C. S. Weisman (1972) Discrimination, Personality, Achievement: A Survey of Northern Blacks. New York: Seminar Press.

Davis, K. (1959) "The myth of functional analysis as a special method in sociology and anthropology." American Sociological Review 24: 757-772.

Dewey, J. (1916) Democracy and Education. New York: Macmillan.

Digest of Educational Statistics (1981) Washington, DC: Government Printing Office.

Dornbusch, S., P. Ritter, P. Leiberman, D. Roberts, and M. Fraleigh (1986) A Report to the National Advisory Board of the Study of Stanford and the Schools on the Main Findings of Our Collaborative Study of Families and Schools. Palo Alto, CA: Stanford University.

Durkheim, E. (1956) Education and Society (S. D. Fox, trans.). New York: Free Press.

Durkheim, E. (1973) Moral Education: A Study in the Theory and Application of the Sociology of Education (E. K. Wilson, trans.). New York: Free Press.

Edwards, H. (1970) Black Students. New York: Macmillan.

Edwards, N. and H. G. Richey (1963) The School in the American Social Order. Boston: Houghton Mifflin.

Ellis, L. (1977) "The decline and fall of sociology: 1975-2000." American Sociologist 12: 56-66.

Farber, B. (1983) Conceptions of Kinship. New York: Elsevier.

Farley, R. (1978) "School integration in the United States," pp. 22-45 in F. Bean and W. Frisbee (eds.) The Demography of Racial and Ethnic Groups. New York: Academic Press.

Farley, R. (1980) "School desegregation and white flight: an investigation of competing models and their discrepancies." Sociology of Education 53: 123-139.

Federal Role in Education (1965) Washington, DC: Congressional Quarterly Service.

Freeman, R. (1976). The Overeducated American. New York: Academic Press.

Glick, P. C. and H. P. Miller (1956) "Educational level and potential income." American Sociological Review 21: 307-312.

Goldberg, A. (1975) Statistical Inferences in the Great IQ Debate. Madison: University of Wisconsin Institute for Research on Poverty Papers.

Goldberg, A. (1981) Coleman Goes Private (in Public). Report for the Stanford University Center for Advanced Studies in the Behavioral Sciences. Palo Alto: Stanford University.

Gordon, C. W. (1958) The Social System of the High School. New York: John Wiley.

Gordon, L. (1969) "Suburban consensus formation and the race issue." Journal of Conflict Resolution XIII: 550-556.

Gordon, L. (1978) Sociology and American Social Issues. Boston: Houghton Mifflin.

Gouldner, A. (1970) The Coming Crisis of Western Technology. New York: Basic Books.

Gross, N. (1953) "Social class structure and American education." Harvard Educational Review 24: 298-329.

Gross, N. (1961) "The sociology of education," pp. 128-152 in R. Merton, L. Broom, and L. Cottrell, Jr. (eds.) Sociology Today: Problems and Prospects. New York: Free Press.

Hanks, M. P. and B. K. Eckland (1976) "Athletics and social participation in the educational attainment process." Sociology of Education 49: 271-294.

Hansen, W. L. (1982) "Economic growth and equal opportunity: conflicting or complementary goals in higher education?" Institute for Research on Poverty. Discussion Paper No. 706-82. Madison: University of Wisconsin Institute for Research on Poverty.

Hardert, R. A. (1986) "Social factors related to adolescent drug abuse among high school students: a test of three theories." Presented at the annual meeting of the Pacific Sociological Association, Denver.

Harriott, R. E. and B. J. Hodgkins (1969) "Social context and the school: an open-system analysis of social and educational change." Rural Sociology (June), pp. 149-166.

Hawley, W. (1981) Effective School Desegregation. Beverly Hills, CA: Sage.

Herrnstein, R. (1973) I.Q. in the Meritocracy. New York: Allen Lane.

Hill, R. J. (1983) "Minorities, women, and institutional change: some administrative concerns." Sociological Perspectives 26: 17-18.

Hoffer, T., A. Greeley, and J. Coleman (1985) "Achievement growth in public and Catholic schools." Sociology of Education 58: 74-97.

Hollingshead, A. B. (1949) Elmtown's Youth. New York: John Wiley.

Inkeles, A. and D. H. Smith (1974) Becoming Modern. Cambridge, MA: Harvard University Press.

Jacobson, D. K. (1977) "Separation, integration, and avoidance among black, white, and Latin adolescents." Social Forces 56: 1011-1027.

Jencks, C. (1979) Who Gets Ahead? The Determination of Economic Success in America. New York: Basic Books.

Jensen, A. (1969) "How much can we boost IQ and scholastic achievement?" Harvard Educational Review 39: 1-123.

Katz, M. B. (1975) Class, Bureaucracy, and Schools: The Illusion of Educational Change in America. New York: Praeger.

Kozol, J. (1967) Death at an Early Age: The Destruction of the Hearts and Minds of Negro Children in the Boston Public Schools. Boston: Houghton Mifflin.

Kulis, S., K. Miller, M. Axelrod, and L. Gordon (1987) "Minority student representation in the U.S. departments of sociology." American Sociological Association Footnotes 15: 9, 11.

Lang, D. (1984) "Education stratification and the academic hierarchy." Research in Higher Education 21: 329-352.

Lewis, L. S. (1964) "Class and perceptions of class." Social Forces 42: 336-341.

Lieberman, M. (1956) Education as a Profession. Englewood Cliffs, NJ: Prentice-Hall.

Madge, J. (1962) The Origins of Scientific Sociology. New York: Free Press.

Mare, R. (1978-1979) "Sources of educational growth in America." Focus 3: 2-12.

Merton, R. K. (1957) "The role-set: problem in sociological theory." British Journal of Sociology 8: 340-363.

Merton, R. K. (1968) Social Theory and Social Structure. New York: Free Press.

Meyer, J. W. (1977) "The functions of education as an institution." American Journal of Sociology 83: 340-363.

Meyer, J. W., F. O. Ramirez, R. Rubinson, and J. Boli (1977) "The world educational revolution, 1950-1970." Sociology of Education 50: 242-258.

Miller, K. A., M. L. Kohn, and C. Schooler (1985) "Educational self-direction and the cognitive functioning of students." Social Forces 64: 923-944.

Moore, W. and M. Tumin (1949) "Some social functions of ignorance." American Sociological Review 14: 787-795.

Myrdal, G. (1975) An American Dilemma. New York: Pantheon.

National Institute on Education (1985) Involvement in Learning: Realizing the Potential of American Higher Education. Washington, DC: Government Printing Office.

Parsons, T. (1961) "The school class as a social system: some of its functions in American society," pp. 434-455 in A. Halsy, J. Floud, and D. Anderson (eds.) Education, Economy, and Society. New York: Free Press.

Parsons, T. (1966) Societies: Evolutionary and Comparative Perspectives. Englewood Cliffs, NJ: Prentice-Hall.

Parsons, T. and Platt, G. (1973) The American University. Cambridge, MA: Harvard University Press.

Patchen, M., J. Davidson, G. Hofmann, and W. Brown (1977) "Determinants of students' interracial behavior and opinion change." Sociology of Education 50: 55-75.

Polgar, S. K. (1976) "The social context of games: or when is play not play?" Sociology of Education 49: 265-271.

Riesman, D. (1956) Constraints and Variety in American Education. Lincoln: University of Nebraska Press.

Riesman, D. (1975) "The future of diversity in a time of retrenchment." Higher Education 4: 461-482.

Riesman, D., N. Glazer, and R. Denney (1950) The Lonely Crowd. New Haven, CT: Yale University Press.

Rosenthal, R. and L. Jacobson (1968) Pygmalian in the Classroom: Teacher Expectations and Pupils' Intellectual Development. New York: Irvington.

Rossi, A. (1977) "A biosocial perspective on parenting." Daedalus 106: 1-31.

Rossi, P. (1981) "The challenge and opportunities of applied research." American Sociological Review 45: 889-904.

Rubinson, R. and J. Ralph (1984) "Technical change and the expansion of schooling in the United States, 1890-1970." Sociology of Education, 57: 134-152.

Sanford, N. (1962) The American College. New York: John Wiley.

Sewell, W. (1971) "Inequality of opportunity in higher education." American Sociological Review 36: 793-809.

Silberman, C. (1970) Crisis in the Classroom: The Remaking of American Education. New York: Vintage.

Singleton, L. and S. Murray (1977) "Peer preferences and social interaction among third-grade children in an integrated school district." Journal of Educational Psychology 69: 330-336.

Smith, A. W. and E. Moore (1985) "Mathematics aptitude: effects of coursework, household language, and ethnic differences." Urban Education 20: 273-290.

St. John, N. (1975) School Desegregation: Outcomes for Children. New York: John Wiley.

St. John, N. and R. Lewis (1975) "Race and social structure of the elementary classroom." Sociology of Education 48: 346-368.

Stockard, J., P. Schmuck, K. Kemper, P. Williams, S. Edson, and M. Smith (1980) Sex Equity in Education. New York: Academic Press.

Thomas, G. C. (1981) Black Students in Higher Education. Westport, CT: Greenwood.

Thomas, G. M. and J. W. Meyer (1984) "The expansion of the state." Annual Review of Sociology, Vol. 10.

Thomas, W. I. and F. Znaniecki (1927) The Polish Peasant in Europe and America. New York: Knopf.

Tilly, C. (1975) The Formation of National States in Western Europe. Princeton, NJ: Princeton University Press.

Trow, M. (1976) "The implication of low growth rates for higher education." Higher Education 5: 377-396.

Turner, R. (1960) "Modes of social ascent through education: sponsored and contest mobility." American Sociological Review 25: 121-139.

UNESCO (1983) UNESCO Statistical Yearbook. Louvain, Belgium: Author.

U.S. Bureau of the Census (1979) The Social and Economic Status of the Black Population in the United States: An Historical View, 1790-1978 (No. 80, p. 23). Washington, DC: Government Printing Office.

U.S. Bureau of the Census (1980) Persons of Spanish Origin in the United States (No. 354, p. 20). Washington, DC: Government Printing Office.

U.S. Bureau of the Census (1985) School Enrollment—Social and Economic Characteristics of Students. Population Characteristics, Series P-20, No. 404 (November). Washington, DC: Government Printing Office.

Vander Zanden, J. (1970) Sociology. New York: Ronald Press.

Waller, W. (1932). The Sociology of Teaching. New York: John Wiley.

Ward, L. (1906) Applied Sociology. Boston: Ginn.

Warner, W. L., R. J. Havighurst, and M. B. Loeb (1944) Who Shall Be Educated? New York: Harper.

Weinberg, M. (1968) Desegregation Research: An Appraisal. Bloomington, IN: Phi Delta Kappa.

Weinberg, M. (1977) A Chance to Learn. Cambridge, MA: Harvard University Press.

Whitehead, A. N. (1929) The Aims of Education. New York: Macmillan.

Wilson, W. J. (1987) The Truly Disadvantaged: The Inner City, the Underclass, and Public Policy. Chicago: University of Chicago Press.

7

FAMILY SOCIOLOGY

Rhonda J.V. Montgomery

Wayne State University

The future of family sociology can be considered in two ways. One can ask what the future of family sociology will be or one can ask what the future of family sociology should be? Neither question is easily answered by a scholar who adheres to the tradition of unbiased observation and description. To answer the first question one must have a crystal ball and to answer the second one must be willing to take a stand based upon personal values. Since the first option is not possible, the second question will be addressed, fully recognizing that the answer will reflect personal biases in terms of goals for the field and processes by which these goals can be reached. Yet, the prescriptions are not offered in the absence of input from colleagues but, in fact, reflect a synthesis of prescriptions that have been offered by numerous scholars in the field (e.g., Berardo, 1980; Hill, 1981; Aldous, 1981; Brown and Kidwell, 1982). Since the future is always grounded in the past, this discussion starts with a review of the relatively short history of family scholarship, noting major contributions, limitations, long-term trends, and legacies.

A HISTORICAL VIEW

Family sociology can trace its earliest beginnings to the latter half of the nineteenth century, an era of social Darwinism. Among the works cited by Christensen (1964) as exemplars of the time are Herbert Spencer's *Synthetic Philosophy,* E. B. Tylor's *The Matriarchal Family System in the Nineteenth Century* and Edward Westermarck's (1921) *History of Human Marriage.* In these earliest of empirical works the family is defined and studied as a social institution, and the primary focus of the works is on the origins and development or evolution of the family over time. Using the comparative method, the scholars of the time searched the literature, including historical and anecdoctal records, to uncover the patterns of marriage and family among "primitive" peoples. The results of these early scholars were large volumes comparing marriage, kinship, and socialization patterns of societies widely separated in time and space. Although the methods of analysis have been characterized as descriptive and impressionistic and producing few firm propositions (Hill, 1962), we will see that these early works have provided a legacy to the field of study in terms of underlying assumptions that can still be observed in family scholarship. In particular, these early scholars looked at the family both as the basic unit of society and as the citadel of its values. They, like many of their successors today, believed that the integrity of a society or nation, "depended upon the stability, the simplicity, the immemorial integrity of the family" (Laslett, 1972: 16).

Not all family scholarship in the late nineteenth century was grounded in evolutionism. The work of Frederic Le Play who published *L'Organization de la famille* in 1875 represented a notable change in focus and methods of study. The concern of Le Play and his followers was not the optimistic documentation of the evolution of the family but instead the moralistic concern for healing of social decay. In this early work we see the beginning of action-oriented research with a concern for the relationship between public policy and family.

As Mogey (1955) notes, Le Play's work is also important for its emphasis on empirical facts. Le Play's work included the creation of data collection instruments, family budget questionnaires, and observation anticipating the empirical studies of the twentieth-century scholars. Despite his contributions to the methods of objective data collection, Laslett (1972) points out that Le Play's work was still colored by his moralistic views. Laying great stress on familial form, Le Play believed that the stem family was the desirable form and therefore, despite his own empirical observations to the contrary, "inevitably tended to join with this expression of preference a historical presumption that the stem family had been the normal arrangement, or at least very much respected as the proper type."

In his discussion of the development of the family field of study, Christensen (1964) characterizes the first half of the twentieth century as an age of emerging science. During this period family scholars benefited from the development of social survey techniques, rediscovered the empirical orientation of Le Play, adopted the scientific method and introduced statistical prediction into the field of study. Komarovsky and Waller (1985) note that in the early decades of the century the focus of study remained on social problems of the family, but the changing methods of study and the more accurate sources facilitated the separation of science from morality.

An equally important trend was the shift in focus from the study of the family as an institution to the study of the family as interacting individuals. Although scholars of the Chicago school, including Cooley, Park, Mead, and Thomas, contributed to this shift in focus, the conceptualization of the family as "a unity of interacting personalities each with a history in a given cultural milieu" had been attributed to W. Burgess (Christensen, 1964). This shift in focus resulted in extensive research on dyadic relationships, including dating, mate selection, marital quality and adjustment, and parent-child relationships.

There is general agreement that the third era of family scholarship began in the second half of the twentieth century. Christensen labeled this era as one of systematic theory building, a topic to which a long series of seminal papers have been devoted. Christensen (1964) suggests that theory building or theory construction is a logical synthesis of the two previous eras. While the early social Darwinists were concerned with generating broad generalizations about the family as an institution, the empiricists of the second era generated a plethora of findings, many of which could be viewed as trivial. What was needed was a means of organizing and synthesizing the many and growing number of findings about the family into some type of cohesive theory or framework. It is this goal of theory development that has been a driving force of family scholars over the past four decades. The progress of the field in achieving this goal has been regularly monitored and has generated an extensive literature. Initial efforts were stock-taking efforts that involved inventorying and codifying the products of family research (e.g., Hill et al., 1957; Goode, 1971; Katz and Hill, 1958). A second stage in theory construction centered on the identification and specification of conceptual frameworks starting with the seminal papers by Hill and his colleagues (Hill et al., 1957), followed by numerous updates including the detailed coverage by Christensen (1964) in the *Handbook on Marriage and Family,* an extension of frameworks in the book by Nye and Berardo (1966), and the two decade reviews by Broderick (1971) and Holman and Burr (1980). More recently, family scholars have devoted much time and effort to the development of axiomatic theory and middle-range theories with the most notable effort culminating in Volume I of the two volume work by Burr and his associates (1979), *Contemporary Theories About the Family.* While most of the work in this tradition has remained focused on the family as an association of interacting individuals, there have also been some pioneering attempts to develop theory that aids in the understanding and prediction of the interface between families and other social structures including Elder's (1985) work on family life courses, an extension of this perspective by Tallman (1986), Kantor and Lehr's (1975) work on the family as a social system, and an article by Nye and McDonald (1979) concerned with family policy research.

Despite the intensive efforts that have been directed toward theory development, there is almost universal agreement that theory development in family sociology is still in need of serious attention. This agreement does not, however, extend to the answer of obtaining useful and viable family theories. While there continues to be a large contingent of scholars who would adhere to the strategies first enunciated and implemented by Hill and his colleagues, others question the need for conceptual frameworks (Rodman, 1980); still others would suggest a greater borrowing of theory from related fields (Wiseman, 1981; Aldous, 1981). In any case, there is a growing agreement among scholars that no single general theory of family is likely to be useful in the understanding of family phenomena since, as Holman and Burr (1980: 734) note, such a theory

> would have to include such diverse concerns as economics, social, biological, physical, aesthetic, spiritual, psychological, historical and governmental factors. As a result it would have to be either extremely massive so that all of the factors could be included at a reasonable level of generality or so over-simplifying that it would provide little information about these complex phenomena.

The extensive attention that has been given to the development of family theory has not been matched by attention given to methodological concerns. With a few notable exceptions (e.g., Brown and Kidwell, 1982), family sociology has been much less interested in how information is obtained than in how it is catalogued and used. As Miller and his colleges (1982: 853) note, most of the methodological advances in marriage and family research are not "radically different or even distinct from those used to study other social behavioral phenomena." Most innovations in methods have been adopted from the larger field of sociology or other disciplines. There is, however, one methodological concern that has received some attention that appears to be unique to family sociology—the adequate measurement of family phenomena. This concern is as much an issue of conceptualization as of technology. As the pluralism and diversity of families have become more widely acknowledged, the identification and measurement of family traits has become a necessity. Yet, little attention has been given to defining or measuring family traits that are essential to understanding different family forms and organizations. This limitation in measurement has corresponding limitations in terms of sampling design, data collection, and data analysis. Some have suggested that family sociologists have been too quick to employ readily available methodological techniques without giving attention to their appropriateness in the measurement of many family concepts (Galligan, 1982).

Just as the research methods of family sociologists have been influenced by the milieu in which they work, the substantive interests of family sociologists have changed and expanded with the growth in diversity among families (Berardo and Shehan, 1984). Changes in patterns of sexual behavior, marriage, divorce, fertility, morality, and women in the labor force have created a greater prevalence of single parent families, unwed mothers, reconstituted families, dual-earner and dual-career families, childless families, and dependent elders. These alternate family forms have all captured the interest and attention of family scholars. Yet, throughout this expansion in specific interests, family scholars for the most part have remained wedded to a focus on the family at the micro level detailing the transactions of family member and the problems experienced by these alternate family forms. Hence much of the work, even when the focus is on alternative family forms, looks at dyadic relationships between intimate partners, spouses, and parents and children.

TURNING TO THE FUTURE

In sum, family sociology has embarked upon the last decades of the twentieth century with a long-standing interest in the family at the micro level, a long history of seeking theory to organize its findings, and an increased awareness of its lack of conceptual clarity and the implications of this for research design and measurement. Family scholars have been some of the most self-searching and self-critical scholars. They have generated numerous articles that have assessed the merits, accomplishments, and shortcomings of their work (e.g., Berardo, 1980; Hill, 1981; Aldous, 1981; Brown and Kidwell, 1982; Klein, 1984; Wiseman, 1981; Fox, 1981).

From these sources it is a relatively easy task to identify and generate a long list of concerns and directions for the future. These concerns include: a need to be less parochial; a need to recognize pluralism in family forms; a need to rethink the family scholar's role in the public arena; a need to focus on families rather than dyads; a need to study minority families; a need to study the family as a changing and dynamic entity; a need to look at the family in relationship to other social units including schools, health care organizations, government agencies, religious institutions, and the work setting; a need to borrow theory; a need to see the family as an independent or mediating variable; a need to listen to practitioners.

When considered together, two distinct but related themes underlay the numerous recommendations and prescription. The first concerns the purpose of family sociologists and the second the focus of family sociology.

THE UTILITY OF FAMILY SOCIOLOGY

It has been suggested that sociology is the discipline that is uniquely qualified to study the family since the family is a human social grouping and sociology, by definition, focuses upon social interaction and group phenomenon (Christensen, 1964: 23). While few among our colleagues would question this assertion, debate is more likely to arise concerning the purpose of such study. The intent here is not to open the whole philosophy of science debate concerning objectivity and value free research, but to raise the question of the utility of research of family sociologists since the issue is closely tied to the focus of researchers and the questions they choose to investigate. It is easy to agree with the position taken by Foote (1954) that the purpose of research is to produce knowledge for the benefit of common wealth. If one agrees with this premise, then it is just one more step to assume that research questions that are formulated should lead to useful information for some "client" either immediately or as a step toward producing answers to a significant problem (see Freese, 1984). It should be emphasized that this viewpoint does not necessarily imply that all research should be applied research nor does it imply that the "client" should dictate the research questions. What it does imply is that research should lead to information that will allow family sociologists to predict patterns of change in family structures and process, predict likely consequences of such change for individuals and society, and ultimately inform the development of public and private policies.

This notion does not imply the taking of sides or even the expression of values among scholars. It does require the questioning of personal and societal values and much attention to the way research questions are phrased and thereby studied. What is being advocated here is what Nye and McDonald (1979) termed research for family policy. Such research is not the same as family evaluation research or family impact analysis, both of which focus on existing or proposed social programs. Research for family policy focuses on the family as a link between the individual and other social units and has the purpose of identifying the consequences of family structures, processes, and behaviors for individuals and society. It is both more general in purpose and incremental in process than evaluation research. It is basic science with the conscious recognition that the information gathered will incrementally build to an understanding of the relationships between the individual, the family, and the society. Like the scholars of the early twentieth century, family sociologists should be concerned with the relevance of their work for the public good, but unlike these early scholars, we need not limit our focus to problems of the family. Rather the intent should be to chart the family's interface with other social structures. Research guided by this purpose is likely to be the avenue by which family sociology acquires its coveted role of expert in the public arena because the results are likely to be relevant to individuals, families, and decision makers.

THE FOCUS OF FAMILY SOCIOLOGY

In the recent past there has been a tendency to study the family in isolation from other social structures and this tendency has inhibited theory development, restricted study designs, prevented the development of useful measures of family, and ultimately prevented family sociologists from being the source of information about families and their relationship to public policies and practice.

While the early social Darwinists focused exclusively on the family as an institution, the trend in the twentieth century has been for family sociologists to shift their focus to the family at the micro level. This trend has been especially prevalent in the past two decades as noted by Berardo (1980: 727). "In sum, research in the sixties and throughout the seventies has been heavily concentrated at the micro level, with a major focus on the internal transactions between family members." What has been absent has been the conceptualization of the family as a mediator.

While the family's role as mediator between society and the individual has long been recognized and discussed in detail (e.g., Vincent, 1966), this conception of the family has been neglected in research. As a consequence, there have been repeated calls for more research on the interface between family and bureaucracy, family and the work world, family and health care system, and family and any number of other social organizations and institutions. Similarly there have been repeated calls for family sociology that addresses family and public policy.

Although any reason for this neglect of the family as mediator would be pure speculation, it may well be tied to our conceptualization of family. As Tallman (1986) notes, there are three distinct conceptions of the family—as institution, organization, and small group of interacting individuals. Our ability to describe the family, understand its role, develop theory, and predict future patterns is restricted to the extent that we restrict our research to any one of these conceptions. For the past three decades, the emphasis of family sociology has been on the small group of interacting personalities to the exclusion of the family as an organization. Whether this exclusion has been a cause or a consequence of our failure to examine and explain the family's role in mediating between the social structure and the individual is not of importance. What is important for the discipline, if it is to have a role in producing knowledge for the common wealth of society, is a shift in focus among scholars to a conception of "families" as organizations. As such, Tallman (1986: 264) suggests that families can be conceived as "separate social units interacting with other social units within a given social collectivity." It is this conceptualization that is required if patterns of interaction between families and the social structure are to be examined.

Multiple benefits will emerge when the study of family is approached from this perspective. First, when the family is viewed as an organization, the fact that the family is not an entity with a single form but is an entity that can assume a number of forms and functions is understood. Tallman (1986: 264) notes that, "From this perspective families are viewed as a type of social organization that varies over time in size, composition, division of labor, role expectations, hierarchical structure, and control over key resources." This notion of the family as an organization goes beyond that of the family life-cycle model in that it underscores the differences that exist across families who are at the same stage in the family life cycle as well as differences between families at different stages. In short, the emphasis of research stemming from this perspective would be pluralism, a distinct contrast with the majority of family research throughout the past four decades.

Perhaps this last statement deserves clarification. Certainly, those scholars who have focused on alternative life-styles, divorce and remarriage, stepparents, family violence, and dual income families might take exception to this statement. Yet, while these scholars have focused on alternative families, the emphasis has been on "alternative," not family. Whether by intent or by tacit acceptance, family scholars have all too frequently approached the study of "alternative" family forms with a notion that there is a normative form that, if not most prevalent, is at least more accepted (and perhaps better) than other forms. This tendency can be witnessed in the formulation of research questions, sample selections, measurement, and the conclusions that are drawn from findings.

The emphasis on pluralism in turn leads to an emphasis on the family as a variable that needs to be adequately described. It is not sufficient to speak of single-parent families or divorced families or dual-earner families. When the family is viewed as an organization, it becomes clear that a description of the unit involves not only a description of the composition of the family, for example, one parent versus two, but also the division of labor, the role expectations, hierarchical structure, and control over resources. Each of these aspects of a family organization can vary independently of the other traits and therefore needs to be measured and described as such. It is not appropriate to assume covariation among these variables in the absence of empirical tests, as is frequently done when "single-parent" households are compared with "two-parent" households or "dual-earner" families are compared with single-earner families or divorced families are compared with nondivorced.

If single-term identifiers such as dual-earner or single-parent family are to be used, it is necessary first to determine whether relationships between characteristics such as composition and control over resources are common patterns among such families. In the absence of such documentation, research questions are inappropriately phrased leading to incorrect conclusions. For example, to ask the question whether the quality of parent-child relationships differs between single-parent families and two parent families is to assume that these two types of families are consistently different and that we know how they are different. That is, either we assume that the only difference between the two types of family is in composition (i.e., number of parents) or we assume that other differences, such as differences in hierarchical structure and control over resources, are consistent across all single-parent families and likewise across all two-parent families. If this is not our assumption then the question must be rephrased to include multiple factors or the conditions under which the two types of family composition are to be compared. In the absence of such specification we open ourselves up to the probability of inadequate conclusions. Either we assert differences in parent-child relations as owing to family composition when, in fact, they may be owing to differences in other key family characteristics or we fail to find differences owing to composition because we have not controlled for the influence of other key family characteristics.

The enhanced ability to describe the family that is associated with the perspective of the family as an organization will, in turn, enhance our ability to understand the family at both the micro level and the macro level. At the micro level, this conceptualization will lead to better measurement primarily because of the improved conceptualization. Guided by a whole literature concerned with organizational characteristics, we can measure family characteristics with parallel, if not borrowed, measures. This conceptualization, will, in part, resolve our quest for "family measures."

At the macro level, the more precise description will help researchers investigate the family as both an independent and dependent variable. This approach makes it very clear that the interface between the family and other social units is two-way. The family is not simply an absorber of other social impacts, but, in fact, has impact. In the past, social historians who have studied the family as an institution, have noted the bidirectional interaction of the family with other social units, but scholars who have focused on the family as interacting individuals have been more inclined to discuss the impact of policies or purposes *on* the family, if such interaction is discussed at all. The possibility that a family unit or a group of family units may influence other social structures (e.g., the dual-earner families may influence the workplace) has not been widely explored through empirical studies. This limitation in the field may stem from an inability in the past to identify the elements of a family organization that may affect other structures or be affected by them. For example, the influence of the "family as an institution" on the workplace may be observed only over an extended period of historical time, but the influence of different types of "division of labor" or family compositions on employees' expectations of the workplace may be empirically studied at a single point in time. By identifying the elements or characteristics of a family that can influence or be influenced by other social units, this conceptualization of the family as an organization can move family studies to a level of precision and specification that is required to describe adequately the role of families in society. This view will prompt scholars to investigate the diverse influences of policies and social change on different types of family organizations.

The increased specification and understanding that will result from work undertaken will in turn improve the ability of family sociology to predict changes in families in the future and predict the corresponding changes and consequences for other social structures. It is this ability to predict rather than simply describe that is a requisite for family sociology if it is to be recognized as an area of expertise that has unique qualifications for providing knowledge for the commonwealth. Only when we are better able to describe the interface between family and other social structures will we be able to predict and thereby make the study of family useful for understanding social change and guiding public policy.

QUESTIONS IN NEED OF RESEARCH

If family sociologists choose to assume the role of expert and provide information that can be used to inform public policy and guide social change, then the future of family sociology will include addressing many difficult but groundbreaking issues that must be confronted by our changing society. If we are to be sources of knowledge rather than chroniclers of history, it is not enough to describe the functions of the family or its internal workings; we must also study the interface between changing technology and demographic patterns and the changing role and composition of the family. When the family is studied as the mediator between individuals and other social units, numerous important and often difficult questions will be raised. Our willingness and ability to apply the scientific method to these issues will determine our future.

To gain insight into the issues that will be of concern to our society in the future, it is not necessary to speculate in a science fiction fashion but only to turn to recent newspaper headlines. For example, the celebrated Baby M case concerning the legality of contracts for surrogate motherhood and the rights of the surrogate mother is fraught with questions that are central to the domain of family sociology. While many scholars would turn away from such issues and maintain that they are issues of morals and values, the fact is that decisions will be made by legislators and the courts. Are these decisions to be based solely on the personal and religious values of the decision makers or are they to be guided by facts concerning the likely consequences for the individuals involved and for society at large?

The Baby M case raises serious and basic questions about the rights and obligations of society, families, and individuals. Does procreation imply the right or the obligation to own and socialize children? Do the rights of biological parents take precedence over rights of children? Do the rights of biological parents take precedence over the rights of society at large?

These are not questions with a single answer but questions that will be answered according to societal values and conditions. It is our task as family sociologists to identify the options and, as far as possible, the implications of these options. Cross-cultural and historical comparison studies will point to differences among societies in their answers to these questions. Certainly China, in its limitation of births to one child per family, has acted to assert the right of society over families in the choice of procreation. Practices that represent the other extreme, that is, individual rights over that of society, include test-tube fertilization with sperm selected for genetic reasons. What are the implications of sperm banks of Nobel Prize winners for families? For society? More important, who should be making the decisions about who should procreate and under what conditions? Once decisions are made, who will decide which fetuses will live? With new technologies such as amniocentesis, the sex and the likelihood of deformity can be determined early in the gestation period.

What do we do with this information? Who is using it? Who should use it? What will be the implications for individuals? For families? For society? Are these questions to be answered only by medical personnel, or are family sociologists going to influence these answers in any way?

Another recent court case that raises similar issues about the relationship among the rights and responsibilities of the individual, the family, and the larger community or society is the Baby Jane Doe case, which concerned the parents' right to refuse medical treatment. If a parent chooses not to opt for medical treatment does the government have the right "to give unsolicited advice either to parents, hospitals, or to state officials who are faced with difficult treatment decisions concerning handicapped children?" (Taylor, 1986). The Supreme Court ruled no. While the court addressed the issue of rights, it did not go on to address the issue of obligations. Had the court ruled yes, who would have been obligated to care for and support that child throughout its life? Is this to be a family function or a government function?

Technological and medical advancements have not only prompted critical questions about the formation of the family and its role in protection and socialization of children, these advancements also have raised questions about families' roles in the protection and care of the elderly and ultimately the death of its members. Once again we can turn to the newspaper headlines to note that the concerns are not futuristic but are here today. In 1985 Roswell Gilbert was convicted of first-degree murder, the mercy killing of his wife who was afflicted with Alzheimer's disease. Having reached his own personal limits in caring for her and watching her degenerate, Mr. Gilbert shot his wife. When the first bullet did not kill her he shot her again. He was later convicted of premeditated murder (New York Times, 1985).

Among the questions that are raised by the case are those that concern the family's responsibility for caring for its disabled members. When a person becomes unable to care for himself or herself who should provide the care? Children? Spouses? The government? When individuals come to a point when they no longer want to live or life is too painful, should they be allowed to take their lives? Should family members be allowed to assist them with this action? When a person is unable to make a decision about death and is in great pain, should a family member be allowed to make this decision?

Once again the questions that are being asked require both values and information to be answered. Are we prepared as scholars of the family to provide information that can be used to make these decisions, or will we allow others, less knowledgeable about the family, to make these decisions based primarily on unquestioned values? There has been no dearth of research undertaken to study the situation of family members who care for elderly persons. Much of this research, however, has been conducted without benefit of the sociological perspective and most of it has been undertaken without critical analysis of values that currently prevail in public policy. Studies including that of the author that attempt to measure the burden and morale of family caregivers or the influence of alternative policies ostensibly are designed and funded on the premise that they will benefit families. However, they are also designed and funded on the premise that families should be responsible for the care. As noted elsewhere, even this most basic premise deserves serious study (Borgatta and Montgomery, 1987). If families are not responsible, then who is or should be? When should responsibility for care end for the individual? For the family? For society?

The future of family sociology rests on our ability and willingness to study the family as a mediator between the individual and other social units. It is a matter of positioning ourselves to have answers to new questions. This requires giving attention to the questions we ask, the design of our studies, the measures we use, and ultimately the theory that guides us. If our questions are phrased narrowly within the existing values, the answers that we obtain will be limited to the present situation. We will continue to be describers and not very good describers at that. For example, if we as a society are to be confronted with the question of who should be parents, then data that would be useful for guiding the answer would tell us about the outcomes of different types of parents at this time. That is, information about the situation and societal contributions of children raised by various types of family structures would be useful. We would give attention to outcome variables, such as the extent of socially destructive or predatory behavior among children, the extent of socially enhancing behaviors, or the level of dependence on societal support. How do children raised in different types of families differ in these critical elements? If they do differ, what aspects of the family organization are correlated with these differences? Is it the family composition? Family resources? Division of labor? Describing relationships between types of family organization and types of outcomes for children and society would be helpful. We need not be engineers or architects, but we are the scientists on which such engineers and architects rely. If there are patterns and they are predictable, then we should find them. If we are afraid to do so, then we might better define ourselves as historians than as scientists.

REFERENCES

Aldous, Joan (1981) "Second guessing the experts: thoughts on family agencies for the eighties." Journal of Marriage and the Family 43 (2): 267-9.

Berardo, Felix M. (1980) "Decade preview: some trends and directions for family research and theory in the 1980's." Journal of Marriage and the Family 42: 723-728.

Berardo, Felix M. and Constance L. Shehan (1984) "Family scholarship: a reflection of the changing family?" Journal of Family Issues, 5 (4): 577-98.

Blalock, H. M., Jr. (1979) "The professional address: measurement and conceptualization problems: the major obstacle to integrating theory and research." American Sociological Review 44 (December): 881-94.

Borgatta, E. and R. Montgomery (1987) "Aging policy and societal values," pp. 7-29 in Critical Issues in Aging Policy. Newbury Park, CA: Sage.

Broderick, C. B. [ed.] (1971) A Decade of Family Research and Action 1960-69. Minneapolis: National Council on Family Relations.

Brown, Lynne H. and Jeannie S. Kidwell (1982) "Methodology in family studies: the other side of caring." Journal of Marriage and the Family 44 (4): 833-839.

Burgess, E. W. (1946) "New foundations for marriage and the family: research." Marriage and Family Living 8: 64-65.

Burr, W. R., R. Hill, F. I. Nye and I. L. Reiss [eds.] (1979) Contemporary Theories about the Family. Volume 1: Research Based Theories. New York: Free Press.

Christensen, Harold T. (1964) Handbook of Marriage and the Family. Chicago: Rand Dobash, R. Emerson and Russell P. Dobash (1984) "Social science and social action: the case of wife beating." Journal of Family Issues 2 (December): 439-70.

Elder, Glen H., Jr. (1985) "Perspectives on the life course," in G. Elder (ed.) Life Course Dynamics. Ithaca, NY: Cornell University Press.

Foote, N. N. (1954) "Research: a new strength for family life." Marriage and Family Living 16: 13-20.

Fox, Greer L. (1981) "Family research theory, and politics: challenges of the eighties." Journal of Marriage and the Family 43 (2): 259-61.

Freese, Lee (1984) "Cumulative problem solving in family sociology." Journal of Family Issues 5: 447-469.

Galligan, Richard Journal (1982) "Innovative techniques: siren or rose." Journal of Marriage and the Family 44 (4): 875-886.

Glick, Paul C. (1984) "American household structure in transition." Family Planning Perspective 16 (5): 205-211.

Goode, W. Journal, E. H. Hopkins and H. M. McClure (1971) Social Systems and Family Patterns: A Propositional Inventory. Indianapolis: Bobbs-Merrill.

Hendrix, Lewellyn (1984) "The increasing mistrust of cross-cultural studies." Journal of Family Issues 5 (4): 542-4.

Hill, R. (1951) "Review of current research on marriage and the family." American Sociology 16: 694-701.

Hill, R. (1955) "A critique of contemporary marriage and family research." Social Forces 33: 268-277.

Hill, R. (1962) "Cross-national family research: attempts and prospects." International Social Science Journal 14: 425-451.

Hill, Reubin (1981) "Whither family research in the 1980's: new horizons." Journal of Marriage and the Family 43 (2): 255-7.

Hill, R., A. M. Katz and R. L. Simpson (1957) "An inventory of research in marriage and family behavior: a statement of objectives and progress." Marriage and Family Living 19: 89-92.

Holman, Thomas B. and Wesley R. Burr (1980) "Beyond the beyond: the growth of family theories in the 1970's." Journal of Marriage and the Family 42: 729-741.

Kantor, D. and W. Lehr (1975) Inside the Family: Toward a Theory of Family Process. San Francisco. Jossey-Bass.

Katz, A. M. and R. Hill (1958) "Residential propinquity and marital selection: a review of theory, method and fact." Marriage and Family Living. 20: 27-35.

Klein, David M. [ed.] (1984) Journal of Family Issues: The Current State of Family Scholarship 5. (complete issue)

Komarovsky, Mirra and W. Waller (1985) "Studies of the family." American Journal of Sociology 50: 443-451.

Larzelere, Robert E. and John H. Skeen (1984) "The method of multiple hypothesis: a neglected research strategy in family studies." Journal of Family Issues 5 (4): 474-92.

Laslett, Peter (1972) Household and Family in Past Time. Cambridge: University Press.

Lee, Gary R. (1984) "The utility of cross-cultural data: potentials and limitations for family sociology." Journal of Family Issues 5 (4): 519-41.

Lewis, Robert A. (1984) "Yes, but no: a reply to cumulative problem solving in family sociology." Journal of Family Issues 5 (4): 471-3.

Miller, Brent C., Boyd C. Rollins and Darwin L. Thomas (1982) "On methods of studying marriages and families." Journal of Marriage and the Family 44 (4): 851-873.

Model, Suzanne (1981) "Housework by husbands: determinants and implications." Journal of Family Issues 2 (2): 225-37.

Mogey, J. M. (1955) "The contributions of Frederic Le Play to family research." Marriage and Family Living 17: 310-315.

New York Times (1985) "Man convicted of killing wife who begged to die." May 10.

New York Times (1985) "Man free in death of ill wife." August 15.

Nye, F. I. and F. Berardo (1966) Emerging Conceptual Frameworks in Family Analysis. New York: Macmillan.

Nye, F., Ivan McDonald, and Gerald McDonald (1979) "Family policy research: emergent models and some theoretical issues." Journal of Marriage and the Family 41 (3): 473-485.

Rodman, Hyman (1980) "Are conceptual frameworks necessary for theory building?: the case of family sociology." Sociological Quarterly 20: 429-41.

Tallman, Irving (1986) "Social history and the life-course perspective on the family: a view from the bridge," pp. 225-281 in James F. Short, Jr. (ed.) The Social Value: Dimensions and Issues. Beverly Hills, CA: Sage.

Taylor, Stuart, Jr. (1986) "High Court upsets U. S. intervention on infants' lives." New York Times (June 10): A22.

Thompson, Linda and Alexis J. Walker (1982) "The dyad as the unit of analysis: conceptual and methodological issues." Journal of Marriage and the Family 44 (4): 889-900.

Vincent, C. E. (1966) "Family spongia: the adaptive function." Journal of Marriage and the Family 28: 29-36.

Walker, Alexis J. and Linda Thompson (1984) "Feminism and family studies." Journal of Family Issues 5 (4): 545-70.

Walters, Lynda Henley, Joe F. Pittman, Jr., and J. Elizabeth Norrell (1984) "Development of a quantitative measure of a family from self-reports of family members." Journal of Family Issues 5 (4): 497-514.

Westermarck, Edward. (1921) The History of Human Marriage. London: Macmillan.

Wiseman, Jacqueline P. (1981) "The family and its researchers in the eighties: retrenching, renewing and revitalizing." Journal of Marriage and the Family 43 (2): 263-5.

8

SOCIOLOGY OF RELIGION

Anson Shupe

Indiana University—Purdue University, Fort Wayne

Jeffrey K. Hadden

University of Virginia

Twenty years ago a sociologist writing about the future of the sociology of religion might well have been hesitant, if not pessimistic, about its fate. During the 1950s and much of the 1960s the relentless logic of the secularization model, a religious analog to the then-popular "convergence" theory of modernization writings, was dominant. Its implications for religion's declining societal and personal importance was uncritically accepted by most sociologists.[1]

Many who put on the prophetic mantle confidently assumed that either the very subject matter of the sociology of religion was slowly disappearing or, as did Harvey Cox in *The Secular City* (1965), evolving urban religion would force sociologists to rethink in radical ways how they understood religion. In a word, the sociology of religion certainly was not considered one of the more exciting or growing specialties of the discipline. In terms of social significance, it was generally regarded as trivial in comparison to emerging areas of interest such as deviance, or economic and political sociology.

All of this has changed today, in part because of the inescapable visibility of religion in culture and, in part, because of significant conceptual and methodological developments in the scientific study of religion.

THE DECLINE OF THE SOCIOLOGY OF RELIGION

Today the sociology of religion is enjoying a resurgence of professional and classroom interest as well as research involvement. That the sub-

120

discipline should have ever experienced a period of slump is ironic, since the religious dimension was fundamental to the thinking of sociology's founding generations. Those who had not received formal theological educations, as did Karl Marx, nonetheless lived and worked within societies where church and state (as well as church and academy) were closely intertwined.

Sociology was born amid the profound tension between religion and liberal culture in early nineteenth-century Europe. In the spirit of the Enlightenment, reason was believed king, and science would pave the way to a world that would soon be rid of archaic obstacles such as tyrants and religious superstitions.

Yet even when social theorists postulated a cultural maturation away from the influence of religious worldviews (e.g., August Comte's evolutionary scheme wherein the *theological* stage of society evolved eventually into a *positivist* stage, or Max Weber's global process of *rationalization*), religion was nevertheless an indispensable ingredient of change. In fact, in Comte's plan the ambitious young science of sociology itself was to be cast as a religion for popular dissemination under the name of the Church of Humanity.

The irony is compounded by rather clear indications that the origins of American sociology were to some extent tied to the reformist motives of many individual sociologists involved in the social gospel movement of the late nineteenth and early twentieth centuries. As Reed (1981: 31) observes, "Prominent among the students of the first [American] sociologists were clergy and other religionists filled with a sense of mission to reshape the social structure along the ethical lines sketched by Jesus." Many of the American founders were committed to social reform and viewed sociology as a moral science. Albion Small, founder of the University of Chicago's Department of Sociology and of the *American Journal of Sociology*, was the leading proponent of this view. The early volumes of *AJS* contained nine articles by Shailer Matthews, a leading figure of the social gospel movement. *Social Forces* and *Sociology and Social Research*, the other two major sociological journals through 1925, were also edited by reform-minded churchmen (Reed, 1975: 112). In fact, the social gospel movement was sometimes referred to at seminaries and divinity schools as "Christian Sociology." Likewise, Lyon (1983: 234) maintains that "the Christian Sociology movement had a major role in the institutionalization of American Sociology, helping to provide its early identity."

But even while Christian sociologists occupied important roles in the early years of the discipline, there is significant evidence to suggest that their views were not the dominant perspective in the discipline. A remarkable

study conducted by psychologist James Leuba in 1914 found that only 29%
of the sociologists in his sample believed in God, and among a subsample
judged to be the elite of the discipline, only 19% were believers (Leuba,
1916). The credibility of these data is enhanced by a replication that Leuba
conducted in 1933 that produced very similar results (1934).

Cases in point are not difficult to locate. For example, Frank Lester
Ward, who was the most influential theorist among the founding
generation of American sociologists, believed religion to be an archaic
institution, and he often expressed antiecclesiastical views (Reed, 1975:
100). And Herbert Spencer, the most widely read non-American for the
first two generations of American sociologists, was adamantly antagonistic
to religion.

Though not all sociologists of religion were professed "religionists," even
among that number who had once taken seminary training, the perception
of them as such existed in the larger discipline. That is likely one important
reason for the slump of interest in the sociology of religion beginning in the
1920s and lasting until the post-World War II era. Lyon (1983: 238) notes
that American sociology's mood grew increasingly secular and positivist in
imitation of natural science and in pursuit of respectability. And clearly, a
second generation of sociologists became concerned with the institutionalization of sociology as a science. As a consequence of this orientation,
religion per se (not just the social gospel) became viewed by many social
scientists as something on the wane, if not already irrelevant.

Likewise, religion—the cosmic, the transcendent, the irrational—
seemed incompatible with science—the orderly, the empirical, the material—
even as a subject matter for investigation.

Reed (1974: 1959) documents the estrangement of the sociology of
religion from the mainstream teaching centers of the discipline. For
example, inspecting 305 masters and doctoral theses completed at the
University of Chicago between 1893 and 1935, he found that 31, or 10%, of
these could be considered as dealing with the sociology of religion, thus
making it one of the most popular fields of inquiry in the new discipline. But
what is most interesting is the fact that those who chose thesis and
dissertation topics on religion invariably did not enjoy careers as illustrious
as those of their peers who chose to study secular topics. Concludes Reed,
"the Chicago students who were to be successful in the profession did not
do sociology of religion."

Furthermore, to the extent that the sociology of religion developed as a
subdiscipline, persons who can be identified as religious were in the
forefront of this area of inquiry (Reed, 1982). And one group of religiously
devout colleagues contributed to the stereotype of religion being "apart"

from the mainstream of sociology by forming a professional association whose organizing principle was the fact that its members were Roman Catholic. The founding of the American Catholic Sociological Association (later the Association for the Sociology of Religion) in 1938 emerged because many Catholic sociologists sensed the persistent relevance of religion in a purportedly secularized society. And yet they confronted a discipline that dismissed their attempts to create a respectable subdiscipline as transparently sectarian or atavistic (Reiss, 1970).

Even in the early postwar years the founders of the Religious Research Fellowship (later the Religious Research Association) in 1951 had denominational rather than academic employers (Hadden, 1974: 129). And it took some revisions before the statement of goals of the Committee for the Scientific Study of Religion (later the Society for the Scientific Study of Religion), established in 1949, "placed stronger emphasis upon the scientific rather than apologetic aspect of studying religion" (Newman, 1974: 139).

It is no wonder that the sociology of religion began to founder in this country, rejected or ignored as it was by the parent discipline. These image problems, coupled with the often inadequate scientific training of early practitioners, popular skepticism about the obstacles or impossibilities of science studying religion, and the lack of funding opportunities for sociologists of religion (Hadden and Heenan, 1970: 164-165) relegated the sociology of religion to a decidedly second-class status within mainstream sociology.[2]

Nevertheless, an important foundation for research and theory in the American sociology of religion was laid during the classical era of the nineteenth century and later, during the first half of the twentieth century. The "giants" such as Marx, Simmel, Durkheim, and Spencer had asked the important questions about religion as a social fact even if they were too closely wed to an ethnocentric evolutionary model of secular development (Nisbet, 1969) that led them to believe that the available "primitive materials" on contemporary preliterate people were glimpses of our own western ancestors at some earlier time.

If later sociologists of religion, particularly in the United States, did not significantly push "beyond the classics" in their theorizing, as some (e.g., Glock and Hammond, 1973) have criticized, they nevertheless brought a middle-range, more empirical orientation into their studies that would be required to develop adequately the scientific (as opposed to the purely philosophical) status of the subdiscipline.

It is to this phase of the sociology of religion's history in the United States that we now turn.

RESURGENCE OF THE SOCIOLOGY OF RELIGION

While the three American professional associations in the social scientific study of religion just mentioned initially may have reaffirmed the correctness of the label of *religionists* for those affiliated scholars who sought to study the sociological side of religious life, they also created permanent networks of professional communication and journals for disseminating research findings (e.g., *Sociological Analysis, Journal for the Scientific Study of Religion,* and the *Review of Religious Research*).

Such developments had no small consequence for the sociology of religion. Despite fashionable predictions during the post-World War II years about the "death of God" and the advent of a postbiblical "secular city" in which urban men and women would dwell, traditional biblical faith among Americans did not retreat nor did unconventional, innovative religions disappear. And social scientists, by patiently monitoring these patterns of faith and practice, if only for themselves in their own publications and meetings, preserved the sociology of religion through the years of slump.

Two dovetailing factors were responsible for the resurgence of interest in the sociology of religion. First, the subdiscipline has benefited enormously from social issues and societal developments involving religion but entirely outside its control. Second, it has witnessed improved theoretical and methodological sophistication in overall graduate training. The result has been that the quality of sociological research on various forms of religious activity has risen and been available when there was widespread "market" demand for information on topics of public discussion. Three recent examples will suffice to illustrate this point.

During the 1960s a new generation of social scientists trained in quantitative survey methods began "mapping out" the dimensions and elements of religious life in the United States. Undoubtedly the seminal work of this era was Gerhard Lenski's monumental study *The Religious Factor* (1961). This work represents a critical turning point in the development of the social scientific study of religion. Lenski's study in Detroit provided a dense mountain of empirical data and the first solid evidence suggesting the need to reassess the theoretical foundations of the sociology of religion in a direction away from the secularization thesis.

More important still, the work of Charles Y. Glock, (along with the students he trained and with whom he was coauthor) was monumental to the development of the sociology of religion. Glock defined the importance of the survey method and the rigorous operationalization of a multitude of concepts for sociologists of religion during the 1960s, significantly altering the field (Glock and Stark, 1965).

A number of studies during this period demonstrated the relevance of religion to important social controversies, such as race relations (Campbell and Pettigrew, 1959), anti-Semitism (Glock and Stark, 1966), black religion and the civil rights movements (Marx, 1967), and clergy activism against both racism (Hadden, 1969) and the Vietnam War (Quinley, 1974). Not only did the sociology of religion demonstrate the contemporary "relevance" both of the religious factor and of its own professional analyses (in an age when that characteristic was elevated to a fetish), but the infusion into the subdiscipline of the larger discipline's newest quantitative methods and modes of analysis undoubtedly made it more attractive to new scholars.

During the 1970s a proliferation of exotic new religious movements and their controversies with the established institutions of media, families, churches, and government became issues of public and professional debate (Shupe and Bromley, 1980; Robbins and Anthony, 1981). While scholars in theology and religious studies largely contained their polemics to traditional apologetics or doctrinal attacks, sociologists were into the field with surveys and both as observers and participants, producing a lively corpus of research that was consumed by journals, magazines, and the mass media (see Shupe et al., 1984).

An entire generation of "new blood," trained by the scholars of the 1960s, came into the sociology of religion during the 1970s largely through interest in various aspects of the so-called cult phenomenon. Phillip E. Hammond, editor of the *Journal for the Scientific Study of Religion*, reminisced in 1982:

> I'm more convinced each year that new religious movements have given a valuable shot in the arm to the scientific study of religion.... Social scientists, it seems to me, responded remarkably well to the challenge brought on by the rich mix of non-traditional religions appearing in the recent past. And in doing so, they have advanced our understanding of religion in society [p. ii].

The 1980s witnessed the rise of two related social movement phenomena: (1) the return of evangelical Christians to a sense of social reform, public commitment, and political activism through the movement that sociologists of religion have dubbed the New Christian Right; and (2) the "electronic church" of burgeoning radio and television ministries. This overall controversy is still ongoing, made the more polemic and ever-shifting by the public relations skills of many of the NCR's leaders and the usually imperfect replicability and limitations of surveys and other studies.

Nevertheless, sociologists of religion have led other scholars in clarifying the claims of NCR/electronic church spokespersons as to their actual constituencies and probable influence, dissecting the origins and varieties of these phenomena, and probing their implications for larger society (Hadden and Swann, 1981; Hunter, 1983; Liebman and Wuthnow, 1983; Bromley and Shupe, 1984).

In addition, many sociologists have begun to regard the events of reemerging social and religious conservatism in the United States as part of a larger worldwide pattern of "global fundamentalism." Cross-cultural studies right up through the 1970s uncritically assumed the validity of the secularization/modernization model's straight-line determinism (D. Smith, 1970; B. Smith, 1976). By contrast, comparative studies of the 1980s have begun to look at the unique histories and structural conditions of various western and non-Western countries (Merkl and Smart, 1983; Lincoln, 1985; Hadden and Shupe, 1986). Furthermore, many scholars have begun to view with a tentative and even skeptical eye the secularization hypothesis' ability to aid their analyses (Hammond, 1985).

Once again, events of conflict and revolution outside the control of sociologists have created pressures for research and knowledge to render these understandable. The willingness of sociologists of religion to respond and capitalize on such opportunities has further integrated the subdiscipline into the mainstream of sociology.

From all indications, these sorts of controversies and issues have drawn new sociologists into the subdiscipline. If nothing else, wider interest in such phenomena has exposed those with only marginal identities as sociologists of religion to the vitality of the field's activities.

THEORETICAL PROGRESS

The religious institution was part of the "grand" theoretical schemes of this century's major sociological theorists, such as Pitirim Sorokin and Talcott Parsons, but overall the modern subdiscipline has witnessed relatively little important theorizing about religion per se. Much of this trend is a result of the widespread disillusionment with such macro theories among members of the sociological profession in general and the desire to investigate more modest topics with greater degrees of concrete verifiability.

Notable exceptions to this lack of theorizing include Andrew Greeley's *Religion: A Secular Theory* (1982) and a series of studies and theoretical essays by Rodney Stark and William Sims Bainbridge culminating in *The*

Future of Religion (1985). Solidly grounded in sophisticated empiricism, Stark and Bainbridge have spent much of the 1980s constructing a deductive set of propositions from exchange theory, aimed at explaining the dynamics of any religious faith (Stark and Bainbridge, 1985). Though this effort has not been without criticisms that it is reductionist (Wallis and Bruce, 1984), the Stark and Bainbridge corpus is the most ambitious attempt at systematic theorizing in recent years.

Most sociologists of religion have preferred to focus on more manageable middle range questions. As a consequence, a great deal of work on a wide array of subjects has accumulated, much of it useful and of interest to both lay persons and policymakers. As during the 1960s, scholars have continued to look at the religious dimensions of various social problems and controversies, such as juvenile delinquency (Knudten and Knudten, 1971; Higgins and Albracht, 1977), alcohol abuse (Peek et al., 1979), sexism (Daly, 1975; Bainbridge and Hatch, 1982), woman abuse and family violence (Shupe et al., 1986), alternative healing practices (McGuire, 1982, 1983), and abortion (Harris and Mills, 1985; Ebaugh and Haney, 1978).

Still, much effort has been directed at criticisms and clarification of classic theoretical concepts, such as the frequently cited Weberian church-sect dichotomy (Swatos, 1976). Perennial phenomena of interest to scholars of comparative religions, such as conversion (Straus, 1979; Long and Hadden, 1983; Snow and Machalek, 1984) and mysticism (Holm, 1982; Hay and Morisy, 1978; Lovekin and Malony, 1977; Greeley, 1975) have also been part of this more empirically grounded middle-range literature.

At the same time, sociologists of religion have appropriated theories and concepts from other areas of sociology and social science, such as phenomenology, exchange theory, role theory, attribution theory, and resource mobilization theory, successfully applying these to topics as diverse as the occupational strains of Southern Baptist ministers (Ingram, 1981) and the dynamics of social control and fund-raising in new religious movements (Richardson, Steward, and Simmonds, 1979; Bromley and Shupe, 1980).

In short, whatever the postwar sociology has lacked in elegant theoretical sophistication (and it has not been entirely devoid of theorizing) it has more than made up in developing a solid, growing base of empirical generalizations and middle-range hypotheses never possessed during the first half of the twentieth century. In that sense the sociology of religion was for a long time theory rich and data poor. It did not begin a systematic accumulation of reliable information to begin rigorously testing theoretical propositions until much later than some other areas of sociology.

METHODOLOGICAL PROGRESS

Weak methods was one standard criticism of early studies in the American sociology of religion. This weakness existed because so many of the "first generation" of practitioners were not rigorously trained in social science methods. Indeed, the precursor of the Religious Research Fellowship was a group known as the Augmented Technical Staff of the Committee for Cooperative Field Research. Affiliated during the 1940s with the Home Missions Council and the Federal Council of Churches, only two of the seven original members had primary research duties and skills in their respective denominations (Hadden, 1974).

By the end of the 1960s this stereotype of methodological naïveté was no longer true. In 1970 Hadden and Heenan could write in assessing sociology of religion research from the previous decade:

> Sociology of religion has not been the birth place of innovative methodologies in social sciences. At the same time, the level of methodological sophistication is now sufficiently strong to escape the label of a weak step-sister in the social scientific enterprise [p. 161].

The case is even more so today. As a generalization, research methodologies in the sociology of religion have reached a par with those of most other specialties.[3] It is true that the subdiscipline still sees a larger percentage of studies involving qualitative methods as well as samples of convenience and modest size, but certainly no more than deviance, social psychology, or ethnomethodology.

Since the descriptive surveys of the 1960s, a great deal of progress has been accomplished. Charles Glock's pioneering efforts in conceptualizing the different ways, or dimensions, by which religiosity could manifest itself (he found five: experience, ritual, ideology, knowledge, and consequence), for example, began a tradition of factor analytic efforts to identify and measure religion in all its complexity (Glock and Stark, 1965; King, 1967; Faulkner and DeJong, 1966; Weigert and Thomas, 1969).

Scaling of such concepts as religious commitment and civil religion has undergone much development, replication, and refinement (e.g., Wuthnow, 1979; Wimberley, 1979; Wimberley et al., 1976), and multivariate analyses in sociology of religion books and journal articles are commonplace. For secondary analysis, sociologists of religion have relied heavily on survey data gathered by the General Social Survey of the National Opinion Research Center in Michigan to test a wide variety of hypotheses on social issues as well as using data from the Roper Corporation and George Gallup's Princeton Religious Research Center. Creative work in coding and statistically analyzing others' qualitative work, as Stark and Bainbridge did in analyzing cult and sect information from Melton's (1978) *Encyclopedia of American Religion* is another prime example.

Likewise, sociological researchers engaged in qualitative fieldwork have become more sensitive to linguistic, phenomenological, and sociology of knowledge issues affecting the research process and their interpretation of actors' experiences in religiously intimate and natural settings (e.g., Damrell, 1977; Rochford, 1985).

In sum, methodological progress in the sociology of religion has advanced considerably since the subdiscipline's North American origins. It is in large measure responsible for the more middle range (as opposed to "grand" or macro) bent of many sociologists of religion discussed in the previous section.

CRITICISMS OF THE SUBDISCIPLINE

American sociology of religion currently suffers from internal and external shortcomings as well as serious omissions in its research agenda. Several of these problems have dogged it since its earliest days.

Internally, many sociologists of religion came to the field by happenstance. Often they stumbled across a topic with an intriguing religious angle and found that the field's professional meetings and journals provided a ready outlet for presentations and publication of findings. A relatively small number have ever trained explicitly to become sociologists of religion. As a result, their training has often poorly prepared them for such research. Specifically, many sociologists (as well as most citizens) have been, and are generally ignorant of:

(1) the extent of religious diversity (and conflict) in the United States and elsewhere;
(2) the history of religion in America and Europe;
(3) the history and theologies of specific religious groups;
(4) the actual parameters of religious life in American (or any other) society.

Probably in no other sociological subspeciality is so much remedial self-education required!

In addition, within the sociology of religion there still lingers some tension between committed religionists and less applied, more academic scholars that Hadden (1974) identified over a decade ago. This tension is not distributed equally across the main professional societies, however. For example, the Association for the Sociology of Religion still possesses remnants of its Roman Catholic heritage, but it has been so "Protestantized" by non-Catholic academic researchers in recent years that its sectarian flavor has been all but erased.

Externally, many of the problems about which Hadden and Heenan (1970) complained earlier still exist. Because of First Amendment fears about violating the separation of church and state, government agencies continue to be poor sources of research funding. The private (e.g., denominational) sector is probably still the largest reservoir of research monies, but it is far from adequate. Through prudent management of its fiscal reserves, the Society for the Scientific Study of Religion has provided limited support for members' research, but this is woefully insufficient to support larger sociological inquiry into religion.

In this light it is interesting to witness the recent debate over the ethics of sociologists accepting financial support for research from controversial religious movements and groups that may, it has been suggested, have something to gain in return from such support (Horowitz, 1978; also see the special Fall 1983 issue of *Sociological Analysis*). The sociology of religion's past dependency on denominational funds makes the current issue of some scholars accepting "new religion" monies a curious one, indeed (see O'Toole, 1983).

The vast amount of research in the sociology of religion is conducted either as a spin-off of projects funded for some other purpose or is done simply without adequate funding. Considering such undersupport, it may be considered remarkable that research on the sociology of religion has attained the quality that it now possesses.

Moreover, prejudice is still extant among colleagues in other specialties to the effect that sociologists interested in studying religion are suspected of being personally devout religionists or having "gone native." The implicit bias of the secularization model has become so thoroughly ingrained in modern social science that a sociologist of religion often has to assume the defensive in explaining his or her substantive interests. (A similar problem has sometimes plagued sociologists studying deviant behavior such as homosexuality or prostitution.)

One consequence of this image problem has been that the employment market for sociologists of religion is weak. Many sociologists of religion, "hedge their bets" by maintaining professional activity in some additional or secondary substantive area of research, such as social movements, complex organizations, family, deviance, or social psychology. Their professional identities may at times even be closer to their secondary specialties, whether in their own minds or of necessity on their curriculum vitae when they apply for jobs.

THE FUTURE OF THE SOCIOLOGY OF RELIGION

Methodologically, the sociology of religion has "arrived." Nevertheless, its future will depend less on the application of sophisticated research methods than on the willingness of scholars to pursue topics of theoretical and popular significance.

We conclude by considering five "megatrends" in American religion that will likely occupy much of the attention of researchers for the balance of this century. Each calls for sociologists to reassess concepts and paradigms they may have taken for granted during the past 50 years.

(1) The challenge to secularization theory. In 1985 Phillip Hammond edited a volume of essays titled *The Sacred in a Secular Age* (Hammond, 1985). Each of the 22 chapters focused on some discrete aspect of the relationship between the sacred and the secular. The essays documented well the degree to which the study of religion has been, and continues to be, influenced by secularization theory. The volume did not add up to a systematic critique of secularization theory, yet in chapter after chapter one could find many of the most productive scholars in the modern scientific study of religion raising doubts about the utility of secularization theory.

Perhaps the most significant aspect of the volume is the fact that this sweeping assessment and critique carries the imprimatur of the Society for the Scientific Study of Religion. It represents, in effect, an "official" beginning of the process of challenging the assumptions of the secularization paradigm that has reigned supreme since the mid-nineteenth century. If it is premature to announce the passing of this long tradition, then at least the essays in *The Sacred in a Secular Age* bear testimony that the search for alternative models has begun.

Four important challenges confront secularization theory (Hadden, 1987). First, a critique of secularization theory itself uncovers a hodgepodge of loosely employed ideas rather than any systematic theory. Second, existing data simply do not support the theory—the new religious and conservative movements in recent years are evidence of that. Third, the effervescence of new religious movements *in the very locations where secularization appears to cut deeply into established institutional religion* suggests that religion may really be ubiquitous in human cultures. Fourth, the number of countries in which religion is significantly entangled in reform, rebellion, and revolution is ever-expanding. This reality challenges the assumptions of secularization theory that would relegate religion to the private realm.

(2) The acceleration of religious conflict in America. These sorts of struggles show no signs of abating. Church/state issues, involving such passionate symbols as aid to parochial schools, the purportedly "secular humanistic" content of public schools texts, and school prayer are not fringe issues. They will increasingly be the subject of political races and referendums. Over such issues as these and others, liberals versus conservatives, and religious versus the irreligious, can be expected to do battle. Polarization seems virtually assured, if the number of recent publicized lawsuits before state supreme courts and the U.S. Supreme Court is any indication.

Meanwhile, conflict over new expressions of religion (e.g., the anti-cultism of the 1970s, now dressed in behavioral science rhetoric) should continue with gusto. Since the arrival in the late 1960s and early 1970s of Oriental and other "cults," such "anticult" groups, both secular and religious, have widened their definitions of possibly harmful groups to include conservative Christians (e.g., witness the emergence of Funda-mentalists Anonymous) and even televangelists.

(3) The entrenchment of privatized religion. The popularization of the "electronic church" and televangelism has given rise to oligarchic fiefdoms, or *parachurches*, which are not under the control of any denomination; rather, they answer only to their creators.

At present such "media" religion is privatized and enjoyed (to judge by the enormous sums of money sent to televangelists by individual viewers) by a considerable audience. Such parachurches compete with more established "nonelectronic" denominations, if only indirectly. There is good reason to think that in organization and size some of the larger parachurches may approximate denominations, centered (at least in the first generation) around the personality cults of their founders.

Such parachurches are not new additions to the American religious scene. They have existed since the nineteenth century and the rise of great evangelists like Charles Finney, Dwight Moody, and Billy Sunday. But the advent of electronic communications, and the capacity of the mass media to present images and coalesce identities and allegiances has never before been used so much by independent evangelistic associations. The dawning of a new generation of nondenominational religious groups, rich and influential, portends to reshape America's religious scene.

(4) The retrenchment of many mainline denominations. By the late 1980s the steady decline of the so-called mainline Protestant denominations has leveled off, but they will not likely recover their former hegemony on the American religious scene anytime soon. Their members are, on the

average, older (if higher socioeconomic class) and less fertile. Moreover, such groups are the least likely to proselytize and seek members from the existing religious marketplace of consumers. And these denominations are the ones least likely to retain their children when they reach adulthood.

The sociology of religion during the past decade or so has made great inroads into the birth and creation of new religious traditions. The mainline Protestant denominations may present it with the further opportunity to record what happens when such traditions reach their zenith and then decline into senility.

(5) New emerging forms of piety. Liberals and conservatives in this generation are reversing their standard roles in terms of social activism. Liberals have discovered the charismatic joys of conservative Christianity and are engaging in glossolalia, spiritual healing, and renewed biblical faith. Some have also turned their spirituality outward in the political sphere, creating "liberation theologies" and sacralized movements to address social ills.

Likewise, some conservatives are rediscovering their activist heritage of the nineteenth century, from abolition and women's suffrage to labor reform and conservation, antipornography and antiabortion efforts, the Christian school movement, Christian advocacy groups such as the Moral Majority and Christian Voice, and even the possibility of a televangelist-turned-presidential candidate in the form of Marion G. "Pat" Robertson. All are part of the religious developments transpiring and emerging in the final years of the twentieth century.

CONCLUSION

The subdiscipline of the sociology of religion has been a part of discipline from its inception, though its decline after World War I might not lead contemporary students to think so. After a struggling renewal period that culminated in professional organizations being founded around mid-century, the sociology of religion has now moved into the mainstream of social science.

Willingness to tackle controversial issues, is a strength of the sociology of religion and ensures its high profile for the rest of this century. For religion and politics, religion and media, religion and science, religion and justice—at every juncture, with every major institution, the interface of society with religion is increasingly becoming manifest. Religion is, after all, the pursuit of ultimate truths and values. And in a shrinking world, with increasingly scarce resources and decisions of allocation to be made, these truths and values may be expected to play a major role.

NOTES

1. One of us did, in fact, express doubts about the future prospects of the subdiscipline from the vantage point of 1970. In words of grim foreboding we said: "We see some compelling reasons to question whether the developments of the 70s will match the progress of the decade we have just concluded. In our pessimistic moments, we see the possibility of all forward movement grinding to a silent halt" (Hadden and Heenan, 1970: 161).

2. There is an interesting parallel between the secondary status of religious studies in sociology and in its sibling discipline, psychology. Spilka, Hood, and Gorsuch (1985: xi) describe how the psychology of religion at the beginning of this century was "a highly respected area of study, dignified by such notables as William James, G. Stanley Hall, and Carl Jung." However, a combination of psychoanalytic bias that regarded religion as childish and neurotic and the crass materialism of behaviorism had turned religion into a taboo field of inquiry by the 1960s.

3. Mills (1983) has found that in terms of being associated with other interests of American Sociological Association members, the sociology of religion is weakly associated with research methods (more weakly than in the case of social theory). However, these data say nothing about the methodological expertise of sociologists of religion, only about the frequency with which sociologists in the ASA put these specialties down on forms about primary teaching and research areas.

REFERENCES

Bainbridge, William Sims and Laurie Russell Hatch (1982) "Women's access to elite careers: in search of a religion effect." Journal for the Scientific Study of Religion 21: 242-55.
Bromley, David G. and Anson Shupe [eds.] (1980) "Financing the new religions: a resource mobilization approach." Journal for the Scientific Study of Religion 19: 227-39.
Bromley, David G. and Anson Shupe [eds.] (1984) New Christian Politics. Macon, GA: Mercer University Press.
Campbell, Ernest Q. and Thomas F. Pettigrew (1959) Christians in Racial Crisis. Washington, DC: Public Affairs Press.
Cox, Harvey (1965) The Secular City. New York: Macmillan.
Daly, Mary (1975) The Church and the Second Sex. New York: Harper & Row.
Damrell, Joseph (1977) Seeking Spiritual Meaning: The World of Vedanta. Beverly Hills, CA: Sage.
Ebaugh, Helen Rose and C. Allen Haney (1978) "Church attendance and attitudes toward abortion: differentials in liberal and conservative churches." Journal for the Scientific Study of Religion 12: 407-13.

Faulkner, Joseph E. and Gordon F. Dejong (1966) "Religiosity in 5-D: an empirical analysis." Social Forces 47: 80-3.

Glock, Charles Y. [ed.] (1973) Religion in Sociological Perspective. Belmont, CA: Wadsworth.

Glock, Charles Y. and Rodney Stark (1965) Religion and Society in Tension. Chicago: Rand McNally.

Glock, Charles Y. and Rodney Stark (1966) Religious Belief and Anti-Semitism. New York: Harper & Row.

Glock, Charles Y., Rodney Stark, and Phillip E. Hammond [eds.] (1973) Beyond the Classics: Essays in the Scientific Study of Religion. San Francisco: Harper & Row.

Greeley, Andrew M. (1975) The Sociology of the Paranormal: A Reconnaissance. Beverly Hills, CA: Sage.

Greeley, Andrew M. (1982) Religion: A Secular Theory. New York: Free Press.

Hadden, Jeffrey K. (1969) The Gathering Storm in the Churches. Garden City, NY: Doubleday.

Hadden, Jeffrey K. (1974) "A brief social history of the Religious Research Association." Review of Religious Research: 128-36.

Hadden, Jeffrey K. (1987) "Toward desacralizing secularization theory." Social Forces 65: 587-611.

Hadden, Jeffrey K. and Edward F. Heenan (1970) "Empirical studies in the sociology of religion: an assessment of the past ten years." Sociological Analysis 30: 153-71.

Hadden, Jeffrey K. and Anson Shupe [eds.] (1986) Prophetic Religions and Politics. New York: Paragon.

Hadden, Jeffrey K. and Charles E. Swann (1981) Prime Time Preachers: The Rising Power of Televangelism. Reading, MA: Addison-Wesley.

Hammond, Phillip E. (1982) "From the editor." Journal for the Scientific Study of Religion 21: ii.

Hammond, Phillip E. [ed.] (1985) The Sacred in a Secular Age. Berkeley, CA: University of California Press.

Harris, Richard J. and Edgar W. Mills (1985) "Religion, values, and attitudes toward abortion." Journal for the Scientific Study of Religion 24: 137-54.

Hay, David and Ann Morisy (1978) "Reports of ecstatic, paranormal, or religious experience in Great Britain and the United States: a comparison of trends." Journal for the Scientific Study of Religion 17: 255-68.

Higgins, Paul C. and G. C. Albracht (1977) "Hellfire and delinquency revisited." Social Forces 55: 952-8.

Holm, Nils G. (1982) "Mysticism and intense experiences." Journal for the Scientific Study of Religion 21: 268-76.

Horowitz, Irving Louis (1978) "Sun Myung Moon: missionary to Western civilization, and science, sin, and sponsorship," in I.L. Horowitz (ed.), Science, Sin, and Scholarship: The Politics of Reverend Moon and the Unification Church. Cambridge, MA: MIT Press.

Hunter, James Davison (1983) American Evangelicalism. New Brunswick, NJ: Rutgers University Press.

Ingram, Larry (1981) "Leadership, democracy, and religion: role ambiguity among pastors in Southern Baptist churches." Journal for the Scientific Study of Religion 20: 119-29.

King, Morton (1967) "Measuring the religious variable: nine proposed dimensions." Journal for the Scientific Study of Religion 6 (Fall): 173-85.

Knudten, Richard and Mary S. Knudten (1971) "Juvenile delinquency, crime, and religion." Review of Religious Research 12: 130-52.

Lenski, Gerhard (1961) The Religious Factor. Garden City, NY: Doubleday.

Leuba, James H. (1916) The Belief in God and Immortality. Boston: Sherman, French.

Leuba, James H. (1934) "Religious beliefs of American scientists." Harper's Magazine (Vol. 169, August): 291-300.

Liebman, Robert C. and Robert Wuthnow [eds.] (1983) The New Christian Right. New York: Aldine.

Lincoln, Bruce (1985) Religion, Rebellion, Revolution. New York: St. Martin's Press.

Long, Theodore E. and Jeffrey K. Hadden (1983) "Religious conversion and the concept of socialization: integrating the brainwashing and drift models." Journal for the Scientific Study of Religion 22 (March): 1-14.

Lovekin, Adams and H. Newton Malony (1977) "Religious glossolalia." Journal for the Scientific Study of Religion 16 (December): 383-93.

Lyon, David (1983) "The idea of a Christian sociology: some historical precedents and current concerns." Sociological Analysis 44 (Fall): 227-42.

Marx, Gary (1967) "Religion: opiate or inspiration of civil rights militancy among Negroes?" American Sociological Review 32 (February): 64-72.

McGuire, Meredith B. (1982) Pentecostal Catholics. Philadelphia, PA: Temple University Press.

McGuire, Meredith B. (1983) "Words of power: personal empowerment and healing." Culture, Medicine, and Psychiatry 7: 221-40.

Melton, J. Gordon (1978) Encyclopedia of American Religions (2 vols., A Consortium Book). Wilmington, NC: McGrath.

Merkl, Peter H. and Ninian Smart [eds.] (1983) Religion and Politics in the Modern World. New York: New York University Press.

Mills, Edgar W. (1983) "The sociology of religion as an ASA sub-discipline." Sociological Analysis 44 (Winter): 339-53.

Newman, William M. (1974) "The Society for the Scientific Study of Religion: the development of an academic society." Review of Religious Research 15 (Spring): 137-51.

Nisbet, Robert (1969) Social Change and History. New York: Oxford University Press.

O'Toole, Roger [ed.] (1983) "Symposium on scholarship and sponsorship." Sociological Analysis 44: 177-225.

Peek, Charles W., H. Paul Chalfant, and Edward B. Milton (1979) "Sinners in the hands of an angry God . . ." Journal for the Scientific Study of Religion 18 (March): 29-39.

Quinley, Harold E. (1974) The Prophetic Clergy. New York: John Wiley.

Reed, Myer S. Jr. (1974) "The sociology of the sociology of religion: a report on research in progress." Review of Religious Research 15 (Spring): 157-65.

Reed, Myer S. Jr. (1975) "Differentiation and development in a scientific specialty: the sociology of religion in the United States from 1895 to 1970" (unpublished dissertation, Tulane University, New Orleans, LA).

Reed, Myer S. Jr. (1981) "An alliance for progress: the early years of the sociology of religion in the United States." Sociological Analysis 42 (Spring): 27-46.

Reed, Myer S. Jr. (1982) "After the alliance: the sociology of religion in the United States from 1925 to 1949." Sociological Analysis 43 (Fall): 189-204.

Reiss, Paul J. (1970) "Science and religion in the evolution of a sociological association." Sociological Analysis 31 (Fall): 119-30.

Richardson, James T., Mary White Stewart, and Robert B. Simmonds (1979) Organized Miracles: A Study of a Contemporary Youth, Communal, Fundamentalist Organization. New Brunswick, NJ: Rutgers University Press.

Robbins, Thomas and Dick Anthony [eds.] (1981) In Gods We Trust: New Patterns of Religious Pluralism in America. New Brunswick, NJ: Transaction Books.

Rochford, E. Burke Jr. (1985) Hare Krishna in America. New Brunswick, NJ: Rutgers University Press.

Shupe, Anson D. Jr. and David G. Bromley (1980) The New Vigilantes: Deprogrammers, Anti-Cultists, and the New Religions. Beverly Hills, CA: Sage.

Shupe, Anson D. Jr., David G. Bromley, and Donna L. Oliver (1984) The Anti-Cult Movement in America: A Bibliography and Historical Survey. New York: Garland.

Shupe, Anson, William A. Stacey, and Lonnie R. Hazlewood (1986) Violent Men, Violent Families. Lexington, MA: D. C. Heath-Lexington.

Smith, Bardwell L. [ed.] (1976) Religion and Social Conflict in South Asia. Leiden, The Netherlands: E. J. Brill.

Smith, Donald E. (1970) Religion and Political Development. Boston: Little, Brown.

Snow, David A. and Richard Machalek (1984) "The sociology of conversion." Annual Review of Sociology 10: 167-90.

Spilka, Bernard, Ralph W. Hood, Jr., and Richard L. Gorsuch (1985) The Psychology of Religion. Englewood Cliffs, NJ: Prentice-Hall.

Stark, Rodney and William Sims Bainbridge (1985) The Future of Religion. Berkeley: University of California Press.

Straus, Roger A. (1979) "Religious conversion as a personal and collective accomplishment." Sociological Analysis 41 (Summer): 158-65.

Swatos, William H. Jr. (1976) "Church-sect typology: Weber or Troeltsdch?" Journal for the Scientific Study of Religion 15 (June): 129-44.

Sweigert, Andrew and Darwin I. Thomas (1969) "Religiosity in 5-D: a critical note." Social Forces 48 (December): 260-3.

Wallis, Roy and Steve Bruce (1984) "The Stark-Bainbridge theory of religion: a critical analysis and counter proposals." Sociological Analysis 45: 11-28.

Wimberley, Ronald C. (1979) "Continuity in the measurement of civil religion." Sociological Analysis 40 (Spring): 59-62.

Wimberley, Ronald C., Donald Clelland, Thomas Hood, and C. M. Lipsey (1976) "The civil religious dimension: is it there?" Social Forces 54: 890-900.

Wuthnow, Robert (1979) The Religious Dimension: New Dimensions in Quantitative Research. New York: Academic Press.

9

ORGANIZATIONAL SOCIOLOGY

Lee Clarke

Rutgers University

Review articles on subfields imply a measure of intellectual consensus within that subfield. Although such an implication regarding organizations is misleading, it is likely that three schools of thought will structure scholarly debate in the foreseeable future. Loose coupling theories of decision making, institutional theories of organizational structure, and population ecology models of organizational change are currently the most exciting sets of ideas about organizations in sociology.[1] Each offers useful ways of thinking about important questions, and sizable claims are being made for their capacities to transform organization theory. Here I review the central ideas of each of these schools, identify their major contributions, and provide a friendly critique.

I warn the reader that the field of organizations is imbued with jargon. To an extent, specialized languages are unavoidable, even desirable, because if organizations have supraindividual qualities, then it is necessary to have concepts that are more or less unique to organizations as a class of social actors. The disadvantages of vernacular are that it insulates researchers from outside criticism and permits the construction of vocabularies whose theoretical utility is suspect. In any case, organizational sociology will probably never be marked by lucidity, and in a short chapter intended to review major perspectives, I must perpetuate our too often esoteric terminology.

Author's Note: My special thanks to Oscar Grusky for comments and support. Others who generously provided critiques were Howard Aldrich, Paul DiMaggio, Marshall W. Meyer, Charles Perrow, Walter W. Powell, Patricia A. Roos, Edward Royce, Pamela S. Tolbert, and Lynne G. Zucker. Work on this chapter was undertaken with support from the National Institute of Mental Health (MH 14583 "Services Research Training Program"). The NIMH is not responsible for the chapter's content.

DECISION MAKING

Classical management theory, human relations, and Weberian analysis assume that organizational leaders set goals and policies, and that organizations respond to such directives. If so, leaders should be found to have a fairly thorough understanding of what goes on within and without their organizations, and be able to implement their directives. These predictions follow from the assumptions of the rational model of decision making, in which individual perception, the formation of alternatives, policy implementation, organizational behavior, and feedback from the environment are stable and predictable. Decision makers collect information that they process in terms of organizational goals, make a decision, and commit the organization to action, which then elicits an environmental response. For rational choice, selection of alternatives is governed by demands of efficiency and criteria of effectiveness. The relevance of rational theory declines proportionately as these demands and criteria (and decision makers' preferences) become less clearly defined (March, 1978).

Garbage Can theory rejects the idea that power and rationality drive decision making (March and Olsen, 1979; Lutz, 1982; Tasca, 1983), arguing instead that decisions result from the fortuitous coincidence of people, problems, solutions, and choices (March and Olsen, 1979; March and Weissinger-Baylon, 1986). Preferences, in this view, are rarely stable and ordered, and criteria for judging the relevance of information are vague (Simon, 1957; March and Simon, 1958). Moreover, since ends and means are not necessarily correlated, individual intention and organizational action are often disjointed. Thus the idea that organizations work toward goals, so important for most models, is a minor part of Garbage Can theory. Instead, organizations act and produce goals only when challenged to render sensible accounts of their actions (March and Olsen, 1979: 71-75; Fine, 1984). By highlighting loose coupling among decision components, Garbage Can models make ambiguity a mainstay of analysis (Weick, 1976; Hickson, 1987). Chance, symbolism, and equivocal meaning shape decision making more than the rational model allows (Long, 1958; Lindblom, 1959, 1979; Edelman, 1964; Feldman and March, 1982; Weick, 1979). Indeed, from a Garbage Can perspective, the rational model is itself a symbol produced by organizations to make sense of their own behavior (Starbuck, 1983).

Where other theories might stress how hierarchy determines who will make decisions, Garbage Can theorists hold that individuals and groups have neither the power, inclination, nor time to choose. Rather, participation in decision making is determined by factors most theories relegate to secondary status: opportunity costs, social obligations outside the organization, and prestige (March and Olsen, 1979: 27). Thus loose coupling arguments provide a way of accounting for organizational outcomes that reflect no one's intentions or preferences.

Contributions

Loose coupling theories make several important contributions to our understanding of decision making in organizations.[2] First, these models are a fundamental challenge to the rational model. Although few would describe themselves as adherents to the theory of rational choice, most organization theory incorporates some of its assumptions. For example, power models, management theory, and human relations models assume a fairly close correspondence between elite decisions and organizational action. By focusing on organizational behavior under ambiguous conditions—situations in which goals are unclear, technologies are ill-defined, and rights to participate in key decisions are in flux—Garbage Can theories sensitize researchers to situations unaccounted for by the rational model.

Second, this school's epistemological skepticism about where organizational structures originate and how those structures operate focuses attention on the *processes* through which information and people are organized. Any theory, regardless of what it is designed to explain, must be able to account for such processes (Mohr, 1982). Moreover, to detect and analyze these processes, researchers have relied on intensive case studies (e.g., the studies in March and Olsen, 1979; Sproull et al., 1978), thus putting to fruitful use ethnographic, field, and observational methods.

Third, the focus on nonrational aspects of organizations adds substance to the stark structuralism of much organization theory. By drawing attention to the mix of nonrational and rational, loose coupling theories provide a useful way of approaching the issue of the tension between individual values and organizational needs. At one time, this issue was framed in terms of formal versus informal structures in organizations (Perrow, 1977). That perspective, however, was not one that questioned the validity of usual bureaucratic theory that understands organizations as coherent systems. Rather, the study of informal structures simply further specified the ways in which behavior was patterned in organizations. Loose coupling models invert these arguments by focusing on how decisions emerge from the interests and values of actors, rather than being dictated by the constraints of organizational structure.

Critique

There are several problems with loose coupling theory.[3] First, the model is probably not applicable to a wide variety of organizations. Most of the studies have been of schools and universities, and thus we lack systematic comparative research to evaluate the power of the theory. One consequence of the lack of rigorous testing is that it is difficult to know if the theory explains particular types of *situations* or if it characterizes types of *organizations*. Are there really organizations whose structures of authority constantly shift and change with particular issues, or are some types of situations more amenable than others to organized anarchy? Do educational organizations have no conception of their goals and how to achieve them, or does the relative openness of such organizations allow groups to infuse them with multiple and sometimes conflicting purposes? One way Garbage Can theory can be made more useful is by according more attention to the question of the *conditions under which* it can and cannot explain organizational behavior.

Second, although loose coupling arguments are appreciatively and frequently cited, its central concept has not been adequately measured. The original article on Garbage Can theory was published in 1972 (Cohen et al., 1972) and Weick's piece on loose coupling was published in 1976. Although a decade has passed since the publication of Weick's classic paper, I know of no reliable instruments designed to measure loose coupling. If the concept is going to be more than a sensitizing device, we need valid and reliable measures of loose-tight coupling.

Third, the focus on symbols and myths and their role in decision making is extremely important, but more study should be given to the purposes symbols serve for groups and organizations. As loose coupling arguments point out, there often is no obvious connection between decision event and organizational response. It is undeniable that organizational members construct and trade in symbols, but it is also true that symbols constrain thought and behavior. Thus it is necessary to establish if there is systematic variation in the likelihood of certain types of problems being matched with certain organizational positions. The studies in March and Olsen (1979) convincingly illustrate that decisions can be opportunities for several agendas to emerge. Thus the ways symbols are used—to set agendas so that some issues rather than others are defined as legitimate, to maintain distributions of authority, to legitimate decisions in technical, bureaucratic terms when decisions are made with other (e.g., political) considerations in mind, or to obscure the source of an organization's goals—is an important, but neglected, issue. Garbage Can theory has lost sight of the fact that *ambiguity itself* is socially constructed. This implies the possibility that pervasive ambiguity may suit the interests of groups inside and outside organizations.

Fourth, the importance of chance, the influence granted opportunity costs of time, and the assertion that decision makers are allocated to decision situations on the basis of "symbolic" and "educational" concerns, rather than because of genuine concern with decision outcomes (March and Olsen, 1979: 47-48), are probably exaggerations. Most organizations are not as 'randomly organized' as Garbage Can theory maintains (see also Aldrich, 1979: 92). For example, in universities (supposedly the ideal-typical organized anarchies), power is certainly more widely dispersed than in a bank, and academic departments are less tightly coupled than companies in an army, but it is rare that lower participants enjoy the same probabilities to affect important decisions as those at the top of the hierarchy. Although an oversimplification, most organizations are more accurately captured by an image of a division of labor, based on legitimated authority, the subunits designed to transform some raw material (including symbols), than an image of disjointed elements, randomly colliding in a system of equivocal meanings.

My final comment is more a suggestion for refinement than a criticism. Garbage Can models are most useful at the level of interorganizational analysis (Clarke, forthcoming). Groups of organizations, under ambiguous conditions, are more like the garbage cans described by loose coupling models than are single organizations. They often lack a stable structure that coordinates members, their members are less likely to share expectations about what constitutes appropriate behavior, and there is less likely to be a centralized office that coordinates people and activities. In *inter*organizational garbage cans, entry and exit into decision opportunities can be much more fluid than in bureaucracies, and there is no well-defined hierarchy that clearly delimits authority and responsibility among organizations. For example, Clarke (forthcoming) modified and extended Garbage Can theory to study how a set of organizations defined and tried to mitigate the effects of a toxic chemical accident, and Laumann et al. (1985) found complementary evidence in their study of national health and energy policies.

INSTITUTIONALIZATION

The second school of thought certain to be part of the future of organizational sociology is composed of institutional theories of organizational structure. These theories are important challenges to usual ways of thinking about how and why organizations change and fail to change. The broad claims for the power of institutional theory to supplant and augment received theory warrant close attention. With tempering and development, the perspective promises valuable contributions not only to organizational sociology but to social theory more generally.[4]

Institutional theories begin with the frequent discrepancies between what organizations say they do and what they actually do. Public schools, for example, proclaim their dedication to instruction and struggle to expand their domains, using the rationale of furthering educational objectives. When examined closely, however, schools do not evaluate their success in achieving these laudable goals and do not fail when these goals are not achieved (Rowan, 1982; Meyer and Scott, 1983). Institutional theory argues that structures, programs, and policies are adopted by organizations not because they contribute to efficiency or because they further official goals. Rather, the major determinants of structural change are found in organizations' cultural or normative environments. Organizations do not innovate as much as they conform; they do not become bureaucratically rational as much they *appear* to do so. By manipulating outside appearances organizations gain legitimacy from their environments, thus allowing them to survive and prosper.

To make the argument clear it helps to contrast it with a more familiar set of ideas. The Weberian organization tries to coordinate its members and raw materials so that goals can be reached efficiently and effectively. Power, authority, and domination are central concepts in this view, partly because those at the top of the hierarchy determine the organization's purposes and partly because conflict, if unchecked, can undermine organizational effectiveness. Thus there is a constant need to monitor and control members' behavior to prevent deviation from organizational goals. To the extent that organizations behave consistently with this portrait, they are bureaucratically rational.

Institutional theory questions each of these tenets of Weberian analysis, representing an important departure from usual views of organizations. Previous research attached causal primacy to technical constraints imposed by environments (e.g., Woodward, 1965; Lawrence and Lorsch, 1967; Thompson, 1967; Pugh et al., 1968), organizational power (e.g., Child, 1972; Perrow, 1986), or functional adaptation (e.g., Aldrich and Pfeffer, 1976; Hannan and Freeman, 1977; Aldrich, 1979). Institutional models argue that exchange dependencies, technical characteristics, demands for efficiency, class analysis, and natural selection ignore ideological and cultural environments.

Some early institutional studies were concerned with how social actors acquire language categories and the uses those categories serve in making sense of organizational life. Zucker (1977) examined how people create social structure in ambiguous situations, focusing specifically on the social construction of myth building. The major organizational studies are more concerned with the connection between organizational structure and environmental pressures. It is not demands for efficiency and control that determine organizational structure. Rather, institutionalized organizations integrate themselves with the larger environment, thus buffering their "technical cores" from outside scrutiny (Meyer et al., 1983: 46-47).

The categories of thought and language that organizational participants acquire are central for explaining the extent to which organizations become isomorphic with their environments. If those cultural categories conform to environmental demands, the organization secures legitimacy (Meyer et al., 1983: 52, 56). By incorporating legitimated symbols, organizations signal technical core from the symbolic front presented to the environment, organizations hide the fact that they are not working as they should (Meyer and Rowan, 1977).

Contributions

Institutional theory is a valuable alternative to conventional theories of organizational behavior, structure, and environments, and there are several important contributions from this school. First, institutional theory augments the critique of the historical necessity of bureaucratic organization and thus moderates blanket assertions for the explanatory power of efficiency (e.g., Williamson, 1975; Chandler, 1977; Chandler and Daems, 1980). The phenomenological underpinnings of institutional models suggest the meaning of the term *efficiency* varies depending on the level of analysis used to address a research topic. Exploring the implications of this observation will add much needed subtlety to unrealistic contrasts of markets versus hierarchies, centralized versus decentralized organizations, and even institutionalized versus rational bureaucracies.

Second, institutional theory complements March and Simon's (1958) and Perrow's (1986) insights concerning premise setting and unobtrusive controls in organizations. Zucker's (1977) experimental evidence shows how perceptions of authority can be shaped so that some alternatives are considered more legitimate than others. A more recent article explores how values and nonrational forces (from an organizational view) facilitate unobtrusive control (Zucker, 1983). By studying processes through which structures and practices come to be accepted as objective and inert, the theory provides a valuable explanation of how alternative social structures become "literally unthinkable" (Zucker, 1983: 25), and of how what might be termed *hegemonic culture* works to maintain dominant modes of control.

Finally, institutional theory's focus on exposé and debunking, as with earlier institutional research (Gusfield, 1955; Messinger, 1955; Clark, 1960; Zald and Denton, 1963; Selznick, 1965), creates new opportunities for making organizational research more useful for explaining important social problems. Much of organizational sociology adopts metaphors devoid of human agency and social problems. There are multilevel systems, niches, biological analogies, dry taxonomies, types of technology, feedback mechanisms, and nebulous environments. While such concepts are certainly valuable, institutional perspectives are better able to explain concrete social problems because they are conceptually better equipped to delineate the multiple purposes served by organizations. For example, by calling into question the power of education to account for economic success, the work of Berg (1971), Jencks et al. (1972), and Collins (1979) raises an important paradox: If usual measures of learning are not clearly related to mobility, but education is necessary for mobility, what exactly is the connection between education and social stratification? The fascinating studies of the relationships between environments, organizational structure, and monitoring of work processes in public schools found in Rowan (1982) and Meyer and Scott (1983) provide a way of specifying how educational organizations work to credential their raw materials. Using organizational analysis to clarify social problems such as these deserves more attention from institutional theorists.

Critique

My criticisms of institutional theory are suggestions for improvement, rather than a basis for refutation. First, the meanings of the terms *institution* and *institutionalization* are too vague, although to the credit of most authors, attempts *are* made to define them. Zucker (1977: 728) argues that "institutionalization is both a process and a property variable"; institutionalized acts are perceived as "objective" and "exterior" to the actor. For Meyer and Rowan (1983: 22), institutionalization "involves the processes by which social process, obligations, or actualities come to take on a rulelike status in social thought and action." Tolbert and Zucker (1983: 25) see institutionalization as "the process through which components of formal structure become widely accepted." Tolbert (1985: 2) argues that institutionalized practices are "fact-like." Obviously the term *institution-*

alization signifies the process through which learning and retention occur. The problem is that there seems to be no clear way to differentiate between structures that are legitimate and institutionalized and structures that are illegitimate and noninstitutionalized. It is easy enough to discover social structures that are not institutionalized by calling attention to what does not exist. But it seems as though any aspects of organizational structure, by virtue of the fact that they are indeed part of an organization, must by definition be socially legitimate. If institutionalized organizations are to be differentiated from, say technical organizations, there must be some indicator of legitimacy that is *independent of factlike and objective structure.*

Second, institutional theories have not satisfactorily answered the question: "Whence legitimacy?" Institutionalists frequently write of structures that are "widely accepted" (Tolbert and Zucker, 1983: 26), "widespread understandings of social reality" (Meyer and Rowan, 1983: 24), and normative understandings "shared by members of society" (Tolbert, 1983: 1). Yet, evidence from *The Confidence Gap* (Lipset and Schneider, 1983) indicates that legitimacy is far from uniformly distributed in society. Much business and government practice is seen as *illegitimate* by sectors of the public, thus calling into question the extent to which at least parts of bureaucratic organization are normatively shared. This observation suggests that that part of institutional theory that asserts *society* bestows legitimacy is at least underspecified, and probably invalid. Society in general is not the arbiter of legitimacy, and some elements of society (such as powerful interest groups) are more capable than others of creating and sustaining cultural myths and institutionalized beliefs. Rowan (1982: 259) is more specific than most about what constitutes the institutional environment of public schools: "lobbying publics, professions, legislatures, and regulatory agencies." Similarly, DiMaggio and Powell (1983: 147) claim the state and professions "have become the great rationalizers of the second half of the twentieth century." As these remarks suggest, the most important grantors of legitimacy to organizations are other organizations, not an undifferentiated society.

Third, institutional theory must resolve the puzzle of how organizations can be so clever as to construct rational fronts to present to their environments, but so senseless as to be unable to control what goes on within them. Meyer and Rowan (1983) show how ineffective public schools are in reaching official goals, but also how remarkably resourceful they are in achieving unofficial goals. To ensure legitimacy, organizations must be vigilant enough to perceive environmental threats, effective enough to process that information, and smart enough to discern which structures will gain them the requisite legitimacy. But, if organizations are adroit enough to do those things, why not *really* become more efficient? If they did so, nonprofits would be more effective, for-profits would increase their profit margins, control would be enhanced, and output would increase, all in addition to maintaining legitimacy.

Fourth, although the institutional argument is an important alternative to functional, contingency, and structural views, the attack may be too selective. Perrow (1985) reproaches institutional theory for failing to consider power as an explanation for the discrepancies between official policy and actual behavior. The force of the critique is that institutional models detach symbols, myths, and ceremonies from their organizational bases, thus ignoring the structural and political implications of institutional analysis. The examples institutionalists use frequently involve programs designed to correct injustices to the dispossessed—affirmative action, desegregation, nursing home reforms, and so forth. Perrow argues that what institutional theory sees as conformity with the environment may actually be highly effective subversion of rules pressed upon organizations by groups trying to have their interests reflected in policy. If what is really going on in institutionalist studies is that the powerless are unable to see through to fruition programs for which they have struggled, then it is not merely myth and ceremony that accounts for the data, but very real differences between groups trying to use organizations for their own purposes.⁵ Organizations not only produce symbols, they also use them.

Finally, insofar as institutional theory tries to account for the historical development of bureaucracy in organizations other than those with unclear goals and unmeasurable outputs (e.g., Zucker, 1983, 1986), it should address the extensive literature on control and the vesting of class interests in organizational transformation (Roy, 1981). Stone's (1974) study of the origins of job structures in the steel industry, Edward's (1975) analysis of how various structural arrangements control labor, and Marglin's (1974, 1975), Braverman's (1975), and Clawson's (1980) analyses of hierarchy in capitalist organizations, provide explanations for bureaucratic change based on the movement of capital, conflicts of interests, and structural constraints of opposing social forces. While materialist arguments such as these may not be complete explanations, they do pose plausible alternative interpretations for organizational development.

POPULATION ECOLOGY

The final set of theories considered here are those from population ecology. Scholarly concern with the environment reaches its apotheosis in population ecology models of organizational change. This school is exemplary of positive science: It has a highly specialized conceptual apparatus, and its methods and formal models are among the most sophisticated in the field. There is little doubt that population ecology will be an important part of the future of organizational sociology.

Previously, environments were conceptualized in terms of organization sets, networks, fields, and sectors. Population ecology models raise the level of environmental analysis to such heights that real organizations barely seem relevant. Usual vocabularies employed in organization theory are not found here. Goals, power relationships, authority, legitimacy, and hierarchies are, for the most part, replaced with organizational forms, foundings, mortality rates, niches, populations, and selecting environments. In these theories, there are populations of organizations, just as there are populations of humans. Populations are collections of organizations that produce similar outputs, a definition similar to that of an industry (Scherer, 1980).[6] Members of a population compete for scarce resources, the amounts of which are set by environments. The mix of resources available for any given population to exploit is an environmental niche. The total amount of resources available is the carrying capacity of an environment; that is, the environment sets upper limits beyond which, if exceeded, organizations die.

The axiom of interdependence is the theoretic starting point for population ecology. Neither individual organizations nor populations of organizations can persist and flourish alone, and so extract resources from environments. Because environments are varied and complex, they resist attempts by single organizations to alter them. The fundamental dynamics that cause changes in the composition of populations are environmental perturbations. When these perturbations occur, "environmental changes affect observed distributions largely by altering birthrates and death rates of populations using different adaptive strategies" (Freeman and Hannan, 1983: 1117). It is through reproductive and mortality processes that particular organizational forms come to predominate. Although there are several possible ways of classifying organizational forms, two classes that have been studied are *generalists*, which are usually large, have a surplus of resources, and are optimal in uncertain and unstable environments, and *specialists*, which are usually small, do not have a surplus of resources, and are optimal in stable and certain environments (Hannan and Freeman, 1977: 946). It is the environment that does the optimizing of these forms (Hannan and Freeman, 1977: 939), driven by the logic of natural selection and differential reinforcement (Langton, 1984: 331). In some formulations, such as that of Hannan and Freeman (1977), organizations are unable to adapt to environmental change; other views accord some adaptive capacity to organizations (McKelvey and Aldrich, 1983).

A basic premise of the population ecology perspective is that if an organizational response to an environmental change increases the probability that an organization will survive, the response will be maintained and spread throughout the population (Hannan and Freeman, 1984: 150). Interestingly, though one would expect that organizations unable to change would be selected out by constantly changing environments, Hannan and Freeman hypothesize that organizations characterized by structural inertia are the most likely to survive (see Aldrich and Auster, 1986). Hannan and Freeman (1984), in an article that seems more akin to institutional than ecological analysis, argue this relationship holds because environments demand that organizations be accountable and reliable (Hannan and Freeman, 1984: 153; Hannan and Freeman, 1986).

Population ecology theories were initially formulated in direct response to the view that the ability of organizations to shape and control their environments is greater than the power of environments to shape and control organizations. Aldrich (1979) devoted an entire chapter to criticizing the notion that organizations enjoy strategic choice within their environments. As the popularity and sophistication of population ecology models has increased, this debate has for the most part receded to the background (see critique by Perrow, 1986: 208-218, and response by Carroll, 1984: 74-77; see also Hrebiniak and Joyce, 1985). It is nevertheless important to bear in mind that the basic assumption of population ecology is that environments determine which organizations will live and which will die. In this sense the theory shares with neoclassical economics a radical environmental determinism (Astley and Van de Ven, 1983). One should also remember that population ecology models are most applicable when a whole population of organizations is available for analysis (Aldrich, 1979; Astley and Van de Ven, 1983; Freeman and Hannan, 1983: 1129; Hannan and Freeman, 1984: 159), although Carroll (1985) shows that at least in the newspaper industry there is interdependence between populations of small and large organizations operating in the same industry.

Contributions

Population ecology enriches organizational theory in a number of ways. First, it puts forth new ways of thinking about how organizations and environments become isomorphic. "The usual argument," Freeman and Hannan point out, "is that any kind of environmental instability favors" organizational strategies designed to secure and maintain a surplus of resources (Freeman and Hannan, 1983: 1142). Their reasoning, by contrast, suggests that this strategy may be optimal only in environments that change frequently and whose populations are characterized by short tenures (Freeman and Hannan, 1983: 1119). This formulation of the connection between organizational and environmental structure thus refines contingency theories of organizational performance.

Second, population ecology's level of analysis and emphasis on interdependence between units sensitizes us to the issue of generalization in organizational sociology. This is one of the most important, though neglected, issues in the field today. In comparison with other areas of sociology, organizational research fares badly in its ability to extrapolate findings to large numbers of its basic unit of analysis. The field has relied instead on the hope that typologies would allow a more limited type of generalization to classes of organizations that share certain characteristics. As Aldrich (1985) argues, population ecology perspectives counter biases of small scale and static analysis in the sociology of organizations. By urging diachronic analysis of large samples of organizations, ecological theories force us to question the frequent assumption that firms are all (more or less) alike, and thus lead us to "search for the possible bounds on [our] generalizations" (Aldrich, 1985). Organizational sociology has a long row to hoe before real generalization is possible, chiefly because of conceptual difficulties: How should the universe be defined? How many dimensions of organizational reality, and of what quality, need to be tapped before it is possible to generalize with confidence? What are the conditions under which generalizations are valid? Theoretic questions such as these mitigate against dependence on probability theory in resolving problems of generalization in the field of organizations. To its credit, population ecology attempts to address these problems, thus challenging researchers to consider issues that have previously eluded systematic investigation.

Third, since population ecology depends on documenting regularities in population changes, the perspective requires longitudinal, rather than cross-sectional, analyses (Carroll and Huo, 1986). In this way, population ecology encourages study of historical changes in organizational forms, a topic that is gaining increasing importance in organizational analysis. More generally, as with Garbage Can and institutional theory, ecological analysis encourages investigation into processes of change, which is necessary for the development of causal theories.

Fourth, the research topics posed by population ecologists have been overlooked for too long in organizational sociology. These topics include: accounting for the rise and fall of industries, types of organizations, and technologies, and the connections between collections of organizations and their surrounding communities. Although its ultimate success in providing explanations for such changes is unclear, population ecology makes major strides toward addressing these important issues.

Finally, population ecology takes more seriously than other schools of thought the interdependencies between organizations and their environments. Although Kasarda and Bidwell's work (1984), for example, is not cast at the level of population ecology, it shows very clearly the utility of ecological analysis in developing a theory of organizational structuring that identifies mechanisms of organizational change, as well as specifies the conditions under which types of change will occur.

Critique

There are some important problems with population ecology models that need further attention. First, for all the conceptual complexities created by population ecology, there are serious ambiguities in the conceptual apparatus. Population ecology has failed to provide a workable definition of *environment,* despite the obvious importance of the concept. One might say an environment is that which is external to an organization, but since population ecology research is, by necessity, unconcerned with single organizations, that definition will not suffice. Alternatively the environment might be defined as that which affects populations of organizations. Although better than the previous definition, this conceptualization is too vague and far-reaching to be of much use. Moreover, there is reason to be skeptical of population ecology's anthropomorphism of the concept "environment." In particular, it is difficult to see how environments act, select, and retain. Most often environments are defined as collections of resources, in various configurations, but how do collections of resources act?

Second, if population ecology is to fulfill its promise of explaining changes in large classes of organizations it must research the processes through which the environment selects organizations. This is a troublesome problem as yet unaddressed by population ecology theorists. On one hand, selection and retention processes are crucial to the theory; on the other hand, it seems unlikely that detail on such processes can be provided without observational studies. Yet, given the resource constraints of researchers' environments, it is unlikely they can provide such detail on more than a small number of organizations, obviously an unacceptable constraint for theories that require whole populations for analysis. For example, the only population ecology study of which I am aware that attempts to precisely document selection and retention processes is Langton's (1984) account of the rise of Wedgwood pottery in England. Yet, although this study is couched in the vocabulary of population ecology and natural selection, it is actually inappropriate for the task since it deals with a single organization rather than a population.

Third, although there are claims that population analysis is best applied to large numbers of small organizations, there are also claims (sometimes by the same authors) that the perspective is applicable to all organizations (Freeman and Hannan, 1983: 1143). Population ecology, I believe, is not going to be successful when applied to powerful organizations in concentrated industries. As Astley (1985) argues, the fit of an organization may not always be optimal since some organizations may create their own domains.[7] This issue is addressed in Carroll's (1984) review of ecological theories. Responding to Perrow's (1986) assertion that small organizations are trivial, Carroll similarly frames the debate in terms of organizational size. But the real issue here is not whether small organizations are important, but whether power can be an important variable in population level analysis. If power *is* important in accounting for structural change in organizations, then it is difficult to see how environments naturally select some organizations over others.

This is a complicated issue. Population ecologists are not insensitive to political variables. For example, the last five chapters of Aldrich's *Organizations and Environments* (1979) are concerned, in one way or another, with organizational power, and Carroll and Delacroix (1982) use political turbulence as an independent variable in their analysis of newspapers in Argentina and Ireland (see also Carroll and Huo, 1986). Nevertheless, Aldrich does not make clear the role power is to play in ecological analysis, and political turbulence is not the same as organizational power. The crux of the problem is the role of power as an independent variable in the creation, persistence, or transformation of organizational forms and in influencing environments. If organizations, either singly or in groups, can wield power in a decisive way to affect these outcomes, then it is a mystification to attribute them to chance or environmental forces.[8] Moreover, the work of Meyer et al. (1985; Meyer, 1986) suggests that organizations are not as helpless in the face of environmental forces as population ecology maintains. Although Meyer et al. find evidence that organizations do indeed respond to environmental demands, their data on municipal finance agencies are explained better by a model of organizations creating the very environments to which they respond than a model of environmental selection (see especially ch. 6).

Fourth, if environments can indeed act, population ecology must resolve the problem of how environments develop criteria for selecting organizational forms with optimal fit. In particular, for population ecology to be an adequate explanation of organizational change, it is necessary to know (1) where these criteria come from, (2) how these criteria are applied so consistently that optima are achieved, and (3) why environments develop some criteria for fitness rather than others.

Fifth, there is an element of functionalism in population ecology theory that decreases its explanatory power. Population ecologists deny this charge, particularly that form of the charge that imputes assumptions of progress to ecological analysis. Carroll (1984: 72) argues that population ecology no longer assumes progress, as had previous formulations, because "evolution is . . . equated . . . simply with change over time." Hannan and Freeman (1984: 150) contend that structures and strategies are not necessarily produced because they are useful, "they are just produced." But this speaks to only half the issue. The other half is that structures and strategies are retained because they fulfill vital functions for organizations or populations (Freeman and Hannan, 1983: 1119; Langton, 1984: 337). In one sense this is a nonissue, as Aldrich (personal communication) points out, because to say that the purpose of some process is to help an organization obtain resources is not the same as engaging in functional analysis. But population ecology implies that organizations that die fail to incorporate strategies and structures retained by organizations left alive. This seems to assert the existence of functional prerequisites for organizational populations.[9] It is obvious that organizations must garner resources to remain viable, but what objective indicators are there that those forms left alive are optimally or even relatively better fit for their environments? The lack of such indicators introduces a dangerous possibility of circularity into population ecology arguments.

CONCLUSIONS

All three perspectives reviewed here are provocative and shape scholarship on organizations. Garbage Can theory challenges rational models of decision making. Institutional theory is an alternative to structuralist explanations of organizational change. Population ecology theory has the potential for generalizing research findings to large numbers of similar organizations. But in evaluating these theories, I noted several criticisms of each school of thought. The reader may have noted some commonalities in these critiques.

To continue to furnish the field with productive research, the key concepts of each set of theories need to be refined, clarified, and operationalized. We need valid and reliable indicators of loose coupling, participation structures, and feedback mechanisms (for Garbage Can theory), institutionalized and technical organizations, sectors, and legitimacy (for institutional theory), and organization, population, and environment (for population ecology theory). The key concepts of Garbage Can and institutional theory have not been matched rigorously enough with data that might disprove the theories; that is, the research has not followed the most conservative strategies that would allow disproof of the theories' major predictions. For population ecology, the tools of analysis have defined the most important concepts, rather than the other way around.

The range of supportive and possibly disconfirming evidence for each school of thought needs to be broadened. Garbage Can and institutional theories have been applied mostly to schools and universities (recent exceptions are, respectively, March and Weissinger-Baylon, 1986; Fligstein, 1985; Zucker, 1986). These studies provided ample material for developing new ideas about organizations, but it is essential that these ideas be applied to other types of organizational settings. Both Garbage Can theory and institutional theory should be applied to profit-making organizations. There is, of course, a broad range of types of profit-making organizations that could be used, for example, insurance companies, banks, steel plants, and high-tech firms. It is no accident that this list includes some organizations with clearly measured outputs and definite hierarchies of authority. Population ecology models, in contrast, have been applied mainly to business organizations, and they need to be tested with data on nonprofits (e.g., Meyer et al., 1985).

By broadening research agendas, scholars will more likely specify the conditions under which the theories are useful explanations. The field of organizations is not well served by overgeneralization, for our credibility is seriously diminished when we are insensitive to the limits of our theory and research. Ambiguity and loose coupling are not central tendencies of organizational life, they are present in some types of organizations (or situations) under certain conditions. Problems of legitimacy and institutional conformity are not properties of modern organizations, they are variables that are valuable in explaining situations in which boundaries between organizations and environments are indistinct and in which the ability to measure organizational outputs can be the subject of intense conflict. Natural selection and stochastic evolution are not omnipresent processes among organizations, they are concepts useful for accounting for organizational change when there are large numbers of units and no stable relationships of power between organizations.

Organizational sociology is one of the most vital and important areas of scholarship in the field. Its future, I think, is promising, given sufficient pluralism of research styles and a munificent environment.

NOTES

1. So, too, is the sociology of economics and economic history, but space limitations prevent their inclusion here. See the relevant citations in Perrow (1986: ch. 7).

2. Some fascinating work from cognitive psychology is relevant here, but because it is not cast at an organizational level of analysis, I exclude it from consideration. For a collection of some of the best work in this area, see the articles in Kahneman et al. (1982). For critiques, see Fischoff (1977), Perrow (1984), Short (1984), and Clarke (forthcoming).

3. Mohr's *Explaining Organizational Behavior* (1982) thoroughly assesses Garbage Can theory, although his view is less forgiving than that taken here (see also Hickson, 1987).

4. I do violence to institutionalist views by writing as if there were only one "institutional theory." In fact, this animal comes in many stripes, ranging from microanalysis of the structure of thought (Zucker, 1977), to culture within organizations (Tolbert, 1987), to interorganizational relations (Meyer and Rowan, 1977; DiMaggio and Powell, 1983; Tolbert, 1983; DiMaggio, 1986; Powell, 1987), to nation-states and the world system (Meyer and Hannan, 1979; Meyer, 1980; Kamens and Lunde, 1987). Nevertheless, these perspectives share basic assumptions about action and social change, and so my violence to the particulars is relatively inconsequential.

5. DiMaggio (1987) argues that the perspective is limited to situations in which actors are unable to control or understand organizations.

6. DiMaggio (1986: 360-362) criticizes population ecology for ignoring the structural implications of ecological analysis, arguing against the usual practice of classifying populations on the basis of attributes such as outputs. One alternative is classification based on comparative advantage among organizations, or what McKelvey and Aldrich (1983) call "competencies." Another alternative, suggested by the technique of blockmodeling, is classification on the basis of shared environmental dependencies, or structural equivalence among groups of organizations. This method, although not without problems of its own, claims the advantage of broadening population ecology's ability to test some of its most important predictions (e.g., the extent to which environmental niches and organizational forms are isomorphic).

7. Further, even if organizations *cannot* affect their domains, it does not follow that optimality results.

8. For important analyses of the issue of environmental versus organizational influence, see Penrose (1952) and Winter (1964).

9. See Hempel (1959: 293-301) on the logical problems with the notion of "functional prerequisites."

REFERENCES

Aldrich, Howard (1979) Organizations and Environments. Englewood Cliffs, NJ: Prentice-Hall.

Aldrich, Howard (1985) "A population perspective on organizational strategy." University of North Carolina, Chapel Hill. (unpublished)

Aldrich, Howard and Ellen R. Auster (1986) "Even dwarfs started small: liabilities of age and size and their strategic implications." Research in Organizational Behavior 8: 165-198.

Aldrich, Howard and Jeffrey Pfeffer (1976) "Environments of organizations." Annual Review of Sociology 2: 79-105.

Astley, W. Graham (1985) "The two ecologies: population and community perspectives on organizational evolution." Administrative Science Quarterly 30: 224-241.

Astley, W. Graham and Andrew Van de Ven (1983) "Central perspectives and debates in organization theory." Administrative Science Quarterly 28: 245-273.

Berg, Ivar (1971) Education and Jobs: The Great Training Robbery. Boston: Beacon.

Braverman, Harry (1975) Labor and Monopoly Capital. New York: Monthly Review Press.

Carroll, Glenn R. (1984) "Organizational ecology." Annual Review of Sociology 10: 71-93.

Carroll, Glenn R. (1985) "Concentration and specialization in populations of organizations." American Journal of Sociology 90: 1262-1283.

Carroll, Glenn R. and Jacques Delacroix (1982) "Organizational mortality in the newspaper industries of Argentina and Ireland: an ecological approach." Administrative Science Quarterly 27: 169-198.

Carroll, Glenn R. and Yangchung Paul Huo (1986) "Organizational task and institutional environments in ecological perspective: findings from the local newspaper industry." American Journal of Sociology 91: 838-873.

Chandler, Alfred D. (1977) The Visible Hand. Cambridge, MA: Harvard University Press.

Chandler, Alfred D. and Herman Daems [eds.] (1980) Managerial Hierarchies: Comparative Perspectives on the Rise of the Modern Industrial Enterprise. Cambridge, MA: Harvard University Press.

Child, John (1972) "Organizational structure, environment and performance: the role of strategic choice." Sociology 6: 1-22.

Clark, Burton (1960) The Open Door Challenge: A Case Study. New York: McGraw-Hill.

Clarke, Lee (forthcoming) Acceptable Risk? Making Decisions in a Toxic Environment. Berkeley and Los Angeles: University of California Press.

Clarke, Lee (1988) "Explaining choices among technological risks." Social Problems 35 (1): 501-514.

Clawson, Dan (1980) Bureaucracy and the Labor Process. New York: Monthly Review Press.

Cohen, Michael, James G. March, and Johan P. Olsen (1972) "A Garbage Can model of organizational choice." Administrative Science Quarterly 17: 1-25.

Collins, Randall (1979) The Credential Society: An Historical Sociology of Education and Stratification. New York: Academic Press.

DiMaggio, Paul (1986) "Structural analysis of organizational fields: a blockmodel approach." Research in Organizational Behavior 8: 335-370.

DiMaggio, Paul (1987) "Interest and agency in institutional theory," in Lynne G. Zucker (ed.) Institutional Patterns and Organizations: Culture and Environment. Boston: Pitman.

DiMaggio, Paul and Walter W. Powell (1983) "The iron cage revisited: institutional isomorphism and collective rationality in organizational fields." American Sociological Review 48: 147-160.

Edwards, Richard C. (1979) Contested Terrain: The Transformation of the Workplace in the Twentieth Century. New York: Basic Books.

Edelman, Murray (1964) The Symbolic Uses of Politics. Urbana: University of Illinois Press.

Feldman, Martha S. and James G. March (1982) "Information in organizations as signal and symbol." Administrative Science Quarterly 26: 171-186.

Fischhoff, Baruch (1977) "Cost benefit analysis and the art of motorcycle maintenance." Policy Sciences 8: 177-202.

Fine, Gary Alan (1984) "Negotiated orders and organizational cultures." Annual Review of Sociology 10: 239-262.

Fligstein, Neil (1985) "The spread of the multidivisional form among large firms, 1919-1979." American Sociological Review 50 (3): 377-391.

Freeman, John and Michael T. Hannan (1983) "Niche width and the dynamics of organizational populations." American Journal of Sociology 88: 1116-1145.

Gusfield, Joseph R. (1955) "Social structure and moral reform: a study of the Women's Christian Temperance Movement." American Journal of Sociology 61: 221-232.

Hannan, Michael T. and John Freeman (1977) "The population ecology of organizations." American Journal of Sociology 82: 929-964.

Hannan, Michael T. and John Freeman (1984) "Structural inertia and organizational change." American Sociological Review 49: 149-164.

Hannan, Michael T. and John Freeman (1986) "Where do organizational forms come from?" Sociological Forum 1: 50-72.

Hempel, Carl G. (1959) "The logic of functional analysis," pp. 271-307 in Llewellyn Gross (ed.) Symposium on Sociological Theory. Evanston, IL: Row, Peterson.

Hickson, David J. (1987) "Decision-making at the top of organizations." Annual Review of Sociology 13: 165-192.

Hrebiniak, Lawrence G. and William F. Joyce (1985) "Organizational adaptation: strategic choice and environmental determinism." Administrative Science Quarterly 30: 336-349.

Jencks, Christopher, Marshall Smith, Henry Acland, Mary Jo Bane, David Cohen, Herbert Gintis, Barbara Heyns, and Stephen Michelson (1972) Inequality: A Reassessment of the Effect of Family and Schooling in America. New York: Basic Books.

Kahneman, Daniel, Paul Slovic, and Amos Tversky (1982) Judgment Under Uncertainty: Heuristics and Biases. Cambridge, MA: Cambridge University Press.

Kamens, David H. and Tormod K. Lunde (1987) "Institutional theory and the expansion of central state organizations, 1960-1980," in Lynne G. Zucker (ed.) Institutional Patterns and Organizations: Culture and Environment. Boston: Pitman.

Kasarda, John D. and Charles E. Bidwell (1984) "A human ecological theory of organizational structuring," pp. 183-236 in Michael Micklin and Harvey M. Choldin (eds.) Sociological Human Ecology: Contemporary Issues and Applications. Boulder, CO: Westview.

Langton, John (1984) "The ecological theory of bureaucracy: the case of Josiah Wedgwood and the British pottery industry." Administrative Science Quarterly 29: 330-354.

Laumann, Edward O., David Knoke, and Yong-Hak Kim (1985) "An organizational approach to state policy formation." American Sociological Review 50(1): 1-19.

Lawrence, Paul and Jay Lorsch (1967) Organization and Environment. Cambridge, MA: Harvard University Press.

Lindblom, Charles E. (1959) "The science of muddling through." Public Administration Review 19: 79-88.

Lindblom, Charles E. (1979) "Still muddling, not yet through." Public Administration Review (November/December): 517-526

Lipset, Seymour Martin and William Schneider (1983) The Confidence Gap: Business, Labor, and Government in the Public Mind. New York: Free Press.

Long, Norton (1958) "The local community as an ecology of games." American Journal of Sociology 6: 251-261.

Lutz, Frank (1982) "Tightening up loose couplings in organizations of higher education." Administrative Science Quarterly 27 (4): 653-669.

March, James G. (1978) "Bounded rationality, ambiguity and the engineering of choice." Bell Journal of Economics 9: 587-608.

March, James G. and Johan P. Olsen (1979) Ambiguity and Choice in Organizations. Oslo: Universitetsforlaget.

March, James G. and Herbert A. Simon (1958) Organizations. New York: John Wiley.

March, James G. and Roger Weissinger-Baylon (1986) Ambiguity and Command: Organizational Perspectives on Military Decision Making. Marshfield, MA: Pitman.

Marglin, Stephen A. (1974) "What do bosses do?" Part I. Review of Radical Political Economics 6: 60-112.

Marglin, Stephen A. (1975) "What do bosses do?" Part II. Review of Radical Political Economics 7: 20-37.

McKelvey, Bill and Howard Aldrich (1983) "Populations, natural selection, and applied organizational science." Administrative Science Quarterly 28: 101-128.

Messinger, Sheldon L. (1955) "Organizational transformation: a case study of a declining social movement." American Sociological Review 20: 3-10.

Meyer, John W. (1980) "The world polity and the authority of the nation-state," pp. 109-137 in Albert Bergesen (ed.) Studies of the Modern World System. New York: Academic Press.

Meyer, John W. and Michael T. Hannan (1979) National Development and the World System. Chicago: University of Chicago Press.

Meyer, John W. and Brian Rowan (1977) "Institutionalized organizations: formal structure as myth and ceremony." American Journal of Sociology 83: 340-363.

Meyer, John W. (1983) "The structure of educational organizations," pp. 71-97 in John W. Meyer and W. Richard Scott (eds.) Organizational Environments: Ritual and Rationality. Beverly Hills, CA: Sage.

Meyer, John W. and W. Richard Scott [eds.] (1983) Organizational Environments: Ritual and Rationality. Beverly Hills, CA: Sage.

Meyer, Marshall W. (1986) "The growth of public and private bureaucracies." Theory and Society.

Meyer, Marshall, William Stevenson, and Stephen Webster (1985) Limits to Bureaucratic Growth. Berlin/New York: Walter de Gruyter.

Mohr, Lawrence (1982) Explaining Organizational Behavior. San Francisco: Jossey-Bass.

Penrose, Edith Tilton (1952) "Biological analogies in the theory of the firm." American Economic Review 42: 804-819.

Perrow, Charles (1977) "Review, ambiguity and choice in organizations." Contemporary Sociology 6: 294-298.

Perrow, Charles (1984) Normal Accidents: Living with High Risk Technologies. New York: Basic Books.

Perrow, Charles (1985) "Review, organizational environments: ritual and rationality." American Journal of Sociology 91: 151-155.

Perrow, Charles (1986) Complex Organizations: A Critical Essay. New York: Random House.

Powell, Walter W. (1987) "Institutional effects on organizational structure and performance," in Lynne G. Zucker (ed.) Institutional Patterns and Organizations: Culture and Environment. Boston: Pitman.

Pugh, D. S., D. J. Hickson, and C. R. Hinings (1968) "Dimensions of organization structure." Administrative Science Quarterly 14: 91-114.

Rowan, Brian (1982) "Organizational structure and the institutional environment: the case of public schools." Administrative Science Quarterly 27: 259-279.

Roy, William G. (1981) "The process of bureaucratization in the U. S. state department and the vesting of economic interests, 1886-1905." Administrative Science Quarterly 26: 419-433.

Scherer, Frederick M. (1980) Industrial Market Structure and Economic Performance. Chicago: Rand McNally.

Selznick, Philip (1965) TVA and the Grass Roots. New York: Harper and Row.

Short, James (1984) "Toward the social transformation of risk analysis." American Sociological Review 49 (6): 711-725.

Simon, Herbert A. (1957) Administrative Behavior. New York: Macmillan.

Sproull, Lee, Stephen Weiner, and David Wolf (1978) Organizing an Anarchy: Belief, Bureaucracy, and Politics in the National Institute of Education. Chicago: University of Chicago Press.

Starbuck, William H. (1983) "Organizations as action generators." American Sociological Review 48: 91-102.

Stone, Katherine (1974) "The origins of job structures in the steel industry." The Review of Radical Political Economics 6: 19-64.

Tasca, Leo (1983) "Power and organization in organized anarchies." State University of New York, Stony Brook. (unpublished)

Thompson, James D. (1967) Organizations in Action. New York: McGraw-Hill.

Tolbert, Pamela S. (1985) "Resource dependence and institutional environments: sources of administrative structure in institutions of higher education." Administrative Science Quarterly 30: 1-13.

Tolbert, Pamela S. (1987) "Institutional sources of organizational culture in major law firms," in Lynne G. Zucker (ed.) Institutional Patterns and Organizations: Culture and Environment. Boston: Pitman.

Tolbert, Pamela S. and Lynne G. Zucker (1983) "Institutional sources of change in the formal structure of organizations: the diffusion of civil service reform, 1880-1935." Administrative Science Quarterly 28: 22-39.

Van de Ven, Andrew (1979) "Review of organizations and environments." Administrative Science Quarterly 24: 320-326.

Weick, Karl (1976) "Educational organizations as loosely coupled systems." Administrative Science Quarterly 21: 1-19.

Weick, Karl (1979) The Social Psychology of Organizing. Reading, MA: Addison-Wesley.

Wholey, Douglas R. and Jack W. Brittain (1986) "Organizational ecology: findings and implications." Academy of Management Review 11 (3): 513-533.

Williamson, Oliver E. (1975) Markets and Hierarchies: Analysis and Antitrust Implications. New York: Free Press.

Winter, Sidney G. (1964) "Economic 'natural selection' and the theory of the firm." Yale Economic Essays 4: 225-272.

Woodward, Joan (1965) Industrial Organizations: Theory and Practice. New York: Oxford University Press.

Zald, Mayer N. and Patricia Denton (1963) "From evangelism to general service: the transformation of the YMCA." Administrative Science Quarterly 8: 214-234.

Zucker, Lynne G. (1977) "The role of institutionalization in cultural persistence." American Sociological Review 42: 726-743.

Zucker, Lynne G. (1983) "Organizations as institutions," pp. 1-47 in Samuel B. Bacharach (ed.) Research in the Sociology of Organizations, Vol. 2. Greenwich, CT: JAI.

Zucker, Lynne G. (1986) "Production of trust: institutional sources of economic structure, 1840-1920." Research in Organizational Behavior 8: 53-111.

10

POLITICAL SOCIOLOGY

Paul Burstein
University of Washington

Political sociologists are often asked what political sociology is and how it differs from political science. The best answer I know of was provided by Giovanni Sartori in his 1969 essay, "From the Sociology of Politics to Political Sociology." According to Sartori, there have been two main social scientific approaches to the study of politics. "Political science" considers how political outcomes are produced by *political* institutions and forces, including political parties, government agencies, and interactions among political leaders. The "sociology of politics" explains political outcomes as the product of *social* forces, including the relations among social classes, ethnic and religious groups, and communities. "Political sociology" would be an interdisciplinary hybrid, employing political *and* social factors to explain political outcomes.

When Sartori (1969) wrote his essay, many sociologists considered themselves political sociologists, but by his definition there was little political sociology. He saw the establishment of political sociology as "more a task for the future than a current achievement" (p. 69) because sociologists and political scientists were committed, not to explaining political outcomes, but, more narrowly, to explaining them using only the variables emphasized by their own disciplines. "Much of what goes under the misnomer of 'political sociology,'" he wrote, "is nothing more than a sociology of politics ignorant of political science" (p. 69). Most political science, in turn, was ignorant of the sociology of politics.

There is a bit more political sociology now than there was when Sartori wrote, but his essay did not have the effect he would have liked. Most studies of politics still focus on few explanatory variables, and attempts to develop broad explanations of political phenomena that disregard disciplinary boundaries are relatively rare. Were I to write about the history and current status of political sociology, therefore, I would have little to say. Instead, I will proceed much as Sartori did. I will assume that political sociology seeks to explain the creation, evolution, and destruction of nation-states and governments, and, within those states, the causes and consequences of government—or "state"—action. I will describe briefly what sociologists of politics have been doing to achieve such explanations, and will then discuss what current work may lead to the development of a true political sociology. Along the way, I will contrast what sociologists of politics have done with what political scientists have done, and with what both should have been doing to explain political outcomes.

THE DEVELOPMENT OF THE SOCIOLOGY OF POLITICS

According to Bendix and Lipset's (1966) classic account, the sociology of politics (or, in their terms, but not Sartori's, "political sociology") achieved formal definition in the 1930s, following up classical political studies by Weber, Michels, Marx, and others. The field reached a form recognizable to today's students in the late 1940s and 1950s, as modern methods of data collection were more or less perfected, automated data processing became possible, money for large research projects became available, and sociologists began to specialize in the sociology of politics. Sociologists who began their careers during this period, including Seymour Martin Lipset, Reinhard Bendix, Morris Janowitz, and S. N. Eisenstadt, in large measure created the field, and continue to influence it.

Any attempt to briefly describe a complex field must be somewhat arbitrary, but I think it fair to say that the sociology of politics, on into the 1960s, focused on three main issues: (1) the conditions necessary for democratic government; (2) political participation and party choice; and (3) the distribution of power and its consequences. Underlying all three was a commitment to democratic values (see Bendix and Lipset, 1966: 15), and a concern that they were threatened by totalitarianism, public apathy and ignorance, and concentration of economic and political power.

As Sartori noted, sociologists tried to explain political outcomes by using variables central to sociological explanations in general, particularly social class and demographic characteristics, such as race, religion, ethnicity, and place of residence.

The style of explanation may best be shown by example. Three of the classic works produced during this period were Berelson, Lazarsfeld, and McPhee's *Voting* (1954), Lipset's *Political Man* (1960), and Lipset and Rokkan's (1967) essay, "Cleavage Structures, Party Systems, and Voter Alignments."

Voting examined how the citizens of Elmira, New York, decided whom to vote for in the 1948 presidential election. Although the study was extremely innovative in its panel design and its concern with how people are influenced by their social networks, its fundamental assumption was the traditional sociological one that citizens' political choices are primarily the product of their demographic characteristics. *Voting* influenced hundreds of studies of party choice and political participation that tried to show how the basic model worked itself out in different countries, ethnic and religious groups, and time periods (see, for example, the chapters in Lipset and Rokkan, 1967).

Political Man was a collection of essays of much greater scope than *Voting*, considering what affects political behavior and the prospects for democracy both cross-nationally and historically. Although the essays in *Political Man* were extremely subtle and provocative—they still stimulate controversy 30 years after they were written—they were begun while Lipset was at Columbia University, where *Voting* was written, and Lipset's basic mode of explanation was the same as Berelson, Lazarsfeld, and McPhee's. Lipset was careful to say that people's political actions are not simply the product of their social positions (see Bendix and Lipset, 1966); nevertheless, political outcomes are very strongly influenced by social organization as defined in conventional sociological terms. Thus, for example, whether a society will become or remain democratic is strongly conditioned on the educational levels, wealth, and values of its inhabitants; individual political action is critically affected by economic position; and elections are in large measure an "expression of the democratic class struggle" (Lipset, 1960).

I think the high point of the post-World War II classic period in the sociology of politics was reached in Lipset and Rokkan's (1967) essay, "Cleavage Structures, Party Systems, and Voter Alignments," and the book it introduced, *Party Systems and Voter Alignments*. They argued masterfully that the seemingly great variety of twentieth-century democratic party systems trace their development to two historical revolutions—the national and the industrial—and to two sets of social cleavages—the cultural, including differences in religion and ethnicity, and the economic, including differences between classes and between farmers and city dwellers. The logical possibilities for group conflict and alliances presented by these cleavages, along with demographic differences between countries and a small number of other factors, determined the development of party systems, and these in turn influenced national political development for generations. Parties and political conflict are thus largely produced by basic social divisions, as these were affected by the rise of nation-states and the industrial revolution.

These three works were models of useful scientific simplification, showing how much apparent complexity in social life resulted from the operation of a small number of fundamental variables.

Nevertheless, it is important to note what they ignored as well as what they included. Most studies in the sociology of politics, including these, fail to consider the impact on politics of public opinion, interest groups, constitutions and other formal rules, the actions of political leaders, international relations, political parties as independent actors, and elections as determinants of government policy. They seldom examine government action, either as the consequence of mass political activity, or as an influence on such activity. Although there were some exceptions, such as Janowitz's (1964) work on the military, Eisenstadt's (1963) on the consequences of government action, and Lipset's (1979) own regarding the impact of constitutional rules on political party formation, the sociology of politics usually ignored most variables that political scientists believed—and sometimes demonstrated—to be determinants of political outcomes. The sociology of politics, for all its virtues, was the study of a world without political organizations, government, or law.

Nevertheless, by the end of the 1960s sociologists of politics understood a great deal more about politics than they had at the end of World War II. At that point, however, the sociology of politics began to change direction. Some subjects, particularly party choice, were more or less abandoned; others, such as the development of nation-states, were still pursued but with new approaches and methods; and subjects formerly on the periphery of the sociology of politics, such as social movements, moved dramatically to the center of attention. Changes in the sociology of politics that became noticeable in the late 1960s and early 1970s have strongly influenced the field since then, and it is to this subject that I now turn.

THE SOCIOLOGY OF POLITICS SINCE THE EARLY 1970s

As sociologists of politics sought simple patterns beneath seemingly complex events through the 1960s, they naturally focused on political phenomena that seemed amenable to simple explanations, particularly conventional, easily studied actions (such as voting) taking place in stable institutional contexts (such as stable party systems). Disorder and instability could hardly be ignored; much of the sociology of politics had been motivated by concerns about how democratic governments could withstand violence and totalitarianism. But the breakdown of orderly politics was nevertheless usually viewed as the exception rather than the rule, and the field was oriented toward preventing disorder by enhancing commitment to democracy.

This orientation changed noticeably in the late 1960s and early 1970s. Sociologists of politics working then had a tremendous advantage over their predecessors—they could take for granted the relatively simple and elegant models of politics developed over previous decades. The new generation of sociologists of politics was therefore ready to reintroduce complexity into the study of politics.

This process began most obviously in the study of social movements, which exemplifies the sociology of politics as a whole. Social movements had been studied before, but they were not considered politically important; involvement in movements was often viewed as irrational, and the movements were seen as potentially dangerous but generally marginal to democratic politics. This attitude changed, however, as the American civil rights movement showed that movements could involve intelligently organized struggle on behalf of democratic values. Sociologists' participation in the civil rights and anti-Vietnam war movements also affected their ideas about the irrationality and destructiveness of those involved (Gamson, 1975).

The study of social movements expanded rapidly in the 1970s, and they have been a central focus of the sociology of politics ever since. Yet what happened was not simply the addition of another subject to the sociology of politics. The study of social movements was accompanied by developments in theory and method that affected all of the sociology of politics and helped begin its transformation into political sociology.

The new study of social movements—particularly as initiated by William Gamson, Charles Tilly, and others at the University of Michigan— led to at least five significant changes in the sociology of politics. First, it moved away from the study of the orderly and routine to the seemingly disorderly and unpredictable. Second, it moved from the study of nominal groups, such as classes and ethnic groups, to the study of organized groups, including unions, the Ku Klux Klan, and the Southern Christian Leadership Conference. Third, the new study of social movements examined neglected types of political action; advances in data collection techniques (see Tilly, 1978; Gamson, 1975; Jenkins and Perrow, 1977) greatly improved sociologists' capacity to describe the actions of social movement organizations, their opponents, and bystander groups. Fourth, while studying social movements, sociologists began to study government action more seriously than before, in order to ascertain whether governments responded to demands for government action (see Gamson, 1975).

Finally, the addition of social movement variables to the political sociologists' repertoire took place in the wake of a revolution in social science data analysis; statistical techniques introduced into sociology in the late 1960s made it possible for the first time to consider simultaneously how both social movements and other political actors affected political outcomes.

Similar changes took place elsewhere in the sociology of politics. Moving toward creating a true political sociology, sociologists of politics began to make government action far more central to their analyses, as both the consequence and cause of social and political change. Harold Wilensky (1975), Alex Hicks (Hicks, Friedland, and Johnson, 1978), and others examined how government policies and expenditures were influenced by a variety of social and political factors. The "world systems" and "dependent development" approaches to economic and political development suggested that social change within countries might be affected by international as well as domestic forces (see Chirot and Hall, 1982). And the work of Tilly (1978), Skocpol (1979) and others (see Goldstone, 1986) showed how revolutionary change and the creation of nation-states could be influenced by the relations among states.

Paralleling changes in the study of social movements, analyses in other areas began to see politics as disorderly and conflictful rather than essentially orderly and consensual. Thus, for example, sociologists analyzing the Third World ceased assuming that development was a unilinear process in which developing nations would become like western nations, and began to view development as highly problematic in both speed and direction. Western nations ceased to be viewed primarily as models and benign helpers in modernization; many sociologists argued that their relations with Third World nations were highly exploitive. Governments came to be seen less as responsive to either citizens or relatively benign elites, and more as active participants in politics, influencing citizens and directing their political activities. The creation of nation-states came to be seen as highly contingent rather than natural; few of the many political units existing in Europe 500 years ago exist today, most having disappeared during violent struggles.

This shift in concern from order to disorder was associated with a shift away from abstract concepts and relatively easily measured variables to detailed examinations of individual and group action. To some extent, this shift grew out of a longstanding controversy about the relationship between sociology and history. Although the best sociologists had always emphasized that historical studies were a critical part of sociology, they tended to view historians essentially as research assistants—that is, historians were seen as gathering vast amounts of historical data that would be most satisfactorily interpreted by sociologists, using their more sophisticated theories and methods.

Tilly and others objected to this attitude, insisting that sociologists could learn a great deal from historians' approach to data and the interpretation of social change. Tilly's own work served as fruitful exemplar of this point, and the result has been a far more finely grained examination of politics. This approach has made it possible to gather the data necessary to analyze groups challenging the accepted balance of power, and to place their actions more sensitively into historical context.

The development of better models of political change stimulated improvements in data analysis. Earlier and simpler models of the political process could be analyzed with statistical techniques available in the 1950s and early 1960s. More self-consciously complex models seemed to require more advanced techniques, however. As greater attention was paid to historical development, sociologists had to learn time-series analysis. As government came to be seen as causing as well as responding to social change, sociologists had to learn how to analyze processes involving feedback. And as sociologists studied more types of political action and collected more of their own data (rather than relying on government statistics), measurement error became a more central concern.

Substantively, probably the single most important concern in the sociology of politics has been the plight of the poor and disadvantaged, and especially whether they can use politics to gain a greater share of the world's resources. This concern has been manifested since the 1960s in three areas in particular, and controversies in these areas are central to the sociology of politics.

The first area is electoral politics. Sociologists now pay little attention to individual party choice, but focus more on a prior and more fundamental question—whether party choice affects government policies and the distribution of income. The relevant studies (such as Wilensky, 1975 and Hicks and Swank, 1984) generally involve cross-national comparisons of change in government expenditures or the national distribution of income. Many early studies seemed to show, much to the surprise of the researchers, that party choice had little effect—it didn't make any difference whether parties of the left or right won national elections.

Subsequent work has gone in two directions, the first toward arguing that party choice *does* make a difference, but only under certain circumstances, and the second toward the claim that because the working class is always a minority of the voting public, it must, if it wants its party to win office, make compromises that prevent electoral victory from influencing the distribution of income (see the review in Korpi, 1983, ch. 2). There is still considerable disagreement as to which point of view is correct. I suspect that the ultimate conclusion will be that the party balance does make a difference, but a modest one, and only under some circumstances.

The second area of great concern has been social movements. Here, as in the study of electoral politics, the focus has shifted from the actions of individuals to more fundamental questions about the consequences of mass action—in particular, whether social movements are an effective means of political action for those who find more conventional political activities impractical or ineffective.

Initial expectations and findings in the study of social movements were quite contrary to those for party choice. Many sociologists did not expect social movements to be effective, but initial studies showed that they were (Gamson, 1975). Not only did movements often win what their supporters wanted, but movement supporters could enhance their chances of success through their choices of movement goals, tactics, and organization. These findings made participation in social movements appear rational, at least in the sense that they could achieve their goals and that planning could help them do so. Such participation could therefore be considered an ordinary alternative for those trying to influence political outcomes—individuals frustrated in electoral politics, for example, might reasonably opt for social movement participation instead.

Subsequent studies have supported the conclusion that social movements may be effective (see, e.g., Jenkins, 1985; Burstein, 1985a). One important controversy in the field is analogous to one about electoral politics: under what circumstances are movements most likely to reach their goals? Gamson (1975) showed that movements seeking modest reforms are more likely to succeed than are movements with radical goals; the latter are likely to call forth intense opposition and be crushed. Among movements with seemingly less radical goals, a critical issue has been the extent to which movement organizations control their goals and resources, as opposed to being co-opted by political parties, foundations, professional activists, or the government itself (Jenkins, 1986). This is essentially an argument about how much impact the disadvantaged can have, and how many goals they must abandon to gain recognition as legitimate participants in conventional politics. This controversy has not been resolved, but the disadvantaged do seem able to attain considerable power. They may get help from established institutions, and such institutions may attempt to channel their efforts, but (and this is an important qualification) so long as their goals have some support among elites or in the society at large, they can attain considerable success on the basis of their own resources while adhering to their original goals (Morris, 1985; Jenkins, 1986).

Recent studies of electoral politics and social movements focus on domestic politics. In the third area, the study of the "world system," the focus is the impact on nation-states of nations and other organizations beyond their borders. A major concern is how nations' positions in the international system affects them, particularly their economic development and distribution of income. Do Western aid, investment, and commercial relations help Third World nations, or do Western nations mainly extract resources from the Third World and keep its nations subordinate? And if there are benefits, do they go mostly to a small elite closely tied to the West, or are they spread more generally among the population? (See, e.g., Chirot and Hall, 1982.) Being in the world's periphery is clearly bad, and it is hard to move out of the periphery; but the reasons for this are unclear and the subject of intense controversy.

Recent research in these three areas leads to three conclusions. First, the disadvantaged may use politics to their advantage. Second, their impact is likely to be limited, and effective only under some circumstances. Most current research, in fact, is devoted to ascertaining which circumstances and explaining them in a theoretically satisfactory way. Third, shifts in the focus of the sociology of politics, combined with advances in data collection and analysis, have paid off, leading to significant advances in our understanding of politics.

Despite this progress, recent work can be strongly criticized. Most criticism occurs within subfields; for example, those studying social movements debate the role of outside aid in movement success, and those studying electoral politics debate how to measure the appropriate political outcomes (see, e.g., the discussion in Wilensky, 1975). But broader criticisms can be raised as well. I will focus on theoretical and method-ological weaknesses stemming from the narrowness of focus so pervasive in the sociology of politics.

Theoretically, the sociology of politics suffers because it is almost entirely inductive. What "theory testing" there is usually involves testing hypotheses derived from the work of the nineteenth-century masters, particularly Marx and Weber. Potentially relevant formal theories in political science and economics are ignored. Thus, for example, most sociologists of politics have been astonished by—almost refused to believe—data showing that election outcomes had little impact on public policy (Burstein, 1982). When such data were believed, the interpretation was generally the conventional cynical one that electoral politics was a sham, that there was no real difference between the parties. Yet there has long been a theory—Anthony Downs's economic theory of democracy and its derivatives—that predicted that under certain conditions the policies of major parties would converge, not because electoral politics was ineffective or corrupt, but because open and effective competition would force parties that wanted to win office to converge in supporting proposals that most voters favored (see Mueller, 1979). This theory has its own limitations, but sociologists of politics could have avoided much confusion had they taken it seriously.

Taking the concept of theory more broadly, and focusing on the specification of models of the political process, it is clear that narrow subdisciplinary concerns often impede the struggle to understand politics. Social scientists *should* seek to broaden their models by including as many variables as are relevant to useful explanation. In fact, however, most sociologists become dedicated to showing that their favored variables— social movement activity, election results, international investment flows, whatever—strongly affect political outcomes, and engage in controversies about only those variables. Thus, for example, most studies of the impact of social movements examine social movements alone, instead of how they relate to other kinds of political activity. As a practical matter, this means devoting great effort to the measurement of movement phenomena and their impact, while ignoring other political phenomena or treating them with much less care. Proceeding this way almost inevitably leads to overestimating the effect of the chosen variables and underestimating the effect of competitors for the explanatory limelight (Jennings, 1983, provides an excellent discussion of this issue).

In addition, still missing from almost all quantitative sociology of politics is serious consideration of the government itself. Analyses of the determinants of political outcomes avoid studying government actions— that is, the outcomes supposedly in question—in two ways. The first is to retreat from the study of political outcomes to controversies about their causes—about movement resources, for example. The second is to devote far fewer resources to the analysis of government action or policy than to their determinants. This may mean, for example, considering only whether a law has been adopted, and not what it says, or using readily available statistical measures of policy outcomes, such as expenditures, without considering the possibility that policies may have important nonmonetary outcomes.

Finally, although some neglected variables have been taken up recently by the sociology of politics, many are still ignored, including public opinion, interest groups, constitutions and other formal rules, and the actions of political leaders. And, as in the 1960s, the concerns of sociologists are largely ignored by members of other disciplines—political scientists, for example, either ignore social movements or bemoan the fact that most of their colleagues do. Some progress has been made in bridging the chasm between the sociology of politics and political science—particularly in studies of the world system and of the consequences of elections (see, e.g., Chirot and Hall, 1982; Hicks and Swank, 1984), but most of the bridge remains to be built. I turn now to some particularly important recent work in the sociology of politics, and consider what it may presage for the future.

TOWARD POLITICAL SOCIOLOGY IN THE 1980s AND BEYOND

Recent work in five areas holds great promise for the future of political sociology, both contributing to our understanding of particular aspects of politics and manifesting real vision about the field as a whole: the areas of government action, public opinion, formal organizations, culture and ideas, and causality in politics. Political scientists as well as sociologists have been contributing to the development of a true political sociology.

Two sorts of work on government action are especially important—those focusing on measurement, and those concerned with theoretical synthesis.

Measurement is critical. It seems obvious that something must be described precisely—that is, measured—before it can be explained. Yet in studies of politics, little effort has been devoted to measuring the core variable, government policy itself. Government action is typically described in ways that have changed little in 50 years—in terms of expenditures, which represent only part of what government does; in terms of when legislation was adopted, which ignores its content; or in discursive narratives about the content of legislation, which cannot be used in quantitative analyses of change.

Government action is so seldom measured systematically because it is so difficult to do so. Most attempts rely on content analysis, which is a notoriously labor-intensive and difficult research technique. It would not make sense to devote the required effort to the task if the same conclusions could be reached without doing so.

Some important recent work shows quite conclusively, however, that systematically measuring government policy can greatly alter our view of politics. A particularly good example is Ronnie Steinberg's book, *Wages and Hours* (1982), a study of American labor laws. Steinberg content-analyzed a vast number of state and federal labor laws, examining how coverage and standards of worker protection changed between 1900 and 1973. She essentially rewrote the history of American labor law by showing that previous narrative works, which focused on adoption, had been misleading—most laws covered only a small fraction of the labor force when first adopted, and it was struggle over the extension of the laws that was crucial to most workers. Steinberg's focus on the extension of coverage reoriented analyses of American legal culture and led her to challenge traditional conclusions about the determinants of change in labor legislation. None of that would have been possible without systematic analysis of the content of legislation.

Other works similarly show how advances in analyzing government policy can change conclusions about what the government does and why. Examples include Berk, Brackman, and Lesser's (1977) book on the California penal code, the work of John Meyer and his collaborators on national constitutions (for example, Boli-Bennett and Meyer, 1978), and my own research on federal policy on the Vietnam War and civil rights (Burstein, 1985a).

Theoretical synthesis has a more continuous tradition. One especially creative attempt at synthesis in political sociology is Alford and Friedland's (1985) book, *Powers of Theory*. They argue that there are three major theoretical perspectives in the study of democratic politics: the pluralist, which emphasizes consensus and the peaceful, evolutionary character of modern politics; the managerial, which focuses on the power of elites; and the class, which sees state action as determined by its role in capitalist society. They claim that none of these perspectives provides a complete picture of democratic politics. Many debates in political sociology, they write, involve proponents of each perspective defending its explanation of a particular phenomenon. In fact, according to Alford and Friedland, the debates often represent wasted effort because each perspective really has a different "home domain"—a different set of phenomena—in which its explanations are appropriate. Proponents of the different perspectives should realize, Alford and Friedland claim, that they are usually not even trying to explain the same things. *Powers of Theory* may stimulate new ways of thinking about democratic politics and channel debate away from useless polemic toward creative synthesis.

When explaining government action, the most absurd result of sociologists' commitment to traditional variables is our ignoring the impact of public opinion on political outcomes in democratic countries. Most political scientists assume that legislators in democratic countries try to satisfy the public when adopting policies; economists who study politics do likewise (see Burstein, 1985b). Political scientists are well aware of barriers to the translation of public preferences into public policy, but have such strong reasons for expecting a strong linkage that they have made its investigation a central theoretical concern.

Until recently, evidence about the link between public opinion and public policy was essentially anecdotal, and there were many anecdotes both supporting and contradicting the hypothesis that public opinion strongly affects public policy. Quantitative research on the relationship began slowly, partly for theoretical reasons and partly because systematically gauging the relationship required measuring not only public policy but public opinion as well (Weissberg, 1976).

The last few years have seen a considerable leap ahead, however, thanks primarily to Page and Shapiro (1983), who examined thousands of American polls asking about public policy, and developed measures of change in public opinion and public policy across a wide range of issues. The findings of this and related work are striking. Though Congress does not follow public opinion on all issues, on many important ones it does; even on issues that are important to relatively small proportions of the public, Congress does what the public wants a very substantial proportion of the time. The same seems to be true of state legislatures.

Sociologists' reactions to these findings are noteworthy—we ignore them. We have no good reason to think that the government should take public opinion less seriously than, for example, protest demonstrations by the disadvantaged, yet we pay a tremendous amount of attention to the latter and none to the former. Political scientists are filling this gap in the study of politics, and the development of a true political sociology would require integrating their results into our analyses.

Although sociologists have disagreed with political scientists about public opinion, we agree with them that political outcomes are affected by nongovernmental formal organizations—trade associations, unions, civil liberties organizations, professional groups, manufacturers, and so on. Some social scientists see such organizations primarily as intermediaries, communicating to legislatures what much of the public wants. Others, in contrast, see such groups representing only a tiny fraction of the public and getting their way at the expense of broader public opinion. But few question the importance of such organizations in politics.

Progress in understanding the role of formal organizations in politics has been slow, however, largely because the concepts and methods used to study them have changed little over the decades. Studies of organizations are largely anecdotal and descriptive; they lack a conception of how large numbers of organizations interact to influence policy, and have failed to develop ways to rigorously study complex patterns of relationships among organizations and government agencies.

This situation is changing, however. Edward Laumann and David Knoke, in particular, are developing an organizational approach to state policy formation that shows how contemporary theory and research methods can improve the study of politics (Laumann and Knoke, in press). Their study of groups trying to influence American health and energy policies gathered extremely detailed data to describe organizational interests, resources, reputed influence, and location in networks of communication and exchange. They use these data to predict organizational participation in policymaking and, ultimately, organizational influence on policy outcomes. Many of their findings are counterintuitive— participation does not seem to depend on resources, for example—and their research is intended to serve as a model for future work on other issues and in other countries. Pursuing this line of work would enable us to increase the scope and precision of our descriptions of politics, and can provide a link between the concerns of sociologists with social groups and the focus of political scientists on political organizations.

One of the most difficult issues in the study of politics is culture. A central problem of politics is how people make choices. We usually assume that people act on the basis of either self-interest or ultimate values, yet at the same time sociologists and political scientists (if not economists) know how inadequate such assumptions are. A diverse group of recent works seem to be converging, however, on the suggestion that analyzing culture may help us understand people's choices. Culture may be viewed as providing a kind of "tool kit" or repertoire of ways for making sense of situations and deciding how to respond (Swidler, 1986; see also Gamson and Modigliani, 1987; Tilly, 1978; Polsby, 1984). Often taking the form of "explicitly articulated cultural models, such as ideologies" (Swidler, 1986: 278) culture provides models of social organization and action that shape political action. Culture, in this view, can be a variable aspect of political life, shaping and being shaped by political action.

One way culture affects political outcomes is in determining, not exactly what people will do in politics, but what they think their range of alternatives is. When a legislature begins to consider an issue, for example, its most critical decisions are often about what policies would be feasible. These decisions, often made by small groups working in private, frequently influence debate for many years, with subsequent discussions focusing on small differences among similar proposals rather than on significant new approaches (Burstein, 1985a; Polsby, 1984). Similarly, when an issue is becoming salient to a large public, those most concerned about it often devote great effort to getting their framing of the issue, including their preferred solutions, to dominate public discourse (Gamson and Modigliani, 1987). Political issues may be decided during the struggle over the language in which they will be debated.

It is extremely difficult to integrate culture into systematic analyses of politics. Culture is difficult to conceptualize; data on culture are difficult to collect; the impact of culture on politics is often indirect and slow to develop (Swidler, 1986; Polsby, 1984); and it is difficult to include cultural variables in conventional statistical analyses of the determinants of political outcomes. Nevertheless, it is becoming clear that culture affects political outcomes, and recent work is beginning to show how to analyze those affects.

A final very important body of work concerns causality. Causal analysis in quantitative studies of politics has had some of the defects its detractors emphasized, particularly overreliance on simple linear, additive models, but it has also added rigor to the analysis of politics. The problem political sociologists confront is how to combine rigor with realism and subtlety. Here we are more at the stage of identifying problems than reaching solutions, but advances over past work are real nevertheless. Progress is being made along four lines.

The first is including statistical interactions in models of politics. As already discussed, recent studies show that many independent variables, such as social movement activity or election results, affect government policy only under some circumstances. Adequate statistical models for describing such contingent relationships must include interaction effects, but the models in published work rarely do. This situation may change, however, if recent work showing interactions to be important begins to influence work in progress (see Hicks and Swank, 1984; Burstein, 1985a).

A second problem in causal analysis is including phenomena taking place at different levels of analysis, over different time spans, in coherent models of politics. Alford and Friedland (1985), for example, argue that comprehensive explanations of democratic politics are problematic because each of the three dominant perspectives deals with a different level of analysis and has a different time perspective. Polsby (1984) and, to some extent, Swidler (1986), describe how difficult it is to incorporate ideas and culture into explanations of political outcomes. Cultural elements often take decades to develop, and form the context of political decisions, but do not cause decisions, in a conventional sense. The problems just described are not close to being solved, but they are being posed sharply enough, in areas sufficiently close to central concerns of political sociology, that significant progress toward solutions can be expected soon.

Crises are a third problem in the study of politics. Most studies are incrementalist, based on the assumption that relationships among variables remain constant, with change in the dependent variable being caused by changes in the independent variables. In times of crisis, however, the very nature of the relationships among the variables may change, and the usual assumptions do not hold. An example is the periodic critical realignments in the American party system, which cause dramatic changes in the relationship between social groups and political parties, the range of alternative policies considered, and political outcomes. How to combine crisis and routine politics in unified models is something we do not yet know, but, at least the problem is receiving increasing attention (see, e.g., Steinberg, 1982). Finally, sociologists' causal analyses, in both quantitative and qualitative studies, rest on the assumption that whatever happens is more or less inevitable, the result of a number of steps bound to one another through tight links of causality (see Tilly's 1975 discussion). Some recent work questions this assumption. In his study of the adoption of no-fault divorce laws in American states, Jacob (1986) argues that significant social and political change can occur despite the absence of change in any of the variables normally thought to be the causes of such change. In my own work on the movement for equal employment opportunity, I discovered that the links between the causes of government action and the consequences were often very loose, partly because of the way circumstances change and affect political outcomes in the course of a movement that has lasted for decades.

What we are finding, I think, is not simply that actions have unintended consequences, or that important variables have not yet been discovered, but something more basic about causality in society. In the immediate future, the practical problem for causal analysis will be balancing a striving for rigor with an openness about the nature of causation, trying to remain aware of the complexity of social processes without giving in to the urge to turn every analysis into an ad hoc search for whatever causal factors come to mind. In the longer term, the analysis of politics must be linked to basic research about the nature of society.

CONCLUSIONS

Since Sartori published his essay in 1969, considerable progress has been made toward creating a true, interdisciplinary political sociology. Some areas, such as the study of social movements, have developed very rapidly. Advances in data collection and analysis have led to widespread improvements in the analysis of politics. Increased attention by sociologists to government action has led to fruitful cooperation with political scientists. As a result, we know much more about politics now than we did at the end of the 1960s. In addition, recent work on government action, public opinion, organizations, culture, and causation contains the promise of further rapid advance.

But progress is not guaranteed. Political sociology faces at least three significant barriers to developing better, more comprehensive explanations of political outcomes.

The first and most important is the academic reward system, which pushes people toward narrow specialization. Most sociologists and political scientists are interested primarily in how their own favored variables influence political outcomes, and not politics as a whole. Those who study social movements, for example, cannot expect to be rewarded for including public opinion in their models; should they do so, they risk of alienating their colleagues by discovering that social movements are less important than they believe. The problems are the worst for those who are concerned with variables studied by disciplines other than their own. A sociologist who suggests studying legislatures—a special concern of political scientists—risks rejection by sociologists for wasting time studying unimportant subjects, and by political scientists for invading their turf. Political scientists who try to study, for example, the impact of race or social movements on politics, feel the same way.

Progress in political sociology thus rests, to a considerable degree, on individuals able to fight the normal reward structures of their disciplines, those who aim for comprehensive explanations in the face of pressures to specialize, and who can stay open to general influences from all the social sciences. Many important changes in the sociology of politics reflect changes in sociology in general—the movements toward and away from simplicity in explanation, increasing concern with formal organizations, advances in methods of data collection and analysis, and so on. The speed with which political sociology will develop depends in large measure on the willingness of those in the field to reward breadth as well as depth.

The second barrier to progress is the amount of effort it will take. Much recent progress has depended upon the willingness of researchers to devote vast amounts of labor to gathering and analyzing data in systematic ways (e.g., Steinberg, 1982; cf. Gamson, 1975; Tilly, 1978). The new methods of data gathering and analysis require far more effort and expertise than does traditional scholarship. Inspired use of the new methods can transform our understanding of politics, but this will happen only if many political sociologists devote the effort required to master them.

The final barrier is money. Once upon a time, sociologists of politics, like other social scientists, could do their studies on a shoestring, having their students interview citizens locally and doing some simple analyses.

Advances in research design, improvements in data collection and analysis, and a period (now over) in which resources were increasing, have raised our standards and expectations. Much of the best recent work could not have been done with the resources available in the 1940s and 1950s. Continuing declines in the resources available to political sociologists, as well as other social scientists, will necessarily slow the development of the field.

In the next 10 to 20 years, political sociology may blossom, or it may wither. The materials needed for progress are available. The question is whether they will be creatively used.

REFERENCES

Alford, Robert R. and Roger Friedland (1985) Powers of Theory: Capitalism, the State, and Democracy. New York: Cambridge University Press.

Bendix, Reinhard and Seymour Martin Lipset (1966) "The field of political sociology," pp. 9-47 in Lewis A. Coser (ed.) Political Sociology. New York: Harper & Row.

Berelson, Bernard, Paul Lazarsfeld, and William McPhee (1954) Voting. Chicago: University of Chicago Press.

Berk, Richard, Harold Brackman, and Selma Lesser (1977) A Measure of Justice. New York: Academic Press.

Boli-Bennett, John and John Meyer (1978) "Ideology of childhood and the state." American Sociological Review 43: 797-812.

Burstein, Paul (1982) "Citizen preferences, electoral competition, and political outcomes." Micropolitics 2: 1-20.

Burstein, Paul (1985a) Discrimination, Jobs, and Politics. Chicago: University of Chicago Press.

Burstein, Paul (1985b) "The United States Congress and the sociological study of politics." Sociology and Social Research 69: 171-188.

Chirot, Daniel and Thomas D. Hall (1982) "World-system theory," pp. 81-106 in Ralph Turner and James F. Short, Jr. (eds.) Annual Review of Sociology, Vol. 8. Palo Alto: Annual Reviews.

Eisenstadt, S. N. (1963) The Political Systems of Empires. New York: Free Press.

Gamson, William A. (1975) The Strategy of Social Protest. Homewood, IL: Dorsey.

Gamson, William A. and Andre Modigliani (1987) "The changing culture of affirmative action," in Richard Braungart (ed.) Research in Political Sociology, Vol. 3. Greenwich, CT: JAI.

Goldstone, Jack A. [ed.] (1986) Revolutions: Theoretical, Comparative, and Historical Studies. San Diego: Harcourt Brace Jovanovich.

Hicks, Alex, Roger Friedland, and Edwin Johnson (1978) "Class power and state policy." American Sociological Review 43: 302- 15.

Hicks, Alex and Duane Swank (1984) "On the political economy of welfare expansion." Comparative Political Studies 17: 81-119.

Jacob, Herbert (1986) "Innovation and emulation in policy diffusion: the spread of no-fault divorce." Presented at the annual meeting of the American Political Science Association, Washington, DC.

Janowitz, Morris (1964) The Military in the Political Development of New Nations. Chicago:
    University of Chicago Press.
Jenkins, J. Craig (1985) The Politics of Insurgency. New York: Columbia University Press.
Jenkins, J. Craig and Craig Eckert (1986) "Channeling black insurgency: elite patronage and
    professional SMOs in the development of the civil rights movement." Presented at the
    annual meeting of the American Sociological Association, New York.
Jenkins, J. Craig and Charles Perrow (1977) "Insurgency of the powerless: farm worker
    movements, 1946-72." American Sociological Review 42: 249-268.
Jennings, Edward T., Jr. (1983) "Racial insurgency, the state, and welfare expension."
    American Journal of Sociology 88: 1220-1236.
Korpi, Walter (1983) The Democratic Class Struggle. London: Routledge and Kegan Paul.
Laumann, Edward O. and David Knoke (forthcoming) National Policy Domains: An
    Organizational Perspective on Energy and Health. Madison: University of Wisconsin
    Press.
Lipset, Seymour Martin (1960) Political Man. New York: Doubleday.
Lipset, Seymour Martin (1967) "Cleavage structures, party systems, and voter alignments,"
    pp. 1-64 in Seymour Martin Lipset and Stein Rokkan (eds.) Party Systems and Voter
    Alignments. New York: Free Press.
Lipset, Seymour Martin (1979) The First New Nation. New York: Norton.
Lipset, Seymour Martin and Stein Rokkan (1967) Party Systems and Voter Alignments. New
    York: Free Press.
Morris, Aldon (1985) The Origins of the Civil Rights Movement. New York: Free Press.
Mueller, Dennis C. (1979) Public Choice. Cambridge: Cambridge University Press.
Page, Benjamin I. and Robert Y. Shapiro (1983) "Effects of public opinion on policy."
    American Political Science Review 77: 175-190.
Polsby, Nelson W. (1984) Political Innovation in America. New Haven: Yale University Press.
Sartori, Giovanni (1969) "From the sociology of politics to political sociology," pp. 65-100 in
    Seymour Martin Lipset (ed.) Politics and the Social Sciences. New York: Oxford
    University Press.
Skocpol, Theda (1979) States and Social Revolutions. New York: Cambridge University
    Press.
Steinberg, Ronnie (1982) Wages and Hours: Labor and Reform in Twentieth-Century
    America. New Brunswick, NJ: Rutgers University Press.
Swidler, Ann (1986) "Culture in action: symbols and strategies." American Sociological
    Review 51: 273-286.
Tilly, Charles (1975) "Reflections on the history of European state-making," pp. 3-83 in
    Charles Tilly (ed.) The Formation of National States in Western Europe. Princeton:
    Princeton University Press.
Tilly, Charles (1978) From Mobilization to Revolution. Reading, MA: Addison-Wesley.
Weissberg, Robert (1976) Public Opinion and Popular Government. Englewood Cliffs, NJ:
    Prentice-Hall.
Wilensky, Harold L. (1975) The Welfare State and Equality. Berkeley: University of
    California Press.

PART III

APPROACHES TO SOCIAL PHENOMENA

This section of the book includes an eclectic selection of chapters
focusing on historical sociology, urban sociology, demography and
social psychology. Each represents a major traditional area of inquiry
within sociology. Historical sociology is the "newest" topic on the list,
but only because what is now recognized as a major subfield in the
discipline was formerly simply a method of inquiry. The importance of
historical inquiry and contextual analysis more broadly has gained a
renewed vigor in the past two decades, in part, Hamilton argues, because
of new ways in which historical analysis is being used in sociology and
because sociologists are becoming more historical minded. Hamilton
refutes the view that all sociological analysis must be historical and the
idea that history and sociology are becoming fused into a single
discipline.

In the chapter on urban sociology Lee rejects the current view that
this is a field on the "wane." He does this by indicating that the demise
of the field has been greatly exaggerated and by suggesting that there is a
coherence to the primary focus of the field that has not changed and
that is not likely to change in the future. As developments occur in the
urban environment, urban sociology will continue to answer important
questions about "urban organization" and the causes and consequences
of urban organizational structure and change over time. This is
dependent, Lee argues, on the availability of funding to obtain better
data sets which extend over time (i.e., are longitudinal) and extend over
space (i.e., include larger samples of cities and other residential units of
analysis). Vitality of the field is dependent upon research developments
as well as theoretical breaks from the confines of past traditions.

For demography, a field with an applied focus from its inception,
Pullum projects a fairly vital future as population pressure and other
world wide events persist in keeping population issues at the forefront in
the social sciences. "Demography is the study of the causes and
consequences of variation and change in human fertility, mortality, and
spatial distribution." All three processes have significant consequences
for the major political, social and economic institutions, and thus, as
Pullum notes, have linkages with the disciplines of sociology, economics,

and, to a lesser extent, biology. As a field, demography has access to relatively rich data sets and to a vast array of well-developed formal modeling and statistical techniques that Pullum claims have strengthened the empirical basis of demography. Furthermore, he claims that the applied bent of demography should be welcomed in sociology as an enriching aspect of the discipline, a feature that has given demography its vitality over the years.

Social psychology is reviewed briefly by Cook and Pike who comment on some of the recent developments in the field. They identify several vital research areas within the discipline and argue for a greater emphasis upon the linkages between social psychological models and micro-level theories with macro-level theory and research. One mechanism is for theorists to develop more extensively models of social interaction, moving beyond the exclusive focus on models of individual level action (or more passive models of actors as "reactive"). A second trend discussed by Cook and Pike is the renewed interest in affect, motivation and emotions, rather than the more narrow focus on cognition and information processing. They conclude with a plea for interdisciplinary work and for attempts to integrate the "three faces" of social psychology.

These approaches to social phenomena are all integral to our basic understanding of the relationship of the individual to society and to social institutions more generally. Each includes special data requirements and new methodologies for obtaining better data. The future of these fields of inquiry is dependent not only upon continued theoretical advances and attempts to break out of the molds of traditional foci and modes of inquiry, but also on continued improvements in the quality of the data available for analysis (e.g., historical or longitudinal data sets, obtained over larger time frames or populations and in multiple settings or locations). This theme emerges in other chapters in this volume. Social scientists now have the tools to do large-scale research and more detailed observational and experimental studies, but funding remains a key resource constraint. Social science is at a point in history when social engineering may even be possible—the self-conscious design and modification of social systems and institutions to achieve clearly defined societal goals.

11

HISTORY IN SOCIOLOGY

Gary G. Hamilton
John Walton
University of California, Davis

It is often said that the surest way to guess the future is to predict more of the present. Were this maxim applied to assessing the future of historical sociology, it would easily lead to the unambiguous conclusion that a glorious future lies ahead. Some 25 years ago, in the early 1960s, historical sociology did not appear in any list of subfields for sociology, but today no such list would be without it. At that time, most sociologists were content to leave all historical studies for historians to do, but today few sociological studies are without, at least, an appreciation of history, and more than a few contain research based on the type of primary source material that only historians would have used previously.[1] Indeed, the growth of a historically oriented sociology has been so rapid and its influence so widespread throughout sociology as well as history that some observers (e.g., Giddens, 1979; Abrams, 1982; Sztompka, 1986) now proclaim that history and sociology will soon be one and the same.

This perception of an imminent disciplinary fusion between history and sociology rests on two normative claims. First, it assumes that, insofar as the present is intrinsically a historical moment, the entire subject matter of sociology is historical and, accordingly, that the only *appropriate* forms of analysis *should* contain a temporal dimension. Second, it equally assumes

Authors' Note: This chapter is the result of many years of discussion between the two authors about historical sociology, and contains their reflection on working with historians in starting an interdisciplinary graduate program in Social Theory and Comparative History at the University of California, Davis. The authors wish to thank Nicole Biggart for her comments on an earlier draft.

that, since all sociology is historical, there *should* be no subfield marked off as the exclusive preserve for those interested in historical analysis.

Anthony Giddens (1979: 230) was one of the first to make these claims: "There simply are no logical or even methodological distinctions between the social sciences and history—*appropriately* conceived" (our emphasis). Similarly, Giddens's late colleague, Philip Abrams (1982: 17), argued that "there is no *necessary* difference between the sociologist and the historian, and [that the] sociology which *takes itself seriously* must be historical sociology" (our emphasis). Several other sociologists (Skocpol, 1984: 356-391; Tilly, 1981, 1984) reach similar conclusions, but none so unequivocally as Piotr Sztompka:

> Contrary to the misleading name, historical sociology is not a subdiscipline, like all those innumerable sociologies of religion, art, organization, work, mass media, industry and anything else that comes to mind. Rather it is an approach, point of view, orientation applicable to all areas of social reality. It does not imply that there is some specialized branch of sociology dealing with history. Rather it stipulates that *all sociology worthy of the name* has to be historical in the sense of acknowledging the historical dimension of social life and incorporating historical method into social research [Sztompka, 1986: 330, our emphasis].

Were we to use these normative statements about what sociology ought to be like to predict the future of historical sociology, we would have to conclude that the future of historical sociology is the future of both sociology and history. Such predictions are not merely excessive; rather they are seriously misleading and quite mistaken.

In this essay, we will present four arguments about the future of history in sociology. First, we demonstrate through an analysis of disciplinary practices that there is no reason to think that sociology and history are merging and every reason to believe that they will continue as distinct disciplines. Second, we argue that the renewal of a historical orientation in sociology does not mark a departure from the goals of "scientific" sociology, in the sense that historical sociology still strives for generalizable theories and causal analyses. Third, we show that, although sociologists are becoming more historically minded, there remains considerable diversity in how historical material is incorporated into sociological research. And fourth, we further suggest that, as the discipline of sociology becomes more oriented toward historical analysis generally, then historical sociology itself will continue, and even strengthen its position as a subfield of sociological analysis.

DISCIPLINARY PRACTICES

Will sociology and history merge into a single discipline? Will historical sociology so permeate sociology that it will disappear as a subfield? Those answering "yes" to these questions do so based more on their wishes for the future than on examinations of actual practice in the present. It is certain, of course, that in the last two decades sociology has become more historical and history more sociological. But it does not follow from these observations that the two fields are merging, that they are becoming part of a single intellectual endeavor. In fact, if examined closely, these extravagant claims do not rest upon an understanding of what practitioners in the two disciplines are doing. Instead these visions of merger are reached as a part of a normative reassessment of sociological theory. Any predictions about the future should, however, grow out of an analysis of current practices and not simply be reflections about what sociological theory ought to be like.

An analysis of these practices may well begin with the different answers that historians and sociologists give to the question, "What is your specialty?" On the one hand, historians identify themselves by areas, periods, and topics of expertise. A historian might reply in a broad way that he or she specializes in, for instance, seventeenth-century English political history. Were that person answering another historian, the reply might be simply "Cromwell." On the other hand, it is inconceivable that a sociologist would answer in either way. Instead, sociologists usually identify themselves, in the first instance, with a substantive label, such as "political sociology" and, if pressed, might further supply an area (e.g., Europe) and a theoretical orientation (e.g., Weberian).

With each term of identification, the meanings differ. For example, a *political* historian and a *political* sociologist connote two widely diverse sets of expectations as to what one's expertise is. *Political* for the historian suggests the study of political figures and of the regimes to which they belonged, so the next questions that would be asked after hearing that a person is a political historian concern who, when, and where. *Political* for sociologists, however, implies the study of states, of elites, of bureaucracy, perhaps even of voting patterns. Therefore, the next questions narrow down the possibilities with inquires about which states (e.g., European), what type of approach (e.g., Weberian or Marxian), and if needed, what method (e.g., quantitative, field, or historical/comparative).

These differences in "official" identities between historians and sociologists suggest that such identities are institutionalized, are embedded in different academic communities that have established distinct standards for scholarly practices.[2] For the present purpose, discussion of two aspects of research is sufficient to demonstrate the institutionalized quality of the differences. These two aspects, data collection and standards of analysis and presentation, relate directly to how practitioners in each discipline legitimize their expertise, and hence gain standing (e.g., reputation, promotion) in their intellectual community.

Among historians, data collection rests upon finding and mastering a body of primary source material about a clearly delineated topic. The topic must be of recognized importance and the material must exist in sufficient quantity to allow the historian to claim expertise in the area. In principle, specific topics, such as the Civil War period, can accommodate only so many experts before that topic would be used up, so to speak. But, in fact, what usually occurs in a crowded field is that the topic becomes further subdivided into an array of smaller topics, ranging from biographies to gender relations in the period. In this way, competition to be an expert in an area promotes ever more refined historical specializations, more exhaustive treatments of increasingly narrow topics, and a revisionist orientation based upon ever closer readings of primary sources. To produce a revisionist interpretation that is the most definitive work on a topic to date becomes the acknowledged strategy for making one's work portentous. The ensuing competition for legitimacy and reputation pushes historians further into primary sources. As a consequence, in the same way that anthropologists become identified with the people among whom they have done fieldwork, historians are drawn into identifying with their primary sources.

In contrast, although many use primary sources, historical and otherwise, sociologists are known not for their sources, but instead for their theories and methods. Therefore, as an area of concern, data collection in sociology emphasizes the process of collection and not the materials being collected. Unlike history departments, which may or may not have a graduate course on historiography, all graduate departments in sociology require methods courses, including in recent times courses on comparative and historical methodology. In sociology, even if one uses primary sources, there is no presumption that all the sources have been exhausted, or even that most have. What is presumed, however, is that, in the course of offering a theoretical interpretation, sociologists have examined "sufficient" data to assess their explanatory value in relation to a theory. To examine more data, presumably, would result in diminishing returns. The preference is always for breadth and not for depth of coverage, because it is the scope of coverage that tests the generality of theories. It is for this reason that secondary sources become not only acceptable, but even necessary forms of data; they are the building blocks of original, generalizable theoretical interpretations. Sociologists, therefore, are pulled from an identification with sources toward an identification with theories, particularly with theoretical traditions, such as Marxian or Weberian or Durkheimian.

The manner in which historians present their research usually features their primary sources. To historians, the perception of originality lies in the analysis and presentation of these sources. Some secondary sources may be used to structure the analysis of the primary sources, but they usually remain peripheral to the task of giving an account of what is new. Historians often cultivate a masterful prose style and deliver their analysis in an essay format. This serves to emphasize better the seamlessness of a properly detailed historical interpretation. Historians reading other historians' works typically turn first to the footnotes and references in order to learn which primary sources were used, and with this information then turn to the texts to see how the sources reveal something that was unknown before. Were no new primary sources found in the references and footnotes, or in the case of some works in historical sociology, were no primary sources found at all, historians would be tempted to dismiss the study as containing "nothing new."

In contrast, sociologists present their research in order to emphasize their theoretical interpretations. They divide the body of the text into sections that represent the building blocks of an argument. They use secondary sources to position the research into a tradition and often to provide opposing theories to test. They discuss the processes of data collection in reference to how the data relate to their theory and to whether they were collected in valid ways. This analysis is purposely methodical, so that a sense of analytic accuracy and replicability is conveyed, and prose style often bends to meet the needs of appearing analytic and theoretically precise. In reading the work of other sociologists, most sociologists pay little attention to footnotes and references and concentrate on the theoretical significance of the argument being made. Were there no theoretical argument or only one buried in much empirical detail, as is the case for the writings of most historians, sociologists would likely dismiss the work as meaningless, as being without an interpretive frame.

We have only touched the surface in this discussion about differences in the disciplinary practices between historians and sociologists.[3] We should note, of course, that many historians and sociologists do not conform to the normative standards of their disciplinary community, so one can always locate exceptions. In general, though, disciplinary practices are institutionalized in academic procedures. For instance, the peer review processes in publishing, promotion, and obtaining support for research are instrumental in cultivating and maintaining these practices. These practices not only produce normative standards for individual evaluation, but also lead to the identification of exemplars of scholarship that direct further research in the fields.

Sociologists and historians read each other's works as never before, and ideas flow from one community of scholars to the other. Nonetheless, the two communities are not merging into one community with one set of standards for what is acceptable historical analysis. To be sure, there are some who see themselves as belonging to both disciplines, and a very few who would actually be accepted in both. Perhaps E. P. Thompson or Charles Tilly would be examples. But the exceptions largely prove the rule, because the usual outcome of straddling disciplines is to belong firmly to neither. History has its professional outsiders, its Toynbees and Tuchmans, those historians whose works stand outside of the academic tradition and are criticized for it. And sociology has its share of prizewinning historical sociologists who encountered problems receiving tenure.

Given the institutionalization of departments in universities, it would be sociologically unsophisticated to predict that history and sociology will merge. We can foresee only continued division, despite increasing exchanges of ideas across these organizational boundaries.

THE DEVELOPMENT OF HISTORICAL
SOCIOLOGY AS A SUBFIELD

In evaluating the future of historical sociology, one should remember that the disciplinary practices in sociology are relatively new. They show no sign of abatement, and have only intensified in the past several decades. Standards have become entrenched as sociology has grown larger and more established, and as entry into academic positions has become ever more difficult. In fact, our analysis suggests that the recent emergence of historical sociology is best understood as a part of the entrenchment of these practices.

Many historical sociologists trace the origins of what they do to the models of analysis worked out by the presumed founders of sociology.[4] Indeed, there is often a sense in the work of historical sociologists of their having returned to the original visions of what sociological analysis should be, which, as we have mentioned, produces the utopian assessments about the future of subfield. Although there is certainly much to admire in the writings of early sociologists, it is well to remember that none of them wrote in the intellectual atmosphere shaped by disciplinary practices. In fact, none of the founders of sociology, from Comte and Marx to Durkheim and Weber, should be seen as trying to combine sociology and history. It is more accurate to see the founders of sociology as trying to rise above established historical practices, in order to create categories of explanation that either complement or subsume chronological analysis. Therefore, when current sociologists (e.g., Sztompka, 1986) call for a return to the classics, they do not actually mean that sociology should be more like history, but that sociologists should formulate a generalizing mode of analysis that sits on top of history and that, purportedly, helps make sense of it in ways that regular historians cannot. In other words, historical sociology is a type of sociology, and not a hybrid product of two disciplines.

This call for a return to the founders' models is best understood in the context of disciplinary practices. Once sociology became a discipline, with its own university enclaves, graduate training programs, and journals, the early disciplinarians began to mark off space between disciplines. There were not many practitioners in any discipline, so the effort to claim intellectual territory could proceed with clarity and confidence. Durkheim's efforts (1964) are transparent in this regard, but the efforts of American sociologists were just as influential.

In the first generation, the founders of sociology, even those in the United States, uniformly incorporated into sociology a temporal perspective. For instance, the founding American sociologists broke organizationally from economics, theoretically from Spencer, but uniformly accepted some variant of Darwin's theory of evolution (Haskell, 1977; Cravens, 1978; Walton, 1985). Most saw evolutionary change from a voluntarist perspective, which in turn emphasized the situational and purely historical qualities of social change. In this sense, the founders were historically minded, and some actually did historical investigations (e.g., Sumner, 1896, 1906; Ward, 1893). Nonetheless, the common goal among sociologists was certainly not to do good historical research; rather it was to go beyond what was then a conventional historical analysis toward developing a sociology of historical change.

As some sociologists are doing today, many of the founding sociologists saw the present as a historical moment. They felt that a concentration of understanding on the present contributed to their goal of building a sociology of change. This is especially the case for the early sociology faculty at the University of Chicago, who claimed present day society as the discipline's particular subject matter. By the early 1920s, the Chicago faculty had established a strong fieldwork tradition that built upon their understanding of the present as an outcome of historical processes. One need only look at Thomas and Znaniecki's *The Polish Peasant in Europe and America* (1918), a key sociological work of the era, to recognize the historical vision that was the bedrock of early American sociology.

By the late 1920s, however, and then with abandon in the 1930s, the fieldwork tradition came under attack from a newly trained generation of sociologists. These new and more professionalized sociologists, including the likes of Ogburn, Stouffer, and Lundberg, criticized the fieldwork tradition as not being scientific enough, as being trapped in small samples and idiosyncratic viewpoints. They wanted a more quantitative sociology, based on public opinion and accurate surveys of actual conditions. These criticisms led to a split in sociology between a social problem-reformist orientation, on the one hand, and academic professionalism, on the other. Later in the 1930s, and continuing in the 1940s, a second split occurred within the academically oriented wing, as some sociologists, including Parsons and Merton, began to berate the atheoretical quality of American sociology and worked to develop sounder theoretical foundations. It is at this point that American sociology began to bifurcate into the Grand Theory and Abstracted Empiricism, two wings of sociology that C. Wright Mills criticized so thoroughly in 1959, in *The Sociological Imagination*.

In that interim between the 1920s and Mills's admonishments in 1959, sociology had become a staple of higher education. Many graduate schools, professional associations, and journals were established in the United States and elsewhere, and sociological subfield began to take shape. The intellectual atmosphere was dominated by survey research and the criticisms of survey research, by structural functionalism and by criticisms of structural functionalism. These were the dominant trends and those who did not partake in the trends, such as Sorokin and MacIver, found they either had to criticize the new movements or be considered antiquated. Usually, both happened. Within the subfields, controversies over theory and method defined the central issues, and reputations were made by those taking up these issues.[5] As grand theory and empiricist techniques occupied everyone's attention, historical mindedness in sociological research receded in importance.

In the 1950s there were a number of sociologists, such as Mills (1951, 1959), Smelser (1959), and Bendix (1956), working with historical materials, but they were not seen as a breed apart, as doing something distinctive. Instead, they were seen as adding some historical depth to particular subfields (e.g., stratification, industrial sociology). However, beginning in the late 1950s (e.g., Dahrendorf, 1959) and gaining wide recognition in the

1960s, sociologists started a comprehensive critique of both structural functional theories and descriptive empirical research. Embroiled in this critique, sociologists began to locate a number of diverse, relatively recent writings as exemplars for a new sociology.[6] Among those exemplars were some stressing sociological theories of historical change.

In reconstructing the emergence of historical sociology as a subfield, most writers (Skocpol, 1984; Tilly, 1981, 1984; Sztompka, 1986) emphasize a fairly small core of exemplary works. The most commonly cited are those of Moore (1966), Thompson (1963), Eisenstadt (1963), Bendix (1956, 1964), Tilly (1964), Perry Anderson (1974a; 1974b), and Wallerstein (1974). Some would include Braudel (1966) and others from the French "Annales school," and Hobsbawn (1962) and others from the English tradition of social history. What books are included in the list of seminal works matters less than the recognition that in the mid-1960s sociologists began doing serious sociological research with historical material and that these exemplars led the way for sociology to become, two decades later, decidedly historical.

HISTORICAL, AHISTORICAL, AND HISTORICALLY MINDED SOCIOLOGY

Is sociology intrinsically historical? Three propositions summarize our answer to this question. First, historical sociology includes a variety of analytical styles that, when taken together, do not exhaust all forms of valid or useful sociological inquiry. Sociology is not "intrinsically" historical in any concise sense. Second, by implication, there are legitimate forms of ahistorical sociology. These forms, such as the situational analysis developed by Goffman, are not necessarily incompatible with historical work—simply distinct. Third, it is not the case, however, that investigators may decide at their own discretion, which topics are susceptible to valid ahistorical analysis. All sociological research that draws conclusions about change over time must be at least historically minded. At a minimum, historical mindedness means that the research subject is understood (1) as the product of a particular intersection of social processes in time, (2) as a phenomenon whose nature changes over time with the shifting concatenation of social processes, and yet (3) as one whose profile at a given time can be validly analyzed under the convenient assumption that time is "held constant." This assumption, of course, is severely limiting and abuses follow quickly if the analyst strays from its limitations. Still, it is also a necessary assumption when one wants to portray a cross-section in time or to combine several cross-sections in a set of periods that may, with a shift of analytic style, be connected in some transformation.

A common failing of sociological research is an insensitivity to historical mindedness that lapses into invalid ahistorical work. The difference is illustrated in a comparison of two well known sociological studies of occupational change. In *White Collar*, C. Wright Mills (1951) analyzed the emergence of a "new middle class" in the United States. The old middle classes of small proprietors and independent professionals were fast being supplanted by the new white-collar salariat of teachers, salespeople, and office workers. For understanding this shift, the "liberal ethos" was irrelevant and the Marxian view inadequate. The change had to be analyzed as the product of capitalist development, which would provide a perspective on how "the occupational structure of the United States is being slowly reshaped as a gigantic corporate group" (p. 70), and how it affects consciousness in the meaning of work, the decline of craftsmanship, and status panic. Although Mills drew on historical evidence to support inferences about the changing occupational structure, his study is not, strictly speaking, historical sociology, but what we call a "historically minded" treatment of contemporary society. "The first lesson of modern sociology is that the individual cannot understand his own experience or gauge his own fate without locating himself within the trends of his epoch and the life-chances of all the individuals of his social layer" (p. xx).

Sixteen years later, Peter M. Blau and Otis Dudley Duncan (1967) published their much acclaimed study of *The American Occupational Structure*, which was based on a cross-sectional questionnaire study of "occupational changes in a generation." In sharp contrast to Mills (whom they do not cite), Blau and Duncan concluded that "The rates of upward mobility in the United States today are still high . . . notwithstanding the changes in historical circumstances that have been held responsible for high mobility rates in the past . . . technological progress has undoubtedly improved chances of upward mobility and *will do so in the future*" (pp. 426–428, emphasis added). These conclusions rest on no historical evidence, but on a quantitative analysis of survey data about intergenerational mobility—specifically, a comparison of the occupational positions of a large sample of men with their reports of their fathers' positions.

The Blau and Duncan study is ahistorical in two senses. Obviously, they make no effort to examine the historical forces that shaped the occupational structure that is their subject. Unlike Mills, they are not historically minded. That much, however, is forgivable under the assumption that Blau and Duncan want to portray the American occupational structure of 1967. But that assumption is not valid since they want to do a lot more, as the passage quoted indicates. Blau and Duncan want to draw conclusions about occupational *mobility*, the nature of the change from the modal occupation of fathers to those of sons. It is at this point that the study lapses into highly questionable ahistorical conclusions. Blau and Duncan have not compared the structure itself at two different times, its changing shape, in order to give meaning to a position within that structure. On the contrary, they have ahistorically assumed a static structure. Blau and Duncan would award the badge of occupational mobility to an office-working "manager" whose father was a shopkeeper. Mills would see the same individual as an anxious cog in the new machinery of mass society. The important differences between these two observations lie in the explanations from which they derive. Mills provides an explicit historical analysis that can be evaluated, perhaps disrupted. Blau and Duncan make implicit historical claims based on an analysis that assumes away the elements of any verifiable explanation.

VARIETIES OF HISTORICAL SOCIOLOGY

The contrast between Mills and Blau and Duncan shows the usefulness of a historical orientation in sociology, but not the variety of the uses. In order to assess the future of historical sociology, therefore, this distinction between historical sociology and historically minded sociology needs elaboration. In our view, historical sociology includes a variety of styles that ranges from pure efforts to explain the past to historically minded reflections on the present. The types of historical sociology we shall propose, however, make no sense as a continuum. Rather, they are strategies that make varied uses of historical research depending upon what is to be explained and what theory is presumed to assist explanation. Historical sociology, like any other kind of sociology, is characterized by a relationship between theory and appropriate observation—what questions we ask and where we look for the answers. The varied forms of that relationship describe the subcategories of historical sociology. Although the following is not intended as an exhaustive list, we shall propose that five types of historical sociology encompass the major relational foci that characterize the field: (1) general theories of social change, (2) sociological narratives of historical processes, (3) cultural and institutional analyses of meaning, (4) historical steps to the present, and (5) sociology as historical benchmark.

General Theories of Social Change

Historical sociology in the service of social change theory involves efforts to discover and document fundamental processes that animate broad sequences of change. Classical social theory is virtually defined by this approach with the grandly integrative schemes of Marx's dialectical analysis of modes of production, Weber's unfolding rationality in history, or Spencer's organic evolution. Sorokin's cyclical cultural values bridge the classics and modern theories. Sharply opposed theories may be equally devoted to this style. For example, Smelser (1959) and Wallerstein (1974) both employ historical detail to support an argument about the causes of the industrial revolution. Smelser emphasizes changes in the family and social values engendered by the broader process of social differentiation, and Wallerstein stresses the accumulation of capital by certain states and classes in the world economic system.

In each instance, the key is that diverse historical changes are analyzed, linked, and traced to core processes that work themselves out in history in the twin senses of orchestrating whole epochs and of explaining their transformation. The essential relationship of theory and observation lies in the connection between an encompassing explanation of change and a focus on decisive societal structure (relations of production and exchange, the state, the family) whose influences diffuse to secondary, if sometimes reciprocal, institutional changes (in ideology, values, or politics). The theory is immanent and finds a place for all concrete social practices as reflections of the emergent principle.

Sociological Narrative of Historical Processes

Historical sociology as narrative attempts to explain delimited processes or events such as revolution, class formation, state making, market expansion, and urbanization. Karl Polanyi (1944) explains the peculiar institution of the free market economy as a product of capitalism and state regulation growing out of historical conditions of the nineteenth century. Charles Tilly (1975) takes another tack on the same problem by explaining the formation of nation states in response to a set of changing conditions in markets, production, population, and class politics. Theda Skocpol (1979) wants to explain big revolutions by relating a number of historical conditions (land, agricultural production, political representation) to the decisive fact of state strength or weakness. Such analyses make no claim to a general theory of social change. Indeed, they are typically skeptical of that enterprise. Yet they are eminently theoretical because the sociological narrative is employed as a method for weighing and integrating the diverse causes of the event or process.

The effect, as Stinchcombe (1978: 13) explains, "is to make the narrative *appear* causal" and cause is inferred from analogies that point to similarities between the actions of people. The relationship of explanation and evidence is between a deductive or analogical principle and specific events that are explained by their inclusion in the principle.

Cultural and Institutional Analysis of Meaning

The analysis of meaning in historical sociology, like Weber's *verstehen*, endeavors to understand the subjective and collective interpretations attached to historical events by contemporary actors. The approach is equally applicable to historical and modern institutional analyses, such as David Reisman's (1950) interpretation in the 1950s of United States society as an overconforming "lonely crowd," or the recent insights of Robert Bellah and associates (1985) that portray a search for moral coherence in the crosscurrents of individualism and community. Weber's *The Protestant Ethic and the Spirit of Capitalism* is the outstanding historical example of a style that has recently enjoyed a renaissance in the convergent work of cultural historians (e.g., Darnton, 1984), symbolic anthropologists (e.g., Geertz, 1980), philosophers of societal mentality (e.g., Foucault, 1977), and political scientists concerned with the real and illusory meanings of hegemony (e.g., Scott, 1985).

In all instances a relationship is developed between consciousness and action, which theorizes action as the product of meanings that people attach to the circumstances of life. The theory is usually implicit, answering to the question "what sorts of meanings do people hold that lead them to act as they do?" Once revealed, these interpretations lend coherence to the most varied and minute details of social life.

Historical Steps to the Present

As previously illustrated with Mills's *White Collar*, historical sociology also analyzes the present by showing how today's social arrangements have evolved—what forces produced prevailing institutions and practices, thereby continuing to affect social life. Far more than "background," the effort here is to understand the changing present, where we came from and may be heading. That posture reveals an interventionist aim akin to Marx's hope that we can "shorten and lessen the birthpangs" of historical development by knowing its trajectory. By figuratively standing outside the present, it is possible to isolate the principal causes and effects of social change and to aim reforms at critical targets. Mills (1959) interpreted the worlds of work and politics as orchestrated by the demands of corporate concentration. Paul Starr (1982) explains the present monopoly of professional medicine, as well as how it is succumbing to profit-oriented bureaucracy, as a result of the interplay of cultural authority and economic change. Viviana Zelizer (1985) argues that the social value of children in modern society, a sentimentalized "pricelessness," is a product of the forces of consumerism and market expansion that undermined nineteenth-century beliefs in the economic value of children as productive members of the household economy. In varying degrees, Mills, Starr, and Zelizer judge contemporary practice harshly and imply that they could be altered with the right hands and the right historical levers.

The relationship between theory and evidence is defined by the problem of emergence, the extent to which the present, on one hand, flows directly from the past or, on the other hand, twists and turns under new conditions. Because change is always a combination of these things, the analytical task becomes one of finding the decisive historical junctures, discovering a new principle, and consequently explaining the transformation from past to present.

Sociology as Historical Benchmark

By now sociology has a 150-year history of its own, a record that includes empirical research and interpretation in and about the past. Henry Mayhew and Charles Booth did social surveys of poverty in London in the 1850s and early 1900s respectively. Robert and Helen Lynd studied social stratification in a midwestern community beginning in the 1920s. Modern historical sociology is increasingly in the fortunate position of possessing a longitudinal benchmark for research. Deliberately (e.g., Hunter, 1980) and inadvertently (e.g., Burawoy, 1979) investigators have returned to the scenes of earlier research, employing similar methods to document and explain the intervening change. And the possibilities are broader. Gareth Stedman-Jones's (1971) historical study of casual labor and poverty in nineteenth-century London makes use of Mayhew's surveys and a variety of additional evidence from the period to develop a more complete history. Frederick Engels's study of Manchester, England in the 1840s invites replication, as do the many investigations of Chicago in the early twentieth century. In another sense, the sociology of earlier periods can provide indicators of the thought of an era—how race or crime were understood by influential "social pathologists" of an earlier day (Mills, 1943). Although we are accustomed to think that "new" sociology uses "old" history as evidence, the reverse is possible and inviting as a method for historical sociology.

This approach raises new problems by focusing on the relationship of continuity between past and present institutions. How is sociology as history to be understood? What does an old sociological study tell us about its own times—what can we trust in Engels's marvelous and slanted account of working-class life in Manchester? What extensions to the intervening years and the present are possible, given the limitations of the original research? Are these problems any different from precautions that must be taken in evaluating the social research of our own time?

CONCLUSION: PROJECTING THE FUTURE

Although this elaboration of types of historical sociology is not intended as definitive, it serves to demonstrate that the field is varied in both the analytical aims of research and the uses of history. The future of historical sociology can be projected only in the sense of a composite of these distinct activities—some the rage today (e.g., analyses of meaning) and others lurking. In the aggregate, however, we can predict confidently that historical sociology will continue to flourish, and we see two general reasons this should be so.

First, within the discipline, the language of historical analysis has become a central part of sociological discourse, which sets the evaluative standards for sociological work. Sociological narrative has become the research style of a new generation of mainstream sociologists whose writings have had a significant impact both within and outside the discipline. Cultural and institutional analyses of meaning comprise a growing interdisciplinary field (of symbolic anthropologists, critical theorists, and cultural historians) as well as a sociological perspective. Increasingly, classical studies in sociology are being deliberately used as a benchmark for longitudinal research (Middletown update). And, of course the new historical mindedness we have noted follows the steps to the present. Presently, only general theories of social change appear out of fashion, perhaps as a result of the many criticisms of "world systems" as an inadequate replacement for grand theories of the past, but this, too, is likely only a temporary lapse.

Therefore, we believe that if historical sociology, with its diversity, is but a type of general sociology, it is certainly a vital part. It would be inconsistent on our part to rhapsodize the social surveys of Henry Mayhew and patronize the vastly more sophisticated, ahistorical survey research of the present. Yet, the value of any time-bound study that can be integrated into a historical interpretation appreciates greatly. This is because historical evidence provides a foundation for causal explanations that are otherwise rare or supported by statistical inference in most sociology. By providing a firmer basis for interpreting causation, historical sociology is more closely related to the evaluation and construction of explanatory theory. In short, historical sociology is more ambitious than other sociology—it asks bigger questions, promises more, and takes greater risks.

A second set of reasons that historical sociology will continue concerns the relations between sociology and other disciplines. Historical sociology has become one of the few locations in social science to build on genuine interdisciplinary, cross-cultural exchanges. To fashion convincing explanatory theories of change, historical sociologists are going beyond conventional disciplinary boundaries to explore issues formerly only in the preserve of historians or economists or political scientists. And they are going beyond the confines of North American society, and even Western society, to explore territory that only area specialists worked in previously. It is this interdisciplinary and cross-cultural expansion that persuades some sociologists that the substantive boundaries between the disciplines are disappearing, that, for instance, history and sociology are merging. As we have shown, this view is highly ethnocentric, it's the insiders' perspective that everyone is really just the same as they are. Nonetheless, historical sociology is generating the kind of intellectual excitement that has been absent in interdisciplinary work for many years. In this regard, historical sociologists increasingly perform the role of intellectual brokers between social science disciplines. As with exchange relations in other arenas, intellectual exchanges do not portend a merger between those parties exchanging ideas. And insofar as these exchanges continue, the role of intellectual brokers—the ones imperious enough to think they can handle more than one discipline—will not disappear. Willing to risk naïveté in the interest of broader generalization, historical sociologist are, in truth, just that imperious.

NOTES

1. See Skocpol (1984, pp. 356-403) for a discussion and bibliography of some of the studies in historical sociology.

2. See Kuhn's (1970) analysis of the processes of consensual validation in scholarly communities and the effects of such community processes upon setting academic standards.

3. See Tilly (1981) for a more detailed analysis of the practices of the two disciplines.

4. Skocpol (1984, pp. 4-5) makes a similar point, as does Hamilton (1987).

5. The most famous of these controversies occurred in the literature on stratification. This controversy was the ongoing debate about Davis and Moore's (1945) structural functional theory of stratification versus various alternative proposed by Tumin (1953), Dahrendorf (1959), and others.

6. Among others, for instance, the works of Erving Goffman became especially cited as examples deserving emulation.

REFERENCES

Abrams, Philip (1982) Historical Sociology. Ithaca, NY: Cornell University Press.

Anderson, Perry (1974a) Passages from Antiquity to Feudalism. London: New Left.

Anderson, Perry (1974b) Lineages of the Absolutist State. London: New Left.

Bellah, Robert N. et al. (1985) Habits of the Heart: Individualism and Commitment in American Life. Berkeley: University of California Press.

Bendix, Reinhard (1956) Work and Authority in Industry. New York: John Wiley.

Bendix, Reinhard (1964) Nation-Building and Citizenship: Studies of Our Changing Social Order. New York: John Wiley.

Blau, Peter M. and Otis Dudley Duncan (1967) The American Occupational Structure. New York: John Wiley.

Braudel, Fernand (1966) The Mediterranean and the Mediterranean World in the Age of Phillip II. New York: Harper & Row.

Burawoy, Michael (1979) Manufacturing Consent: Changes in the Labor Process under Monopoly Capital. Chicago: University of Chicago Press.

Cravens, Hamilton (1978) The Triumph of Evolution. Philadelphia: University of Pennsylvania Press.

Dahrendorf, Ralf (1959) Class and Class Conflict in Industrial Society. Stanford, CA: Stanford University Press.

Darnton, Robert (1984) The Great Cat Massacre and Other Episodes in French Cultural History. New York: Basic Books.

Davis, Kingsley, and Wilbert Moore (1945) "Some principles of stratification." American Sociological Review 10.

Durkheim, Emile (1964) The Rules of Sociological Method. New York: Free Press.

Eisenstadt, S. N. (1963) The Political System of Empires. New York: Free Press.

Foucault, Michel (1977) Discipline and Punishment: The Birth of the Prison. New York: Random House.

Geertz, Clifford (1980) Negara: The Theatre State in Nineteenth-Century Bali. Princeton, NJ: Princeton University Press.

Giddens, Anthony (1979) Central Problems in Social Theory. London: Macmillan.

Hamilton, Gary (1987) "The 'new history' in sociology." International Journal of Politics, Culture and Society 1: 89-114.

Haskell, Thomas L. (1977) The Emergence of Professional Social Science. Urbana: University of Illinois Press.

Hobsbawn, Eric J. (1962) The Age of Revolution, 1789-1848. New York: Mentor.

Hunter, Floyd (1980) Community Power Succession: Atlanta's Policy-Makers Revisited. Chapel Hill: University of North Carolina Press.

Kuhn, Thomas S. (1970) The Structure of Scientific Revolutions (2nd ed.). Chicago: University of Chicago Press.

Mills, C. Wright (1943) "The professional ideology of social pathologists." American Journal of Sociology 49: 165-180.

Mills, C. Wright (1951) White Collar: The American Middle Classes. New York: Oxford University Press.

Mills, C. Wright (1959) The Sociological Imagination. New York: Oxford University Press.

Mills, C. Wright (1967) The Power Elite. New York: Oxford University Press.

Moore, Barrington, Jr. (1966) Social Origins of Dictatorship and Democracy: Lord and Peasant in the Making of the Modern World. Boston: Beacon Press.

Polanyi, Karl (1944) The Great Transformation: The Political and Economic Origins of Our Time. New York: Holt, Rinehart.

Reisman, David (1950) The Lonely Crowd: A Study of the Changing American Character. New Haven, CT: Yale University Press.

Scott, James C. (1985) Weapons of the Weak: Everyday Forms of Resistance. New Haven, CT: Yale University Press.

Skocpol, Theda (1979) States and Revolution: A Comparative Analysis of France, Russia, and China. Cambridge: Cambridge University Press.

Skocpol, Theda (1984) Vision and Method in Historical Sociology. Cambridge: Cambridge University Press.

Smelser, Neil (1959) Social Change in the Industrial Revolution. Chicago: University of Chicago Press.

Starr, Paul (1982) The Social Transformation of American Medicine. New York: Basic Books.

Stedman-Jones, Gareth (1971) Outcast London: A Study in the Relationship between Classes in Victorian Society. London: Oxford University Press.

Stinchcombe, Arthur L. (1978) Theoretical Methods in Social History. New York: Academic Press.

Sumner, William Graham (1896) History of Banking in the United States. New York: The Journal of Commerce and Commercial Bulletin.

Sumner, William Graham (1906) Folkways. New Haven, CT: Yale University Press.

Sztompka, Piotr (1986) "The renaissance of historical orientation in sociology." International Sociology 1: 321-337.

Thomas, William and Florian Znaniecki (1918) The Polish Peasant in Europe and America. Chicago: University of Chicago Press.

Thompson, E. P. (1963) The Making of the English Working Class. New York: Vintage.

Tilly, Charles (1964) The Vendee. Cambridge, MA: Harvard University Press.

Tilly, Charles (1975) The Formation of National States in Western Europe. Princeton, NJ: Princeton University Press.

Tilly, Charles (1981) As Sociology Meets History. New York: Academic Press.

Tilly, Charles (1984) Big Structures, Large Processes, Huge Comparisons. New York: Russell Sage.

Tumin, Melvin (1953) "Some principles of stratification: a critical analysis." American Sociological Review 18: 387-394.

Wallerstein, Immanuel (1974) The Modern World System: Capitalist Agriculture and the Origins of the European World-Economy in the Sixteenth Century. New York: Academic Press.

Walton, John (1985) Sociology and Critical Inquiry. Chicago: Dorsey.

Ward, Lester (1893) The Psychic Factors of Civilization. Boston: Ginn.

Zelizer, Viviana A. (1985) Pricing the Priceless Child: The Changing Social Value of Children. New York: Basic Books.

12

URBAN SOCIOLOGY

Barrett A. Lee

Vanderbilt University

Despite its venerable place within the larger discipline, urban sociology is regarded by many as a specialty area that is on the wane. Outsiders (those who are not urban sociologists) point to the field's descriptive emphasis and atheoretical bent; insiders voice concern over fragmentation and lack of direction. At the institutional level, urban sociology appears to be declining as well, with membership in the ASA's Community Section (composed largely of urbanists) down by one-third since 1975 and fewer graduate faculty members claiming urban expertise.[1] Even casual expressions of affinity for the field are often subtly ominous. Consider, for example, a colleague's remark (overheard at a professional meeting) that he enjoys the label *urban sociologist* because it "gives me enough room to do any kind of research I please."

Carried to an extreme, this "anything goes" attitude could ultimately confirm the critics' doubts, diluting urban sociology beyond recognition. In moderation, however, such an attitude can encourage a healthy diversity of research topics, theoretical perspectives, and methodological styles. A major thrust of the present chapter is that urban sociology has been a vital enterprise—and will remain so in the future—in part because of the differences in viewpoint that exist among its practitioners. These differences are kept from getting out of hand by implicit agreement on a small set of questions about cities and urban life that seem worth asking. Although

Author's Note: This chapter grew out of a panel session, "Urban Sociology Yet to Come," at the 1986 Pacific Sociological Association meeting in Denver; my thanks to Lyn Lofland and Dennis Judd for their stimulating remarks as panel participants. I am also indebted to Harvey Choldin, Claude Fischer, Avery Guest, John Logan, and Barry Wellman, who provided helpful readings of an earlier draft, and to Peter Wood for his able research assistance. Work on the chapter was supported by a grant from the National Institute of Child Health and Human Development (1 R23 HD19537).

most of the questions have been around since the Chicago School era and before, how we phrase and answer them will continue to change. This ongoing process of revision should be sufficiently exciting to attract new adherents and ensure a number of institutional niches for urban sociology well into the next century.

In the pages that follow, I defend in more detail my conviction that the critics' reports of urban sociology's demise—like that of Samuel Clemens—have been greatly exaggerated. I begin with a glance backward in time, at the foundation laid for the field by its pioneers and at the influence of subsequent events. The focus then shifts to the present, to the forces responsible for the contemporary "identity crisis," the central questions bounding (however loosely) urban sociology, and the range of research emphases apparent within those boundaries. Finally, I adopt the role of wishful prognosticator, suggesting directions in which we urban sociologists might fruitfully head and assessing objectively our likelihood of doing so.

THE CHICAGO SCHOOL AND ITS LEGACY

Any effort to trace the historical development of the field must pay due respect to the Chicago School. This group of eminent sociologists, affiliated with the University of Chicago during the period 1915-1940, was responsible for putting urban sociology—and, to some extent, American sociology—on the intellectual map. At a time when the discipline as a whole was struggling to establish itself, Robert Park, Ernest Burgess, and their colleagues and students advocated a scientific sociology that could help make sense of the complex social milieu of an industrial society. That this approach was initially pursued most energetically in an industrial city is far from coincidental. Members of the Chicago School lived in the midst of a great urban laboratory where social phenomena of all kinds were expressed in problematic form.

The challenge provided by the urban environment evoked a variety of responses from the Chicago sociologists. Perhaps the response for which they are best remembered was a theoretical one, the formulation of an ecological perspective on cities. Park (1952) was instrumental in borrowing ideas from the biological (plant and animal) ecology that flourished early in the century. He used these ideas to build a conceptual framework for sociological (human) ecology, stressing the similar "biotic" processes—competition, succession, and the like—that generated a spontaneous or "natural" order in both human and nonhuman communities. The task of making the framework testable was left to Burgess (1925), whose famous concentric zone theory of intraurban structure and growth rested on the assumption that biotic processes have predictable spatial outcomes. Eventually, one of the department's star pupils, Roderick McKenzie (1968), would extend ecological concepts beyond the city limits, examining relations between places that were part of larger settlement systems such as regions or metropolitan areas.

Members of the Chicago School fostered important nonecological traditions in urban sociology as well. In his agenda-setting essay, "The City," for example, Park (1925) posed a question—about the fate of local sentiment, solidarity, and other manifestations of community in the urban setting—that has stimulated countless ethnographic case studies and given the field a heavy neighborhood flavor (for reviews, see Choldin, 1984; Olson, 1982; Suttles, 1976). And in another essay that has inspired extensive research, a former student of Park's, Louis Wirth (1938), argued that increases in the size, density, and heterogeneity of a city's population reduce value consensus, increase the likelihood of conflict, and generally affect the social fabric in a deleterious manner. Wirth's concern with the disruptive aspects of city growth reflects the reformist sentiments and alarm over urban "disorganization" underlying many of the investigations conducted by the Chicago School.

As most urbanists recognize, the issues addressed by Wirth were not new at the time he wrote about them, having been discussed previously by Simmel (1950), Toennies (1957), and Durkheim (1933), among others. These European founding fathers of sociology also devoted attention to the community question well before Park and his students did, and path breakers like Adna Weber (1899) and Charles Booth (1902-1903) had completed statistical analyses of urban growth and structure decades in advance of Burgess. But while the Chicago sociologists followed in the wake of these early efforts, they still managed to stamp urban inquiry with their own distinctive style: an empirical, multimethod orientation that balanced scholarly objectives with practical, policy-oriented ones in attempting to understand the social organization of an individual neighborhood, city, or metropolis.

Over the last 50 years, several types of events have modified the stylistic imprint of the Chicago School. The expansion of the U.S. Census and the rising popularity of the sample survey since the Second World War have increased the availability of large-N datasets, permitting urban sociologists to venture beyond the case study. Technical innovations in computing and electronic data processing have made possible more sophisticated statistical analyses, which in turn have encouraged theoretical revision and development. World trends, such as the rapid urbanization of non-Western societies and the growing accessibility between places due to transport and communications advances, have also shaped the course taken by urban sociology. In contrast to the intraurban predilection of the Chicagoans, many scholars during the postwar period have carried out cross-national investigations of the urbanization process or have studied systems of cities (Timberlake, 1985; Wilson, 1984).

A final type of event with implications for the Chicago School legacy has occurred on a periodic basis, originating within the field of urban sociology itself. I refer here to serious theoretical challenges, a number of which have been made since the "golden age" of the Chicago sociologists. To give but one illustration, the value of human ecology for understanding the internal spatial organization of cities has been questioned since its inception. Early critiques were aimed at ecologists' inattention to cultural and institutional influences on urban structure (Firey, 1945; Form, 1954). More recently, the so-called new urban sociology has injected neo-Marxism into the debate (Jaret, 1983; Smith, 1984). According to the neo-Marxists, conventional ecology has shed light on the intermediate determinants of structure—transportation technology, housing characteristics, mobility rates, and the like—but has neglected "fundamental causes," which are to be found in the capitalist mode of production. To rectify this shortcoming, Castells (1977), Harvey (1973), and others have argued that the ecological paradigm should be replaced by one emphasizing the spatial ramifications of work-based class interests and conflicts.

In the face of these theoretical challenges and the other events just noted, there can be little doubt that the Chicago School version of urban sociology enjoys less of a monopoly than it once did. Nevertheless, its influence remains disproportionate, for obvious reasons. As evidenced by research reviews that tie contemporary areas of inquiry directly to Park (Guest, 1984a), Wirth (Fischer, 1972), and their colleagues, many urban scholars believe the Chicagoans' general orientation continues to be appropriate. Even those who do not share this belief have difficulty overlooking the long line of classics written by Chicago faculty and graduate students more than a half-century ago. Consider, too, how many of us received our training from intellectual descendants of Park and Burgess, or whose initial exposure to sociology was from one of the hundreds of introductory textbooks modeled after the Park-Burgess prototype (1921). That the Chicago School has survived across generations is testimony not only to the leadership of its members within urban sociology, but to their active involvement in the launching of the sociological discipline as a whole.

IS THERE AN URBAN SOCIOLOGY?

Given the central role of urban sociologists in the development of American sociology, it may seem reasonable to expect the urban specialty area to be highly visible and prestigious relative to other areas of the discipline. Yet urban sociologists today often lament that our field suffers from the same problem as Rodney Dangerfield, getting little respect from nonurban colleagues. Taking much of the blame for urban sociology's current woes is an "identity crisis" of unknown proportions, apparent in the frequency with which the question heading this section arises during informal discussions among urbanists. The identity crisis is most conveniently explained as a function of differences in methodological style, absence of theoretical consensus, diversity of topics pursued, and other characteristics internal to the field. However, to comprehend fully why urban sociology may seem to lack direction and coherence, external factors must also be taken into account.

In an ironic twist, the trend toward an increasingly modern urban world has probably weakened rather than strengthened urban sociology as a subdiscipline. Although the connection is not inevitable, urbanization has traditionally been associated with gains in the scale and complexity of social organization. During the past half-century, this relationship has progressed to the point that the organizational units of primary interest to urban sociologists—neighborhoods, cities, and metropolitan areas—can no longer be assumed automatically to exert a dominant influence on people's lives. In fact, against the backdrop of nation-states, corporate actors, and similarly powerful elements that constitute the international economic order, it is tempting to dismiss any type of locality-based unit as trivial (Cohen, 1981; Molotch and Logan, 1985). A number of scholars have done just that, causing others to wonder what—if not urban places— urban sociologists should be investigating.

The pervasive nature of urbanization in countries like the United States, with virtually everyone living in cities or exposed to urban ways of life, has also helped precipitate the identity crisis in urban sociology. Historically, an important justification for studying the urban environment was the Wirthian suspicion that it generated values, attitudes, and behaviors at odds with—and presumably inferior to— those prevalent in rural settings. While urban-rural differences are still registered today (Glenn and Hill, 1977), the difficulties involved in maintaining the integrity of the comparison have become considerable. In an age of diffuse urbanization, there are fewer options concerning the types of communities with which cities can be legitimately contrasted.

As truly rural areas have faded from the scene, the "action" of interest to many kinds of sociologists has become disproportionately concentrated in urban locations. An unfortunate consequence of this development is that research into collective behavior, family structure, voluntary association activity, and all manner of topics winds up being misleadingly labeled *urban* on the basis of where a study is conducted rather than what it's about. This confusion of sociology *in* cities with a sociology *of* cities tends to be greatest when dramatic events or social problems attract attention to the metropolis and enhance funding opportunities for research proposals liberally spiced with urban buzzwords. Such was the case during the urban crisis of the 1960s and early 1970s. At the same time that business was booming for urban sociologists, the meaning of *urban* as an area of intellectual inquiry was gradually being undermined by a proliferation of pseudourban research projects.

The urban crisis contributed in another, related way to the identity crisis in urban sociology: by stimulating interest in interdisciplinary scholarship on cities. Though cross-fertilization has long taken place between urbanists in sociology and their counterparts in economics, history, geography, political science, psychology, and planning, it is no coincidence that many university programs in urban studies were initiated 15-20 years ago, during a period when the inner city was officially "in turmoil" and hence the object of intense scrutiny by social scientists. Underlying the concept of urban studies then and now is the assumption that cities are too complex to be understood without the benefit of insights from a variety of academic disciplines. Few urban sociologists today would challenge the wisdom of that assumption; if anything, the commitment to an interdisciplinary perspective has grown stronger over the past two decades (Kasarda and Lineberry, 1980). As a result, however, the boundaries of urban sociology have become more difficult to discern. Reading the literature on some topics, it is almost impossible to say where ideas drawn from urban economics or geography end and those from urban sociology begin.

That the identity crisis afflicting urban sociology has external as well as internal sources seems clear. What remains uncertain is how serious the crisis is. My own review of indicators of institutional vitality suggests a cautiously optimistic prognosis: when measured by the existence of specialized journals, sessions at meetings, job openings, topical conferences, and chapters in collections like this, urban sociology appears to be alive if not entirely well.[2] Such measures may seem superficial, attesting more to rigidity in the way academic turf is divided than to the health of a subdiscipline. I am convinced, however, that urban sociology receives institutional legitimation for a reason. As with other durable specialties in the social sciences, at the core of urban sociology lies a handful of key questions that have guided the efforts of its devotees since the heyday of the Chicago School. The questions are rarely made explicit, but most urbanists exhibit some level of awareness of them.

Reduced to their essentials, the questions are as follows:

(1) What patterns or regularities can be detected in urban organization at a particular point in time?

(2) How does urban organization change over time?

(3) Which factors account for geographic (between-place) and temporal differences in urban organization?

(4) What are the consequences of urban organizational structure and change?

The first two questions are concerned with description (both cross-sectional and longitudinal), the last two with explanation. All four questions have urban organization as their central concept. I use the term *urban organization* in its conventional sociospatial sense, to refer to dimensions of human settlement (density, segregation, population size and composition, degree of urbanization, and so on) that reflect the distribution of people, housing, and functional activities across territorial units. Depending upon the topic under investigation, the territorial units in which urban organization is observed may be as small as city blocks or as large as nations. Similarly, the antecedents of urban organization mentioned in the third question can range from household residential preferences to institutional actions; the consequences mentioned in the fourth may be experienced by individuals, groups, communities, or whole societies.

As these examples indicate, the core questions of urban sociology are quite general in nature. Generality should not be confused with imprecision, however. Like all subdisciplines of sociology, urban sociology is a bit rough around the edges, overlapping with human ecology, demography, political sociology, and other areas of specialization. Yet the questions that define the urban sociological agenda are sufficiently specific to permit the imposition of boundaries on the field. And to the degree that consistent judgments can be made concerning what falls inside and outside those boundaries, an identifiable urban sociology can be said to exist.[3]

WHAT URBAN SOCIOLOGISTS DO

But if urban sociology is so readily delimited, why all the talk of an identity crisis? Because the generality of the guiding questions just discussed is double-edged. While the questions make it possible, in theory, to assert the existence of a singular urban specialty area, they provide enough latitude for many urban sociologies to be practiced. The purpose of this section is to describe briefly some of the more prominent of those sociologies.

I have decided to proceed topically, dividing the field along lines of research. That decision is based partly on convenience, but also on my perception of the field's structure. People studying the same aspect of urban organization tend to employ similar concepts, data, and methods. There is less similarity with respect to theoretical perspective, thanks to the challenges to the Chicago School noted earlier. Even in matters of theory and interpretation, however, certain topical areas are dominated by camps of like-minded investigators. Given this occasional coalescence of research styles and theoretical preferences, a topic-specific focus on what urban sociologists do seems reasonable. Obviously, we do much more than can be covered in one section of one chapter. Out of necessity, then, I limit my review to eight active areas of research.

The first area, which I label *microurbanism* and whose origins can be traced to the writings of Toennies, Simmel, and Wirth, deals with the fourth core question of the field at a microsociological level: What are the consequences of the urban setting for the behavior, values, and psychological well-being of the persons who live there? Examples of research in this area include Lofland's qualitative (1973) analysis of urbanites' adaptations to encounters with strangers in the "public spaces" of a city, and Fischer's (1976; 1982: 45-76) numerous survey inquiries into the relationship between urbanism (typically operationalized as population size) and tolerance, alienation, happiness, and other individual orientations. Also falling within the first research area is the voluminous literature on the density-pathology connection (Baldassare, 1979; Choldin, 1978; Verbrugge and Taylor, 1980). At present there seems to be little evidence, either from the density studies or from those like Lofland and Fischer have conducted, that people are seriously harmed by the scale of urban organization.

A second area of urban sociological research considers the *quality of residential life* experienced by inhabitants of cities. Emerging from the social indicators movement of the 1960s and 1970s, research in this area sometimes makes use of "objective" measures—air pollution readings, crime rates, and so forth (Appelbaum, 1978; Liu, 1976)—but more frequently emphasizes residents' subjective reactions to objective conditions (Marans and Rodgers, 1974; Michelson, 1977). The most common dependent variables are survey items that tap respondents' global (overall) levels of neighborhood and community satisfaction or that ask for evaluations of specific features of the residential environment (service adequacy, housing upkeep, traffic or noise volume, safety, and so on). As in microurbanism research, quality-of-life scholars are ultimately concerned with the personal impact of urban scale and thus address the fourth central question mentioned previously (Baldassare, 1981; Dahmann, 1985; Lee and Guest, 1983).

While the rational expressions of satisfaction examined in quality-of-life investigations appear to be based primarily on the head, research on the *community question*—the third of the eight topical areas—strikes nearer the heart (for reviews, see Hunter, 1978; Suttles, 1972; Wellman and Leighton, 1979). Since the founding of sociology, the effects of the urban setting have been gauged in part by assessing residents' sentiments toward and ties to their localities. The most common way to accomplish this has been through ethnographic observation of life in a single neighborhood (Gans, 1962, 1967; Kornblum, 1974; Suttles, 1968). Over the past two decades, however, the sample survey has gained ground, if not caught up entirely (Fischer, 1982; Guest and Lee, 1983; Hunter, 1974; Kasarda and Janowitz, 1974; Wellman, 1979).

Regardless of methodological strategy, research in this third area suggests that attachment to community is highly variable, depending upon one's investment or stake in a particular location (through home ownership, child rearing, and so on), the presence of an issue to bring residents together, the availability of alternative avenues of social integration (such as relations with relatives or co-workers), and a host of other factors. Many scholars have interpreted such variability as a refutation of the decline-of-community thesis: neighborly relations and local solidarities do not inevitably break down in the face of urbanization. Complicating that interpretation is the longitudinal nature of the thesis. With few exceptions (Hunter, 1975; Lee et al., 1984), the evidence brought to bear on the decline of community has been cross-sectional.

The fourth area of inquiry—into *intraurban structure and change*—stresses the description and explanation of urban organization rather than its consequences (see Choldin, 1985; Guest, 1984b; LaGory and Pipkin, 1981; Schwirian, 1974). The principal data source is the U.S. Census, which permits researchers to look at the density gradient, residential segregation, and other facets of population and housing allocation across small spatial units such as census tracts or blocks. In terms of theory, the area continues to be dominated by revised versions of the ecological perspective, although—as will be noted later—several alternative viewpoints are becoming popular.

Illustrative of this area is a substantial body of research on neighborhood change (see Schwirian, 1983). Some investigations, such as those conducted by Choldin and Hanson (1982) and Guest (1973), have tested the idea that neighborhoods pass through a standard sequence of stages—or a life cycle—in density, SES composition, and housing stock as they mature. A larger number of studies (reviewed by Aldrich, 1975) have employed the ecological concept of succession, usually to examine racial patterns. In light of recent findings, it appears that certain of the generalizations about racial change based on these studies may be historically and geographically specific (Lee, 1985; Lee et al., 1985). Furthermore, the generalizations tell us little about the exact mechanisms—demographic processes, household decision making, and the like—through which changes in the internal structure of a city take place.

Traditionally, the fifth and sixth topical areas in urban sociology—here referred to as *city growth* (concerned with changes in the size of individual places) and *urban redistribution* (concerned with population shifts between and within larger territorial units such as metropolises, regions, or countries; see Kasarda, 1980)—have resembled the work on neighborhood change in several respects. Until about 15 years ago, most persons analyzing growth and redistribution addressed the second and third core questions of the field, relying primarily on census data and ecological theory to do so (Hawley, 1971; Taeuber, 1972). Since that time, however, the growth and redistribution literatures have been transformed. Neighborhood change remains largely the domain of ecologists, but political-economic and neo-Marxist interpretations have gained momentum in attempts to explain urban change on a grander scale (Jaret, 1983).[4]

Differences between the conventional ecological perspective and these newer, critical approaches are apparent in work on regional variation in the rate of urban growth. While ecologists characterize population movement from the Frostbelt to the Sunbelt as part of a long-term adaptation process, with greater system equilibrium the beneficial result (Long, 1981; Poston, 1980), urbanists who favor a political economy perspective are less sanguine. They believe such shifting to be a form of uneven development spurred by the desire of footloose corporations to maximize profit, often at the expense of communities and local governments desperate for jobs and revenue (Perry and Watkins, 1977). Similarly, the suburbanization process has been treated by ecologists as a function of improvements in transportation technology and the increasing accessibility of affordable, desirable residential locations (Guest, 1984b; Tobin, 1976). In contrast, neo-Marxists argue that suburbanization reflects "the needs of the capitalist class, the demands of labor, . . . capital accumulation circuits and their mediating infra-structures, and . . . the array of interests organized around the use and exchange of land" (Gottdiener, 1983: 246).

The old urban sociology and the new appear to be achieving a more harmonious blend in the seventh area of research, which deals with *systems of cities* (Chase-Dunn, 1983; Timberlake, 1985; Wilson, 1984). This area rests on an assumption palatable to ecologists and neo-Marxists alike: that urban places do not exist in isolation but are part of some larger division of labor. The issue that has commanded the most interest is the degree of influence wielded by specific cities in a particular (regional, national, global) interurban context. Early investigations had difficulty conceptualizing that influence, and used oversimplified, cross-sectional measures of dominance that captured only a few aspects of a place's position in the urban hierarchy. But during the last five years, long-term regional shifts in the U.S. metropolitan system have been identified on a variety of functional dimensions (South and Poston, 1982), and trade linkages, commodity flows, and other indicators of between-city exchanges have permitted a fine-grained assessment of the different roles played by places within the system (Eberstein and Frisbie, 1982). In terms of synthesizing older and newer perspectives, recent attempts to enhance ecological analyses with insights from world system theory seem especially promising (Meyer, 1986).

In the eighth and final area, research examines *urban institutions* that are related in some way to the spatial distribution of population, housing, and land uses. Institutional investigations touch on many of the same topics as the first seven areas do, but regard the behavior and structure of the institutions themselves as key variables. Examples of work in this mold include efforts to: (1) show how the actions of real estate agents (Pearce, 1979), developers (Feagin, 1983), and government agencies (Shlay and Rossi, 1981) result in residential segregation and other forms of spatial inequality, (2) trace community population growth to the activities of a local business elite or "growth machine" (Molotch, 1976; Logan, 1978; Lyon et al., 1981), and (3) demonstrate the impact of multinational corporations on interurban systems (Cohen, 1981; Hill, 1977). In each of the examples, institutions are considered causes rather than consequences of urban organization, attesting to the area's preoccupation with the third central question of urban sociology. The most obvious exceptions to this rule can be found in the literatures on community power structures and local government policies and outputs (Clark, 1975; Lineberry, 1980), in which—consistent with the fourth question of the field—city characteristics are employed to explain variation in the phenomena of interest.

WHAT URBAN SOCIOLOGISTS SHOULD BE DOING

As the critical comments made so far suggest, there is room for improvement and additional work to be done in each of the eight topical areas. Indeed, eight separate chapters could be written outlining future programs of research. I leave that area-specific task to others, concentrating instead on changes in the conduct of urban inquiry that have the potential for wider impact. Though not relevant to all lines of research in urban sociology, the proposals offered here are intended to benefit a variety of areas. Their cross-cutting character derives from the fact that they tend to be methodological in the broadest sense, that is, they are concerned with how existing questions might be better answered. Because of their methodological orientation, these proposals may seem to set a rather conservative agenda for the field. As I hope to show, however, some of their ramifications are far-reaching.

An initial proposal has to do with the *samples* used in research on microurbanism, residential satisfaction, and community attachment, areas in which individuals normally constitute the cases.[5] While students of macro-level topics enjoy ready access to census information for a large number of places, those of us working at the micro end of the continuum must frequently engage in primary data collection with modest resources. Thus our results wind up being based on analyses of smaller, less demographically diverse samples. Aside from the obvious problems of generalizability that arise, limited, homogeneous Ns make it difficult to answer many interesting questions that require direct comparison of subgroups.

By way of illustration, consider the question of whether women stress different dimensions than men do when evaluating the desirability of their residential environments. A recent article by Shlay and DiGregorio (1985) concludes that they do, and that the criteria of evaluation are further differentiated according to the marital and employment statuses that women occupy. These conclusions were made possible by the authors' prudent choice of sample design. Unfortunately, special steps like stratification and disproportionate sampling, which can be taken to ensure sufficient numbers of respondents for the kinds of subgroup comparisons featured in Shlay and DiGregorio's investigation, have commonly been overlooked. In my opinion, such steps could help fill the gaps in our knowledge left by a long line of low-budget surveys and field studies employing race-, sex-, age- and/or class-homogeneous samples. An alternative strategy—resorting to secondary analysis of the General Social Survey file and other large-sample data sets—could also prove valuable, assuming all of the variables pertinent to the problem at hand have been measured.

The data bases used by urban sociologists are often deficient in capturing temporal variation as well. Even in topical areas that are devoted exclusively to understanding longitudinal phenomena such as neighborhood change and urban redistribution, researchers only occasionally examine shifts between more than two time points or over spans longer than a decade. Consequently, we are restricted to estimating the effects of characteristics measured at t_1 on changes occurring between t_1 and t_2. We learn little about the influence that changes taking place prior to t_1 may have on the $t_1 - t_2$ period, however cumulative or unfolding the process of interest is suspected to be. Temporally limited data can also obscure instances of historical specificity, allowing periods of unusual change to provide the basis for broad generalizations.

Outside of those topical areas with a trend or change focus, my criticism of the length of temporal coverage afforded by our data might appear frivolous, since longitudinal designs of any kind are rare. As noted earlier, few urban sociologists have given the community question the over-time treatment it deserves, despite a supply of t_1 case studies that are candidates for replication at t_2. Similarly, temporal changes in urbanites' interaction styles, psychological states, and reactions to dense conditions—changes theoretically hinted at as a product of successful adaptation to the urban setting—remain largely unexplored by microurbanists.

For one last example of an area that could profit from longitudinal data, I turn to research on the urban organizational influences of lenders, real estate firms, and other institutional actors. In the typical institutional investigation, with observations at a single time point, the likelihood that the behavior of such actors has lagged effects cannot be taken into account empirically. Nor can the existence of any effects be asserted with much assurance, since cross-sectional data leave the direction of causal influence ambiguous: Do lending policies stimulate neighborhood decline or respond to it? Assuming that one could somehow resolve the directional issue cross-sectionally, the magnitude of institutional effects may still change as new legislation or the pressure of public opinion prompts lenders to alter their policies.

Of course, the behavior of lenders could vary across cities or states as well as over time. This possibility leads to another general proposal about samples and data sets in urban sociology: that they be expanded to incorporate a greater variety of *locations* than current practice dictates. My proposal is intended to apply to all areas of research, but with full appreciation that methodological norms differ from one area and style of urban inquiry to the next. Clearly, it would be unrealistic to expect a neighborhood ethnographer to cover as many sites as someone studying segregation patterns with census tract data. Nevertheless, just a one- or two-site increase over the current single-case norm prevailing in ethnographic circles would facilitate comparisons between neighborhoods, substantially enriching the analysis.

Implicit in this recommendation is a concern with several distinct locational dimensions of the data bases employed in urban research. The first dimension is quantity, and my general guideline for the future is straightforward: the larger the number of locations represented, the better. The guideline should be followed both when locations constitute the actual units of analysis—as they normally do in samples of tracts, cities, or metropolitan areas—and when they serve as catchment areas for individuals, institutional actors, and other types of cases.

A second dimension—the range of locations included in a sample—probably surpasses sheer number in importance. In fact, one reason for boosting the locational N is to extend the range of variation in whatever site characteristics happen to be germane to the problem of interest. Yet a large N produces that outcome only accidentally; purposive procedures are necessary to ensure it. Oddly, urbanists have been more likely to truncate than extend the locational range, focusing on inhabitants of certain kinds of housing or neighborhoods or on cities in a single region of the country. Perhaps the most problematic form of truncation is by population size. Do we really want to limit our analyses to the largest (or smallest) places, given the many aspects of community life that are hypothesized to covary with size? Fischer's (1982) investigation of interpersonal networks demonstrates the value of not doing so with respect to at least one topic. By interviewing people living in semirural settings and towns as well as in the major metropolitan centers of Northern California, he was able to test several competing theories of urbanism in a direct and illuminating fashion. More of us need to follow this lead in other areas and for attributes of place besides size.

More of us should also be attempting to build multiple levels of location into our data sets. This objective seems like a natural for urbanists to pursue, since many of the things that we study are found within nested geographic entities—tracts, municipalities, regions, and so on—for which data are plentiful. Furthermore, the objective can be justified theoretically: the dominant perspectives in virtually every area of research hold that "context counts," though social psychologists, human ecologists, and neo-Marxists disagree over how and why it does. Despite such differences of opinion, one would expect the compatibility of the contextual approach with existing data and theory to attract many proponents. To date, however, urban sociologists have been content to relegate contextual analysis to the concluding sections of articles, as a "promising direction for future inquiry."

Suppose for a moment that we decided to practice what is being preached in those concluding sections. What new light could a systematic treatment of context shed on a subject like neighborhood or community satisfaction? Obtaining survey responses from persons living in urban settings throughout the United States, we might discover that levels of satisfaction differ across cities, even after individual- and neighborhood-level predictors have accounted for as much variation as possible. By adding relevant city- or metropolitan-level characteristics to our data file, we could then move beyond a crude demonstration of "total-city" effects to a more sophisticated specification of particular features of the larger context—population size and growth, climate, local taxes, and so forth—that may color residents' judgments of their neighborhoods. In short, a contextual analysis could pay both descriptive and explanatory dividends.

Taking context more seriously is only one of the many innovative approaches that urban sociologists should be encouraged to explore. We need such encouragement to overcome the enduring influence of the Chicago School. In particular, the human ecological paradigm pioneered by the Chicago sociologists has instilled in many of us a series of methodological assumptions and biases that guide our work. The ecological legacy is two-sided. On the positive side, it lends a degree of coherence to the field; on the negative, it blinds us to new opportunities.

One opportunity that remains largely unexploited has to do with the way we conceive of and operationalize place. Implicit in much ecological writing is a view of urban places as "objective" entities, as clearly demarcated territories well represented by census units and data. Despite early objections to such a view (Firey, 1945), only occasional attempts have been made to examine the *subjective* meanings, images, and boundaries associated with various physical locales (Hunter, 1974; Guest and Lee, 1984; Suttles, 1972). The potential of the subjective domain has recently been underscored by Logan and Collver (1983: 432), who contend that "residents' perceptions of what their community and other communities are like are as important to urban theory as the information on objective characteristics on which most urban research is based." If Logan and Collver are correct, city growth, population redistribution patterns, and a host of other phenomena could be fruitfully analyzed as partial functions of areal "reputations."

How do such reputations have an impact on urban organization? Presumably they convey information that increases or decreases the appeal of alternative locations to households, businesses, developers, and other key players in the real estate market. Put differently, subjective aspects of place are likely to affect the decisions made by land-interested actors. When home seekers believe—rightly or wrongly—that a neighborhood has a crime problem, they may elect to look elsewhere. When, on the other hand, a neighborhood is known as a good area for raising children, housing demand there will probably be strong. The place reputations to which home seekers respond come from a variety of sources, but the role played by real estate agents is of particular significance. Agents specialize in reputation management, exaggerating an area's virtues and covering up its blemishes, always with an eye to influencing locational decisions.

Clearly, these decisions are not made entirely on the basis of subjective information; the objective characteristics of a place matter, too. The point is that urbanists know very little about decision-making processes or any of the individual behaviors that collectively produce urban structure and change. This deficiency can be traced to the ecological predisposition toward the macro (read community) level of analysis, which has effectively proscribed reductionism. Fortunately, the normative barrier to micro-analysis appears to be weakening, if recent treatments of neighborhood change (Taub et al., 1984) and residential segregation (Massey and Denton, 1985) are an accurate indication. My hope is that the micro path will become even more heavily traveled by urban sociologists in the years ahead. I do not wish to see the traditional macroscopic orientation abandoned completely in favor of a microscopic one, but rather a better balance achieved between the two.

Growing out of the ecological preference for macro units is a pervasive concern with the *structure* of such units. To the extent that structure refers to relations between entities, a structural emphasis sounds eminently sociological. In urban research, however, structure is usually operationalized as the mean characteristics of places or the distribution of demographic groups, housing types, or functional activities across places. Even some investigations of systems of cities reflect this bias, defining position in the system as a city's rank on internal characteristics rather than as a set of linkages with other communities. Given data limitations, it is unclear what strides can be made toward a truly structural handling of urban structure. In a few topical areas, the concepts and techniques of network analysis may eventually prove helpful (Laumann et al., 1978; Wellman and Leighton, 1979).

Short of drastic conceptual and operational revamping, there are several things that might be done to upgrade standard practice with respect to structure. One is to supplement our analyses of mean structural patterns or changes with a disaggregated look at the number of individual cases that conform to or depart from the mean. Another is to devote more energy to potentially important dimensions of structure that have been neglected in the past. Finally, the value of structural attributes as independent variables should be recognized. Aside from those persons contributing to the microurbanism, quality-of-life, and community-question literatures, most of us tend to think about urban structure primarily as explanandum.

The topic of residential segregation provides an illustration of how these suggestions can be applied. Disaggregating over-time data by region, city, or section of a city could expose variation in the level and trend of racial segregation, forcing researchers to qualify broad generalizations (Lee et al., 1985). Researchers should also be urged to examine the life cycle dimension of segregation as thoroughly as they have the racial dimension, given the dramatic changes in household composition since 1970. The distinctive housing needs associated with each life cycle stage imply that segregation statistics calculated for attributes of the housing stock itself could help us better understand life cycle differentiation in urban areas (see White, 1988). Beyond analysis of such unexplored dimensions, students of segregation should consider some of the consequences the phenomenon is likely to have for individuals, neighborhoods, and larger urban units. For example, while there is speculation about the ways in which residential isolation affects black well-being, such influences are only beginning to be documented empirically (Massey et al., 1987).

The lack of attention paid to structural consequences is actually a manifestation of a more general problem in urban sociology: an emphasis on *description* over *explanation*. Once again, the historical antecedents of the problem lie in the Chicago School, both in the mapping activity of the early ecologists and in the neighborhood and community case studies conducted by their ethnographer colleagues. Having followed in the Chicagoans' footsteps on a few occasions myself, I naturally consider description a scientifically legitimate activity. At the same time, I appreciate the value of theoretical or explanatory frameworks as devices for directing our research efforts and making sense out of the findings those efforts yield. To date, however, most of us have been content to leave urban theory to others. The result is mounting dissatisfaction with the theoretical perspectives currently available.

What can be done about this situation? Because of space limitations, I offer only a handful of general guidelines that are intended to apply to theory creation and revision in more than one area of the field. First, explanations of urban phenomena that synthesize insights from a variety of perspectives should have greater value—and hence be considered a more worthy goal—than those founded on a single perspective. The danger with single perspectives is that they too often rely on single independent variables. In my opinion, the intricacies of urban organization defy such monocausal theories, regardless of whether human ecologists (micro-economic rationality) or neo-Marxists (capital accumulation) have formulated them.

Second, future theoretical work should concentrate on the specific processes or mechanisms through which urban organization is changed and through which it registers its effects. I make this suggestion partly to compensate for the structural overburden that has characterized urban sociology, but partly out of fear that the increasingly idiosyncratic, formless nature of urban places may one day frustrate traditional cross-sectional, community-level approaches, particularly in the study of intraurban population distribution. It remains unclear if our methods are up to the task of detecting ever-fainter organizational detail. We may, however, be able to explicate the underlying processes responsible for shifts in the overall mosaic.

A third suggestion, implicit in the processual thrust being advocated, is that the urban theoretical agenda give high priority to "bringing actors back in." The Chicago ecologists believed that the key actors on the urban scene were individual households that competed for desirable locations under free-market conditions. However accurate this view may once have been, a more sophisticated perspective is now required. As my previous comments indicate, an adequate framework for understanding contemporary urban organization must take into account: (1) institutional as well as individual actors, (2) the types of relationships, ranging from conflict to collusion, that exist between them, (3) the influence that these relations and other elements of the larger context—as perceived by the actors—have on their behavior, and (4) the various ways in which their behavior generates organizational outcomes.

The kind of actor-oriented framework I have in mind rests on the assumption that economic and status interests, which provide the primary behavioral motivation, are normally pursued via political channels and the market place. As Logan and Molotch (1987) argue, however, neither the polity nor the market should be regarded as impartial referees determining which actors succeed in urban space and which fail. To the contrary, both realms are socially constructed; they may set limits on what developers, corporations, neighborhood associations, and other actors can accomplish, but they are shaped and manipulated by these actors as well. This line of thinking, outlined provocatively in Logan and Molotch's (1987) new book, avoids the economic determinisms present in both human ecological and neo-Marxist approaches. Elaborated more fully, it could represent a uniquely sociological contribution to urban theory.

A REALISTIC FUTURE

In light of the preceding recommendations, my position on the state of urban sociology should come as no surprise: There are many things we should be doing differently. But will we? How many of my recommendations are likely to be followed? More to the point, what are the chances that any significant improvements will be achieved in the years ahead? Though I much prefer writing prescriptions for the future to making predictions about it, the questions just raised deserve an answer.

The odds of urban sociologists being enthusiastic innovators may seem rather slight, based on what I have said about the hold maintained on us by the Chicago School. The Chicago influence should not be considered an intellectual straitjacket, however; numerous conceptual, theoretical, and methodological advances have moved us well beyond confinement to a single school or camp. What I find reassuring is that many of the proposals made in the previous section, which should further free us from the limiting aspects of tradition, are already being explored. To the degree that the proposals constitute projections of nascent trends, the prospects for their eventual fulfillment are brighter than they might otherwise appear.

Of course, not all of the suggestions for enhancing urban sociology are equally likely to be acted upon. For a variety of reasons—including the complexity of urban phenomena, deep-seated paradigmatic loyalties, and the inherent difficulty of the task—theory building and revision will probably proceed at a slow pace. In contrast, fairly rapid gains can be anticipated in methodology, contingent (as noted below) on a continuation of funding. Computer-related technological developments have shaped the nature of sociological work in the past, and should do so in the future, permitting samples to be expanded, temporal and locational detail to be incorporated into data bases, and other needed changes in design and analysis to be initiated.

These incidental benefits of the computer revolution serve as a reminder that urban sociologists, like the cities we study, are affected by the milieu surrounding our research. The technological dimension of that milieu is certainly important, but the political dimension is even more critical. As usual, the agenda for urban sociology in the decades ahead will not be set by its practitioners alone: how sympathetic those in control at the national level are to the social sciences will have a decisive impact on funding opportunities and, ultimately, on research topics and styles. Will sources of support dry up, restricting our options to neighborhood observational studies and small-scale surveys? Or, in a more optimistic vein (belied by the discipline's recent track record, some would claim), will abundant funding enable the computers to roll on, perhaps at an accelerating pace? While my crystal ball guarantees a future for urban sociology, it is not powerful enough to reveal which one.

NOTES

1. According to unpublished information provided by the ASA executive office, the number of community section members decreased from 500 in 1975 to 335 in 1986. Over roughly the same period (from 1976 through 1986), the number of faculty members with any kind of urban specialty listed in the *ASA Guide to Graduate Departments* dropped from 416 to 336, or from 10.3% to 8.3% of the total faculty.

2. The *ASA Guide to Graduate Departments* indicates that approximately 53% of all departments ranked urban sociology among their specialty areas in 1986. This figure is actually a few percentage points higher than it was a decade earlier.

3. Employing the four questions as boundary criteria, for example, much of the older work on community power structure—through its neglect of both causes and consequences of urban organization—would fall outside of urban sociology's domain.

4. The lack of interest in neighborhood change among neo-Marxists stems in part from their view of neighborhoods as "residual" phenomena whose viability depends entirely upon the needs of the capital accumulation process (see Molotch, 1979).

5. Although terms like *sample* and *case* crop up frequently in this section, I use them primarily for convenience. My choice of quantitative language is not meant to exclude participant observation research and community studies from the discussion.

REFERENCES

Aldrich, Howard (1975) "Ecological succession in racially changing neighborhoods: a review of the literature." Urban Affairs Quarterly 10: 327-48.
Appelbaum, Richard P. (1978) Size, Growth, and U.S. Cities. New York: Praeger.
Baldassare, Mark (1979) Residential Crowding in Urban America. Berkeley: University of California Press.
Baldassare, Mark (1981) The Growth Dilemma: Residents' Views and Local Population Change in the United States. Berkeley: University of California Press.
Booth, Charles (1902-1903) Life and Labour of the People in London (3rd ed., 17 vols.). London: Macmillan.

Burgess, Ernest W. (1925) "The growth of the city: an introduction to a research project," pp. 47-62 in R. E. Park and E. W. Burgess (eds.) The City. Chicago: University of Chicago Press.

Castells, Manuel (1977) The Urban Question: A Marxist Approach. Cambridge: MIT Press.

Chase-Dunn, Christopher (1983) "Urbanization in the world system: new directions for research." Comparative Urban Research 9 (2): 41-6.

Choldin, Harvey M. (1978) "Urban density and pathology," pp. 91-113 in R. H. Turner, J. Coleman and R. C. Fox (eds.) Annual Review of Sociology, Vol. 4. Palo Alto, CA: Annual Reviews.

Choldin, Harvey M. (1984) "Subcommunities: neighborhoods and suburbs in ecological perspective," pp. 237-76 in M. Micklin and H. M. Choldin (eds.) Sociological Human Ecology: Contemporary Issues and Applications. Boulder, CO: Westview.

Choldin, Harvey M. (1985) Cities and Suburbs: An Introduction to Urban Sociology. New York: McGraw-Hill.

Choldin, Harvey M. and Claudine Hanson (1982) "Status shifts within the city." American Sociological Review 47: 129-41.

Clark, Terry Nichols (1975) "Community power," pp. 271-95 in A. Inkeles, J. Coleman, and N. Smelser (eds.) Annual Review of Sociology, Vol. 1. Palo Alto, CA: Annual Reviews.

Cohen, Robert B. (1981) "The new international division of labor, multinational corporations and urban hierarchy," pp. 287-315 in M. Dear and A. J. Scott (eds.) Urbanization and Urban Planning in Capitalist Society. New York: Methuen.

Dahmann, Donald C. (1985) "Assessments of neighborhood quality in metropolitan America." Urban Affairs Quarterly 20: 511-35.

Durkheim, Emile (1933) The Division of Labor in Society (G. Simpson, trans. and ed.). New York: Macmillan.

Eberstein, Isaac W. and W. Parker Frisbie (1982) "Metropolitan function and interdependence in the U.S. urban system." Social Forces 60: 676-700.

Feagin, Joe R. (1983) The Urban Real Estate Game: Playing Monopoly with Real Money. Englewood Cliffs, NJ: Prentice-Hall.

Firey, Walter (1945) "Sentiment and symbolism as ecological variables." American Sociological Review 10: 140-8.

Fischer, Claude S. (1972) "'Urbanism as a way of life': a review and an agenda." Sociological Methods and Research 1: 187-242.

Fischer, Claude S. (1976) The Urban Experience. New York: Harcourt Brace Jovanovich.

Fischer, Claude S. (1982) To Dwell Among Friends: Personal Networks in Town and City. Chicago: University of Chicago Press.

Form, William H. (1954) "The place of social structure in the determination of land use: some implications for a theory of urban ecology." Social Forces 32: 317-23.

Gans, Herbert J. (1962) The Urban Villagers: Group and Class in the Life of Italian-Americans. New York: Free Press.

Gans, Herbert J. (1967) The Levittowners: Ways of Life and Politics in a New Suburban Community. New York: Random House.

Glenn, Norval D. and Lester Hill, Jr. (1977) "Rural-urban differences in attitudes and behavior in the United States." Annals of the American Academy of Political and Social Science 429: 36-50.

Gottdiener, Mark (1983) "Understanding metropolitan deconcentration: a clash of paradigms." Social Science Quarterly 64: 227-46.

Guest, Avery M. (1973) "Urban growth and population densities." Demography 10: 53-69.

Guest, Avery M. (1984a) "Robert Park and the natural area: a sentimental review." Sociology and Social Research 69: 1-21.

Guest, Avery M. (1984b) "The city," pp. 227-322 in M. Micklin and H. M. Choldin (eds.) Sociological Human Ecology: Contemporary Issues and Applications. Boulder, CO: Westview.

Guest, Avery M. and Barrett A. Lee (1983) "The social organization of local areas." Urban Affairs Quarterly 19: 217-40.

Guest, Avery M. and Barrett A. Lee (1984) "How urbanities define their neighborhoods." Population and Environment 7: 32-56.

Harvey, David (1973) Social Justice and the City. Baltimore: Johns Hopkins University Press.

Hawley, Amos H. (1971) Urban Society: An Ecological Approach. New York: John Wiley.

Hill, Richard Child (1977) "Capital accumulation and urbanization in the United States." Comparative Urban Research 4 (2, 3): 39-60.

Hunter, Albert (1974) Symbolic Communities: The Persistence and Change of Chicago's Local Communities. Chicago: University of Chicago Press.

Hunter, Albert (1975) "The loss of community: an empirical test through replication." American Sociological Review 40: 537-52.

Hunter, Albert (1978) "Persistence of local sentiments in mass society," pp. 133-62 in D. Street (ed.) Handbook of Contemporary Urban Life. San Francisco: Jossey-Bass.

Jaret, Charles (1983) "Recent neo-Marxist urban analysis," pp. 499-525 in R. H. Turner and J. F. Short, Jr. (ed.) Annual Review of Sociology, Vol. 9. Palo Alto, CA: Annual Reviews.

Kasarda, John D. (1980) "The implications of contemporary redistribution trends for national urban policy." Social Science Quarterly 61: 373-400.

Kasarda, John D. and Morris Janowitz (1974) "Community attachment in mass society." American Sociological Review 39: 328-39.

Kasarda, John D. and Robert L. Lineberry (eds.) (1980) "The political economy of cities" (entire issue). American Behavioral Scientist 24: 155-317.

Kornblum, William (1974) Blue Collar Community. Chicago: University of Chicago Press.

LaGory, Mark and John Pipkin (1981) Urban Social Space. Belmont, CA: Wadsworth.

Laumann, Edward O., Joseph Galaskiewicz, and Peter V. Marsden (1978) "Community structure as interorganizational linkages," pp. 455-84 in R. H. Turner, J. Coleman and R. C. Fox (eds.) Annual Review of Sociology, Vol. 4. Palo Alto, CA: Annual Reviews.

Lee, Barrett A. (1985) "Racially mixed neighborhoods during the 1970s: change or stability?" Social Science Quarterly 66: 346-64.

Lee, Barrett A. and Avery M. Guest (1983) "Determinants of neighborhood satisfaction: a metropolitan-level analysis." Sociological Quarterly 24: 287-303.

Lee, Barrett A., R. S. Oropesa, Barbara J. Metch, and Avery M. Guest (1984) "Testing the decline-of-community thesis: neighborhood organizations in Seattle, 1929 and 1979." American Journal of Sociology 89: 1161-88.

Lee, Barrett A., Daphne Spain, and Debra J. Umberson (1985) "Neighborhood revitalization and racial change: the case of Washington, D.C." Demography 22: 581-602.

Lineberry, Robert L. (1980) "From political sociology to political economy: the state of theory in urban research." American Behavioral Scientist 24: 299-317.

Liu, Ben Chieh (1976) Quality of Life Indicators in U.S. Metropolitan Areas: A Statistical Analysis. New York: Praeger.

Lofland, Lyn (1973) A World of Strangers: Order and Action in Urban Public Space. New York: Basic Books.

Logan, John R. (1978) "Growth, politics, and the stratification of places." American Journal of Sociology 84: 404-16.

Logan, John R. and O. Andrew Collver (1983) "Residents' perceptions of suburban community differences." American Sociological Review 48: 428-33.

Logan, John R. and Harvey L. Molotch (1987) Urban Fortunes: Making Place in the City. Berkeley: University of California Press.

Long, John F. (1981) Population Deconcentration in the United States. U.S. Bureau of the Census, Special Demographic Analyses, CDS-81-5. Washington, DC: Government Printing Office.

Lyon, Larry, Lawrence Felice, and M. Ray Perryman (1981) "Community power and population increase: an empirical test of the growth machine." American Journal of Sociology 86: 1387-1400.

Marans, Robert W. and Willard Rodgers (1974) "Toward an understanding of community satisfaction," pp. 299-352 in A. H. Hawley and V. P. Rock (eds.) Metropolitan America in Contemporary Perspective. New York: Halsted.

Massey, Douglas S., Gretchen A. Condran, and Nancy A. Denton (1987) "The effect of residential segregation on black social and economic well-being." Social Forces 66: 29-56.

Massey, Douglas S. and Nancy A. Denton (1985) "Spatial assimilation as a socioeconomic outcome." American Sociological Review 50: 94-105.

McKenzie, Roderick D. 1968. On Human Ecology (A. H. Hawley, ed.). Chicago: University of Chicago Press.

Meyer, David R. (1986) "The world system of cities: relations between international financial metropolises and South American cities." Social Forces 64: 553-81.

Michelson, William (1977) Environmental Choice, Human Behavior, and Residential Satisfaction. New York: Oxford University Press.

Molotch, Harvey L. (1976) "The city as a growth machine: toward a political economy of place." American Journal of Sociology 82: 309-32.

Molotch, Harvey L. (1979) "Capital and neighborhood in the United States: some conceptual links." Urban Affairs Quarterly 14: 289-312.

Molotch, Harvey L. and John R. Logan (1985) "Urban dependencies: new forms of use and exchange in U.S. cities." Urban Affairs Quarterly 21: 143-70.

Olson, Philip (1982) "Urban neighborhood research: its development and current focus." Urban Affairs Quarterly 17: 491-518.

Park, Robert E. (1925) "The city: suggestions for the investigation of human behavior in the urban environment," pp. 1-46 in R. E. Park and E. W. Burgess (eds.) The City. Chicago: University of Chicago Press.

Park, Robert E. (1952) Human Communities: The City and Human Ecology. New York: Free Press.

Park, Robert E. and Ernest W. Burgess (1921) Introduction to the Science of Sociology. Chicago: University of Chicago Press.

Pearce, Diana (1979) "Gatekeepers and homeseekers: institutional factors in racial steering." Social Problems 26: 325-42.

Perry, David C. and Alfred J. Watkins [eds.] (1977) The Rise of the Sunbelt Cities. Urban Affairs Annual Reviews, Vol. 14. Beverly Hills, CA: Sage.

Poston, Dudley L., Jr. (1980) "An ecological analysis of migration in metropolitan America, 1970-1975" Social Science Quarterly 61: 418-33.

Schwirian, Kent P. [ed.] (1974) Comparative Urban Structure: Studies in the Ecology of Cities. Lexington, MA: D. C. Heath.

Schwirian, Kent P. (1983) "Models of neighborhood change," pp. 83-102 in R. H. Turner and J. F. Short, Jr. (eds.) Annual Review of Sociology, Vol. 9. Palo Alto, CA: Annual Reviews.

Shlay, Ann B. and Denise A. DiGregorio (1985) "Same city, different worlds: examining gender- and work-based differences in perceptions of neighborhood desirability." Urban Affairs Quarterly 21: 66-86.

Shlay, Anne B. and Peter H. Rossi (1981) "Keeping up the neighborhood: estimating the net effects of zoning." American Sociological Review 46: 703-19.

Simmel, Georg (1950) The Sociology of Georg Simmel (K. H. Wolff, trans. and ed.). Glencoe, IL: Free Press.

Smith, Michael P. [ed.] (1984) Cities in Transformation: Class, Capital, and the State. Urban Affairs Annual Reviews, Vol. 26. Beverly Hills, CA: Sage.

South, Scott J. and Dudley L. Poston, Jr. (1982) "The U.S. metropolitan system: regional change, 1950-1970." Urban Affairs Quarterly 18: 187-206.

Suttles, Gerald D. (1968) The Social Order of the Slum: Ethnicity and Territory in the Inner City. Chicago: University of Chicago Press.

Suttles, Gerald D. (1972) The Social Construction of Communities. Chicago: University of Chicago Press.

Suttles, Gerald D. (1976) "Urban ethnography: situational and normative accounts," pp. 1-18 in A. Inkeles, J. Coleman, and N. Smelser (eds.) Annual Review of Sociology, Vol. 2. Palo Alto, CA: Annual Reviews.

Taeuber, Irene K. (1972) "The changing distribution of the population of the United States in the twentieth century," pp. 29-107 in S. M. Mazie (ed.) Population, Distribution, and Policy. Research Reports of U.S. Commission on Population Growth and the American Future, Vol. 5. Washington, DC: Government Printing Office.

Taub, Richard P., D. Garth Taylor, and Jan D. Dunham (1984) Paths of Neighborhood Change: Race and Crime in Urban America. Chicago: University of Chicago Press.

Timberlake, Michael (ed.) (1985) Urbanization in the World Economy. Orlando, FL: Academic Press.

Tobin, Gary A. (1976) "Suburbanization and the development of motor transportation: transportation technology and the suburbanization process," pp. 95-111 in B. Schwartz (ed.) The Changing Face of the Suburbs. Chicago: University of Chicago Press.

Toennies, Ferdinand (1957) Community and Society (C. P. Loomis, trans. and ed.). East Lansing: Michigan State University Press.

Verbrugge, Lois M. and Ralph B. Taylor (1980) "Consequences of population density and size." Urban Affairs Quarterly 16: 135-60.

Weber, Adna F. (1899) The Growth of Cities in the Nineteenth Century: A Study in Statistics. New York: Macmillan.

Wellman, Barry (1979) "The community question: the intimate networks of east New Yorkers." American Journal of Sociology 84: 1201-31.

Wellman, Barry and Barry Leighton (1979) "Networks, neighborhoods, and communities." Urban Affairs Quarterly 14: 363-90.

White, Michael J. (1988) Neighborhoods and Residential Differentiation. New York: Russell Sage.

Wilson, Franklin D. (1984) "Urban ecology: urbanization and systems of cities," pp. 283-307 in R. H. Turner and J. F. Short, Jr. (ed.) Annual Review of Sociology, Vol. 10. Palo Alto, CA: Annual Reviews.

Wirth, Louis (1938) "Urbanism as a way of life." American Journal of Sociology 44: 1-24.

13

DEMOGRAPHY

Thomas W. Pullum

University of Texas at Austin

Demography is the study of the causes and consequences of variation and change in human fertility, mortality, and spatial distribution. The field cuts across all of the social sciences as well as several of the health and biological sciences. In the United States, most demographers are members of the Population Association of America (PAA), and internationally they are members of the International Union for the Scientific Study of Population (IUSSP). Most are social scientists; more specifically, they tend to be affiliated by training and employment with academic departments of either sociology or economics. However, in relating the field of demography to the future directions of sociology, it is essential to appreciate that demography is not properly viewed as a specialization within sociology. The field has its origins and continues to receive much of its vitality from the world outside of academia.

This brief chapter will focus on the impact that sociology and demography have had upon one another and may have in the future. To an extent they will be regarded as two overlapping disciplines, although the honor of recognition as a "discipline" is presently bestowed more upon sociology than upon demography. In the United States there are only a couple of doctoral programs in demography, and internationally there are perhaps a handful more. Reference will also be made to the discipline of economics, because it is the other most common disciplinary attachment of demographers and economic paradigms are expected to figure significantly in the future of both demography and sociology.

THE PAST

Historically, demography has two principal lines of descent or ancestry. The older of these is based in the collection and analysis of census data.

Governments have conducted censuses for thousands of years for reasons related to internal politics, taxation, and military preparedness. During the nineteenth century, as more questions came to be asked in censuses and they were conducted more regularly, the emerging central statistical offices in Europe and North America began to make a more thorough use of these data. Means, percentage distributions, rates, and cross-tabulations began to be produced. Sensitivities to patterns of misreporting and underreporting emerged. Techniques and devices (such as the Hollerith card) were developed simply to cope with the sheer volume of data. Many of the data processing and data analysis techniques now used for surveys as well as censuses can be traced to the evolution of the United States and British censuses, in particular, and to their mandatory character and relentless expansion of purpose.

The second line of descent for demography was based on the registration of vital events, particularly deaths. A census counts the living; a life table measures the force of mortality, particularly summarized by the average age at death, or the expectation of life, of a synthetic cohort. The life table continues to be the central distinctive method of demography, and appears in many contexts other than mortality, including the study of durations of marriage, breast-feeding, and contraceptive use. Some of the basic ideas of event history analysis and hazard models can be traced back to the life table.

The motivation for the analysis of bills of mortality by John Graunt and others in the mid-seventeenth century was partly scientific curiosity, but to a very considerable extent it was a response to commercial interests. Insurers of lives, sailing ships, and anything else of value needed to calculate expected lifetimes or durations, the present value of future annuities, the future value of present premiums, and so on, in order to be competitive and to make a profit at the same time. Today's actuaries (who must pass the notoriously difficult actuarial examinations) continue to be distinguished from demographers by their more specialized and commercial activities, but there remains a sense of kinship.

The field can also be traced back through the concerns of some political economists, most notably Thomas Malthus in the early nineteenth century. Here again, the interest was a practical one, the consequences of rapid increases in the population of Britain during the early decades of the industrial revolution, but Malthus wrote in terms of general propositions and mechanisms that were more abstract than technical.

Many respected demographers continue to be affiliated with government censuses and the collection and analysis of vital statistics, including mortality, but also data on fertility and nuptiality, migration and immigration, morbidity, disability, and retirement. Other noted demographers began their careers in these technical activities and then shifted more toward the perspectives of sociology and economics.

A point to be stressed is that demography began with the need—defined largely by nonacademic, nonscholarly interests—for the analysis and interpretation of data. The individuals who taught themselves how to analyze and interpret such data gradually became affiliated with academic disciplines, but the government and commercial interests that required their services in the first place have continued to have the same kinds of needs, albeit more sophisticated than ever.

Sociology represents a confluence of many traditions and interests, which is of course a reason for the lack of consensus about a central paradigm. Social workers, social reformers, journalists, social philosophers, social statisticians, or demographers, and other strands and heritages are loosely tied together under the label "sociology." Many students who enter the field lack perspective on its history, and many practitioners seek consensus when there is no particular reason, given the multiplicity of origins, that consensus should be expected or even desirable.

Demography became a legitimate academic specialization within sociology or economics relatively recently. This is particularly true if demography is regarded strictly in terms of the analysis of fertility, mortality, and migration, and distinct from some of the collateral self-identified subdisciplines within sociology, such as marriage and the family, race and ethnicity, stratification, urban sociology, and human ecology, and within economics the study of the labor force. Certainly, one favors the development of links between related specialties, and in practice most individuals identify with several of these specialties. But distinctions and definitions are perpetuated and even enhanced through academic committees, special area reading lists for graduate students, professional associations, journals, and even the chapters of this volume.

At any rate, what we would now label demography did not become a legitimate specialization in sociology departments until approximately the 1920s and 1930s. During those years the first generation of academically based demographers did their graduate study and took their first academic positions. Before them, there is little evidence of such a specialization, and to a large degree these founders were self-taught. Two of the most notable events during this period were the founding of the PAA in 1931 and the establishment of the Office of Population Research at Princeton University in 1936.

The first generation of academic demographers included Kingsley Davis, Philip Hauser, Frank Notestein, Calvin Schmid, Dorothy Thomas, and several others, each of whom subsequently produced many intellectual descendants. (The names given here are representative but not complete. It is impossible to present a complete list of the "first generation" of academic demographers and difficult to distinguish them from a "second generation.") The founding "sociologist/demographers," in accordance with their own origins and interests, maintained strong nonacademic links and activities. In terms of the character of their contributions, they are difficult to distinguish from some demographers who lacked professorial appointments, such as Irene and Conrad Taeuber, P. K. Whelpton, Clyde Kiser, Louis Dublin, and Alfred Lotka (this list also is incomplete). By and large, the academic demographers were somewhat more concerned with causes and consequences, and somewhat less concerned with measurement and description, but this is a very unreliable distinction. There is no question that the field has broadened and deepened as it has become transformed into a legitimate academic enterprise—even though, as stated earlier, it rarely is regarded as a discipline on a par with sociology or economics.

The content of demography and the reinforcement of one's identification as a demographer have been shaped to a very large extent by the PAA, the IUSSP, and the major journals—*The Milbank Memorial Fund Quarterly* in the early years (from 1923 until it moved its focus to health in the early 1970s), *Population Studies* (begun in 1947), *Demography* (begun in 1968), and *Population and Development Review* (begun in 1975). These associations and journals, and the listings in *Population Index,* probably provide the best working determination of the scope of the field.

If the presidency of the PAA is traced from its beginnings to the present, there has been a gradual shift to individuals with academic affiliations rather than government or foundation affiliations (although, much to the credit of the PAA, the transition has not been complete). There has been a similar shift in the authorship and orientation of the major journals.

The academic status of the field increased during the post-World War II years, with such events as the establishment of professorial chairs in Britain and Australia, the creation of university-based centers for population research, and the involvement of the United Nations, the Ford Foundation, and the National Institutes of Health in sponsoring research and training.

Not until the 1970s was a sociology of population section established within the American Sociological Association. The delay in this event was undoubtedly a reflection of the viability of the PAA. It would be revealing to undertake a comparison of the content of demography as defined by the program of the annual meetings of the PAA and alternatively by the more limited sessions of the ASA Section. We have not done this systematically but have the impression that the differences are not large.

THE PRESENT

Some of the preceding discussion refers to the present rather than the past, but we now turn specifically to the current state of demography and its current relationship to sociology. These comments will be undeniably subjective. We shall not attempt in this brief space to describe findings or concepts that are at the leading edge of current research, as interesting as these are. It will also be impossible to make systematic comparisons with "health indicators," so to speak, from other fields; such comparisons may emerge from this volume as a whole. Rather, we shall review a few of the indicators and issues that seem most relevant.

Much of the strength of demography resides in its techniques for data analysis. In some ways it serves as a conduit through which techniques developed by statisticians and biostatisticians make their way into mainstream sociology. Because demography is indisputably one of the most quantitative fields practiced within sociology, there is a tendency for demographers to serve as resident experts in the analysis of quantitative data and to teach courses on the methods of social statistics. This simple reality facilitates the diffusion process. Log linear models and hazard models are recent examples of procedures that, although not originated by demographers, are used more in demographic applications.

Organizations that exist primarily in order to monitor or measure demographic variables have contributed to general methodology. For example, the World Fertility Survey (WFS), an international research program that extended from 1972 to 1984, produced estimates of sample design effects in most of its surveys. WFS sponsored the development of a computer program for design effects that could be applied to more general surveys. This was a significant potential contribution to social survey methodology in general, because most survey researchers in sociology (in accordance with the computer packages they use) completely ignore the loss of efficiency of multistage cluster samples compared to the ideal of a simple random sample. Both the U.S. Bureau of the Census and Statistics Canada have made substantial contributions to quantitative methodology, including data collection procedures, editing and imputation, checks on reliability, data processing, and analysis and presentation.

Demography has a major impact upon sociology simply through data that were first collected primarily for demographic purposes. In some developing countries, virtually the only national surveys ever conducted are related to health, fertility and family planning, labor force activity, and migration. Nearly all countries conduct regular censuses, and many have government-conducted surveys of employment and other demographic indicators similar to the Current Population Survey. Public use samples have been prepared for all the twentieth-century United States censuses except for 1920 and 1930. All these data sets are used by sociologists and economists as well as demographers.

It can be argued that the availability of specific data sets, software, and statistical techniques have a very significant impact on the substantive interests of researchers and on their conceptualization of issues and questions. These artifacts of the research process have been particularly important in the recent exchanges among demography, sociology, and economics.

The most significant of these influences, we believe, has been the progressive shift from aggregates to individuals as the units of analysis. It is possible that this shift indicates the natural development of a scientific field, a steady reduction to smaller and smaller units, as in nuclear physics, that awaits only the tools by which those smaller units can be observed. Alternatively, it may be that the development of data and of computing and statistical procedures has altered our conception of social processes in a fashion that is not altogether beneficial.

When demographic analysis was limited to the use of census and vital statistics data, results were routinely phrased in terms of aggregates, defined by geographical or political criteria, ethnicity or race, age, sex, marital status, occupation, and so on; analysis consisted of examining differentials between these aggregates. Early sociologists, notably Emile Durkheim in his analysis of suicide in Europe, also used such data, sometimes with remarkable insight, and generally with an interest in explanation rather than description. Inferences were made, but usually could not be verified, about processes that link individuals and the aggregate, such as alienation and anomie, diffusion, acculturation, and so on.

In just the past couple of decades, there has been a remarkable increase in the amount of research by sociologists (and even more remarkably, given their origins, by demographers) in which the individual is treated as the unit of analysis. Race and ethnicity, characteristics of the place of residence, and so on, are included in regression analyses and treated solely as individual characteristics, rather than as social identities. The statistical methods do not distinguish between the various levels of aggregation at which the variables are defined; nothing reflects the fact that individuals with shared characteristics tend to reinforce one another's attitudes and behavior. It can be argued that the most *efficient* way to analyze multi-level data is in units at the lowest level of aggregation; the danger is that aggregates at higher levels will be robbed of their social meaning.

The statistical techniques that now dominate sociology and, increasingly, demography, have an additional subtle impact on our conceptualization of social phenomena through their suggestions of causal inference. Instead of seeking patterns of interrelationship, we are now required or at least invited to estimate complex causal structures, sometimes with little concern for the quality and appropriateness of the data, and sometimes with cross-sectional measurements for which the causal logic is very shaky.

Certainly the advances in software and statistical procedures in recent decades have had many beneficial effects. Demographers have made the transition from working with census and registration data, for which statistical variability is not an issue, to working with complex sample data. It is now common for life tables to be prepared with standard errors and for population projections to be accompanied by confidence intervals. Demographic techniques, once a jumble of *ad hoc* procedures developed for a number of specific and different kinds of data, have become more consistent with one another and with accepted statistical methods. However, what we perceive as the steamroller effect of the multifaceted general linear model, with its implicit emphasis on the individual as the unit of analysis and upon a highly structured causal order, threatens to obscure two of the main traditional strengths of demography: the conceptualization of homogeneous aggregates as proper units of analysis and the willingness to describe patterns rather than to force causal inferences from data inadequate for such purposes.

The main positive influence of sociology upon demography at present is in the area of theoretical perspectives and devices. Examples are the notion of the life course in connection with migration and, of course, fertility; the notion of competing roles of women in interpreting the relationship between childbearing and labor force activity; the importance of household dynamics in the definition and projection of households; the importance of the extended family and social identities upon desired family size. Economic concepts have also helped in the interpretation of demographic phenomena such as the post-World War II baby boom and the adoption of family planning in developing countries. Perhaps because of their greater technical sophistication, interpretations derived from neoclassical economics are probably more influential at present than are interpretations based on social influences. This is ironic because there are far more demographers working within the discipline of sociology than within economics.

Although we acknowledge that demography does not in itself have a rich heritage of formal theory, it has contributed important concepts to sociology and related fields. These include the concept of exposure to risk, which has been applied to crime rates; the effect of population density and diversity, measured in different ways, upon adherence to norms; the importance of migration and mobility for other kinds of social and political change; the relevance of the age distribution and population growth for modernization and development.

Finally, we shall suggest some mechanisms by which demography has affected the research and training environment in several departments of sociology. Because of the relatively applied character of demographic research, it has generated a disproportionately large fraction of training programs and research grants and contracts within sociology for at least two decades. In the 1960s, NIMH, and since then, the National Institute for Child Health and Human Development (NICHD) within NIH, have supported several predoctoral training grants. The Hewlett Foundation currently sponsors several training grants for international students, and the United Nations and several foundations provide graduate students with fellowships on an individual basis. Many students who receive support from these programs were attracted to demography after, rather than before, entering graduate school. Other students, particularly foreign students, are admitted to sociology departments precisely because of the demography programs within those departments, with the funding providing an additional inducement.

NICHD, to a lesser extent NSF, and a few other agencies also provide grants and contracts for demographic research. Approximately seven universities in the United States also have center grants for population research from NICHD. Although these grants have a strong interdisciplinary character, at least within the social sciences, and are not administered formally by sociology or economics departments, it is generally these two departments whose members are most active in such centers. These centers are frequently a mechanism by which colloquia, data sets, software, and computing equipment become available for the larger community of social scientists. They also provide a model for the research enterprise that is perhaps more structured than in other specialties, simply because of the process of preparing proposals, writing reports, and meeting deadlines that accompanies funded research.

The applied character of demography has occasionally led to master's and special degree programs within sociology departments. In fact, there is currently a strong movement within demography to strengthen links with business and government, to provide greater legitimation to demographers working in those settings, and to produce more researchers for nonacademic positions. To sociologists at large, this may seem a rather bizarre trend, because demographers are already regarded as perhaps a bit too applied to be fully respectable as academics. In the past, applied master's programs have been fraught with tension with the mainstream program, and such tensions are likely to characterize future programs as well.

THE FUTURE; CONCLUSIONS

Substantively and technically, demography is proceeding on many fascinating research fronts. For example, in the study of fertility, much work concerns the proximate determinants, those mechanisms (mainly marital exposure, contraception, abortion, and breast-feeding) through which socioeconomic variations in numbers of children actually come about. The demography of the family and the household is concerned with articulating the lives of individuals with the formation, modification, and dissolution of households. The analysis of historical data (censuses, registers, genealogies, and so on) is burgeoning and permits a broader analysis of population dynamics than is possible with just contemporary data. American demographers are estimating the flows of undocumented immigration into the United States, its economic consequences, and the patterns of assimilation. Worldwide, there is much research on the impact of high levels of both international and rural-to-urban migration, and also on the determinants of contraceptive adoption and continuation. Demographers are concerned with the consequences of increased life expectancy and with the continuing divergence between the life expectancies of men and women. The impact of early childbearing upon subsequent employment and the interaction between fertility and employment are promising topics of research. This list indicates only some of the areas under investigation.

Rather than describe in any detail the questions that are currently under study, and rather than speculate on substantive directions, we shall conclude with some comments on the future of demography as it is linked to the discipline of sociology. We shall indicate some of the more significant issues that relate to the fact that this large and successful field cuts across several disciplines in content but is often classified institutionally as a subdivision of sociology. Obviously, it is in this part of the chapter that subjectivity will be greatest.

A set of issues concerns the applied character of demography. We offer three related propositions. First, demography derives its vitality from its general use of actual data and its frequent relevance to nonacademic concerns. Second, to the extent that demographers are located within an environment of sociologists, this applied orientation is at some risk of being eroded. Third, the discipline of sociology would be enriched if sociologists would accept—perhaps even welcome—the stimulus of applied research that demographers provide.

As observed earlier, the discipline of sociology is a confluence of several traditions. The enterprise will benefit if a diversity of perspectives is retained, at least broadly, including the simultaneous acceptability of theoretical concerns, on the one hand, and descriptive or applied concerns, on the other. Ideally, these perspectives would coexist in a relationship of mutual reinforcement. However, at least within an institutional context, it can be difficult for a balance to be maintained, and for all fields within the discipline to benefit from this intimate contact.

A pertinent analogy may be drawn to the relationship between statistics and mathematics, or to the relationship between numerical analysis (much of which has moved to the new field of computer science) and mathematics. In most universities, until rather recently, statistics was structurally located within departments of mathematics, but was regarded by mathematicians as a less scholarly field because of its use of actual data, its emphasis on computing and calculation, and its involvement with commercial applications. A true mathematician, like a philosopher, depended only on pencil and paper and reference works. Statisticians, on the other hand, were frustrated by the high level of abstraction of mainstream mathematics. Most of today's departments of statistics emerged as a faction in departments of mathematics; the tensions were too great to permit coexistence. The crude generalization can be made that statisticians who remain in departments of mathematics prefer to be known as probabilists.

The point here is that some costs result because demography is relatively more applied than is sociology as a whole. As seen above, this fact improves the availability of funding, the opportunities for government and commercial involvement, the possibilities for research and training programs, even the marketability of demographers. At the same time, it costs the field some degree of credibility and prestige within a community of scholars that values detachment from worldly pressures. The result is a tension that ideally will enrich both demography and sociology, rather than result in fissions and the creation of academic departments of demography. We would argue that it is this applied versus theoretical tension, rather than differences of content, that occasionally has produced separate degree programs in demography (e.g., at Princeton and for a period at Berkeley).

Another issue concerns the impact of the discipline of economics upon both demography and sociology. This is relevant in the present context because demography serves as a territory from which the competition between the methods and perspectives of economists and sociologists can be observed, and upon which it takes place constantly.

The term *competition* may seem inappropriate to describe the application of alternative methods and intellectual perspectives to the understanding of specific problems. To a considerable extent the boundaries of the various social science disciplines are arbitrary. The same phenomena can and should be approached from a diversity of angles. The concern is that many sociologists, including many who practice demography, appear to be abandoning the sociological perspective, to the potential detriment of demography.

Much of the impact of economics has been highly beneficial, as we have tried to indicate. The concepts of economic rationality, utilities, costs and benefits, and so on, are very powerful. Again, however, the issue concerns the balance of alternative emphases and perspectives and the subtle hierarchy of statuses within the academic world. I am convinced that socially defined aggregates, the core concepts of norms, roles, social influences, and other sociological ideas are every bit as powerful as the ideas of economics. One hopes that demography will foster the integration of these perspectives, rather than the abandonment of one in favor of the other, largely for no reasons other than fashion and superficial technical sophistication.

We emphasize that it is the historical and present diversity of both sociology and demography that we hope will continue. The preceding comments are in favor of a plurality of approaches.

The adoption of new methods within any field should be based on their superiority in producing interpretations and enhancing our understanding. One observes, however, an attraction to increasingly sophisticated methods with no real evidence that they have any payoff. For example, in the analysis of survey data, it is common for analysts to ignore totally any evidence of the unreliability of the responses, to ignore design effects that substantially reduce the effective sample size, not to check for the importance of outliers, and not even to balk at the causal analysis of cross-sectional data—and yet to insist on the use of logistic regression even when the dependent variable is not skewed. Great quantities of computer time are devoted to complex and expensive estimation and controlling procedures when simpler analysis would yield essentially the same results and be more easily interpreted. Where the maxim of Henry David Thoreau might wisely be adopted, we see instead countless colleagues and graduate students who gauge their productivity in terms of thousands of dollars of computer time, inches of computer output, monthly data storage charges, and hours spent at the terminal. Both demographers and sociologists would benefit from starting every analysis at a simple, straightforward level and adding complexity only at the suggestion of well-motivated hypotheses and in proportion to the basic quality of the data.

For nearly two decades, demographers have allied themselves with statisticians in attempting to retain a high level of government activity in the collection, analysis, and publication of demographic data, as this activity has been threatened. They have also participated in numerous presentations to congressional committees and such, arguing for the continued funding of population research. It is hoped that these government activities will continue, and that when they become endangered, this kind of activism will continue. NICHD has supported many data collection activities, including a current survey on household and family structure, questions every June as part of the Current Population Survey, and so on. USAID currently subsidizes demographic and health surveys in many developing countries through the successor to WFS. The United Nations assists in census and household survey activities in many countries. These data collection activities are vital for obvious policy and documentary reasons, but they also provide grist for the mills of many demographers and sociologists as well. It is appropriate to argue for their retention and expansion.

As a concluding summary, it is our assessment that demography is at this time a field of remarkable health and productivity. It has experienced growth of many kinds during the past few decades, and through its alignment with sociology and economics has taken on a more interpretive and explanatory character. Despite this maturation the field remains close to its roots, which lie in the diverse and ever-changing demographic patterns and structures of real populations.

REFERENCES

The few items listed here are not intended to substantiate the interpretations or arguments of this chapter, nor to summarize the content of demography or its overlap with sociology. These are simply a few historical landmarks that help to illuminate the character and growth of demography in relation to sociology.

Freedman, Ronald (1961) The Sociology of Fertility: A Trend Report and Bibliography. Current Sociology X, XI.

Hauser, Philip, and Otis Dudley Duncan [eds.] (1959) The Study of Population: An Inventory and Appraisal. Chicago: University of Chicago Press.

Notestein, Frank (1971) "Reminiscences: the role of foundations, the Population Association of America, Princeton University, and the United Nations in fostering American interest in population problems," in Clyde V. Kiser (ed.) Forty Years of Research in Human Fertility, Retrospect and Prospect. Milbank Memorial Fund Quarterly XLIX, 4 (part 2): 67-84.

14

SOCIAL PSYCHOLOGY
Models of Action, Reaction, and Interaction

Karen S. Cook
Kenneth C. Pike
University of Washington

Why should sociologists be interested in the future of social psychology? Perhaps most sociologists will be persuaded by a historical tradition closely linking these fields and resulting in social psychology becoming one of the foremost areas of specialization within sociology (Rosenberg and Turner, 1981). Even the most ardent structuralist would benefit from a knowledge of social psychology since macro-level theories often rest on either explicit or implicit (usually the latter) social psychological assumptions about individuals and social processes.

Investigating the link between micro and macro levels of analysis, though of great import, is not a new endeavor for either sociology or social psychology. Whether couched in more general terms, such as examining the relationship between sociology and psychology, as was the case in the 1903 Fifth International Congress of Sociology (Jaspars, 1983), or in more specific terms, as in Coleman's (1986) attempt to ground social theory in a theory of purposive action, the issue is essentially social psychological in nature. Social psychology has always regarded the integration of theories concerning individuals and society as its primary task (see Cartwright, 1979; Jaspars, 1983). Thus all sociologists should have an interest in the future direction of social psychological theory and research.

To summarize the history and assess the current trends of an academic field is not easy. These tasks are especially problematic in the case of social psychology because the field has roots in two distinct disciplines. Although the founding of social psychology as a separate field of study is traditionally viewed as coinciding with the publication in 1908 of the first two textbooks, appropriately titled, *Social Psychology* by E. A. Ross, a sociologist, and W. McDougall, a psychologist, its origins are best understood in light of historical developments within its parent disciplines. Space limitations preclude a detailed look at the disciplinary roots of social psychology, however, the interested reader can refer to excellent treatments of this subject by Farr (1983), Forgas (1983), and Pepitone (1981), among others.

Social psychology's current failure to explain Comte's question of how the individual can be both cause and consequence of society is to be found, at least in part, in the parochialism of theorists who have sought to explain social psychological phenomena exclusively in terms of either its individual or social antecedents (Cartwright, 1979). Unfortunately Stryker's comments of 11 years ago remain true today:

> There are now, two social psychologies (ignoring variations within each). Occasionally, these touch and influence one another; more often, they proceed essentially independently of one another . . . the two tend to differ in definition and in execution. For psychological social psychology, the field is defined by its focus on psychological processes of individuals; the task is to understand the impact of social stimuli on individuals. For sociological social psychology, the field is defined by the reciprocity of society and individual; and the fundamental task is the explanation of social interaction [Stryker, 1977: 145].

For significant progress to be made, more social psychologists will have to accept and practice a social psychology defined by Cartwright (1979: 91) as "that branch of the social sciences which attempts to explain how society influences the cognition, motivation, development, and behavior of individuals and, in turn, is influenced by them." This social psychology must also be capable of explaining the behavior of interacting individuals and the structures generated by these interactions.

Our first task is to summarize some of the current trends in the two distinct branches of social psychology. We will highlight those trends that have the potential to inform a more holistic social psychology that truly seeks to explain the linkages between actors and social structures. These complex interrelationships are currently being addressed in different ways within at least four research traditions in social psychology: social cognition, structural symbolic interactionism, social exchange theory, and the tradition often referred to as "social structure and personality." We will briefly sketch the distinctive features of these traditions and comment on their strengths and weaknesses.

CURRENT TRENDS AND HISTORICAL ROOTS

Social Cognition

The dominant perspective in psychological social psychology is cognitive, focusing upon individual-level models of cognitive processing (e.g., information encoding and retrieval, inferential processes such as attribution, as well as the cognitive structures associated with each of these stages in cognitive processing). Psychologists, Markus and Zajonc (1985: 137), argue that the cognitive revolution has impelled "nearly all investigators to view social psychological phenomena from the cognitive perspective. . . . The cognitive approach is now clearly the dominant approach among social psychologists, having virtually no competitors."

The primary aim of theories of social cognition is to explain how people cognize their social world and social relationships (Taylor, 1981). Given this broad scope, it is not surprising that seemingly conflicting processes must be posited. Social cognition must explain not only how a vast amount of incoming information is reduced to manageable levels, but also how those selected bits of information are elaborated so that inferences can be made about a constructed social reality. Research in social cognition can thus be classified in terms of two distinct but supplementary branches: (1) a social representational branch involving its reductionist aspects, and (2) a social-inference branch involving its elaborational aspects (McGuire, 1986).

Cognitively oriented psychologists and social psychologists since the late 1970s have conducted a vast amount of research on cognitive representations, generally termed schemas, and their role in information processing. In a recent review Markus and Zajonc (1985: 163) conclude: "that schemas are multidetermined and multiply activated and that they have diverse and varied consequences depending on the goals of the perceiver and the content of the stimulus information." Thus it becomes readily apparent that the conception of schema cuts across both the representational and social-inference branches of social cognition. Schemas structure incoming information to fit preexisting categories, serving a reductionist function. However, structure fades into process as schematic thought, in combination with memorial and inferential processes, elaborate existing information and help to guide an individual's course of action.

The elaborational aspects of social cognition (i.e., the social inference branch) can best be illustrated by research on attribution, the process of constructing causal explanations for behavior. Attribution is a pervasive activity undertaken by individuals in an attempt to facilitate prediction and control of their complex social environment (Harvey, Weary, and Stanley, 1985). Heider (1958), Jones and Davis (1965), Kelley (1973) and Weiner (1974) all developed theoretical frameworks that can be classified as attribution theories.

While these theories address different aspects of the attribution process, they have several methodological and conceptual features in common. As one would expect of theories promulgated by psychological social psychologists, they have most often been investigated in laboratory experiments, although this need not be the case (Crittenden, 1983). In addition, most of the theory and research concerning attribution could be classified as asocial, conceiving of attributional processes only at the individual or intraindividual level (Hewstone et al., 1985). This critique of attribution theory by sociological social psychologists is, of course, an indictment of the "social" cognition perspective as a whole. Indeed, many psychologists have even questioned the "social" nature of social cognition (Markus and Zajonc, 1985; McGuire, 1986; Taylor, 1981).

For social cognition to make a significant contribution to the task of bridging the gap between microprocesses and macrostructures, the influence of the social context upon ongoing social interaction must be examined. Researchers recently have begun to address this major criticism. For example, within attribution research, several studies have examined the influence of status and role variables (e.g., Hamilton and Sanders, 1981; Howard, 1984; Howard and Pike, 1986); while others (e.g., Fincham, 1985) have investigated attributional patterns in ongoing personal relationships. However, as Howard and Pike (1986: 165) argue:

> Even these recent attempts to incorporate social context are limited . . . focusing on the influence of societal structures on cognition to the virtual exclusion of their influences on normative, moral and affective processes as well as on the relationships between norms, values and cognition. . . . Social psychologists have far to go in developing both theories and research that can adequately address the influence of societal structures on cognition [Howard and Pike, 1986: 165].

Structural Symbolic Interactionism

Symbolic interactionism is one of the main branches of sociological social psychology. The attraction of this perspective is its explicit recognition of the reciprocity of the individual and society. Stryker (1977) views this focus as fundamental, distinguishing sociological social psychology from psychological social psychology. Symbolic interactionism's intellectual development can be traced from the Scottish moral philosophers (Smith, Hume, Ferguson, Hutcheson, and others), through the American pragmatic philosophers (Pierce, Royce, James, Dewey, and particularly, Mead), to early American sociologists (Cooley, Thomas, and others). Space limitations preclude a discussion of these roots; however, readers interested in the genesis and historical development of symbolic interactionism as well as in recent trends are referred to excellent reviews by Meltzer, Petras, and Reynolds (1975) and Stryker (1981).

We will focus upon "structural symbolic interactionism," an emergent synthesis of the insights of symbolic interactionism and role theory (Stryker and Statham, 1985), because it has the greatest potential to help bridge the micro-macro gap in sociological research. Many theorists have attempted to combine insights from these perspectives to varying degrees (e.g., Burke, 1980; McCall and Simmons, 1978; and especially Turner, 1978). Stryker (e.g., Stryker and Statham, 1985) has placed greater emphasis on social structural concerns and has developed the most formalized presentation of these views, thus our discussion draws heavily upon his work. We begin by briefly outlining the strengths and weaknesses of the two distinct, but complementary frameworks, highlighting the comparative advantages of the emergent theoretical synthesis.

Symbolic interactionism. The major consistent appeal of this approach is its explicit linkage of the social person to the social world. Ironically, many question whether or not this goal has been or even is capable of being achieved using a symbolic interactionist framework (e.g., House, 1977; Wilson, 1983). Two major criticisms are addressed by the emergent structural version of symbolic interactionism. (For a summary of recent criticisms, see Stryker and Statham, 1985.) The first, is the failure to address social structure (and thus macroprocesses such as stratification and its implications for the distribution of wealth, power, and status in society) and the subsequent ideological biases that this introduces. The second related criticism is that symbolic interactionists hold an overly dynamic view of human behavior, positing that social structures and roles are continually breaking down and must be negotiated anew in each recurring instance of interaction.

Role theory. Turner (1986: 355) succinctly summarizes the image of the social world held by structural role theorists: "The social world is viewed as a network of variously interrelated positions, or statuses, within which individuals enact roles. For each position, as well as for groups and classes of positions, various kinds of expectations about how incumbents are to behave can be discerned." (For an in-depth analysis of role theory see Heiss, 1981; Turner, 1986.) It is readily apparent that the major advantage of structural role theory is its ability to specify the potential ways in which normative expectations affect behavior.

Structural role theory, however, has limitations owing in part to its ties to structural functionalism. The frequently stated, and major criticism of structural role theory is that it relies on an overly structured view of social life, overemphasizing the influence of norms, roles, and the enactment of normative expectations (Turner, 1986). Thus what is lacking in structural role theory, a realization of the processual, negotiated aspects of social life, is the strong point of symbolic interactionism. Conversely symbolic interactionism's failure to address social structural concerns could be remedied by turning to structural role theory.

The emergent synthesis. Structural symbolic interactionism and, more explicitly, identity theory that is derived from that framework (Stryker and Serpe, 1982; Serpe, 1987) both reflect the fact that social behavior is influenced by structural constraints and by the emerging, dynamic aspects of the interaction process. This synthesis uses the concept of role to link the self and social structure. As Stryker (1983: 209-210) puts it: "It is the idea that persons must be located in role relationships embedded in a larger structure, as well as the more traditional symbolic interactionist idea that persons' behaviors are mediated by self and other meanings derived from social location and interaction, that contains theoretical lessons important to social psychology." (For a detailed statement see Stryker and Serpe, 1982).

In spite of the promise this synthetic framework holds for linking the social person and social structure, much theoretical and empirical work must be completed before this goal is attainable. Although the general framework is well developed, few testable propositions have been advanced. There are also serious methodological issues that must be resolved before progress can be made. Stryker and Statham (1985: 368) note that "few, if any, of the concepts . . . of a structural symbolic interactionism have been adequately measured." As a result, there is a paucity of relevant empirical research (however, see Serpe, 1987).

Exchange Theory

Exchange theory is a framework that links actors and structures. The exchange perspective has deep roots in all of the social sciences including psychology, anthropology, philosophy, sociology, and economics. Different variants of this perspective are based on different underlying assumptions about motivation, cognition, social structure and, in particular, the linkage between microprocesses and macro level structures. Homans (1974), Blau (1964), Coleman (1972), and Emerson (1981) all developed theoretical frameworks that can be classified as social exchange theories. All of these theorists, to varying degrees, emphasized the relations between actors and structures. Homans (1974), for example, at one end of the continuum, focused on the more "subinstitutional" level of analysis and attempted to explain, on the basis of behavioral principles (which Emerson, 1981, later formalized and extended), the processes of formation, maintenance, and the dissolution of social exchange relations. Blau (1964), at the other end of the continuum, developed a much more elaborate theoretical conception of complex exchange systems and the processes that regularize and stabilize exchange (referred to as institutionalization).

A fundamental premise, now accepted by most exchange theorists, is the important notion that exchange relations extend beyond direct, dyadic relations to encompass "indirect" exchange and complex systems or networks of exchange. Until the recent resurgence of interest in social networks, there seemed to be no easy way to bridge the conceptual and empirical gap between "mass" society, organizations, and individual actors, or between formal and informal social structures. Interest in social networks, Seeman (1981: 408) claims, has grown "precisely because the network idea is one that can join social psychological interests in the person with structural interests in the situation and its broader social context." Emerson (1981), to some extent, Coleman (1972), and more recently, Marsden (1982) and Cook et al. (1983), have all contributed to this development within exchange theory.

The aim of current theory is to formulate specific propositions concerning the relationship between exchange processes and the emergence and modification of various structural forms. The most challenging aspect of this task is the specification of the mechanisms, both psychological (on the part of the actors) and sociological (as they relate to structural change and elaboration) that produce particular structural forms, institutions, and alterations in them over time. A related problem is the clarification of the role of norms and values in these processes. Norms, it is widely argued, come into existence to regulate exchange activity, but the specific mechanisms that result in the formation of particular normative structures are not well specified in exchange theory. Development of a theory of values, in particular, specification of the processes that result in the emergence of concrete value orderings and preferences on the part of actors, is also frequently treated as outside the purview of exchange theory.

Social exchange theorists, like economists in this respect, assume the existence of values or preference orderings. A notable exception is the last paper Emerson (1987) wrote, titled "Toward a Theory of Value."

We will briefly comment on some of the current weaknesses of exchange theory. The theory, though often described as a micro-level theory, ironically does not have a very complete model of the actor or of social interaction. Even though all theoretical frameworks must abstract from concrete reality in order to make general statements of some utility, exchange theory, or at least much of the empirical work, has been too narrowly focused on the exchange of resources of direct monetary value. More is often exchanged in the process of social interaction and the symbolic aspects of exchange and information transmission need further examination. Existing models of the actor also include only very crude statements of motivation. If the theory is to encompass actors as well as structures, a more complete investigation of the motivations resulting in exchange processes needs to be undertaken. Two additional weaknesses seem to be paramount. First, the theory offers an incomplete analysis of the mechanisms of structural change, relying too heavily on the notion of power-balancing structural tendencies. Second, as already indicated, the theory does not offer a satisfactory explanation of the emergence of norms that are hypothesized to circumscribe and regulate exchange.

Social Structure and Personality

The final tradition we will mention is known as "social structure and personality" (House, 1977, 1981) or "contextual social psychology" (Pettigrew, 1986). Its proponents not only do greater justice to the study of the impact of culture and structure on individuals, but also provide some insight into the effects of macrostructural factors on micro-level (primarily intraindividual) processes. This tradition connects more directly than some of the other research traditions in social psychology with applied issues (e.g., in family, organizational and urban settings.) Typically, however, it does not focus on interaction or the interdependence between actors, and more often it takes the psychological or social functioning of the individual as its primary dependent variable.

House (1981) notes that research in this area has moved from a very macro and cultural view to a more differentiated and structural view of the relationship between social structure and personality. The former approach emphasized the relationship between characteristics of total societies and unitary conceptions of personality culminating in studies of "national character." The current approach emphasizes the relationship between aspects of social structure and aspects of individual personality (e.g., Kohn and Schooler, 1983).

House (1981) and others, have noted major flaws in the theoretical and empirical work on "national character" or "culture and personality." These flaws include: the failure to collect systematic and representative data; the application of theories of personality development to social and cultural data; and, perhaps most importantly, "students of culture and personality had largely *assumed* that which they purportedly were to *demonstrate* empirically" (House, 1981: 534, emphasis in original). In no small part these criticisms resulted in a decline of work in this area as noted by House (1981). This need not be the case, however. House (1981) convincingly argues that (1) delineating the major theoretical variables; (2) specifying the causal mechanisms through which social structure exerts its influence on personality and behavior; and (3) examining the cognitive processes through which individuals respond to the proximate effects of social structure can go far in explaining the relationship between social structure and personality.

We must limit our consideration to one representative body of work in this area. While acknowledging the important contributions of others (e.g., Rosenberg and Pearlin, 1978), we will examine briefly the work of Kohn and his colleagues (see Kohn and Schooler, 1982, 1983; Miller et al., 1986). Their work exemplifies the potential contributions an empirically valid theory of social structure and personality can make to social psychology's fundamental task. Kohn and his colleagues have sought to explain how various stratification factors (particularly aspects of occupational conditions and work experience) affect aspects of an individual's personality (particularly self-direction). By continually building upon their findings and using methodological advances that occurred during the course of their research, they have clearly demonstrated how a variety of dimensions of work are related to specific aspects of personality. In so doing, they have not only demonstrated the utility of House's (1981) three analytical principles, but also have revived interest in the field of social structure and personality.

In spite of this reemergence, however, much work remains to be done on the topic of social structure and personality. Even House (1977, 1981) claims that it must establish greater connection with the other major "faces" of social psychology. It is disappointing, but perhaps not surprising, that this has not occurred either within or between disciplinary boundaries. Furthermore, if the current imbalance in research, focusing predominately on how social structure affects personality and not vice versa (House, 1981), is to be seriously addressed, both theoretical and methodological advances will be required.

FUTURE TRENDS IN SOCIAL PSYCHOLOGY

Moving Beyond Cognition: Affect, Emotions, and Motivation

Jones (1985: 82) argues that "there have been peaks and valleys in the emphasis on cognitive factors and that, relative to earlier periods, social psychology has been undergoing its own less dramatic cognitive revolution since the ascendance of attributional approaches in the late 1960's." The increasing focus on the more cognitive aspects of behavior in all likelihood will persist into the next decade as investigators develop more complete models of cognitive processing. However, Jones (1985: 93) predicts that "the role of affect is likely to receive greater attention" in the near future, in part, because "the precise relations between cognition, affect and behavior remain very much a mystery." A related trend is the renewed interest in emotions and motivation (see Turner, 1987).[1]

Sociologists and social psychologists working on emotions (e.g., Kemper, Lofland, Cancian, Gordon, Clark, and Hothschild) are generally concerned with examining the role of the emotions in social interaction and the management of work and family relations (see Berg, 1987). Methodologies, as described by Berg (1987), range from highly personal accounts to interview and survey approaches. Substantive tasks include: identifying the rules of emotion work (see Hochschild, 1983), examining gender ideologies in relation to emotions, linking theories of interaction and decision making to the expression of emotions, and specifying the cultural and situational determinants of emotional responses. Kemper (1978) and Gordon (1981), among others, are also interested in studying the links between the domains of physiology and sociology through research on emotions like fear and anger, as well as sentiments such as romantic love and jealousy.

As McMahon (1984) suggests, the early study of social psychology was dominated by a heavy emphasis on trait theories and studies of the motivational properties of these "socially acquired internal traits." It is interesting that as the next decade approaches social psychologists and sociologists like Turner (1987) are expressing renewed interest in motivational dynamics. McMahon (1984: 129) notes that "as one might expect, a number of social psychologists within psychology are now studying social motivation (e.g., Deci and Ryan). "The general thrust of this work," she continues, "is that motivation is not a unitary process." Turner (1987: 15) points out that though the topic was abandoned for awhile, "Brody (1980) emphasizes, in his review of social motivation, there is almost always a model of motivation in the analysis of cognitive processes; and . . . there is typically an implicit theory of motivation in most sociological approaches to the study of interaction." Turner attempts to develop a composite model of the motivational dynamics of human interaction drawing upon insights from five long-standing theoretical traditions in the social sciences (e.g., psychoanalytic approaches, the phenomenological perspective, ethnomethodology, utilitarianism, and Durkheim's structuralism, among others). Though major problems remain concerning the utility of such models in the construction of testable hypotheses (not to mention measurement issues), the sociological and social psychological study of motivation has certainly gained renewed vigor. Turner (1987: 26) argues that model building activities of this sort represent "one potentially useful strategy for reopening a serious consideration of a topic that has been submerged in sociological theory."

Another notable development in social psychology is the recent formation of a new journal and now, an international, interdisciplinary association concerned with the study of personal relationships. While this trend is linked to Jones' prediction that "affect" will become a more important focus of research than it has been in the past, it may also be the result of an overemphasis in the field in general upon cognition and individual-level models of action (see also Steiner, 1986). Missing in much of this cognitive work, at least that based heavily in psychology, is the concept of interaction or interdependence. Individuals, in these theories, often seem disembodied from the complex web of relations, networks, and structures that engulf them on a daily basis. The notion of different roles or scripts is about as close as some of this work comes to representing the social structural reality of the actors it seeks to analyze.

From Models of Action and Reaction to Models of Interaction

Turner (1986: 2) argues that "the basic unit of analysis for a sociologist is interaction." Steiner (1986: 285), in a commentary addressed primarily to psychologists, claims that "individualistic social psychology should be combined and coordinated with an almost nonexistent social psychology of collective behavior, without which it often provides a distorted picture of the individual's functioning." (The long-standing tradition of work on collective behavior in sociology is rarely noted by psychologists.) For Steiner it is the intellectual climate within the discipline (in this case, psychology) as much as any other factor that accounts for the neglect of collective phenomena.

The recent volume by Kelley et al. (1983) on close relationships is evidence of another influential voice in psychology calling for renewed interest in interaction and interdependence. Even though sociologists have been oriented from the earliest days of social psychology toward the study of groups and other collective phenomena, to a large extent this work has not been influential in psychology (with a few exceptions: Bales' early work; the work of Thibaut and Kelley, 1959, and Kelley and Thibaut, 1978, because they were psychologists; and some of the early work on symbolic interaction, primarily Goffman's work). Steiner (1986: 285) argues convincingly that the "dominant paradigmatic preferences of the field (psychology) are unlikely to change very rapidly in the near future." In his words, "A discipline that highlights the proximal (often internal) antecedents of the individual's behavior in experimental situations, focuses on specific acts of individuals rather than sequences of acts, and relies heavily on self-report data is not likely to encourage scholars who wish to examine the system-like qualities of groups."

An increased understanding of both individual and group-level phenomena is necessary in order to "augment or correct our understanding" of each level (Steiner, 1986: 284). But as Steiner has pointed out in 1986 as well as 1974, "the group is the neglected member of this partnership." One major factor contributing to the neglect of groups or collective phenomena in Steiner's opinion (1986: 264) is the "universally and habitually accepted paradigmatic assumption" of contemporary social psychology, that "actions are performed by individuals rather than by social systems." Steiner (1986: 264) puts the issue even more succinctly: "As statements of Cooley, Murphy and Lewin suggest, discovering the self-sufficient individual may require no less intellectual agility than discovering the invisible group."

The individual, Steiner (1986) argues, is often portrayed simply as "reacting" to the group, not as participating in it. What passes for the study of groups, he contends, is likely to be an examination of the "impact of a collection of people called 'the group' on the thoughts, feelings, and actions of the individual" and less likely to be concerned with the "system-like interpersonal transactions of the people who are called a group (Tajfel, 1972)" (see Steiner, 1986: 264). In short, models of action and reaction abound in social psychology (in sociology as well); there are far fewer models of interaction. Or, in Steiner's (1986: 264) words, "the responding individual is the social psychologist's favorite protagonist."

Bridging the Micro-Macro Gap

Linked to the renewed interest in relationships is the concern, voiced perhaps only in sociology, with understanding the interplay between "micro-level" theory and "macro-level" structures and events. Not only are some social psychologists looking more closely at macro-level phenomena with an eye toward attempting to understand the social psychological underpinnings, but also some macro-level theorists have gained a renewed interest in more sophisticated, less naive conceptions of the social psychological processes that underlie aggregate or group-level and collective phenomena.

The debate over the specific ways in which micro-level theory and macroprocesses relate is a complex one. Turner (1986) recently concludes that talk of linking the micro and macro levels in sociology is "premature." Blau (1987) agrees and goes further to argue that wholly different concepts and theories are required for these different levels of analysis; thus the aim is not only premature, but definitely unobtainable, given current knowledge and theoretical progress (or lack of it) in sociology. Despite these voices of pessimism, the renewed awareness of the general issue of the relationship between micro-level theories and macro-level phenomena is an important development (see also Pettigrew, 1986). Efforts to bridge this "gap" are worthy of pursuit since such efforts may provide more pay-off in the long run for sociology than persistence at the task of constructing ever more complex theories of intraindividual processes.

Examples of this renewed concern with understanding the linkages between various levels of analysis in social psychology are found in Kelley et al.'s (1983) conceptual framework for studying relationships and Pettigrew's (1986) diagram linking levels of analysis. The Kelley et al. (1983) framework (not yet a "theory" of interdependence) includes three levels that could be considered macro, meso, and micro levels to use Pettigrew's (1986) terminology. The framework includes society, relationships, and individuals. It directs attention to interaction processes as well as the macro-level determinants of these processes and incorporates individual-level factors (i.e., intraindividual or personal variables).

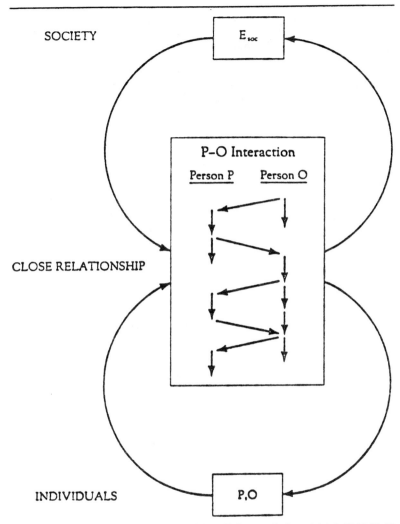

SOURCE: *Close Relationships*, by Harold H. Kelley et al. Copyright © 1983 W. H. Freeman and Company. Used with permission.

NOTE: The interaction within the close relationship both (1) affects and is affected by the social environment (E_{soc}) and the causal conditions of both Person P (P) and Person O (O) and (2) mediates effects from society to individuals and from individuals to society.

Figure 14.1 Schematic Outline of Kelley et al.'s Model of a Close Relationship's Causal Links with Its Social Environment and Personal Causal Conditions

Implications of These Trends

The trends just identified have methodological as well as theoretical implications. Psychologists have tended to rely more heavily than have sociologists upon the experimental method. In fact, symbolic interactionists in sociology, among others, have traditionally categorically rejected this method of inquiry. On the other hand, sociologists, as House (1977, 1981) and Pettigrew (1986) note, have relied more on nonexperimental, survey research methods, especially those identified as belonging to the "social structure and personality" camp. The debate over experimental versus nonexperimental methods is no longer a useful debate in the discipline. Instead, the more important issues relate to data quality. It is generally agreed that what is needed is higher quality data, observational in addition to subjective data, longitudinal in addition to cross-sectional data, and data (perhaps collected on-line) on interactive sequences of events, not retrospective accounts of reconstructed interaction events.

Better data and improvements in our understanding of interaction and interdependence go hand in hand. Data of this type will also give us the chance to begin to sort out both theoretically and methodologically the complex relationships between micro-level phenomena and macro-level events and structures. This is a big agenda for social psychology as practiced by sociologists; but, if Steiner (1986) is correct, this work is much less likely to come from psychologists in the future.

CONCLUSION: THE NEED FOR A RENEWED COMMITMENT TO INTERDISCIPLINARY EFFORTS

Jones (1985: 47) recently concludes that "proponents of both the interdisciplinary and the separate disciplinary approaches have failed in their efforts and social psychology has clearly evolved as a subdiscipline of psychology ... with some resonating pockets of highly compatible interest in sociology." He cites as evidence for this conclusion three facts: (1) the repeated failure of interdisciplinary programs in social psychology in the United States, (2) the dominance of psychologists in the social psychology textbook market, and (3) the disproportionate publication of social psychology in psychology journals (Jones, 1985: 48).[2]

This assessment is based on professional more than on intellectual grounds. The problem with interdisciplinary programs generally may be more a function of university and professional "politics" and "turf" battles than a fundamental incompatibility in the underlying frameworks. There is great merit in interdisciplinary, intellectual ventures despite professional or political obstacles to their success. In Kelley et al.'s words (1983: 503): "We must finally return to a recognition of the interdependence between different levels of knowledge and the mutual interrelatedness among scientific efforts at the individual, close relationship, and societal levels . . . relationship research (for example) can not afford . . . to be isolated from the efforts and results in neighboring disciplines." Neither can other major foci of social psychological inquiry.

House (1977), Pettigrew (1986), Stryker (1977) and others have urged the field to move toward synthesis. What was labeled "the crisis" in social psychology in the 1970s may in fact have resulted more from the increasing specialization and insularity of research traditions within the field, than anything else; or, as Pettigrew (1986) puts it, "the absence of bold theory." In the next decade social psychology may well become truly interdisciplinary. If this is to happen, however, both psychologists and sociologists must be open to discourse and mutual influence. Within sociology the traditional boundaries between levels of analysis must be trespassed as researchers begin to articulate more definitively the nature of the relationship between the individual and society, or, as we have referred to it, the linkage between structure and action.

The biggest shortcoming of this chapter is the omission of other major perspectives in the field that have contributed over the years to the development of social psychology. This is true not only of important work in psychology and sociology, but also of significant work in related disciplines and fields, such as developmental psychology, anthropology, political science, economics, complex organizations, applied sociology, and applied social psychology (Rodin, 1985). In general, the compartmentalization of theoretical and empirical work into distinct, bounded pigeon holes must give way to genuine efforts to build bridges and interdisciplinary links. Without these efforts attempts to create better, more comprehensive theories of social psychological phenomena are ultimately doomed to failure.

NOTES

1. This particular trend is evidenced within sociology in the formation of a new section on the sociology of emotions in the American Sociological Association.

2. Pettigrew (1986) notes that the assessment made by Jones (1985) may be biased because relevant journals in sociology, such as *Symbolic Interaction,* are omitted from his analysis.

REFERENCES

Berg, E. (1987) "New sections probe: emotions and culture." Footnotes 15 (1): 1.

Blau, P. M. (1964) Exchange and Power in Social Life. New York: John Wiley.

Blau, P. M. (1987) "Microprocess and macrostructure," in K. S. Cook (ed.) Social Exchange Theory. Beverly Hills, CA: Sage.

Brody, N. (1980) "Social motivation," pp. 143-168 in M. R. Rosenzwieg and L. W. Porter (eds.) Annual Review of Psychology. Palo Alto, CA: Annual Reviews.

Burke, P. J. (1980) "The self: measurement requirements from an interactionist perspective." Sociometry 43: 18-29.

Cartwright, D. (1979) "Contemporary social psychology in historical perspective." Social Psychology Quarterly 42: 250-258.

Coleman, J. S. (1972) "Systems of social exchange." Journal of Mathematical Sociology 2: 145-163.

Coleman, J. S. (1986) "Social theory, social research, and a theory of action." American Journal of Sociology 91: 1309-1335.

Cook, K. S., R. M. Emerson, M. R. Gillmore, and T. Yamagishi (1983) "The distribution of power in exchange networks: theory and experimental results." American Journal of Sociology 89: 275-305.

Crittenden, K. (1983) "Sociological aspects of attribution." Annual Review of Sociology 9: 425-46.

Emerson, R. M. (1981) "Social exchange theory," pp. 30-65 in M. Rosenberg and R. H. Turner (eds.) Social Psychology: Sociological Perspectives. New York: Basic Books.

Emerson, R. M. (1987) "Toward a theory of value," in K. S. Cook (ed.) Social Exchange Theory. Beverly Hills, CA: Sage.

Farr, R. M. (1983) "Wilhelm Wundt (1832-1920) and the origins of psychology as an experimental and social science." British Journal of Social Psychology 22: 289-301.

Fincham, F. D. (1985) "Attributions in close relationships," pp. 203-34 in J. H. Harvey and G. Weary (eds.) Attribution: Basic Issues and Applications. Orlando, FL: Academic Press.

Forgas, J. P. (1983) "What is social about social cognition?" British Journal of Social Psychology 22: 129-44.

Gordon, S. (1981) "The sociology of sentiments and emotion," pp. 562-92 in M. Rosenberg and R. Turner (eds.) Social Psychology: Sociological Perspectives. New York: Basic Books.

Hamilton, V. L. and J. Sanders (1981) "The effects of roles and deeds on responsibility judgments: the normative structure of wrongdoing." Social Psychology Quarterly 44: 237-54.

Harvey, J. H., G. Weary and M. A. Stanley (1985) "Introduction: attribution theory and research—still vital in the 1980s," pp. 1-4 in J. H. Harvey and G. Weary (eds.) Attribution: Basic Issues and Applications. Orlando, FL: Academic Press.

Heider, F. (1958) The Psychology of Interpersonal Relations. New York: John Wiley.

Heiss, J. (1981) "Social roles," pp. 94-129 in M. Rosenberg and R. H. Turner (eds.) Social Psychology: Sociological Perspectives. New York: Basic Books.

Hewstone, M., F. D. Fincham and J. Jaspars (1985) Attribution Theory and Research: Conceptual, Developmental, and Social Dimensions. New York: Academic Press.

Hochschild, A. R. (1983) The Managed Heart: Commercialization of Human Feeling. Berkeley: University of California Press.

Homans, G. C. (1974) Social Behavior: Its Elementary Forms (rev. ed.). New York: Harcourt, Brace, Jovanovich.

House, J. S. (1977) "The three faces of social psychology." Sociometry 40: 161-77.

House, J. S. (1981) "Social structure and personality," pp. 525-62 in M. Rosenberg and R. H. Turner (eds.) Social Psychology: Sociological Perspectives. New York: Basic Books.

Howard, J. A. (1984) "Societal influences on attribution: blaming some victims more than others." Journal of Personality and Social Psychology 47: 494-505.

Howard, J. A. and K. C. Pike (1986) "Ideological investment in cognitive processing: the influence of social statuses on attribution." Social Psychology Quarterly 49: 154-67.

Jaspars, J.M.F. (1983) "The task of social psychology: some historical reflections." British Journal of Social Psychology 22: 277-88.

Jones, E. E. (1985) "Major developments in social psychology during the past five decades," pp. 47-107 in G. Lindzey and E. Aronson (eds.) The Handbook of Social Psychology (Vol. 1). New York: Random House.

Jones, E. E. and K. E. Davis (1965) "From acts to dispositions: the attribution process in person perception," pp. 219-66 in L. Berkowitz (ed.) Advances in Experimental Social Psychology (Vol. 2). New York: Academic Press.

Kelley, H. H. (1973) "The process of causal attribution." American Psychologist 28: 107-28.

Kelley, H. H., E. Berscheid, A. Christensen, J. H. Harvey, T. L. Huston, G. Levinger, E. McClintock, L. A. Peplau, and D. R. Peterson (1983) Close Relationships. New York: W. H. Freeman.

Kelley, H. H. and J. W. Thibaut (1978) Interpersonal Relations: A Theory of Interdependence. New York: John Wiley/Interscience.

Kemper, T. (1978) A Social Interactional Theory of Emotions. New York: John Wiley.

Kohn, M. L. and C. Schooler (1982) "Reciprocal effects of job conditions and personality." American Journal of Sociology 87: 1257-86.

Kohn, M. L. and C. Schooler [in collaboration with J. Miller, K. Miller, C. Schoenbach, and R. Schoenberg] (1983) Work and Personality: An Inquiry into the Impact of Social Stratification. Norwood, NJ: Ablex.

Markus, H. and R. B. Zajonc (1985) "The cognitive perspective in social psychology," pp. 137-230 in G. Lindzey and E. Aronson (eds.) The Handbook of Social Psychology, Vol. 1. New York: Random House.

Marsden, P. V. (1982) "Brokerage behavior in restricted exchange networks," pp. 201-18 in P. V. Marsden and N. Lin (eds.) Social Structure and Network Analysis. Beverly Hills, CA: Sage.

McCall, G. J. and J. L. Simmons (1978) Identities and Interactions (rev ed.). New York: Free Press.

McDougall, W. (1908) Introduction to Social Psychology. London: Methuen.

McGuire, W. J. (1986) "The vicissitudes of attitudes and similar representational constructs in twentieth century psychology." European Journal of Social Psychology, 16: 89-130.

McMahon, A. M. (1984) "The two social psychologies: post crises directions." Annual Review of Sociology 10: 121-40.

Meltzer, B. N., J. W. Petras, and L. T. Reynolds (1975) Symbolic Interactionism: Genesis, Varieties and Criticism. London: Routledge and Kegan Paul.

Miller, K. A., M. L. Kohn, and C. Schooler (1986) "Educational self-direction and personality." American Sociological Review 51: 372-90.

Pepitone, A. (1981) "Lessons from the history of social psychology." American Psychologist 9: 972-85.

Pettigrew, T. F. (1986) "Toward unity and bold theory." Presented at the Pacific Sociological Association Meetings, Denver.

Rodin, J. (1985) "The application of social psychology," pp. 805-81 in G. Lindzey and E. Aronson (eds.) The Handbook of Social Psychology (Vol. 2). New York: Random House.

Rosenberg, M. and L. I. Pearlin (1978) "Social class and self-esteem among children and adults." American Journal of Sociology 84: 53-77.

Rosenberg, M. and R. H. Turner (1981) "Preface," pp. xv-xxiv in M. Rosenberg and R. H. Turner (eds.) Social Psychology: Sociological Perspectives. New York: Basic Books.

Ross, E. A. (1908) Social Psychology. New York: Macmillan.

Seeman, M. (1981) "Intergroup relations," pp. 378-410 in M. Rosenberg and R. H. Turner (eds.) Social Psychology: Sociological Perspectives. New York: Basic Books.

Serpe, R. T. (1987) "Stability and change in self: a structural symbolic interactionist explanation." Social Psychology Quarterly 50: 44-55.

Steiner, I. D. (1974) "Whatever happened to the group in social psychology?" Journal of Experimental Social Psychology 10: 94-108.

Steiner, I. D. (1986) "Paradigms and groups," pp. 251-289 in L. Berkowitz (ed.) Advances in Experimental Social Psychology (Vol. 19). New York: Academic Press.

Stryker, S. (1977) "Developments in 'two social psychologies': toward an appreciation of mutual relevance." Sociometry 40: 145-60.

Stryker, S. (1981) "Symbolic interactionism: themes and variations," pp. 3-29 in M. Rosenberg and R. H. Turner (eds.) Social Psychology: Sociological Perspectives. New York: Basic Books.

Stryker, S. (1983) "Social psychology from the standpoint of a structural symbolic interactionism: toward an interdisciplinary social psychology," pp. 181-218. in L. Berkowitz (ed.) Advances in Experimental Social Psychology (Vol. 16). New York: Academic Press.

Stryker, S. and R. T. Serpe (1982) "Commitment, identity salience and role behavior," pp. 199-218 in W. Ickes and E. Knowles (eds.) Personality, Roles and Social Behavior. New York: Springer-Verlag.

Stryker, S. and A. Statham (1985) "Symbolic interaction and role theory," pp. 311-78 in G. Lindzey and E. Aronson (eds.) The Handbook of Social Psychology (Vol. 1). New York: Random House.

Tajfel, H. (1972) "Experiments in a vacuum," pp. 69-119 in J. Israel and H. Tajfel (eds.) The Context of Social Psychology. New York: Academic Press.

Taylor, S. E. (1981) "The interface of cognitive and social psychology," pp. 189-211 in J. H. Harvey (ed.) Cognition, Social Behavior, and the Environment. Hillsdale, NJ: Lawrence Erlbaum.

Thibaut, J. W. and H. H. Kelley (1959) The Social Psychology of Groups. New York: John Wiley.

Turner, J. H. (1986) The Structure of Sociological Theory (4th ed.). Chicago: Dorsey.

Turner, J. H. (1987) "Toward a sociological theory of motivation." American Sociological Review 52: 15-27.

Turner, R. H. (1978) "The role and the person." American Journal of Sociology 84: 1-23.

Weiner, B. (1974) Achievement Motivation and Attribution Theory. Morristown, NJ: General Learning Press.

Wilson, J. (1983) Social Theory. Englewood Cliffs, NJ: Prentice-Hall.

PART IV

SOCIAL CONTROL, COMMUNICATION, AND CHANGE

Concern with the study of social change is pervasive in sociology, so a section that includes this emphasis is constructed rather arbitrarily, and could include other arrangements of topics, as for example emphases on the major institutional areas of politics and economics. In a modest size book such as this, coverage has to be selective, and the topics here have been chosen as areas that have timely importance for the discipline.

The study of deviance has declined as an area of attention in sociology in recent times, according to DeFleur and Meier. They trace the rise of interest in deviance and social control, noting the factors that made it such an exciting area during recent decades. After reviewing the current status of the area, they indicate that while some aspects of the theoretical debates have passed, work has been both significant and of high quality.

The major developmental roots of the sociology of law are outlined by Ross and Teitelbaum, who then go on to review the ways in which sociologists have attended to the area over time. The interaction with the legal profession is noted, particularly with the influence of the legal realists. The sociology of law is seen as often involved in the evaluation of legal rules according to their effects in practice, and the ramifications of this in a number of areas of research is noted. The future of the sociology of law is outlined through a review of both pragmatic considerations about the law and how it operates and related sociological concerns and epistemology.

Criminology may be seen as a more narrow concern than a field like the sociology of law or social control, but still, as an area, it has had an important place in sociology in part for the pragmatic reasons of the importance to society. Kercher notes that decades of research have led to knowledge of many factors associated with crime, but few major predictors. He indicates that in the study of crime there has been a growth of methodological and statistical sophistication, and the models for examining causal relationships in the prediction (or explanation) of crime are those at the forefront of social science generally. The predictors of crime are reviewed, and he notes, for example, that "socioeconomic status no longer constitutes the 'master variable' in sociological theories of lawbreaking, particularly in accounting for juvenile delinquency." The meager findings in the prediction of crime are seen as disheartening, but grounds for optimism in the future are seen in the refinement of variables and data collection procedures, the design of studies, and further exploration into the complexities of behavior in the models for prediction.

The study of media and mass communications has not only involved sociologists, but also most social sciences and several professions or applied areas. Interest in the study of the media among sociologists is seen as having declined in the last quarter century, and the features of this decline are examined. Ball-Rokeach indicates how a number of reconceptualizations of broad research questions have generated new theoretical and research efforts that accompany a resurgence of sociological interest in the area.

The field of social change involves a whole range of phenomena, in contrast to substantive areas, and Moore indicates that there cannot be a single, encompassing theory of social change. He notes his interest in a large-scale and long-term perspective, and he gives critical attention to social evolution. More recent sociological attention has focused on "world system theory," which Moore identifies as an alternate approach to large units and processes. Moore examines the concept of social inequality, giving attention to the limitations of using class concepts. After reviewing some large trends, Moore discusses issues on methodology and how these relate to effective analysis of social change.

15

DEVIANCE AND SOCIAL CONTROL
Revisiting Our Intellectual Heritage

Lois B. DeFleur
University of Missouri, Columbia

Robert F. Meier
Washington State University

Within the last decade, trends in the sociological study of deviance and social control have been carefully dissected and analyzed (e.g., Gibbs and Erickson, 1975; Scull, 1984). Generally, these reviews agree, *inter alia*, that the central place of deviance in the field of sociology has been displaced as interest in renowned theories in the area declined. The intellectual excitement that once characterized the study of deviance has gradually but inescapably faded. In this chapter, we present an analysis and diagnosis of this state of affairs. We also outline some directions for future work. However, a warning: We offer absolutely nothing that is new. We advocate not novelty, but a return to basic concepts and perspectives.

It is not difficult to document the displacement of interest in the study of deviance. A surge of excitement during the 1950s and another in the late 1960s and 1970s piqued the intellectual curiosity of many sociologists, but work during most of the 1980s has generally failed to generate a match to that earlier enthusiasm. After decades of dominance by theoretical perspectives and research methods generally identified with the "Chicago school," the 1950s witnessed scholarly work on deviance that was more accurately identified with a "Harvard school," one dominated by consensual models of society and a concern with structures of support and opportunity as they affected deviant behavior. Studies of delinquent gangs and theories of subcultural delinquency appeared in almost staccato fashion. The work of Cohen (1955) was followed quickly by still-influential statements by Miller (1958), Bloch and Neiderhoffer (1958), Cloward and

Ohlin (1960), and Short and Strodtbeck (1965). This work provided a new focus—in the form of new theoretical and empirical questions—and a sense of élan among students of deviance. Soon, this work became routine but the general feeling was that progress was being made. Few claimed to know all the answers but the questions were interesting and the work challenging.

On the heels of this work, another burst of enthusiasm occurred in the late 1960s and 1970s as "new conceptions" of deviance emerged with special attention to legal and social reactions to deviant acts and to political motives of official agencies. Optimism swelled once again. The new perspectives tended to dominate *Social Problems* and the then newly created *Crime and Social Justice*.[1] The papers in these publications, as well as others that contained the labeling and radical orientations, were spirited, provocative, and relevant. They conveyed a sense of urgency and relevancy, two key conditions for success during this era. Many observers surely agreed with Jack Douglas (1970: 368) when he stated that the field of deviance was one of the most creative in sociology, and was then in the midst of a conceptual and theoretical revolution.

Unfortunately, by the 1980s this intellectual excitement waned as certain promises of the labeling perspective and those of the "new criminology" failed to materialize. The concepts of the new approaches were not well-developed or well-defined. For example, few sophisticated propositions were developed by interactionist theorists regarding how labels evolve and are applied and the precise social impact of labels was difficult to trace. With respect to the new criminology, most sociologists embraced positivism too strongly to be swayed by unoperationalized notions like "elite" and "false consciousness." Frustration mounted and critics became more vocal. As Gibbs and Erickson (1975: 39-40) stated, "just as something is missing from older theories, so is there a glaring gap in the reactivist perspective . . . and the new criminologists will not make a contribution unless they recognize that exhortations about power, interest, and conflict do not constitute a testable theory." Other critics characterized the situation as a "chaos of competing factions" mired "in a state of profound epistemological and theoretical confusion" (Scull, 1984: 281). It was apparent that there was and is a void and that new directions would be needed.

Clearly, there is much current work done from a labeling and from a radical perspective, but such work seems now to have become conventional in the sense that it draws little reaction outside of persons already committed to the perspective. The case can be made that labeling theory has now joined the ranks of other theoretical perspectives that could be classified, in Kuhn's terms, as "normal science." The major theoretical and empirical questions have now been posed and scholars working within this tradition are plodding along, cleaning up issues left in the wake of the excitement of an earlier decade. This is not to say that labeling theory is either uninteresting or wrong, but merely that labeling theory is no longer stimulating the debates it once did. Radical theory seems to have fared no better but at least radical theorists address contemporary problems and new political struggles present the possibility of another application of theory.

It is not our intention to join the chorus of critics and doomsayers who bemoan the seeming lack of controversy in the study of deviance and social control.[2] Rather, we intend to examine the problems and prospects in the field of deviance and social control through somewhat different lenses. Our goal is to review some of the intellectual and social foundations of deviant behavior and social control to help us better understand where future development may be possible. We will also review some of the social and political factors that influence the changing character of the study of deviance in sociology.

BIOGRAPHICAL, HISTORICAL, AND POLITICAL FOUNDATIONS

The roots of the sociology of deviance, social control, and social problems are so embedded in the more general history of sociology that it is necessary to identify and discuss that history as it has affected current conditions. It is also necessary to consider briefly the backgrounds of those people who were attracted to sociology and the study of deviance. In other words, it is necessary, following C. Wright Mills's dictum, in *The Sociological Imagination* (1959) to consider both the biographical context of sociology in the histories of its practitioners and the historical context of sociology in the development of that discipline. While the two areas are closely related, we will begin with the biographical, more individualistic, context and move to the former, more general, issue.

Biography and the Study of Deviance

Gouldner (1970) maintained that intellectual developments in a discipline are shaped by the thinkers' world view and culture. He claimed that the *gestalt* of social scientists is a function of the ethos of the broader society as well as their personal experiences. Mills's (1943) well known analysis of the biographies of early sociologists illustrated this view. Mills concluded that the similar individual backgrounds of early sociologists produced a like view of society and conceptions of social problems. These early sociologists were largely either clergymen or the sons of clergymen from rural middle America. They focused their attention on urban problems and their interest extended beyond a simple understanding of these problems to a reform of them (see also Lantz, 1984). A similar analysis by the Schwendingers (1974) concurs with that of Mills, although these authors emphasize more of a "class" influence than a religious or rural one. It is inescapable, however, that early sociologists were recruited from similar social, economic, and political roots.

The work of these sociologists was largely descriptive and often unashamedly reformist. Frequently, their "research" was little more than routine journalism—a mere reporting of "facts" concerning the exposure of undesirable social conditions. By the standards they brought with them, these early sociologists found much to describe, much that was socially "undesirable." Gradually, however, sociologists moved away from the descriptive cataloguing of city gangs, suicide, and other problems and began to develop and use scientific approaches and theoretical frameworks for understanding deviance. The use of empirical and quantitative methods was seen as a better way to define, locate, and understand, as well as treat social deviations and social problems.

By the late 1960s, sociologists were no longer recruited exclusively from the midwest and with lower middle-class, rural and religious backgrounds. More modern sociologists, in fact, have been said to reject conventional religion and conservative and moderate political views (Glenn and Weiner, 1969). It was not surprising, therefore, that by the 1960s and 1970s there was a growing disenchantment with many sociological explanations and ideologies that resided on conservative ideologies. Lantz (1984) characterizes this time as a period when sociological concerns were focused primarily on the ideological underpinnings of the field. It was a time for disciplinary introspection in the form of a rather self-conscious "sociology of sociology" (e.g., Friedrichs, 1970; Reynolds and Reynolds, 1970).

The rejection of conservative discipline orthodoxy coincided with events in the larger society. This was the era of the civil rights and women's movements, and challenges to the legitimacy of the war in Vietnam. It was, in fact, an era of challenges to authority in general, whether that authority resided in political, welfare, religious, or educational institutions. It was an era of the affirmation of persons in previously disvalued statuses (Merton, 1972). Those persons included, among others, blacks, women, welfare recipients, homosexuals, and prostitutes. The sense of political assertiveness was too strong for students of society to ignore. As a result, sociologists turned more of their attention to examinations of the social antecedents and consequences of power and to the operations of the dominant social institutions in American society.

Sociologists in the 1960s and 1970s followed a very different intellectual agenda, one that was developed in an atmosphere of conflict and disruption. Perspectives that assumed a consensus on values just did not fit the society that sociologists were then living in. Perspectives that emphasized the gently restraining role of communities—as well as other primary groups—and the benevolence of the state were rejected outright as false or belonging to an earlier never-to-return-to time. A different conception of society as conflict-ridden was more appropriate to the immediate surroundings of sociologists during this time. And most of the data for the appropriateness of such a conception was found every evening on the six o'clock news. It was from this milieu that the new conceptions of deviance and the critical and radical criminology emerged.

The 1980s provide yet different social conditions for sociologists and their work. Much of the concern with the legitimacy of social institutions has waned, accompanied by a growth of more conservative political milieu. To some, the 1980s signal the return to more traditional values in religion, work, and family.[3] The death penalty has been reinstated in many states accompanied by a call for law and order. During this same period there has been a substantial decline in support for social science research, specifically in deviance and social control, although research to make crime control programs more effective has continued to receive support.

These general conditions have fostered considerable reexamination and criticisms of prevailing paradigms and methodologies in deviance. Some observers of the academic scene claim that sociology as a field, and certainly the study of deviance, is at a crossroads (e.g., Sumner, 1983), particularly since sociological perspectives and methodologies increasingly have been taken over by other fields. The size and quality of many graduate programs in sociology have declined as substantial numbers of the best and the brightest students are attracted to more lucrative, vocationally oriented areas such as business, computer science, and engineering. During this period, many applied fields have also emerged out of sociology and have attracted increasing numbers of students. At least one of these fields, criminal justice, has affected the area of deviance.

The extensive growth in criminal justice research and education took place largely in the late 1970s and 1980s. The exponential growth of criminal justice programs in American colleges and universities in part was a result of federal funds from LEEP—the Law Enforcement Education

Program. Students initially were recruited mainly from law enforcement and crime control agencies with federal grants; students were also recruited from traditional sociological criminology and social deviance who were attracted to the more vocational emphasis found in most criminal justice programs. Faculty from the area of deviance and social control, as well as related social sciences, were also recruited into criminal justice programs and they provided the intellectual foundation for this new field (Senna, 1974).

Programs of criminal justice in the 1970s were generally split between two broad orientations, one a practical, crime control approach that emphasized the training of criminal justice personnel, the other a more academic, research-oriented approach designed to train evaluation researchers and university personnel. These two orientations, often in conflict with one another, provided a good deal of vitality for the field and criminal justice is now being described not only as a rapidly developing academic discipline but as a separate profession as well (Willis, 1983; Adams, 1976; see also report by Greene, Bynum, and Webb, 1982).

While precise generalizations are difficult, it seems fair to characterize much work in criminal justice as mainly descriptive or applied. The substantive focus is in the areas of crime, juvenile delinquency, legal institutions, and corrections. This is reminiscent in content and approach of early sociological research. Over one-half of criminal justice faculty come from sociology and the majority received their degrees during the late 1970s and 1980s (Greene, Bynum, and Webb, 1982: 31). The field is obviously young in terms of its knowledge base as well as its practitioners and still awaiting theoretical growth and direction.

One implication of the development of criminal justice is that intellectual energy has been diverted from the study of deviance and may have contributed to factionalism in the field. As personnel and interest was siphoned off into many of the practical concerns that preoccupy criminal justice specialists, those who remained intellectually wed to the field of deviance had to adjust to fewer colleagues (and students in deviance classes), theory that appeared passé, and a general feeling that the "action" with respect to the topic had moved to another discipline.

But it is not simply the effects of personal backgrounds and recent professional opportunities for sociologists in other fields that affect researchable questions and theoretical frameworks. As Mills (1959: 143) points out, it is the intersection of biography, history, and society that are the coordinate points for a proper study of humanity.

History and the Study of Deviance

The growth of intellectual and practical interest in the sociology of deviance parallels closely the history and growth of sociology itself (e.g., Hinkle and Hinkle, 1954). The first sociology department, at the University of Chicago in 1892, was born at a time of rapid industrialization and urbanization. The city of Chicago was experiencing the consequences of these larger processes, so it was an ideal location from which to study major social problems firsthand.

The problems were easy to identify: housing shortages, health problems, high rates of crime, suicide, and alcoholism to name only a few. Schools were straining to accommodate newcomers and the physical environment in the central city and those areas surrounding the central city area were beginning to show the wear and tear of numerous short-term residents who lacked long-term pride in their temporary homes. Sociology came to be defined—at least in terms of the work that was done by these early sociologists—as the study of the problems of the new industrial, urbanized society. Not content merely to study these problems, sociology was also a form of social reform directed toward the reduction of these problems as well as their understanding (Davis, 1980, chapter 3).

Most of the sociology courses offered in colleges and universities at the turn of the century were centered around pauperism, child labor, poverty, crime, and juvenile delinquency, as well as other social consequences of urbanization and industrialization (see Gibbons, 1979: 20-21). The most righteous writing was saved for chapters on charity and philanthropy. The most influential textbook was probably Charles Richmond Henderson's *Introduction to the Study of the Dependent, Neglected, and Delinquent Classes* (1893).

Sociological concern with social control is directly related to sociological concern with social problems and deviant behavior. Ross began writing about social control in the 1890s. The breakdown of traditional forms of control, found most forcefully in the family and other primary groups, suggested that a replacement must be found if social order was to be maintained. Industrialization and urbanization were not causes of social problems; they merely gave rise to them by destroying older, more intimate forms of social organization. Persons who came to violate group expectations (norms) were simply adjusting to changing social circumstances. Ross never explicitly developed a theory of deviance or social problems, but like other early sociologists, he was a social Darwinist in that he maintained that those who survived socially were able to compete in the market place in legitimate occupations while others languished in marginal

jobs flirting with poverty, the law, and other personal forms of maladjust-
ment, such as alcoholism, mental disorder, and suicide.

While there was a good deal of sociological attention directed toward
pathological individuals and their conduct, there was also growing concern
over the larger, more general conditions that gave rise to those individual
acts. In other words, there was emerging a dual concern both with what
would later be called social deviance (which focuses on individuals and their
behavior) and with social problems (which focuses on roles and institutionalized relations and conditions).

Sociologists usually identified urbanization as some ultimate cause of
social and individual problems, but these sociologists were not about to call
for a radical reform of United States society. The early sociologists were
reactionaries. They searched for alternative forms of social control in the
city, such as Clifford Shaw's Chicago Area Projects for delinquents, but
never called into question the legitimacy of the new industrial order. By
virtue of their personal biographies (Mills, 1943) or their class membership
(Schwendinger and Schwendinger, 1974), these sociologists were committed to the new order, but a new idea or perspective was needed to
capture the sociological meaning of what it was about this new order that
produced social ills.

By about 1920, sociologists had a new perspective—called "social
disorganization" in a book by Thomas and Znaniecki (1919) on problems
experienced by Polish immigrants—to apply to social problems. Empirical
investigation of these problems required firsthand observation, so students
(largely as a result of Henderson's insistence) were sent into the city for their
research. Studies of such diverse social locales as taxi dance halls, hobo
jungles, taverns, slums frequented by delinquent gangs, hotel lobbies,
suicide prevention centers, as well as nondeviant organizations, such as real
estate boards and unemployment offices, were all legitimate arenas in
which to look for the effects of social disorganization. No longer were
individuals pathological; instead groups were disorganized. "The Chicago
School," as Matza (1969) points out, did not rid sociology of the notion of
"pathology." It merely moved it. The concept of pathology had been
effectively transferred from the individual to the group level.

A New Sociological Concept: Social Deviance

The effect of the shift from individual to group pathology was to blur the
distinction between social problems and social deviance, a conceptual
problem that existed well into the 1950s. The social disorganization

approach did not generate strong competition until functionalist and learning approaches developed and subsequently combined at midcentury. The influence of these perspectives was seen in major theoretical work (Cloward and Ohlin [4] as well as an influential textbook, Marshall Clinard's *Sociology of Deviant Behavior* [1957]). Rubington and Weinberg (1971: 126) observe: "Shortly after [Clinard's] book came out, numerous courses, once called either Social Problems or Social Disorganization were renamed Sociology of Deviant Behavior. This renaming attested to a new dilemma— namely, is the notion of deviant behavior to include all that comes under the classification of social problems?"

The distinction between deviance and social problems relates to a lack of conceptual clarity. Deviance has been defined both in terms of departure from norms and in terms of the reactions of others. Social problems are said to represent undesirable social conditions, but there is no agreement on how many must find the condition undesirable before it is "social" or how undesirable the condition must be. The determination of what is deviant presumably goes beyond individual normative preferences about desirable conduct but disputes among sociologists interested in deviance have failed to produce consensus about its meaning. Sociologists interested in social problems usually adopt loose definitions of social problems simply to get on with their lectures or research. They maintain that the determination of what is a social problem must go beyond individual values about long-term desired social conditions but no definition of social problems is able to specify satisfactorily when a problem in the environment becomes "social." This is so because any statement of numbers of persons sharing that perception would be arbitrary. This is also so because we are still not sure how individual deviant acts influence our perception of what is or what should be a social problem. A claim that "Whether deviant acts become social problems depends on the number involved and the degree of conflict engendered" (Tallman and McGee, 1971: 38) merely begs the question.

But surely the determination of what is and what is not a social problem and an act of deviance depends not on our ability to define these concepts, but on events in the larger social world we find ourselves in. As norms and values change, so too does the nature of deviance.

DIRECTIONS IN DEVIANCE AND SOCIAL CONTROL

The directions we propose are, in a real sense, old ones. We maintain that the study of deviance and social control is central to the field of

sociology and to the study of modern society. In this context, we believe
that we need to look to social life for the meaning of deviance and be
sensitive to changing social processes as well as the processes of change and
differentiation in social norms. This requires that we reaffirm the
sociohistorical and sociopolitical contexts of deviance and determine the
character, definition, and context of deviant behavior.

Deviance and Stratification

To explore the sociological context of deviance and social control
requires a commitment to examine what makes behavior deviant and
control "social." Let us illustrate with an example. There is a close
relationship between the nature of stratification and deviance (for a brief
statement on this relationship, see Clinard and Meier, 1985: 324-325).
Following the arguments in Dahrendorf's (1970) classic essay on "The
Origin of Inequality," we believe that the conditions that promote social
differentiation also promote deviance. Dahrendorf reduces the nature of
social stratification to constituent parts—the creation of norms, their
violation, and the exercise of sanctions by persons in power. Dahrendorf
maintains that only by understanding normative expectations and the
sanctioning of social behavior is it possible to understand the nature of
inequalities among individuals and positions. The existence and maintenance of norms through the application of sanctions creates systems of
stratification. Social differentiation, in this view, is, in the language of
measurement, merely an ordinal level phenomenon; social stratification is
an interval-level phenomenon for which distinctions of "higher" and
"lower" (or "ought" and "ought not") are appropriate, depending on the
nature of norms and who has sanctioning power.

It might be said that social control is merely something that a
superordinate does to a subordinate, often with the motivation of obtaining
normative compliance from the subordinate. But the very idea of
"superordinate" and "subordinate" represents ranked differences (i.e., a
system of stratification), and such differences are applicable to both
individuals and to groups. We can, for example, speak of subordinate
persons or subordinate classes. In each instance, we are speaking of the
power to control, to create and maintain norms, and to sanction violations
of those norms.

Students of stratification and students of deviance could profitably ask
many similar questions about social phenomena. For example: Where do
the norms that regulate social behavior come from? Under what historical

conditions do these norms change and do societies change? Why must the near-compulsory character of certain norms be enforced by sanctions? We do not wish to overstate the connection between the study of deviance and stratification, but we believe that the answers to such questions would be helpful in understanding the derivative nature of deviant behavior in various societies, and they would also extend greatly our knowledge about the nature of stratification systems.

In this sense, there is much overlap between questions about the origins of social problems and the origins of specific deviant acts. Studies of the origins of social problems, for example, point to a remarkably similar process to that described here. Gusfield (1963), for one, identifies particular groups with norms prohibiting the consumption of alcoholic beverages and the influence of these groups—largely white, middle-class women—on the passage of the Prohibition amendment. The creation of legal institutions may also follow a similar path of norm promotion. Platt (1969) argues that this type of process is so general it might also account for the creation of legal institutions. He points to groups of moral entrepreneurs, called "child savers," who were very instrumental in the creation and operation of the juvenile court.

Other examples suggest that the general processes by which social problems are identified and those by which forms of deviant behavior are identified are quite similar. These processes point to the central role of power in the form of norm promotion. The relative power of those promoting the norm vis-à-vis those being influenced by that promotion is certainly one aspect. In fact, so general are these processes that sociologists have failed thus far to specify the general conditions under which norms are created and successfully promoted. Surely, a general theory of the origins of deviance and social problems requires more precision than this now trite observation. But, at the same time, it must be recognized that a sophisticated theoretical statement would end up being a theory of deviance, social problems, *and* social control—and that seems too much to ask even of our brightest social thinkers.

Whatever form preliminary theory might eventually take, there is an additional consideration. The concept of social control has *also* often been defined in terms of social influence or norm promotion (see Meier, 1982; Gibbs, 1981, 1986). To the extent that the process of defining social problems and deviance is a process of social control, labeling theorists are clearly correct in their assertion that social control leads to deviance, not the reverse (Lemert, 1972, p. ix). As with the more general theory of the creation of social problems and social deviance, whether such insights can be developed more precisely—to permit empirical tests, for example—

remains questionable. For whatever reason, labeling theorists, who have grappled with such matters for more than two decades have been slow to formulate testable propositions and, as a result, consequent insights of this perspective have remained undeveloped. Of course, other scholars have been free to develop ideas about the interrelationships among the concepts of deviance, social problems, and social control, but to date no agreed-upon theoretical connections have been proposed.

The Context of Deviance and Social Control

As interactionist theorists have maintained, and we agree, an important concern in the study of deviant behavior is understanding how some norms are promoted to a greater or lesser extent than are others. Given the terminology adopted here, this is a processes of normative differentiation and promotion. Such a focus cannot be maintained without a concern with the cultural, political, and historical context in which deviance takes place.

We are fully aware that there are sociologists whose work is focused precisely on understanding deviance in context. Scull (1984) and Piven (1981), for example, are two scholars who have called for locating deviance within the political and historical context of all types of societies.[5] Scull's (1977) own work on the origins of the insane asylum adopts a historical and political perspective. Scull challenges the prevailing view (advanced mainly by Rothman, 1971) that the asylum was a response necessitated by increasing urbanization and industrialization. He accounts for its development by understanding the larger context or in this case the segregative control mechanisms brought about by a highly rationalized capitalistic social order.

Several recent analyses also underscore the importance of examining deviance within a larger context. Troyer and Markle (1983), for example, have traced the sociohistorical and political forces that affect the changing norms and sanctions associated with cigarette smoking. They use this case study as part of their attempt to unravel the more general processes of norm development and the designation of deviant categories of individuals and acts. According to the authors, the smoking controversy is particularly appropriate for an understanding of these general phenomena because it has extended over a long period of time and has evoked responses ranging from vindication to stigmatization. Also, smoking is an unusual controversy in that the behavior in question is distributed across various social class levels and a very powerful economic interest group (the tobacco industry) is actively *opposing* the designation of tobacco consumption as deviant. Thus this debate is rich in sociological detail and it merits further discussion.

A brief history of the controversy reveals its checkered past. In the late 1870s cigarette smoking was strongly condemned and more than 14 states banned smoking entirely. In spite of being considered deviant, cigarette smoking increased in the United States in the early 1900s and attitudes toward it changed between World War I and World War II. As the norms associated with smoking changed, the formal and informal sanctions associated with it were eliminated. Troyer and Markle discuss a variety of sociopolitical and economic conditions that affected these changes but they focus primarily on the economic impact of the tobacco industry, as well as economic interests associated with tobacco advertising in the mass media. By the end of World War II, smoking was acceptable and even socially desirable. This continued until quite recently as teenagers, wishing to emulate adult and "cool" behavior, used chewing tobacco and smoked cigarettes.

Attitudes and behavior began to change in the 1960s and 1970s as the 1965 United States' Surgeon General's Report stimulated a critical examination of tobacco consumption. Conflict and competition among various political and economic interests associated with these issues gained force, and during the 1970s and 1980s, smoking began to be defined increasingly as deviant and was legally banned in many public places. Additional regulation of smoking advertisement is under discussion and attitudes of many people toward smoking have become significantly more negative. With increasing regulation and sanctions, the deviant definition of smoking has increased so swiftly that it has extended to other forms of smoking (e.g., cigars and pipes) as well as chewing tobacco. Smokers are becoming increasingly defensive about their behavior and nonsmokers are becoming bolder in their objections.

The primary thesis of this historical analysis is that changes in definitions of smoking norms and sanctions are not explainable by reference to individual-level conduct, but by examining institutional and organizational forces. Troyer and Markle (1983: 5) maintain that these changes can best be understood as conflicts between competing status groups over the conferral of legitimacy and prestige. What is particularly interesting about the smoking controversy is the finding that sociopolitical and economic forces—and not health fears from the Surgeon General's 1965 report— were decisive in shaping the social response to smoking. Troyer and Markle demonstrate that health reports about the harmfulness of smoking were *not* catalysts for official sanctioning actions toward smokers; rather, sanctioning efforts occurred in response to pressures and lobbying from strong economic groups. In any case, as the authors point out, many products with fewer health claims against them, compared to cigarettes, have been severely regulated and even banned from the American marketplace. The stakes in this controversy are high as opposing groups battle over tactics of norm promotion. If the norms of nonsmokers are officially endorsed, which is largely what has happened thus far, smokers will drop in status and power as they are labeled as "deviants."

As the Troyer and Markle analysis demonstrates, we must continue to track the conflicts between these interest groups in order to understand the milieu in which norms and sanctions change. In these natural social processes we find the larger context of social deviance. This context is one in which conditions and types of people are identified as undesirable, and in which the use of power creates systems of stratification, not in the sense of ranked occupations but in the original meaning of that term as any ranked social differentiation. And, as Sagarin (1975) and others have long argued, much of the meaning of the concept of deviance can be found in conduct and people that are disvalued.

A Concluding Remark

Recent laments about the unhealthy state of sociological conceptions of deviance must surely be tempered not only by the significant amount of work ongoing but also by the high quality of that work. While it is true that there are few spirited theoretical debates now underway compared to earlier decades, this observation alone does not lead logically to the conclusion that the study of deviance and social control is moribund. Rather, we would point out that there are several exciting strands of ongoing research, scholars are still posing interesting theoretical questions, and, in general, work in the field seems to be increasing in methodological and statistical sophistication.

We wish to offer more than idle optimism about future sociological developments. But constructive suggestions must be grounded in that which makes the sociological enterprise distinct among other approaches to the study of deviance and social control: a concern with forces that go beyond the individual or the particular with focus on the historical and political context in which processes of deviance and social control are located. We wish simply to remind each other that there is much that is powerful in sociological explanations and that much of that power is found in basic sociological concepts.

It is less important that one holds allegiance to any particular theoretical approach (e.g., "labeling," "conflict," "control," "learning," "eclectic") than it is that one holds allegiance to getting the big picture. Many colors and types of brushes may be used to construct portraits of the social fabric and even then it may be incomplete or misleading. One image may highlight one aspect to the neglect of another, and sociology is no less susceptible to pentimento than is the art world. There is, in short, much work to do and the efforts of all are welcome.

NOTES

1. *Crime and Social Justice* began publication in 1974 in an effort to revive an earlier criminology journal associated with the School of Criminology at the University of California at Berkeley, *Issues in Criminology*. *Crime and Social Justice* grew out of a commitment to a radical perspective and a concern that this type of work was not being published elsewhere. With respect to *Social Problems*, Spector (1976) has argued that *Social Problems*, rather than merely serving as a publication outlet for labeling theory, actually launched the perspective, and that labeling theory might not have generated the excitement it did without the editorial guidance of Howard Becker at that journal in the early 1960s.

2. The chorus is, by now, an old one and one of us joined for a refrain chorus a few years ago. See Meier, 1980. But concern over the direction should not be confused with criticism of that discipline even if that concern is not coupled immediately with a proposed solution to the problem.

3. The shift to the right has occurred as well in the university community, particularly in terms of fiscal restraints and the general tone of accountability. Collins (1986) traces some discontent in sociology to an increase in the number of sociologists since the mid-1960s and to a continuing specialization among them. This is reflected in the relatively narrow subspecialities of many sociologists. The danger, as Collins (1986: 1355) puts it, is "that we over-particularize our knowledge and we polemicize the localistic ideologies that masquerade as our basis of methodologies and metatheories."

4. The influence of social learning and strain perspectives on Cloward and Ohlin's thinking is reflected not only in the content of their book but on the dedication page as well. The book is dedicated to Robert K. Merton and Edwin H. Sutherland.

5. Collins (1986) stresses the continuing importance of comparative historical analyses for creative work during the next 10 years in general sociology. Such work, Collins speculates, will be directed around issues that deal with the following substantive areas: the relative role of emotion and cognition in social action; the integration of micro and macro approaches to social life; integrated theories of organizations, networks, and markets; and issues dealing with sex and gender.

REFERENCES

Adams, Reed (1976) "Criminal justice: an emerging academic profession and discipline." Journal of Criminal Justice 4: 303-314.

Bloch, Herbert A. and Arthur Neiderhoffer (1958) The Gang: A Study in Adolescent Behavior. New York: Philosophical Library.

Clinard, Marshall B. (1957) Sociology of Deviant Behavior. New York: Holt, Rinehart & Winston.

Clinard, Marshall B. and Robert F. Meier (1985) Sociology of Deviant Behavior (6th ed.). New York: Holt, Rinehart & Winston.

Cloward, Richard A. and Lloyd E. Ohlin (1960) Delinquency and Opportunity: A Theory of Delinquent Gangs. Glencoe, IL: Free Press.

Cohen, Albert K. (1955) Delinquent Boys: The Culture of the Gang. New York: Free Press.

Collins, Randall (1986) "Is 1980s sociology in the doldrums?" American Journal of Sociology 91: 1336-1355.

Dahrendorf, Ralf (1970) "On the origin of inequality among men," pp. 151-178 in Essays in the Theory of Society. Stanford, CA: Stanford University Press.

Davis, Nanette J. (1980) Sociological Construction of Deviance: Perspectives and Issues in the Field (2nd ed.). Dubuque, IA: Brown.

Douglas, Jack (1970) "Deviance and order in a pluralistic society," pp. 367-401 in J. C. McKinney and E. A. Tiryakian (eds.) Theoretical Sociology: Perspectives and Developments. New York: Appleton-Century-Crofts.

Friedrichs, Robert W. (1970) A Sociology of Sociology. New York: Free Press.

Gibbons, Don C. (1979) The Criminological Enterprise: Theories and Perspectives. Englewood Cliffs, NJ: Prentice-Hall.

Gibbs, Jack P. (1981) Norms, Deviance, and Social Control: Conceptual Matters. New York: Elsevier North Holland.

Gibbs, Jack P. and Maynard L. Erickson (1975) "Major developments in the sociological study of deviance." Annual Review of Sociology 1: 21-42.

Glenn, Norval and David Weiner (1969) "Some trends in the social origins of American sociologists." American Sociologist 4: 291-4302.

Gouldner, Alvin W. (1970) The Coming Crisis of Western Sociology. New York: Basic Books.

Greene, Jack R., Timothy S. Bynum, and Vincent J. Webb (1982) Crime Related Education: Faculty Roles, Values and Expectations. Washington, DC: U.S. Department of Justice.

Gusfield, Joseph R. (1963) Symbolic Crusade: Status Politics and the American Temperance Movement. Urbana: University of Illinois Press.

Hinkle, Roscoe C., Jr. and Gisela J. Hinkle (1954) The Development of Modern Sociology: Its Nature and Growth in the United States. Garden City, NY: Doubleday.

Lantz, Herman R. (1984) "Continuities and discontinuities in American sociology." Sociological Quarterly 25: 581-596.

Lemert, Edwin (1972) Human Deviance, Social Problems, and Social Control (2nd ed.). Englewood Cliffs, NJ: Prentice-Hall.

Matza, David (1969) Becoming Deviant. Englewood Cliffs, NJ: Prentice-Hall.

Meier, Robert F. (1980) "The arrested development of criminological theory." Contemporary Sociology 9: 374-376.

Meier, Robert F. (1982) "Perspectives on the concept of social control." Annual Review of Sociology 8: 35-55.

Merton, Robert (1972) "Insiders and outsiders: a chapter in the sociology of knowledge," pp. 9-47 in Varieties of Political Expression in Sociology. Chicago: University of Chicago Press.

Miller, Walter B. (1958) "Lower-class culture as a generating milieu of gang delinquency." Journal of Social Issues 14: 5-19.

Mills, C. Wright (1943) "The professional ideology of social pathologists." American Journal of Sociology 49: 165-180.

Mills, C. Wright (1959) The Sociological Imagination. New York: Oxford University Press.

Piven, Frances Fox (1981) "Deviant behavior and the remaking of the world." Social Problems 28: 489-508.

Platt, Anthony M. (1969) The Child Savers: The Invention of Delinquency. Chicago, IL: University of Chicago Press.

Reynolds, Larry T. and Janice M. Reynolds [eds.] (1970) The Sociology of Sociology. New York: David McKay.

Rothman, David J. (1971) The Discovery of the Asylum. Boston: Little, Brown.

Rubington, Earl and Martin S. Weinberg (1971) The Study of Social Problems: Five Perspectives. New York: Oxford University Press.

Sagarin, Edward (1975) Deviants and Deviance: An Introduction to the Study of Disvalued People and Behavior. New York: Praeger.

Schwendinger, Herman and Julia R. Schwendinger (1974) Sociologists of the Chair. New York: Basic Books.

Scull, Andrew T. (1977) "Madness and segregative control: the rise of the insane asylum." Social Problems 24: 337-351.

Scull, Andrew T. (1984) "Competing perspectives on deviance." Deviant Behavior 5: 275-289.

Senna, Joseph J. (1974) "Criminal justice higher education—its growth and directions." Crime and Delinquency 20: 389-397.

Short, James F. and Fred L. Strodtbeck (1965) Group Process and Gang Delinquency. Chicago: University of Chicago Press.

Spector, Malcolm (1976) "Labeling theory in social problems: a young journal watches a new theory." Social Problems 24: 69-75.

Sumner, Colin (1983) "Rethinking deviance: toward a sociology of censures." Research in Law, Deviance, and Social Control 5: 187-204.

Tallman, Irving and Reece McGee (1971) "Definition of a social problem," pp. 19-58 in E. O. Smigel (ed.) Handbook on the Study of Social Problems. Chicago: Rand McNally.

Thomas, William I. and Florian Znaniecki (1919) The Polish Peasant in Europe and America: Monograph of an Immigrant Group. Life Record of an Immigrant, Vol. 3. Boston, MA: Richard G. Badger.

Troyer, Ronald J. and Gerald E. Markle (1983) Cigarettes: The Battle Over Smoking. New Brunswick, NJ: Rutgers University Press.

Willis, Cecil L. (1983) "Criminal justice theory: a case of trained incapacity?" Journal of Criminal Justice 11: 447-458.

16

SOCIOLOGY OF LAW

H. Laurence Ross
University of New Mexico

Lee E. Teitelbaum
University of Utah

The sociology of law can be defined provisionally as reasoned inquiry into the nature of legal institutions and the relationship of those institutions to their social context. It has its origins in both academic sociology and legal scholarship. Leadership in the development of this field has passed from the ancestral figures of sociology itself—Marx, Weber, and Durkheim—to reform-minded lawyers and, more recently, back to sociologists.

These shifts, to nobody's surprise, reflect the changing interests of these disciplines over time. Early modern sociologists were infatuated with mechanisms of informal social control; insofar as they concerned themselves with law-related matters as in the case of criminality, their focus rested on deviant behavior rather than on the norms defining deviance. For them, as for Weber, Marx, and Durkheim, law itself was not regarded as problematic. During the first half of this century, it was lawyers, such as Pound, Llewellyn, and Felix Cohen, and the Yale school of legal realists who discovered the problematic nature of law and its relation to social institutions. Around the middle of the century, however, the innovative thrust of sociological jurisprudence and legal realism faded into mild acceptance, whereas sociologists gained both interest in, and technical skills to study, the legal system. To a considerable extent, their unique command of investigatory methods maintains sociologists in the forefront of sociology of law as it is currently practiced.

Authors' Note: We wish to thank Joseph Gusfield, George Huaco, Stewart Macaulay, Philippe Nonet, Eric Steele, and Joyce Sterling for their helpful comments and criticisms of this chapter. We, of course, are responsible for all omissions, errors, and infelicities.

Our review finds in the work of the founding fathers of sociology and of the sociological jurisprudence and legal realists who succeeded them the fundamental acknowledgment that law is not only a doctrinal system that defies sociological analysis, but a social institution that invites such analysis. This insight has been the basis of a contemporary renaissance in the sociology of law centering on studies of the empirical effect of legal rules. The current paradigm consists of comparing the reality of law in action with an ideal based on black-letter law. A gap is almost always perceived and traced to the operation of attitudes, structural pressures, and incentives among actors possessing considerable discretion. Our vision of the future of the sociology of law consists in part of a continuation of this paradigm, using more sophisticated quantitative methodology. However, this work seems likely to be supplemented by studies focusing on less formal types of social control and their interaction with state law, and by studies employing microsociological or "interpretive" methodologies that explore more deeply the social construction of legal reality.

SOME INITIAL OBSERVATIONS

Candor requires us to admit that of all sociological specialties, the sociology of law seems the least well established. It also seems to be among the most interdisciplinary of sociological interests. Indeed, its relationship to mainstream sociology is now as hard to define as the relationship of sociology to other disciplines has sometimes been. The American Sociological Association, for example, has no section on the sociology of law, yet the Law and Society Association is a flourishing alliance that includes large numbers of sociologists, along with lawyers, political scientists, and others interested in law broadly understood. No journal of the sociology of law is published in this country, yet more than a dozen periodicals, such as the *Law and Society Review, Law and Policy,* and the *Journal of Legal Studies,* devote considerable space to research and theory in this field (Galanter, 1985: 538).

This curious marginality of the sociology of law is not new. Moreover, its causes have long been identified. More than 40 years ago, Georges Gurvitch observed that "Despite the constantly increasing attention which it has aroused during the last decades . . . the sociology of law still has no clearly defined boundaries. Its various exponents are not in agreement as to its subject, or the problems requiring solutions, or its relation with other branches of the study of law" (Gurvitch, 1942: 1). This problem of defining and delimiting the field remains acutely with us. The sociology of the family or of small groups is limitable because each concerns itself with bounded social systems. The sociology of youth or of stratification can be limited by relying on themes that are subject to convenient, if arbitrary, operationalization (Luhmann, 1985: 2). Convenient limitations to the sociology of law doe not seem readily available, however. Taking a broad view, it appears that all collective and much individual human life is directly or indirectly shaped by law (Rheinstein, 1966). Moreover, to the extent that the study of legal institutions rests upon comparisons over time and across cultures, it is hard—indeed impossible—to separate the sociological study of law from historical or anthropological inquiry.

Finally, the sociology of law necessarily has something of a reflexive character. Law frequently defines categories and then accepts as natural for analysis the categories that it has created. Whereas a sociologist of the family might be able to assume some operational notion of the family, the sociologist of law must remember that the law defines the groups that are regarded as families and then assumes that definition in discourse about the relationship of law to these groups.

We do not propose a path out of this forest; on the contrary, both multidisciplinary complexity and reflexiveness appear to be constituent elements of sociolegal study. We will be concerned to see how these elements insist on manifesting themselves as sociology of law has emerged and will develop.

ORIGINS OF THE SOCIOLOGY OF LAW

It is conventional and justifiable to say that sociology of law did not emerge until the appearance of sociology itself in the late nineteenth century (Luhmann, 1985; Podgorecki, 1974). In respecting that convention, we exclude deliberately a considerable body of writing, such as the work of Montesquieu and Maine, that not only was employed extensively by early sociologists but is identical in kind with sources currently employed in sociological discourse about law.

The ancestral figures in sociology of law were primarily concerned with the relationship between law and social development. Durkheim saw law as derivative from and reflective of social organization. Society developed, in his scheme, from a stage of mechanical solidarity in which cohesion was achieved through universally held norms to one in which integration is founded on mutual interdependence arising out of the division of labor (organic solidarity). This development, essentially one of moral order, can be traced and measured by the shift from simple court systems directly backed by force to more specialized agencies that are concerned with restitutory sanctions and cooperative legal arrangements (Durkheim, 1964).

Although Weber was less overtly committed to judgments sounding in progress, his theory of law implies a relationship between social development and the movement from irrational to rational modes of adjudication. Particularly in Western law, this movement has been toward formal or procedural rationality at the expense of substantive rationality or perhaps "justice."

Weber and Durkheim, as did Maine before them, saw law as a set of institutionalized norms that was distinguishable from, although interdependent with, society. The principal goal of a sociology of law was, accordingly, to derive empirically testable hypotheses about the relation between law and society that could be verified by historical and comparative observation of the contest and direction of variation. Thus occurs the familiar emphasis on understanding the relationship of law and society within an evolutionary framework and typically by reference to normative labels such as "progress."

It is now widely agreed that the central thrust of Marxian analysis is likewise evolutionary. In its original formulation, Marxist theory viewed law as a cultural expression of social structure, primarily in its economic aspects. For bourgeois or capitalist society, it sees the main role of law as the protection of private property. The critical difference between Marxist and other macrosociological theories lies in its insistence upon the repressive or coercive, rather than integrative, character of law. The divisive (class conflict) character of law is emphasized precisely because Marx viewed the integrative emphasis as part of the ideology that helps support the dominant class. But as with other constructions, law itself was largely unproblematic (Cain and Hunt, 1979) and, in regarding law primarily as a manifestation of other relations, the views of Marx, Durkheim, and Weber bear close resemblance.

Pursuit of these classical themes failed, however, to attract the builders of American sociology during the first half of the twentieth century. Informal control, whether in the workplace or the immigrant ghetto, largely monopolized the attention of sociologists during this period. When deviance and crime were addressed, it was without critical inquiry into the legal context defining the wrongfulness of conduct (see Merton and Nisbet, 1971). Those who found themselves in conflict with the law may have arrived there through the operation of overarching social forces: racial prejudice, the system of social stratification, subcultural norms, or the like. The legal system itself, however, figured nowhere in these lists. Whereas the founding fathers may have regarded law as generally unproblematic, early American sociologists tended to think it generally uninteresting as well.

While American sociologists were discovering informal social control, lawyers were discovering the social nature of formal control and, in doing so, they maintained and developed the sociology of law. Two somewhat overlapping lines of thought explored this aspect of law during the first half of this century. The first is the sociological jurisprudence of Roscoe Pound and, in less developed fashion, Benjamin Cardozo.

The classical jurisprudence of the late nineteenth century and early twentieth century largely regarded law objectively—that is, as independent of specific social choices and policies. Law developed deductively ("scientifically") from a body of existing concepts that were a priori valid. It was this scientific or mechanical notion of jurisprudence that Pound denounced, heavily influenced by Jhering's rejection of the jurisprudence of concepts in Germany and by William James's pragmatism in this country.

Pound's sociological jurisprudence starts not with metaphysical propositions about human nature and law, but with an inquiry concerning the meaning of a rule or decision in practice (Pound, 1908). The study of law should accordingly be directed to the "actual social effects of legal institutions and legal doctrines" (Pound, 1912: 513).

Once the controlling force of concepts and deduction was denied, the place of courts as well as legislatures seemed very different. Legal precepts were not to be regarded as certain statements but as general guides to judges, whose duty was now to find reasonable and just solutions to individual cases. Law was thus a social institution that might be improved by intelligent human effort, and the task of judges was to discover the best means of furthering and directing the enterprise of social improvement.

This critique was pursued, in ways that Pound himself did not uniformly admire, by the legal realist movement that once dominated and, in a transformed version, again dominates a segment of academic legal discussion. It is conventional to say, as Karl Llewellyn did at the time, that there was no genuine realist school but only a loosely aligned movement that agreed only in "their negations, and in their skepticism, and in their curiosity" (Llewellyn, 1931). Some of that skepticism went very far indeed. Judge Jerome Frank's reliance on the irrational element in human nature inherent in psychoanalytic theory led him to deny both continuity in law and the possibility of rational adjudication of factual or legal matters (Frank, 1963).

A short-lived but striking aspect of the realist enterprise is the empirical research with which the Yale Law School, in particular, hoped to make its reputation. Those were, it should be said, major research enterprises that Dean Hutchins hoped would show "how the judicial system actually works and how it is affecting the community"; how that system might be reformed to attain "more readily the object for which it had developed"; and "to make clear the part of the law in the prediction and control of behavior." Charles Clark set out to discover the "actual effects of procedural rules on the process of litigation in state and federal courts" William O. Douglas undertook to find the root causes of business failure primarily through investigation of bankruptcy practices.

Most of this research enterprise ended by the mid-1930s, within a few years of its inception, and it has largely been forgotten. In fairness, these studies were not entirely barren. Clark, for example, discovered the modern administration of criminal justice—the routine and expeditious processing of almost all cases, with few jury trials and little time invested in procedural niceties. However, neither Clark nor Douglas did accomplish or could they have accomplished the grandiose plans that they described. More important, the fit between what they found and the specific reform agenda that inspired their inquiries was at best problematic.

Notwithstanding the disagreement between Pound and the realists and the failure of the latter's applied research program, several central propositions emerged from the ferment of the early part of this century that informed the renaissance of sociology of law in the 1960s. Among these were the convictions that law is a means to a social end rather than an end in itself; that law must be viewed and judged in terms of its purpose and results and the fit between them, rather than according to its logical relationship some metaphysical conceptual corpus; and that a priori propositions about the binding force of authority and about the effect of law upon courts and community must be rejected.

THE SOCIOLOGY OF LAW TODAY

Although research activity on the part of the legal realists had largely disappeared by the middle 1930s, their premises reemerged with the renaissance of sociology of law in the 1960s. Their critique of the formalist theory of law was so successful that it now appears self-evident; few lawyers believe that legal rules are entirely determined by logical processes. It is also true that many of the realists themselves, and most legal commentators since, stopped short of denying any independent force to legal forms—that is, to precedent and to logical procedures for employing precedent.

The view that judicial decisions are significantly influenced, but not wholly determined, by existing doctrine generated many of the central concerns of modern sociology of law. At a general level, the issue was often framed in terms of the extent to which the legal system could be regarded as autonomous. Everyone seems to agree that the question is one of relative autonomy; law is generated to some extent by internal, self-defining principles and to some extent by social, political, and economic circumstances. The obvious question is, how much of each? (See Friedman, 1985: 28). As Friedman observes, more or less orthodox legal scholars tend to emphasize the autonomous aspect of law. This, we suspect, is the result of two things. One is largely a consequence of the face validity of looking to doctrine, which tends to suggest an internal coherence of a sort amenable to logical explanation. We can apparently explain outcomes in terms of prior decisions, and therefore it seems fair to infer that those prior decisions do control their successors. The second reason for emphasizing autonomy derives from a commitment to liberal political theory, according to which law is interposed between, and bilaterally constrains, the conduct of individuals and governments. Those whose bent is more sociological, on the other hand, seem inclined to emphasize the interdependence of legal and social, political, or economic phenomena.

The principal concern of sociology of law has not been with general questions, however. Abandonment of the view of law as a closed logical system invited the evaluation of legal rules according to their effects in practice. A variety of research interests are linked by a conceptual approach in which law figures primarily as a specialized vehicle of social control and which attends less to the development of law as a social institution and more to the social significance of that institution. This theme regards law as an independent variable or hypothesis, and the questions that arise concern the extent to which laws or law-dispensing agencies successfully discourage or promote certain behavior.

This sort of inquiry does not compare legal institutions across jurisdictions or over time to determine how those institutions have developed, but compares theoretical expectations about the operation or effects of legal institutions with the observed behavior of organizations, groups, or individuals. It is this model that has produced the "gap research" that typifies much of American sociology of law: The comparison of "legal reality" with a "legal ideal" expressed or assumed by law on the books (see Black, 1972). These "legal ideals" most commonly reflect legal rules that are reasonably clearly stated. Studies of compliance with Supreme Court decisions provide the most familiar instances of this focus. The hypothesis to be tested is drawn directly from an announced legal norm—the *Miranda* rules, for example, or the ban on public school prayer, or the requirement of counsel in juvenile delinquency proceedings—and the research question is whether the expectations announced by those rules are met in practice.

From this research, naive faith in a hypodermic model of command and response, if it ever existed, fell by the wayside. Observed patterns of conduct often were not amenable to neat categorization as compliance or deviance, but were far more complex. Judicial rules, it transpired, often lacked the clarity in content or extension presupposed by crude versions of the rule of law (Teitelbaum, 1982-83; Becker & Feeley, 1973). Moreover, those charged with execution of commands were influenced by community and personal attitudes nowhere accounted for by the hypodermic model of law. Studies of the police revealed that they did not arrest all and only offenders they saw (Black and Reiss, 1970). Prosecution and defense attorneys did not conduct their business strictly according to the likelihood of each suspect's guilt, but according to bureaucratic concerns that were extrinsic to formal criteria of guilt or degree of culpability (Blumberg, 1967; Skolnick, 1967). The effect of counsel in delinquency cases turned on structural factors in juvenile courts rather than on statutory definitions of offense (Stapleton & Teitelbaum, 1972). From these studies, as with those of courts, emerged a theme of discretion mediating between rules and administration that constituted an important limitation on the function of law as an instrument of social control (Ross, 1980).

Most of the large body of recent research on police, prosecutors, defense attorneys, and other agencies associated with the administration of justice falls within the social control model. These studies typically rely on role theory, which focuses on the normative prescriptions for behavior associated with certain social positions. For purposes of sociolegal research, those prescriptions were often derived from formal legal expectations. The significance of observed police behavior initially lay in its nonconformity to what we suppose legal rules require of policemen. The significance of caseload and collegial restraints on the performance of lawyers lay in the deviation from a model of client-centered aggressive advocacy they produced.

A related line of inquiry took as the hypothesis to be tested, not legal rules themselves, but certain fundamental assumptions about the impact of those rules on the behavior of nonlegal actors. The considerable body of research on deterrence illustrates this concern. Studies addressing the death penalty for murder have considered the effectiveness of that particular sanction, with no clear conclusion. Other studies have centered on penalties for drunk driving, which of all criminal behaviors, is among the easiest to measure and therefore peculiarly suitable for testing deterrence assumptions (Ross, 1980). Experimental forms of police patrol have supplied the occasion for studies of deterrence in connection with street crimes (Kelling and Pate, 1974).

Research with a similar agenda has been directed to alternative legal responses to deviance. Liberals during the 1950s and 1960s tended to favor rehabilitation either as a theory of, or a crucial practice in, punishment. Intuitively, it seemed sensible to think that changing the attitudes of wrongdoers would reduce recidivism more than would inflicting pain alone. Research on community-based treatment, vocational programs, and other "rehabilitative" strategies has not borne out that intuition, however. In consequence, current liberal opinion is heavily opposed to predicating penal response upon that theory of intervention (von Hirsch, 1976: 11-18).

Finally, much research over the last 10 years investigates nonjudicial settings and techniques for dispute resolution. Whereas the gap research just described typically concerns itself with a disparity between specific legal rules and the behavior of law-dispensing agents or the community, this last line of inquiry addresses systems or methods of dispute resolution that, although not inconsistent, are also not intended to comply with formal legal norms. Macaulay's (1963) demonstration of a well-defined and widely followed normative system for regulating commercial dealings among businessmen that differed substantially from what courts would have decreed under the formal law of contracts is one seminal study of this sort; Ross's study of how insurance companies settle claims arising out of automobile accidents is another (Ross, 1970).

Trend studies of litigation rates have likewise revealed that relatively few disputes that might result in litigation in fact go to court. Toharia's research on litigation in Spain between 1900 and 1940 indicates that, contrary to expectations, the number of lawsuits declined during this period of considerable economic growth (Friedman, 1983). Friedman and Percival (1976) found no evidence of an increase in litigation in two California trial courts between 1890 and 1970. There is no reason to think that the incidence of *disputes* failed to increase with economic development over these periods; rather, business and even individuals decided for one reason or another not to litigate about them.

Studies of particular strategies for dispute resolution have also proliferated. One focus under this rubric has been negotiation, an intersection of interests among political scientists (e.g., Ikle, 1964), economists (e.g., Schelling, 1963), social psychologists (e.g., Rubin and Brown, 1975), and law professors (e.g., Macaulay, 1963), as well as sociologists (e.g., Strauss,

1978). Theories of negotiation have been formally modeled (von Neumann and Morgenstern, 1947), and empirical studies have probed the rules and techniques actually used in both experimental simulations of negotiation as well as actual bargaining behavior (see Rubin and Brown, 1975; Ross, 1980; Sudnow, 1965; Williams, 1983).

The dispute-resolution literature also contains a variety of empirical studies of mediation and arbitration, although most have been conducted by lawyers motivated by policy rather than by theoretical concerns (Rosenberg and Schubin, 1961; McEwen and Maiman, 1984). This literature has identified important differences between the outcomes of mediated or arbitrated cases and what might be expected from litigation, and has indicated the usefulness of these alternative dispute resolution mechanisms both in general and in particular kinds of cases.

Although these studies concern apparently non- or extralegal methods, their impetus and interpretation nonetheless are often closely linked to the central model of inquiry just described. Trends and practices in dispute settlement are measured against a legal ideal of "full access to justice" which, at least implicitly, is defined in terms of access to courts. Lawrence Friedman, for example, sees in the litigation trend research clear evidence that "courts in Western industrial societies do not seem well-suited to resolving certain kinds of disputes. Thus they fall short of the ideal of 'justice for all' if by justice we mean a cheap, fair, effective tribunal close at hand" (Friedman, 1983: 21). It is also common to compare the outcomes reached through mediation, negotiation, or industry practice with what litigation might be expected to produce, yielding yet another sort of "gap."

THE FUTURE OF THE SOCIOLOGY OF LAW

To a considerable extent, American sociology of law has been driven by one paradigm, although it goes under a number of names and is expressed in a variety of ways. Law is conceived as a social control mechanism of such distinctive importance that it can be regarded as an independent variable or exhaustive source of hypotheses. Its distinction lies in possessing the privilege of force to exact compliance with its rules, its independence of control by other systems of social order, and its capacity to require those other systems to conform to its rules. This approach has been taken by sociological jurisprudence and legal realism, and by most American sociologists as well (Van Houtte, 1985). It is also possible to understand some recent European writing in this way; Luhmann's theory of the progressive separation of law and community values (the "process of the positivation of law") seems to reflect this emphasis (Luhmann, 1982).

Much of value has been learned through this paradigm, particularly about the structure and functions of institutions. It has invited increasing sophistication in methodology; in which the central research task lies in testing hypotheses, a central concern must be to resolve obvious problems of internal and external validity. The extensive but relatively crude research strategies of the realists and even of Kalven and Zeisel (1966) would not now be thought sufficient. To the extent that evaluation of behavioral changes in direct response to legal innovation is sought, new techniques such as interrupted time series analyses have emerged (McCleary & Hay, 1980). A sense of the increased reliance by sociolegal research on sophisticated analytical strategies may be found by reviewing work published in *The Law and Society Review*. From 1966 (when *The Review* first appeared) until the last five years or so, statistical techniques for evaluating data were either nonexistent or simple. Recent writing, however, often employs regression analyses and other relatively elaborate evaluative strategies, presenting for law and social science the familiar tension between accessibility and sophistication.

These developments are congenial to the public activities of legal sociologists. Law reform interests heavily influenced the appearance of sociolegal studies during the first part of this century and the same interests guided its resurrection in the 1960s. This policy relevance of sociology of law has been explicit from the outset. The Yale researchers of the 1930s consulted with and provided data to governmental and advisory bodies, and sociologists of law now are asked—far more than are their confreres in other fields—to provide information to legislators regarding current and proposed laws. They may also be asked to help devise efficient procedures for courts and administrative agencies and even to serve as advisers or expert witnesses in litigation (Saks and Brown, 1978). These opportunities, garnished by the allure of small-scale celebrity, have tended to confirm the appropriateness of the rule-of-law paradigm, because that is the paradigm familiar to legislatures and courts and it is the functioning of elements within that scheme that typically interests those agencies.

The same factors are significant even for "academic" research. One of the valuable things sociologists of law have to offer decision makers is a "scientific" testing of, or alternative to, purely intuitive assumptions about how the world works or would work if some reform were adopted. This evidence is not, however, cost-free; its production requires a methodology that is both professionally defensible and attractive to lay consumers. This, in turn, typically requires external funding by an agency that seeks a recognizable product, and within tolerable time limits. On the one hand, these interests have generated much of the valuable research just described; on the other, it pushes strongly toward maintenance of a paradigm familiar to those who commission that research.

Presumably, work within this paradigm will continue, in part for ideological reasons and in part for practical ones. However, there are signs that the paradigm is breaking down, and that a more complex picture has begun to emerge. Some features of that revised picture seem worth mentioning, as lines of thought that will become clearer as sociology of law develops.

(1) Expansion of the idea of law. It has long been urged by European sociologists that identification of law with one specialized form of social control—that backed by the force of politically organized society—is far too narrow (Gurvitch, 1942; Van Houtte, 1985). This view reflects a different intellectual tradition than has been common in England and America. The treatment of law as a university subject rather than as a practical vocation, a philosophical rather than an applied approach to law, and the greater influence of phenomenological theory in Europe led Europeans to regard law as referring to all social control phenomena rather than to only one specialized form. In their view, the state is one of the social groups, and law is one of the social orders, found in society; other groups exist and have their law as well.

The orientations of American and European schools are conventionally described in terms of *sociology in law* and *sociology of law*. The difference between them sometimes is reflected in views of what is appropriate to study and sometimes in interpretation. American legal sociologists, for example, discovered that the practices of businessmen and insurance companies did not coincide with formal legal expectations. However, the general temptation has been to regard these findings as evidence of deviance if they contradict some state-announced legal norm and otherwise as parallel *non*legal systems of dispute resolution. Thus it has been common to describe such mechanisms as "informal" (by contrast to judicial resolution) and as evidence of problems in access to law (understood as access to courts).

The image of subcultural or parallel systems no longer seems quite sufficient, however. The various forms of social control and the various understandings and practices of community members interact with one another at various points, so as to influence substantially the social meaning of each (Engel, 1980). In the most obvious instances, legal terms (such as *reasonable* and *negligent*) are not intended to announce a specific requirement of conduct. The Uniform Commercial Code, that product of moderate realism, designedly left much of its meaning to be supplied by various business communities as they worked out, from industry to industry and place to place, what behaviors amounted to a "reasonable" acceptance of goods. Custom here is law. In other cases, as with businessmen, community rules have much to do with deciding when the formal legal system will be employed—far more, perhaps, then the substantive and jurisdictional rules of the formal legal system itself have to do with that decision.

The constitutive activities of legal communities can also be found at the trial court level. Juries may be asked to decide whether a certain pattern of conduct constitutes *premeditation,* a term that is not typically regarded as intentionally vague. Premeditation surely supposes forethought, but the amount and quality of forethought may plainly be variously understood.

However, courts generally need not themselves define terms that can be variously understood, as long as the evidence in cases will support all plausible understandings. This circumstance not only allows but authorizes juries to define crucial legal terms according to community attitudes toward killing under various conditions. Moreover, their decisions are not deviations from or alternatives to government by the commands of positive law, but constitute ways in which various communities give meaning within the adjudicative system to what is formally understood as the positive law itself.

This interaction runs, of course, both ways. It is clear that communities and individuals daily make decisions with an eye to what formal law commands or may command. While appellate courts may, and on accepted principles of adjudication should, act on a case-by-case basis, program administrators and their employees ordinarily cannot do so. These latter must carry on comprehensive systems of activity without interruption. The Supreme Court may hold that due process in some way applies to short suspensions of students from school, but reserve decision about expulsions: school principals, however, must interpret the requirements of due process for all the forms of discipline they currently or may subsequently employ. In some genuine sense, a law of school discipline will be developed that cannot be evaluated by comparison with existing legal norms, because none yet exists, but whose development is strongly informed by the distinctive discourse and even the threat of formal law (Teitelbaum, 1982-1983).

Less grandly, it is also clear that much negotiation and mediation takes place in the shadow of the formal law. While formal legal categories here do not, as in litigation, provide the only basis for discussion and decision, they are nonetheless important to positions and claims of disputants, and to the outcomes regarded as tolerable.

These observations take us beyond the traditional emphasis on discretion, which emerged from a sharp focus on gaps between legal ideals and legal practices. The discovery of discretion was exciting for a variety of reasons, not least its impeachment of traditional approaches in legal education. However, a discretion-based sociology finally seems too narrow. For one thing, it does not adequately take account of the effects of legal rules and agencies. Not only do they actually resolve some disputes, but they affect decisions not to go to court or, once there, to settle matters prior to or even after adjudication. For another thing, the significance usually assigned to discretion lies in explaining a gap between a positivist version of law that defines precisely the conduct expected of legal and other actors and the actual behavior of those actors. As we have seen, however, legal rules and procedures do not uniformly share this pretension. In one direction, courts and legislatures expect the community to contribute to the definition of law when they use terms that invite this activity. In the other direction, judicial decisions formally govern only a small set of activities carried out under conditions narrowly defined by the circumstances of that case, which requires laymen to predict the commands courts will issue in situations for which no legal command yet exists (See Holmes, 1897).

One direction sociology of law may take, then, is the tracing and analysis of the interactive and constructive activities of various legal communities. This enterprise, however, raises a series of methodological issues.

(2) "Objective" and "interpretive" methodology. The dispute between advocates of objective or scientific methodologies on the one hand, and of interpretive or other microsocial techniques on the other, has sharply divided sociologists (Knorr-Cetina and Cicourel, 1981). It has recently emerged in connection with sociolegal inquiry. At their most virulent, interpretavists accuse their opponents of uncritical "scientism" or "positivism," whereas "conventional" sociologists find in microstrategies a self-indulgent, a theoretical, and highly political subjectivism.

In the sociology of law, the trend has been toward "scientific" research, although not always quantitative (see, for instance, the work of Goffman, 1963, and Lemert, 1970). The reasons for this emphasis lie not only in the reflection of mainstream sociology but also in the interest of legal sociologists to provide policy makers with convincing evidence about the operation of legal rules. It seems to us that much of value has come from this enterprise. One who is militantly antipositivistic may, of course, insist that all observational terms are defined by the theory in which they occur and thus defy objectification. However, it is one thing to say that the notion

of "mass" is differentially understood and another to say the same of
propositions such as, "Look, this stuff turned green" or "The needle is
pointing to 4" (Newton-Smith, 1981: 12). Some kinds of observational
propositions are practically acceptable in general, and some legal rules are
clear enough that inconsistency with them can be discussed intelligibly.

On the other hand, it no longer seems tolerable, for a variety of reasons,
to insist that only "objective" research in sociology of law should be valued.
There is, in the first place, something of a conflict between the imperatives
of the legal system and the structure of classical social science methodology.
The ideal evaluative study is the classical experiment, in which the
researcher controls for theoretically relevant variables that may be related
to outcomes by random assignment of subjects or cases to experimental
and control groups. Assuming randomization is successful, causal statements about the relationship of the experimental variable to outcomes can
be advanced. However, true experimental research is rarely available in
sociolegal settings. When state participation in the research, through
funding or direct cooperation is necessary, due process and equal
protection issues immediately present themselves. In general, people who
are for relevant purposes equal must be treated equally by the state, and
once benefits have been created by law, they cannot be withdrawn from
some individuals without a substantively justifiable purpose (Teitelbaum,
1983).

There are, of course, exceptional occurrences when random assignment
is possible. It was done for legal service in juvenile delinquency cases before
the Supreme Court held that access to counsel was required by due process
(Stapleton & Teitelbaum, 1972) and it has been done with minor differences
in the application of penalties for trivial offenses (Blumenthal & Ross,
1973). By and large, however, sociological research has relied on second-
best alternatives using statistical devices in place of experimental control
(Campbell & Stanley, 1963). In general, the empirical study of law proceeds
by means of quasi-experimental or even preexperimental methods, the
results of which may rest hazardously on a variety of questionable
assumptions.

In the second place, even sophisticated methodologies can answer only
certain questions. This, by itself, is no indictment, but it becomes one when
methodological possibilities serve as the principal criteria for deciding what
should be examined or for interpreting the meaning of social behavior.
Take, for example, crime. The view of the criminal law is that the
significance of behavior lies in assessments of the harm done by and the
culpability of individuals. For some purposes it is significant to know
whether reported rates of these circumstances rise or fall; when certain

penalties are used; and what are the measurable costs of those penalties. One should not confuse those phenomena, however, with the incidence or significance of behaviors that may or may not ultimately be compressed into the formal categories of the penal code at the end of a multicommunity process. The significance of behavior in the community is far more variable than any code can capture.

Whether a blow by one person is a battery or merely an unpleasant social exchange is largely defined by the victim, who in turn draws on values and experiences in his or her culture and circumstances. A schoolyard fight may be an incident if no one sees it and no one is badly hurt, but a battery if a teacher witnesses the fight at the end of a long day, or the loser is knocked unconscious and taken to the hospital. Even if the loser is injured, the fight may be treated, at the practical election of the loser's parent, as a problem for civil compensation rather than criminal complaint. And, to the extent that middle-class parents can pay for injuries more readily than can poor parents, the meaning of a fight differs from neighborhood to neighborhood.

Victims are not the only definers of crime. The police surely have much to do with this enterprise, in choosing how to characterize behavior on the street. Whether hanging around is loitering turns largely on the individual judgment and temperament of policemen and on their relationship with the community in which people are seen hanging around. Many decisions in the field are influenced by a variety of factors, some personal, some adventitious, and some peculiar to the community of policemen.

The role of attorneys in creating criminality is also crucial. Prosecutors decide whether behavior resulting in death will be presented as accidental, negligent or reckless and thus whether the potential defendant faces no charge, a manslaughter charge, or a murder charge. Decisions are influenced both by the availability of evidence shedding light on the characterization of ambiguous conduct and by organizational concerns. Often, the two bear some relationship to each other.

The activities of these groups are not merely serial, but interactive in various ways. Police judgments and values are influenced both by perceived community attitudes and by other organizations within and without the criminal justice system. Whether an event is treated by police as a curfew or alcohol violation may depend on the attitude of prosecutors toward those categories. Prosecutors in turn are influenced in choosing and negotiating charges by general public attitudes toward certain crimes and criminals and by internal bureaucratic concerns, such as caseload management and the importance of a favorable success ratio in trials.

If, however, crime is understood not as an "event," but as a social construction created by all of these communities and others not named, and by their interactions, it is no longer possible to measure the activity of law, broadly understood, by looking at conviction or punishment rates. These data distort by oversimplification an elaborate and highly contingent process. It is this recognition that creates the methodological problems associated with a broad view of law. Identification of the conditions under which conduct is defined and responded to seemingly demands intensive and exhaustive investigation of an entire social process, with a central focus on the subjective understandings that make its various aspects significant for the participants. And, of course, the subjectivity of the researcher must also be taken seriously into account.

Interpretive and other microsociological approaches sometimes make the same claim to exclusive authority that quantitative methodologies have advanced. At their most radical, they deny any possibility of generalization or comparison. Too much, it is said, depends on the subjective and active relationships of individuals to their cultures and of researchers to informants for statements beyond description of their interchanges. Even among proponents of microsociology, however, this view is relatively uncommon; that path seems to lead to a solipsism with which few can live.

A somewhat more modest approach is to urge that any macrosocial theory must be built upon microsocial premises. It is still unclear, however, that this can be done or how it can be done. Microsocial approaches attend more carefully to contextual factors and to the understandings, both express and tacit, of individuals than does the conventional view, but they do not yet seem to offer an avenue by which the influence of social forces, formal authority, or class structure can be systematically considered. As important as the former may be, the latter cannot be ignored.

These observations may seem to imply a resort to eclecticism in the service of buying a little peace. That rather depends on what one has in mind by eclecticism. There is a difference between, on the one hand, proposing eclecticism as an escape from philosophical issues upon which social science research is predicated and, on the other hand, accepting the propriety of various forms of research in the absence of philosophical consensus. The former suggests that philosophical problems may safely be ignored, on one ground or another. The latter supposes that these problems should be explored, but that they can be explored in connection with applied research programs and that they may yet be variously resolved.

While some social science propositions do take the form, "The needle is pointing to 4" and seem capable of verification in every useful sense, many significant sociological propositions are not of this form. On the other hand, while the social world may be socially constructed, some kinds of predictions are surely possible. Wittgenstein's language game analysis rests precisely upon the assumption of shared meanings associated by community members with specific expressions; those shared meanings form a basis for prediction within the game in which those terms are employed. Chess players can predict that rooks will not move diagonally, because if they did the game would not be chess.

These are unresolved questions of epistemology. There are, as well, ethical problems to be faced by all and metaphysical questions to be faced by all but the most convinced positivist. Even if it is possible to treat people as objects in some settings and for some purposes, it does not follow that one should do so. Following such an approach is a matter of choice, which may have direct and indirect significance for ideology, and ideology may, in turn, provide apparent (but ultimately circular) justification for that approach.

All of these questions must be addressed. The problem is not with pursuing a variety of understandings of social conduct, but in failing to consider their premises and implications. It is considered variety, rather than unconsidered eclecticism, that we expect to emerge as the sociology of law progresses.

REFERENCES

Becker, Theodore and Malcolm Feeley (1973) The Impact of Supreme Court Decisions (2nd ed.). New York: Oxford University Press.

Black, Donald (1972) "The boundaries of legal sociology." Yale Law Journal 81: 1086.

Black, Donald and Albert Reiss (1970) "Police control of juveniles." American Sociological Review 35: 63.

Blumberg, Abraham (1967) "The practice of law as a confidence game." Law and Society Review 1: 15.

Blumenthal, Murray and H. Laurence Ross (1973) Two Experimental Studies of Traffic Law: The Effect of Legal Sanctions on DWI Offenders and The Effect of Court Appearance on Traffic Law Violators. Technical Report DOT HS 249-2-437. Washington, DC: National Highway Traffic Safety Administration.

Boyum, Keith and Lynn Mather [eds.] (1983) Empirical Theories About Courts. New York: Longman.

Cain, Maureen and Alan Hunt (1979) Marx and Engels on Law. New York: Academic Press.

Campbell, Donald T. and Julian C. Stanley (1963) Experimental and Quasi-Experimental Designs for Research. Chicago: Rand McNally.

Durkheim, Emile (1964) The Division of Labor in Society (G. Simpson, trans.). New York: Free Press.

Engel, David (1980) "Legal pluralism in an American community." American Bar Foundation Research Journal, p. 425.

Fisher, Roger and William Ury (1981) Getting to Yes. Boston: Houghton Mifflin.

Frank, Jerome (1963) Law and the Modern Mind (1930). New York: Anchor.
Friedman, Lawrence (1983) "Courts over time: a survey of theories and research," in K. Boyum and L. Mather (eds.) Empirical Theories About Courts. New York: Longman.
Friedman, Lawrence (1983) "The radiating effects of courts," in K. Boyum and L. Mather (eds.) Empirical Theories About Courts. New York: Longman.
Friedman, Lawrence (1985) Total Justice. New York: Russell Sage.
Friedman, Lawrence and Robert V. Percival (1976) "A tale of two courts: litigation in Alameda and San Benito counties." Law & Society Review 10: 267.
Galanter, Marc (1985) "The legal malaise, or justice observed." Law & Society Review 19: 537.
Gibbs, Jack P. (1975) Crime, Punishment and Deterrence. New York: Elsevier.
Giddens, Anthony (1976) "Itermeneutics, ethnomethodology, and problems of interpretative analysis," in Lewis A. Coser and Otto N. Larsen (eds.) The Uses of Controversy in Sociology. New York: Free Press.
Goffman, Erving (1963) Stigma: Notes on the Management of Spoiled Identity. Englewood Cliffs, NJ: Prentice-Hall.
Gurvitch, Georges (1942) Sociology of Law. New York: Philosophical Library.
Holmes, Oliver W., Jr. (1897) "The path of the law." Harvard Law Review 10: 457.
Ikle, Fred C. (1964) How Nations Negotiate. New York: Harper & Row.
Kalven, Harry and Hans Zeisel (1966) The American Jury. Boston: Little, Brown.
Kelling, G. and A. Pate (1974) The Kansas Preventive Patrol Experience. Washington, DC: Police Foundation.
Knorr-Cetina, Karin and Aaron V. Cicourel (1981) Advances in Social Theory and Methodology. Boston: Routledge & Kegan Paul.
Lemert, Edwin (1970) Social Action and Legal Change: Revolution within the Juvenile Court. Chicago: Aldine.
Llewellyn, Karl (1931) "Some realism about realism—responding to Dean Pound." Harvard Law Review 44: 1222.
Llewellyn, Karl (1956) "On what makes legal research worthwhile." Journal of Legal Education 8: 399.
Llewellyn, Karl (1962) Jurisprudence: Realism in Theory and Practice. Chicago: University of Chicago Press.
Luhmann, Niklas (1982) The Differentiation of Society (S. Holmes & C. Larmore trans.). New York: Columbia University Press.
Luhmann, Niklas (1985) A Sociological Theory of Law (E. King & M. Albrow trans.; M. Albrow, ed.). London: Routledge & Kegan Paul.
Macaulay, Stewart (1963) "Non-contractual relations in business: a preliminary study." American Sociological Review 28: 55.
McCleary, Richard and R. A. Hay (1980) Applied Time Series Analysis for the Social Sciences. Beverly Hills, CA: Sage.
McEwen, Craig and Richard Maiman (1984) "Mediation in small claims court: achieving compliance through consent." Law and Society Review 18: 11.
Merton, Robert K. and Robert Nisbet [eds.] (1971) Contemporary Social Problems. New York: Harcourt Brace Jovanovich.
Mnookin, Robert and Lewis Kornhauser (1979) "Bargaining in the shadow of the law. The case of divorce." Yale Law Review 88: 950.
Nader, Laura [ed.] (1980) No Access to Law: Alternatives to the American Judicial System. New York: Academic Press.
Newton-Smith, W. H. (1981) The Rationality of Science. Boston: Routledge & Kegan Paul.
Podgorecki, Adam (1974) Law and Society. London: Routledge & Kegan Paul.

Pound, Roscoe (1908) "Mechanical jurisprudence." Columbia Law Review 8: 605.

Pound, Roscoe (1912) "The scope and purpose of sociological jurisprudence." Harvard Law Review 25: 489.

Pound, Roscoe (1931) "The call for a realist jurisprudence." Harvard Law Review 44: 697.

Pound, Roscoe (1942) "Preface," in G. Gurvitch, Sociology of Law. New York: Philosophical Library.

Pound, Roscoe (1943) "Sociology of law and sociological jurisprudence." University of Toronto Law Journal 5: 1.

Rheinstein, Max (1966) "Introduction," in Max Weber, On Law in Economy and Society (E. Shils & M. Rheinstein trans.). Cambridge, MA: Harvard University Press.

Rosenberg, Maurice and Myra Schubin (1961) "Trial by lawyer: compulsory arbitration of small claims in Pennsylvania." Harvard Law Review 74: 48.

Ross, H. Laurence (1980) Settled Out of Court (2nd ed.). Chicago: Aldine.

Ross, H. Laurence (1982) Deterring the Drinking Driver: Legal Policy and Social Control. Lexington, MA: D. C. Heath.

Ross, H. Laurence and Gary La Free (1986) "Deterrence in criminology and social policy," in Neil J. Smelser and Dean R. Gerstein (eds.) Behavioral and Social Science: Fifty Years of Discovery. Washington, DC: National Academy Press.

Rubin, Jeffrey Z. and Bert R. Brown (1975) The Social Psychology of Bargaining and Negotiation. New York: Academic Press.

Saks, Michael J. and Charles H. Baron [eds.] (1978) The Use/Nonuse/Misuse of Applied Social Research in the Courts. Cambridge, MA: Abt.

Schelling, Thomas C. (1963) The Strategy of Conflict. New York: Oxford University Press.

Skolnick, Jerome (1967) "Social control in the adversary system." Journal of Conflict Resolution 11: 52.

Stapleton, W. Vaughan and Lee E. Teitelbaum (1972) In Defense of Youth: The Role of Counsel in American Juvenile Courts. New York: Russell Sage.

Strauss, Anselm (1978) Negotiations: Varieties, Contexts, Processes, and Social Order. San Francisco: Jossey-Bass.

Sudnow, David (1965) "Normal crimes: sociological features of the penal code in a public defender's office." Social Problems 12: 255.

Teitelbaum, Lee (1982-1983) "School disciplinary procedures: some empirical findings and some theoretical questions." Indiana Law Journal 58: 547.

Teitelbaum, Lee (1983) "Spurious, tractable, and intractable legal problems: a positivist approach to law and social science research," in R. Boruch and J. Cecil (eds.) Solutions to Ethical and Legal Problems in Social Research. New York: Academic Press.

Van Houtte, J. (1985) "Les fondements scientifiques de la sociologie du droit." Presented at the Congres Mondiale de Sociologie du Droit, Aix-en-Provence, France, August 29-31.

von Hirsch, Andrew (1976) Doing Justice: The Choice of Punishments. New York: Hill & Wang.

von Neumann, J. and D. Morgenstern (1947) Theory of Games and Economic Behavior. Princeton, NJ: Princeton University Press.

Weber, Max (1966) On Law in Economy and Society (E. Shils & M. Rheinstein trans.). Cambridge, MA: Harvard University Press.

Williams, Gerald (1983) Legal Negotiation and Settlement. St. Paul, MN: West.

17

CRIMINOLOGY

Kyle Kercher
Case Western Reserve University

Periodically, it is appropriate to take stock of the accumulated knowledge in a field and to suggest where the discipline is or should be moving. As always, the present informs the future. Thus a major portion of this chapter reviews current research on the causes and correlates of crime. The emphasis is on the magnitude of the relation between a given variable and illegal acts. Decades of research have revealed a host of factors associated with crime but few major predictors. The present review highlights this point and provides examples of how greater attention to measurement and design issues will likely clarify and expand criminology's list of strong predictors.[1]

More specifically, the discussion to follow will spotlight the trend among researchers to use multiple indicator measurement models and to test (through longitudinal designs) for reciprocal effects between crime and its predicator. Thus the present chapter documents the growing evidence that future etiological studies of crime will likely focus on issues of reducing measurement error and decreasing the confounding effects of reciprocal causation.

We now turn to a discussion of important methodological issues in weighing the evidence for and against a potential predictor of lawbreaking; a subsequent section presents the empirical evidence for the variables that theories identify as major causes of illegal behavior; and a final section uses current trends in etiological studies of crime to project future concerns and research agendas.

Author's Note: I would like to thank George Bridges and Robert Crutchfield for comments on earlier drafts of this chapter. This final version, however, does not necessarily reflect their views.

SELECTED METHODOLOGICAL ISSUES

Before assessing our present knowledge about the causes and correlates of crime, it is important to establish methodological criteria with which to judge the quality of empirical research on etiological factors. Such a review of methodological issues also serves to indicate current practices and trends. When this section is combined with the subsequent one on evaluating the strength of various predictors, one has a more solid base from which to forecast those correlates of crime that are most likely to receive increased attention, and the methodological techniques that criminologists will use to study these explanatory variables.

With rare exception, research on causes and correlates of crime uses correlational as opposed to experimental designs. Thus the methodological problems of *causal order* and *spuriousness* are always present. Unfortunately, although researchers are generally sensitive to the issue of spuriousness, the problem of causal order is often not acknowledged and even less frequently assessed (see Orsagh, 1979).

But, as noted, there is an initial thrust among criminologists to use longitudinal designs to establish an appropriate causal order. Typically, researchers assess the lagged effects of a predictor variable (i.e., measured at a point prior to the measure of criminal activity), while controlling for the potential reciprocal effects of crime (Harry and Minor, 1986; Saltzman et al., 1982; Paternoster et al., 1983a; McCarthy and Hoge, 1984; Agnew, 1985, 1987).

The criticism these researchers voice of the more common cross-sectional designs is that measures of criminal activity are for a designated period in the *past* (the last six months, year, and so on), whereas the typical measures of predictor variables (parental attachment, moral beliefs, and so on) are for the *present*. That is, the cross-sectional correlation between crime and "predictor" variables has a temporal sequence that is more appropriate for measuring the effect of crime on the explanatory variables rather than vice versa.

There are problems created, however, when using the lagged effects of predictor variables to create a more appropriate temporal sequence. Generally, we would expect the instantaneous effects of variables to be considerably stronger than their lagged effects (see Biddle and Marlin, 1987: 13). Thus the lagged effects of predictor variables are likely to *underestimate* the total influence of these variables on crime. Conversely, cross-sectional studies estimate the instantaneous effects of predictor variables that are biased by an inappropriate temporal sequence (as noted). How can we resolve this issue?

Ideally, the instantaneous (cross-lagged) effect would incorporate a similar measurement period with that for crime. Thus, for example, if we asked teenagers to report their criminal activities from a year ago to the present, then we should also ask teenagers to report levels of the predictor variables (e.g., mean level of parental attachment) for the same year period. Given that researchers typically have not collected such information, what is a reasonable alternative procedure?

Several longitudinal studies have attempted to estimate both the "instantaneous" (cross-sectional) and lagged effects of predictor variables (Meier et al., 1984; Thornberry and Christenson, 1984; Liska and Reed, 1985; Burkette and Warren, 1987). But the measurement periods for current levels of crime and current levels of the predictor variables are the same as those used in cross-sectional studies (i.e., criminal activity for the past six months or more versus measures of the predictor variables at the present time). Thus these longitudinal studies have been subject to the same criticism leveled at cross-sectional studies; namely, they are using an inappropriate causal order (Agnew, 1987: 15).

Longitudinal studies that assess the instantaneous effects of predictors differ from cross-sectional studies, however, in one important aspect: They typically control for the lagged and instantaneous *reciprocal* effects of *crime*—that is, the influence of crime (measured at six-month intervals or longer) on present levels of the predictor variables. Thus the use of mismatched measurement periods (six months or longer for crime versus current levels for predictors) should not spuriously inflate the estimates of the predictor variable's instantaneous effect on crime. Indeed, to the extent that the predictor variable is not stable (i.e., highly correlated with previous levels of the same variable), then one might argue that its instantaneous effect on crime is underestimated. That is, a more temporally contiguous measurement period for the explanatory factor and criminal activities (e.g., both assessed for the past six months) would indicate an even *greater* instantaneous effect for the predictor variable.

The issue of whether current measures of instantaneous effects are valid is a critical one for future research. Invariably criminologists find that the lagged effect of a predictor variable on lawbreaking is not as strong as the instantaneous effect (see Meier et al., 1984; Thornberry and Christenson, 1984; Liska and Reed, 1985; Burkette and Warren, 1987). Thus until the field resolves the issue of how to accurately measure instantaneous effects, we cannot assert with any confidence whether certain variables (such as criminal associates or moral beliefs) have strong or weak effects on crime.

In addition to the trend toward modeling the reciprocal effects of crime and its predictors, one also encounters the first signs of a movement to model measurement error, that is, to assess and reduce the confounding effects of random and nonrandom measurement errors through use of multiple indicators. Still, the majority of studies in criminology use single-indicator measures of predictor variables. Less often, researchers include multi-item (and thus more reliable) measures. Even rarer are factor analyses of multiple items to establish the unidimensional character of assumedly distinctive predictor variables (see Wiatrowski et al., 1981). And in very few instances researchers have used explicit multiple indicator models that correct for random and nonrandom measurement error (see Matsueda, 1982; Patterson and Dishion, 1985; Patterson, 1986). Of particular significance, these latter studies show much stronger effects on crime (for moral beliefs and parental supervision) than do other studies that have not provided such elaborate controls for measurement error. Unfortunately, although correcting for measurement error moves the predictor variables from a minor to a major influence on crime, the studies are cross-sectional. Thus their design opens them to the criticism of an inappropriate causal order (i.e., crime influencing the predictors rather than vice versa).

In addition to the methodological problems studies create through use of cross-sectional designs and single item measures, many studies fail to provide estimates of the *strength* of a statistically significant correlation. Given the large sample sizes typical in criminological research (particularly in analyses using individual-level rather than aggregate data), statistically significant results often represent trivial effects. Moreover, when criminologists do provide estimates of effect size, they frequently use gamma coefficients rather than measures based on explained variance (part r's and betas). Unfortunately, gamma coefficients are prone to grossly exaggerate the relationship between variables (see Kercher, 1987a).

Another methodological problem concerns the *level* at which crime is measured. When the absence of individual-level measures of crime force researchers to use aggregate data, the results are subject to the "ecological fallacy" (see particularly, Orsagh, 1979; but also Robinson, 1950; and Blalock, 1982: 252-259). The ecological fallacy does not occur, however, when using aggregate (contextual) measures of independent variables with individual level measures of crime (e.g., Simca-Fagan and Schwartz, 1986). Furthermore, if one is interested only in explaining *where* as opposed to *why* crime occurs, then even aggregate measures of crime are appropriate.

In the review of the empirical literature to follow, this chapter includes only research using individual-level measures of crime (i.e., studies appropriate for answering questions about why crime occurs). Additionally, the chapter gives precedence to studies that: (1) use longitudinal designs, particularly when they assess both the instantaneous and lagged reciprocal effects of crime and its predictors, (2) attempt to control for measurement error, particularly through explicit multiple indicator measurement models, and (3) measure effect size based on explained variance rather than gamma coefficients.

Furthermore, in summarizing the effect of an independent variable on lawbreaking, r's or betas approaching .30 and above are described as "substantial," values from the midteens to midtwenties are designated "modest," and coefficients of .10 or below (assuming they are statistically significant) are called "weak." Although some might argue that "substantial" effects occur at lower levels, others reserve the label for even higher levels than are used in this chapter (see Blalock, 1963).

The section to follow first reviews the effects of variables that measure stratification, and subsequently examines the influence of social control variables. Space limitations require us, however, to be very selective in which studies and what issues are highlighted.

EMPIRICAL EVIDENCE

Stratification and Crime

Social stratification has dominated past research on the causes of crime. Race and particularly social class have been the subject of numerous studies. Additionally, two statuses that criminologists traditionally have not included when considering stratification—age and gender—have recently received more attention.

In examining the influence of social class, race, sex, and age on crime, researchers have not had to focus on the methodological issue of causal order. With the exception of SES, crime cannot logically influence any of the stratification variables. And even in the case of SES, there are only limited conditions under which causal order is a potential problem. It would seem unlikely, for example, that juvenile delinquency affects *parental* SES—the most common measure of social class that researchers use. Indeed, a reverse causal order is plausible only when one examines the relation between an individuals' *own* SES and crime (e.g., a criminal record could affect one's employment opportunities).

Just as causal order does not create serious problems for most analyses of stratification effects, there would appear to be few methodological issues raised by using single-item measures of the stratification variables. Single-item indicators would seem sufficient to reliably measures SES, race, sex, and age. A measurement issue that researchers more frequently raise, however, concerns the distinction between self-reported versus officially-recorded crime (see especially, Hindelang et al., 1981). Official crime assumedly taps more serious lawbreaking than does self-reported crime. But as we will see, stratification variables display only marginal increases in explanatory power when official records are substituted for self-reported crime.

Socioeconomic status. Socioeconomic status no longer constitutes the "master variable" in sociological theories of lawbreaking, particularly in accounting for juvenile delinquency (see Hirschi, 1969; Johnson, 1979; Elliott et al., 1985). Empirical research consistently finds little or no relationship between parental SES and the illegal behavior of teenagers, whether one measures SES at the individual level or as a neighborhood rate or whether one examines officially-recorded or self-reported crimes (Kercher, 1987a; Weis, 1987).

The findings are more mixed when one examines research on adult populations. Two recent studies of *young adults* (age 26 and younger) lend support to the thesis that one must distinguish between the status of parents and self. The studies indicate a substantial negative correlation between a person's *own* SES and illegal behavior (Thornberry and Farnworth, 1982; Thornberry and Christenson, 1984), especially when SES is restricted to measures of education or unemployment and the analysis concerns blacks engaging in violent crime.

Further qualifications are necessary, however, in interpreting the findings of Thornberry and his associates. There is evidence to suggest that the relationship between educational achievement and lawbreaking may be correlational rather than causal. Bachman et al. (1978) show that the differences in criminal activity among adults of varying educational levels are already present in *early adolescence.*

The findings of Thornberry and his associates are also constrained by contradictory evidence from studies based on cross-sectional samples of the *general population.* Unlike research on young adults, investigations that focus on a much broader range of ages (typically 16 and older) find little support for an SES/crime relation, even when social status is measured by education or unemployment (Stark and McEvoy, 1970; Meier and Johnson, 1977; Minor, 1977; Tittle and Villemez, 1977; Tittle, 1980; Grasmick et al., 1983). Furthermore, very preliminary evidence would indicate that the discrepant findings are not a product of the SES/crime relation declining with age (Tittle, 1980: 92; Tittle and Villemez, 1977: 488-489; but see Greenberg, 1985: 8).[2]

Nor do the contradictory results appear to be an artifact of the more serious crimes examined in research on young adults as compared to the mostly trivial lawbreaking considered in studies of the general population (see Grasmick et al., 1983). In their study of young adults, Thornberry and Farnworth (1982) obtain a substantial association (beta = -.36) between education and *total self-reported crime* for blacks—that is, a crime category dominated by *trivial* offenses (Hindelang et al., 1979; Elliott and Ageton, 1980). Conversely, among studies of the general population, SES shows no association even with assault—that is, a crime category that would appear at least as serious as the average offense contained in self-reported crimes among young adults.

In summary, current research indicates a strong effect for SES under only very restricted circumstances; specifically, for young adults only, primarily among blacks, when SES is measured by education and unemployment rather than by income and occupation, and more for violent than for property crimes. Furthermore, preliminary evidence suggests that the association between education and crime may be correlational rather than causal. Additionally, the research on young adults would seem inconsistent with findings based on broader samples of the population.

Age. Given the restricted circumstances under which SES/crime relationships hold, criminologists have begun to refocus theories to incorporate other, more robust correlates of lawbreaking. Age has received particularly close scrutiny more recently. Indeed, Hirschi and Gottfredson (1983: 553) note, "there is reason to believe that age could replace social class as the master variable of sociological theories of crime."

Few would dispute that there is a substantial inverse association between age and at least some types of illegal behavior (Rowe and Tittle, 1977; Empey, 1978; Nettler, 1984; Gove, 1985; Stark and McEvoy, 1970; Meier and Johnson, 1977; Minor, 1977; Tittle, 1980; Kercher, 1987b). More controversial is Hirschi and Gottfredson's statement (1983: 554) that "the age distribution of crime cannot be accounted for by any variable or combination of variables currently available to criminology."

An initial attempt to test this proposition (Rowe and Tittle, 1977) produced controversial results (compare Greenberg, 1985: 10-11 with Hirschi and Gottfredson, 1985b: 24-25). Correcting for a number of the shortcomings in the Rowe and Tittle study, a reanalysis of their data set reveals less ambiguous results (Kercher, 1987b). Age has little if any direct effect on theft, assault, income tax evasion, illegal gambling, or marijuana smoking, when controlling for a large number of intervening sociological variables. Thus contrary to the contentions of Hirschi and Gottfredson

(1983), sociological factors apparently can explain the age/crime relation. More uncertain, however, is the extent to which age *interacts* with other variables in its effect on crime (see Hirschi and Gottfredson, 1983, 1985; Greenberg, 1985; LaGrange and White, 1985; Farrington, 1986; Snyder et al., 1986; Agnew, 1987: 13; Kercher, 1987a).

Race and sex. Although race was never as prominent as SES in explanations of illegal behavior, it has played a central role in a number of criminological theories (Hindelang, 1978). Additionally, beginning in the early 1970s, the criminality of women and their experience in the criminal justice system have become issues of increasing interest (Simon, 1977; Weis, 1976; Smith and Visher, 1980; Bainbridge and Crutchfield, 1983).

The empirical evidence is mixed regarding the race/crime and sex/crime relation. Studies using officially recorded arrests and victimization data (see Hindelang, 1978, 1979, 1981; Wilbanks, 1984) find large differences in black/white and male/female ratios of illegal behavior. Conversely, among investigations using self-reported teenage and adult crime data, race and gender display only a modest to weak correlation (Jensen and Eve, 1976; Kraut, 1976; Meier and Johnson, 1977; Tittle, 1980; Elifson et al., 1983; Paternoster et al., 1983a; Farnworth, 1984; Pestello, 1984).

Some criminologists have argued that these results simply demonstrate that race and sex have a stronger effect on serious (official) than nonserious (self-reported) crime (Hindelang et al., 1979, 1981). But large ratio differences—as found among black/white and male/female ratios of official crime—do not necessarily translate into large correlations (see also Elliott and Ageton, 1983: 158; Blalock, 1963). In other words, a large *unstandardized* coefficient does not imply a large *standardized* coefficient (i.e., a substantial effect).

A meta-analysis of 74 studies illustrates the preceding point. Using standardized (beta) coefficients, the results indicate that race has a weak relationship with official (serious) as well as self-reported (nonserious) violent crime (Bridges, 1987). Regrettably, there are no corresponding analyses that examine the effect of sex on serious crime. Granted, sex does display much larger gamma coefficients with measures of more serious crime (Hindelang et al., 1981: 148; Smith and Visher, 1980). Unfortunately, large differences in gamma values frequently represent small differences in explained variance (see Kercher, 1987a).

For the present, we can conclude only that race and sex are not strong predictors of less serious crime and, additionally, that there are doubts whether sex and particularly race are major predictors of serious lawbreaking.

Social Control and Crime

Social control may influence illegal behavior through a number of channels; family, peer group, religiosity, moral beliefs, community, and the criminal justice system. Although not exhaustive, the list of social control factors examined here includes those variables to which researchers have given more recent attention (for a more complete list, see Kercher, 1987a). The variables are not, however, as easily analyzed as stratification factors: Social control variables are particularly subject to the confounds introduced by unreliable measures and reverse causal order. Thus the use of multiple indicators and longitudinal designs becomes especially important in estimating the effects of social control on crime.

Family. Two features of family life appear to be most important in current criminological research (see Loeber and Stouthamer-Loeber, 1986): (1) attachment to parents (supervision, involvement, and affectional ties) and (2) the nature of discipline in the home (physical punishment/deprivation, strictness, inconsistency, and unfairness of discipline, nagging and scolding, and lack of reasoning). Research frequently finds that parental attachment inhibits delinquency (McCord, 1979; Johnson, 1979; Loeber and Dishion, 1983; Wiatrowski et al., 1981; Gove and Crutchfield, 1982; Matsueda, 1982; Jensen and Brownfield, 1983; Paternoster et al., 1983a, 1985; Menard and Morse, 1984; Patterson and Stouthamer-Loeber, 1984; Agnew, 1985, 1987; Elliott et al., 1985; Hagan et al., 1985, 1987; LaGrange and White, 1985; Liska and Reed, 1985; Patterson and Dishion, 1985; Harry and Minor, 1986; Marcos et al., 1986; Paternoster and Iovanni, 1986; Snyder et al., 1986). Estimates of the strength of the effect, however, vary greatly among studies. But a careful examination of this research suggests that very substantial effects occur only where measures of parental attachments are most thorough (e.g., McCord, 1979; Patterson and Stouthamer-Loeber, 1984; Patterson and Dishion, 1985).

The powerful effects McCord (1979) obtains are particularly noteworthy. In addition to using more refined (multiagent, multiitem, multihome visit) measures of parental attachment, she assessed its lagged rather than instantaneous effects. In contrast, other research has found the lagged effects to be particularly weak (see Paternoster et al., 1983a; Agnew, 1985, 1987; Elliott et al., 1985; Liska and Reed, 1985). These latter results have led some researchers (e.g., Agnew, 1985, 1987) to attribute the stronger instantaneous effects obtained in cross-sectional research to a reverse causal order, that is, crime influencing attachment. But McCord's results (combined with Patterson and associates) suggest that measurement error, not a reverse causal order, is the primary determinant of how strong an effect parental attachment will display.

Furthermore, a meta-analysis of family correlates of delinquency finds that parental discipline has a weaker effect on illegal behavior than does parental attachment (Loeber and Stouthamer-Loeber, 1986). However, further refinements in measuring parental discipline—not attainable in the survey format criminologists typically use—may be necessary before studies can capture its full effects (see Patterson and Stouthamer-Loeber, 1984; Patterson, 1986; Patterson and Dishion, 1987). Additionally, given the evidence of a bidirectional effect between inept discipline and antisocial behavior (Patterson, 1986), controlling for the reciprocal effects of crime would seem important.

School. For the most part, when examining the effects of education on delinquency, criminologists have been concerned with "school attachment." This term has encompassed many different school-related attitudes and behaviors (Liska and Reed, 1985). A factor analysis of a number of these variables indicates four major dimensions (Wiatrowski et al., 1981): (1) school performance, (2) educational aspirations/expectations, (3) involvement in school activities, and (4) satisfaction/affectional ties with school.

Depending on the dimension of school attachment analyzed, research finds different levels of association with delinquency. Among the four dimensions, school performance generally displays the strongest association with illegal behavior. But even this effect is only weak to moderate (Johnson, 1979; Krohn and Massey, 1980; Wiatrowski et al., 1981; Paternoster et al., 1983a; McCarthy and Hoge, 1984; Menard and Morse, 1984; Agnew, 1985; Denno, 1985; Patterson and Dishion, 1985; Minor and Harry, 1982; Agnew, 1987; but see also Johnson, 1979: 127; LaGrange and White, 1985: 20 for evidence of stronger effects; and for contradictory evidence of a reverse causal order, compare Patterson, 1986: 438-439, with McCarthy and Hoge, 1984: figure 2; Paternoster et al., 1983a: figure 2; and Agnew, 1985: 57).

Educational aspirations/expectations has essentially no effect on delinquency (Krohn and Massey, 1980; Wiatrowski et al., 1981; Agnew, 1985, 1987). The influence of school involvement is also negligible (Wiatrowski et al., 1981; Paternoster et al., 1983a; Agnew, 1985, 1987; Elliott et al., 1985: 111-116; but see Krohn and Massey, 1980). And school-related satisfactions and affectional ties likewise display little effect (Johnson, 1979: 117; Menard and Morse, 1984; Harry and Minor, 1986; Agnew, 1985, 1987; Paternoster and Iovanni, 1986; but see also Wiatrowski et al., 1981).

The conclusion concerning school-related satisfactions/affectional ties requires some qualification, however. There is evidence that these variables have a much stronger (instantaneous) effect on delinquency for females

(Johnson, 1979: 127) and blacks (Liska and Reed, 1985). Furthermore, when considering the four dimensions of school attachment as a whole, it is certainly possible that future refinements in their measurement could increase their association with illegal behavior.

Peer group associations. With the possible exception of prior lawbreaking, association with criminal others is consistently the strongest predictor of illegal behavior (Meier and Johnson, 1977; Johnson, 1979; Matsueda, 1982; Strickland, 1982; Dull, 1983; Meier et al., 1984; Menard and Morse, 1984; Elliott et al., 1985; LaGrange and White, 1985; Patterson and Dishion, 1985; Harry and Minor, 1986; Marcos et al., Paternoster and Iovanni, 1986; Burkette and Warren, 1987; but see Tittle, 1980; Tittle et al., 1986; Agnew, 1987).

A considerable controversy, however, has arisen over the appropriate causal ordering of criminal friends and delinquency (Johnson, 1979; Conger, 1980; Lanza-Kaduce et al., 1982; Stafford and Ekland-Olson, 1982; Elliott et al., 1985; Simca-Fagan and Schwartz, 1986; Agnew, 1987). Three investigations have provided explicit tests for bidirectional effects (Meier et al., 1984; Harry and Minor, 1986; Burkette and Warren, 1987). Meier et al. report that criminal associates have large instantaneous but no lagged effect on delinquency (marijuana smoking), and that delinquency has weak to substantial lagged effects (that vary by measurement period) on criminal friends. In an additional analysis of the same data set, Burkette and Warren confirm these findings. Furthermore, using a broader measure of delinquency and a cross-sectional rather than longitudinal design, Harry and Minor (1986) also find that illegal behavior has no instantaneous effect on criminal friends, and that the instantaneous effect of criminal associates on delinquency is substantial. Thus the preliminary evidence (see also, Patterson and Dishion, 1985, 1987; Patterson, 1986; Snyder et al., 1986; Farrington et al., 1986: 73) suggests that criminal associates continue to display a substantial influence on illegal behavior even when the reciprocal effects of crime are controlled.

Religious commitment. A number of studies indicate that religious commitment has only a weak effect on crime (Tittle, 1980; Elifson et al., 1983; Marcos et al., 1986; Burkette and Warren, 1987). In contrast, Stark et al. (1982) find that the effect of religious commitment is conditional: An individual's religiosity has a stronger effect on crime in religious than secular communities—a result that others dispute (Tittle and Welch, 1983). Indeed, two investigations just cited (Elifson et al., 1983; Burkette and Warren, 1987) report a uniformly weak effect for religiosity in communities from, respectively, "churched" and "unchurched" regions of the U.S.

The Burkette and Warren study is noteworthy for its control of lawbreaking's reciprocal effects on religious commitment (which are minimal). But none of the investigations attempt to correct for measurement error.

Moral beliefs. Most of the recent literature finds that "moral beliefs" has only weak to moderate effects on illegal behavior (Johnson, 1979; Strickland, 1982; Krohn and Massey, 1980; Tittle, 1980; Wiatrowski et al., 1981; Paternoster et al., 1983a, 1985; Agnew, 1985, 1987; Elliott et al., 1985; Marcos et al., 1986; Paternoster and Iovanni, 1986; Snyder et al., 1986; Tittle et al., 1986; Burkette and Warren, 1987).

In contrast, Matsueda (1982) obtains a very substantial (cross-sectional) effect for moral beliefs. His study is noteworthy for its control of measurement error through Lisrel procedures. Unfortunately, he does not introduce controls for the potential reciprocal effects of crime on moral beliefs. Thus more conclusive results must await designs that model reciprocal effects as well as measurement error.

Community. Few individual-level investigations of crime include an assessment of community (contextual) effects (Simca-Fagan and Schwartz, 1986: 669-670). And most of these studies focus on the influence of area SES (see Kercher, 1987a, for a review). But a recent study (Simca-Fagan and Schwartz, 1986) provides a much broader analysis consistent with the more comprehensive list of variables implicated in ecological theories (see Kornhauser, 1978; Sampson et al., 1981; Cohen and Felson, 1979). The study includes a factor analysis of community characteristics extracted from census tract and survey data. The analysis reveals four community dimensions—area economic level, area of disorganization/criminal sub-culture, community participation in organizations, and community residential stability. None of the factors display more than weak direct and indirect effects on officially recorded or self-reported crime. Furthermore, given that the measure of community characteristics are aggregated variables and include multiple methods (survey and census tract), measurement error seems an unlikely explanation of the weak effects.

On the other hand, the study samples adolescents only. If community is to have an impact, it would seem that its strongest effects should occur when persons are older and thus more likely to take part in community life. One study of an older population (Tittle, 1980) has, however, provided at least a limited analysis of community variables (community social integration, community spirit, community deterrence, and urbanicity). The results indicate negligible effects.

The legal system. A number of empirical studies have examined the relation between perceived risk of punishment and criminal activity. And some investigations have considered the possibility of differential effects based on a person's social background, moral beliefs, and experiences with the legal system. The most methodologically advanced cross-sectional and longitudinal studies, however, find only negligible effects for perceived risk of punishment, even when the analyses consider fear of sanctions from less formal sources such as family and friends (Meier and Johnson, 1977; Tittle, 1977, 1980; Johnson, 1979; Minor and Harry, 1982; Saltzman et al., 1982; Stafford and Ekland-Olson, 1982; Strickland, 1982; Paternoster et al., 1983a, 1983b, 1985; Bishop, 1984; Meier et al., 1984; Paternoster and Iovanni, 1986; Tittle et al., 1986).

Some have interpreted these results to indicate the refutation of deterrence theory specifically and reinforcement theory more generally (see Stafford and Ekland-Olson, 1982). But such claims are premature. There are a number of methodological issues that taint the research findings. Establishing an appropriate causal order constitutes one major problem. Longitudinal studies should not automatically assume that the cross-sectional fear/crime correlation represents the influence of crime on fears (i.e., an experiential rather than deterrent effect). The cross-sectional relationship between sanctions and crime is invariably stronger than their lagged association. Thus assigning causal priority in the cross-sectional relationship is critical to estimating the strength of sanctions' effects. An alternative procedure would not assign causal order a priori. Instead, the analysis would statistically control for the lagged and cross-sectional reciprocal effects of crime, while simultaneously estimating both the cross-sectional (instantaneous) and lagged effects of perceived sanctions on crime. At least one study (Meier et al., 1984) has attempted such an analysis and found that, indeed, the instantaneous effect of perceived sanctions was stronger than its lagged effect. But even the instantaneous effect was not substantial—a finding also supported by cross-sectional studies that include a number of control variables (e.g., Tittle, 1980; Johnson, 1979; Strickland, 1982; see also Lanza-Kaduce et al., 1982).

Measurement error is a second and potentially more serious methodological flaw in research on deterrent effects. Recall that studies of parental discipline (one type of informal sanction) and attachment found really strong influences on crime only when researchers used very sophisticated multiitem, multicontact measures of the predictor variables. Indeed, in the case of parental discipline, there is considerable doubt whether survey research, no matter how sophisticated, can measure it—possibly because persons are not even aware of the subtle sanctioning processes that govern their own and others' behavior (Patterson, 1986). Preliminary results indicate that accurate measures of discipline requires trained observers to record both microscopic and macroscopic aspects of the sanctioning process (Patterson and Stouthamer-Loeber, 1984; Patterson, 1986; Patterson and Dishion, 1987; Dishion, personal communications). In short, these results would suggest that researchers should consider alternatives to the traditional, survey-based measures of sanctions. Specifically, measures of "actual" rather than "perceived" sanctions would seem the more promising procedures to capture the effects of sanctions on crime.

Furthermore, informal sanctions would appear more likely than formal sanctions to benefit from use of these alternative measurement procedures. Indeed, research originally did measure actual risks of formal sanctions. The studies changed from measuring the actual to the perceived risk of formal sanctions precisely because objective measures of risk were thought to be less accurate indicators of deterrent effects than were subjective evaluations (see Tittle, 1980). Possibly researchers can return once again to analyzing actual risks of formal sanctions, but this time substituting individual-level crime data for the aggregate-crime data used in the original studies.

THE FUTURE OF CRIMINOLOGY

Predicting the future of any scientific discipline is presumptuous and ripe with the possibilities of making oneself appear foolish. In one sense, we are fortunate that the field of criminology does not advance so rapidly that our conjectures about its future become almost immediately dated. Nevertheless, this chapter has chosen a relatively safe course in which a review of current research provides insight into trends that may then be projected into the future. Inevitably, our particular biases will color our speculations such that what "might" be becomes, in part, what "should" be.

A review of current research on causes of crime can be disenhartening. Among a host of potential determinants, only a very few show more than a negligible association with lawbreaking. It would seem unlikely that criminologists will discover a large number of, if any, major new correlates—at least not while using present theories to guide research. In short, we are probably "stuck" with the list of current predictors for the foreseeable future.

There are grounds for optimism, however. If we are able to piece together a large number of factors that each have a small impact on crime, then their accumulated effect could be considerable. Similarly, the absence of a strong association with crime does not mean that a given variable cannot substantially reduce lawbreaking. For example, involvement in school activities may not display enough variation in real-life settings to explain much variation in delinquency. But active interventions might manipulate school involvement enough to realize significant changes in illegal behavior.[3]

Furthermore, although the list is short, we have uncovered a few major correlates of crime. Chief among these predictors is criminal associates. Age also indicates a strong effect on lawbreaking, though its demographic nature does not lend itself to crime prevention strategies.

There is also promise that methodological advances in measurement will move a number of weak to modest predictors of crime into the category of substantial correlates. Parental attachment indicates very strong effects on delinquency when researchers use multiagent, multicontact measures (see McCord, 1979; Patterson and Stouthamer-Loeber, 1984; Patterson and Dishion, 1985; Patterson, 1986). Likewise, parental discipline displays significant increases in effect with better measurement, though the results can currently be applied only to childhood conduct disorders (Patterson and Stouthamer-Loeber, 1984; Patterson, 1986; Dishion, personal communication).

Given the promise of substantial increases in the ability of family variables to predict delinquency, we might anticipate a growing interest among sociologists in studying parental influences. Indeed, there are some preliminary signs of such a trend (Hagan et al., 1985, 1987) and, additionally, there has been a recent attempt to unite the disparate fields of sociology and developmental psychology in their analysis of family relations (Loeber and Stouthamer-Loeber, 1986). But the complexity and expense of the multiagent, multicontact measurement techniques (particularly for analyzing parental discipline) will tend to discourage widespread participation.

Parental discipline is one type of informal sanction. If the influence of parental discipline on delinquency does receive increasing attention from criminologists, it would parallel a broader trend away from examining formal sanctions in favor of emphasizing the informal controls of significant others. Although the new interest in informal sanctions appears to be a response to the discouraging results obtained for criminal justice sanctions, informal controls have likewise failed to show substantial effects on crime. Possibly the advances in measuring parental discipline will eventually also benefit the measurement of informal sanctions in general.

Moral beliefs also shows of benefiting from better measurement. As noted earlier, it displays very strong effects when measurement error is modeled and thus corrected (Matsueda, 1982). The evidence is of course very preliminary and subject to an alternative explanation based on a reverse casual order (see Agnew, 1985).

Conversely, it would appear doubtful that refinements in the measurement of crime—specifically, distinguishing between serious and less serious lawbreaking—will salvage the predictive power of such variables as race, sex, and SES. Although it is true that official data and self-report measures more sensitive to serious crime show stronger effects for race, sex, and SES, the effects do not appear to be more than modest increases over those indicated for less serious (common) crimes—at least when the effects are evaluated according to explained variance rather than differences of means (unstandardized) measure of association (see Tittle et al., 1978; Thornberry and Farnworth, 1982; Bridges, 1987).

SES does show some signs of revival as a correlate of crime but not, as noted, owing to refinements in the measurement of lawbreaking. Recent research indicates that education and unemployment may have a substantial negative effect on crime among young adults, particularly for blacks engaging in violent crime (Thornberry and Farnworth, 1982; Thornberry and Christenson, 1984). (These findings have not, however, been replicated in studies that analyze broader ranges of ages in the adult population.) Furthermore, when SES is reconceptualized based on Marxian notions of power, there is evidence that the higher the mother's occupational status relative to the father's, the greater the delinquency of daughters (Hagan et al., 1987). Given that SES has had such a dismal record of predicting crime, one would assume that criminologists interested in the effects of social stratification will enthusiastically pursue these promising new findings.

Additionally, as a consequence of the initial success in reviving such variables as moral beliefs and parental attachment through refinements in their measurement, one might also expect an increasing concern over measurement issues and continued growth in the use of multiple indicator models. Consistent with this trend, there is a growing recognition that criminologists must establish the distinctiveness of their various concepts. For example, there is some question whether the criminal activities of friends and self are separate concepts (see Gottfredson and Hirschi, 1987). In particular, the ambiguous concepts of parental and school attachment would appear to require clarification. Initial attempts to illuminate these and other criminological concepts are already underway (see Wiatrowski et al., 1981; Paternoster, 1986; Patterson, 1986; Patterson and Dishion, 1987).

Advances in our knowledge of the causes of crime are also likely to occur as a result of improvements in the *design* of studies—specifically, the greater use of longitudinal and experimental analyses. Concern over the establishment of an appropriate causal order has led criminologists to search for alternatives to the cross-sectional survey designs that have so dominated past research. This concern with causal order appears justified. A growing list of studies demonstrate a reciprocal causal relationship between crime and its predictors (Minor and Harry, 1982; Saltzman et al., 1982; Paternoster et al., 1983a, 1983b; McCarthy and Hoge, 1984; Meier et al., 1984; Thornberry and Christenson, 1984; Agnew, 1985, 1987; Greenberg, 1985: 2-5; Liska and Reed, 1985; Burkette and Warren, 1987). The trend toward analysis of panel data is not, however, without controversy (see Hirschi and Gottfredson, 1983; Gottfredson and Hirschi, 1986, 1987). Indeed, the reciprocal effects of crime are not uniformly strong. Furthermore, a number of panel studies have prematurely assigned crime causal priority in its cross-sectional relationship with potential predictor variables. Future research will need to establish appropriate techniques for assessing the instantaneous effects of predictor variables on crime.

Furthermore, although longitudinal survey designs are superior to cross-sectional analyses, they still fall short of experimental designs in establishing an appropriate causal order and controlling for other sources of spurious correlations. There are initial indications of a move to make greater use of experimental methodology (see Farrington et al., 1986).

Several other trends are likely to occur or continue. As a consequence of the pioneering work of Simca-Fagan and Schwartz (1986), the near future is likely to see more analysis of community contextual effects on individual-level measures of crime. The preliminary results are not, however, very promising. If subsequent studies do not show stronger effects, interest may wane.

In the search for aspects of social control that influence lawbreaking, future criminologists are also likely to focus more frequently on early childhood. There is increasing evidence that early antisocial and delinquent behaviors are strong predictors of later illegal behavior (Loeber, 1982; Loeber and Dishion, 1983: 78-81; Loeber and Stouthamer-Loeber, 1986) and, more generally, that crime predicts crime (Minor and Harry, 1982; Paternoster et al., 1983a; McCarthy and Hoge, 1984; Meier et al., 1984; Thornberry and Christenson, 1984; Agnew, 1985; Elliott et al., 1985: 109-118; Liska and Reed, 1985). Given this evidence that critical determinants of illegal behavior occur at an early age, criminologists may become more interested in examining the relation between parental control and antisocial behavior in early childhood. There is likely to be some resistance among sociologists, however, to analyzing an area that child psychologists have traditionally claimed, particularly given the evidence that cherished survey techniques may be an inappropriate format to study family interactions (see Patterson, 1986).

The focus on early precursors of delinquency and adult crime is also likely to fuel interest in genetic influences. Genetic explanations of crime have gathered considerable empirical support (Mednick and Voavaka, 1980; Gabrielli and Mednick, 1984; Rowe and Osgood, 1984; Loeber and Stouthamer-Loeber, 1986: 127-128; Farrington et al., 1986: 52; Rowe, 1986; Rushton et al., 1986; Patterson and Dishion, 1987: 29, 32). Although many sociologists feel uncomfortable with such explanations, the genetic perspective complements rather than contradicts the social control viewpoint. Indeed, there have been recent attempts to mesh biological with environmental explanations of crime (Baldwin, 1985; Denno, 1985; Wilson and Herrnstein, 1985).

Finally, a brief comment is appropriate on the future of criminology as a profession. There has been a recent drop in crime after decades of apparent increase (Farrington et al., 1986: 38). The aging of the population in the United States is likely to continue this trend. It would seem unlikely, however, that the potentially dramatic decrease in crime will put criminologists out of business in the foreseeable future. Indeed, the decline in "street" crime may promote greater interest in white-collar crime—illegal behaviors that show no evidence of abating.

NOTES

1. The original intention in writing this chapter was to consider the future of all the major fields in criminology. Because of space constrictions, however, the present chapter addresses only issues concerning the etiology of crime. Although this choice restricts the focus of the chapter, causes and correlates of crime would certainly constitute the predominant field in criminology.

2. The findings of Tittle and associates are displayed in a format that examines the age/crime relation by low, medium, and high categories of SES. But interaction effects are symmetrical. Thus if the results were displayed in the alternative format, they would indicate that the SES/crime relation does not vary greatly by age group.

3. I would like to thank Herbert Costner for suggesting this more optimistic perspective.

REFERENCES

Agnew, R. (1985) "Social control theory and delinquency: a longitudinal test." *Criminology* 23: 47-61.

Agnew, R. (1987) A Longitudinal Test of Social Control Theory and Delinquency. Atlanta: Emory University, Department of Sociology.

Bachman, G., P. O'Malley, and J. Johnston (1978) Youth in Transition, Vol. VI. Adolescence to Adulthood: Change and Stability in the Lives of Young Men. Ann Arbor: University of Michigan, Institute for Social Research.

Bainbridge, W. and R. Crutchfield (1983) "Sex role ideology and delinquency." Sociological Perspectives 26, 3: 253-274.

Baldwin, J. (1985) "Thrill and adventure seeking and the age distribution of crime: comment on Hirschi and Gottfredson." American Journal of Sociology 90: 1326-1329.

Biddle, B. and M. Marlin (1987) "Causality, confirmation, credulity and structural equation modelling." Child Development 58: 4-17.

Bishop, D. (1984) "Legal and extralegal barriers to delinquency." Criminology 22: 403-419.

Blalock, H. (1963) "A double standard in measuring degree of association." American Sociological Review 28: 988-989.

Blalock, H. (1982) Conceptualization and Measurement. Beverly Hills, CA: Sage.

Bridges, G. (1987) "Toward understanding of racial differences and interpersonal violence." University of Washington, Department of Sociology. (unpublished)

Burkette, S. and B. Warren (1987) "Religiosity, peer association and adolescent marijuana use: a panel study of underlying causal structures." Criminology 25:109-131.

Cohen, L. and M. Felson (1979) "Social changes and crime rate trends: a routine activity approach," American Sociological Review 44: 588-608.

Conger, R. (1980) "Juvenile delinquency: behavioral restraint or behavior facilitation," pp. 131-142 in T. Hirschi and M. Gottfredson (eds.) Understanding Criminals: Current Theory and Research. Beverly Hills, CA: Sage.

Datesman, S. and F. Scarpitti (1980) Women, Crime, and Justice. New York: Oxford University Press.

Denno, D. (1985) "Sociological and human developmental explanations of crime: conflict or consensus." Criminology 23: 711-741.

Dull, R. (1983) "Friends' use and adult drug and drinking behavior: a further test of differential association theory." Journal of Criminal Law and Criminology 74: 1608-1619.

Elifson, K., D. Petersen, and C. Hadaway (1983) "Religiosity and delinquency." Criminology 21: 505-527.

Elliott, D. and S. Ageton (1980) "Reconciling race and class differences in self-reported and official estimates of delinquency." American Sociological Review 45: 95-110.

Elliott, D. and D. Huizinga (1983) "Social class and delinquent behavior in a national youth panel." Criminology 21: 149-177.

Elliott, D., D. Huizinga, and S. Ageton (1985) Explaining Delinquency and Drug Use. Beverly Hills, CA: Sage.

Empey, L. (1978) American Delinquency. Homewood, IL: Dorsey.

Farnworth, M. (1984) "Male-female differences in delinquency in a minority-group sample." Research in Crime and Delinquency 21: 191-212.

Farrington, D. (1986) "Age and crime," in M. Tonry and N. Morris (eds.) Crime and Justice Review: An Annual Review of Research, Vol. 7. Chicago: University of Chicago Press.

Farrington, D., L. Ohlin, and J. Wilson (1986) Understanding and Controlling Crime: Toward a New Research Strategy. New York: Springer-Verlag.

Gabrielli, W. and S. Mednick (1984) "Urban environment, genetics and crime." Criminology 22: 645-652.

Gottfredson, M. and T. Hirschi (1986) "The true value of lambda would appear to be zero: an essay on career criminals, criminal careers, selective incapacitation, cohort studies, and related topics." Criminology 24: 213-234.

Gottfredson, M. and T. Hirschi (1987) "The methodological adequacy of longitudinal research on crime." Criminology 25: 581-614.

Gove, W. (1985) "The effect of age and gender on deviant behavior: a biopsychosocial perspective," in A. Rossi (ed.) Gender and the Life Course. Chicago: Aldine.

Gove, W. and R. Crutchfield (1982) "The family and juvenile delinquency." Sociological Quarterly 23: 301-319.

Grasmick, H., D. Jacobs, and C. McCollom (1983) "Social class and social control: an application of deterrence theory." Social Forces 62: 359-374.

Greenberg, D. (1985) "Age, crime, and social explanation." American Journal of Sociology 91: 1-21.

Hagan, J., A. Gillis, and J. Simpson (1985) "The class structure of gender and delinquency: toward a power-control theory of common delinquent behavior." American Journal of Sociology 90: 1151-1178.

Hagan, J., J. Simpson, and A. Gillis (1987) "Class in the household: a power-control theory of gender and delinquency." American Journal of Sociology 92: 788-816.

Harry, J. and W. Minor (1986) "Intelligence and delinquency reconsidered: a comment on Menard and Morse." American Journal of Sociology 91: 956-962.

Hindelang, M. (1978) "Race and involvement in common law personal crimes." American Review 43: 93-109.

Hindelang, M. (1979) "Sex differences in criminal activity." Social Problems 27: 143-156.

Hindelang, M. (1981) "Variations in sex-race-age-specific incidence rates of offending." American Sociological Review 46: 461-474.

Hindelang, M., T. Hirschi, and J. Weis (1979) "Correlates of delinquency." American Sociological Review 44: 995-1014.

Hindelang, M., T. Hirschi, and J. Weis (1981) Measuring Delinquency. Beverly Hills, CA: Sage.

Hirschi, T. (1969) Causes of Delinquency. Berkeley: University of California Press.

Hirschi, T. and M. Gottfredson (1983) "Age and the explanation of crime." American Journal of Sociology 89: 552-584.

Hirschi, T. and M. Gottfredson (1985) "Age and crime, logic and scholarship: comment on Greenberg." American Journal of Sociology 91: 22-27.

Jensen, G. and D. Brownfield (1983) "Parents and drugs." Criminology 21: 543-554.

Jensen, G. and R. Eve (1976) "Sex differences in delinquency: an examination of popular sociological explanations." Criminology 13: 427-448.

Johnson, R. (1979) Juvenile Delinquency and its Origins. Cambridge, MA: Cambridge University Press.

Kercher, K. (1987a) "Causes and correlates of crime committed by the elderly: a review of the literature," in E. Borgatta and R. Montgomery (eds.) Critical Issues in Aging Policy. Beverly Hills, CA: Sage.

Kercher, K. (1987b) Explaining the Relationship Between Age and Crime: The Biological Versus Sociological Model. Cleveland: Case Western Reserve University, Department of Sociology.

Kornhauser, R. (1978) Social Sources of Delinquency: An Appraisal of Analytic Models. Chicago: University of Chicago Press.

Kraut, R. (1976) "Deterrent and definitional influences on shoplifting." Social Problems 23: 358-368.

Krohn, M. and J. Massey (1980) "Social control and delinquent behavior: an examination of the elements of the social bond." Sociological Quarterly 21: 529-543.

LaGrange R. and H. White (1985) "Age differences in delinquency: a test of theory." Criminology 23: 19-45.

Lanza-Kaduce, L., R. Akers, M. Krohn, and M. Radosevich (1982) "Conceptual and analytical models in testing social learning theory." American Sociological Review 47: 169-173.

Liska, A. and M. Reed (1985) "Ties to conventional institutions and delinquency: estimating reciprocal effects." American Sociological Review 50: 547-560.

Loeber, R. (1982) "The stability of antisocial and delinquent child behavior: a review." Child Development 53: 1431-1446.

Loeber, R. and T. Dishion (1983) "Early predictors of male delinquency: a review." Psychological Bulletin 94: 68-99.

Loeber, R. and M. Stouthamer-Loeber (1986) "Family factors as correlates and predictors of juvenile conduct problems and delinquency," in M. Tonry and N. Morris (eds.) Crime and Justice Research: An Annual Review of Research, Vol. 7. Chicago: University of Chicago Press.

Marcos, A., S. Bahr, and R. Johnson (1986) "Test of a bonding/association theory of adolescent drug use." Social Forces 65: 135-161.

Matsueda, R. (1982) "Testing control theory and differential association: a causal modeling approach." American Sociological Review 47: 489-504.

McCarthy, J. and D. Hoge (1984) "The dynamics of self-esteem and delinquency." American Journal of Sociology 90: 396-410.

McCord, J. (1979) "Some child-rearing antecedents of criminal behavior in adult men." Journal of Personality and Social Psychology 37: 1477-1486.

Mednick S. and J. Voavaka (1980) "Biology and crime," in N. Morris and M. Tonry (eds.) Crime and Justice: An Annual Review of Research. Chicago: Chicago University Press.

Meier, R., S. Burkette, and C. Hickman (1984) "Sanctions, peers, and deviance: preliminary models of a social control process." Sociological Quarterly 25: 67-82.

Meier, R. and W. Johnson (1977) "Deterrence as social control: the legal and extralegal production of conformity." American Sociological Review 42: 292-304.

Menard, S. and B. Morse (1984) "A structuralist critique of the IQ-delinquency hypothesis: theory and evidence." American Journal of Sociology 89: 1347-1378.

Minor, W. (1977) "A deterrence-control theory of crime," pp. 117-137 in R. Meier (ed.) Theory in Criminology: Contemporary Views. Beverly Hills, CA: Sage.

Minor, W. and J. Harry (1982) "Deterrent and experiential effects in perceptual deterrence research: a replication and extension." Journal of Research in Crime and Delinquency 19: 190-203.

Nettler, G. (1984) Explaining Crime. New York: McGraw-Hill.

Orsagh, T. (1979) "Empirical criminology: interpreting results derived from aggregate data." Journal of Research in Crime and Delinquency 16: 294-306.

Paternoster, R. (1986) "The use of composite scales in perceptual deterrence research: a cautionary note." Journal of Research in Crime and Delinquency 23: 128-168.

Paternoster, R. and L. Iovanni (1986) "The deterrent effect of perceived severity: a reexamination." Social Forces 64: 751-777.

Paternoster, R., L. Saltzman, G. Waldo, and T. Chiricos (1983a) "Perceived risk and social control: do sanctions really deter?" Law and Society Review 17: 457-479.

Paternoster, R., L. Saltzman, G. Waldo, and T. Chiricos (1983b) "Estimating perceptual stability and deterrent effects: the role of perceived legal punishment in the inhibition of criminal involvement." Journal of Criminal Law and Criminology 74: 270-297.

Paternoster, R., L. Saltzman, G. Waldo, and T. Chiricos (1985) "Assessments of risk and behavioral experience: an exploratory study of change." Criminology 23: 417-436.

Patterson, G. (1986) "Performance models for antisocial boys." American Psychologist 41: 432-444.

Patterson, G. and T. Dishion (1985) "Contributions of families and peers to delinquency," Criminology 23: 63-79.

Patterson, G. and T. Dishion (1987) Understanding and Predicting Adolescents' Antisocial Behavior Networks: The Oregon Youth Study. Eugene: Oregon Social Learning Center.

Patterson, G. and M. Stouthamer-Loeber (1984) "The correlation of family management practices and delinquency." Child Development 55: 1299-1307.

Pestello, H. (1984) "Deterrence: a reconceptualization." Crime and Delinquency 30: 593-609.

Robinson, W. (1950) "Ecological correlations and behavior of individuals." American Sociological Review 15: 351-357.

Rowe, A. and C. Tittle (1977) "Life cycle changes and criminal propensity." Sociological Quarterly 18: 223-236.

Rowe, D. (1986) "Genetic and environmental components of antisocial behavior: a study of 265 twin pairs." Criminology 24: 513-532.

Rowe, D. and W. Osgood (1984) "Heredity and sociological theories of delinquency: a reconsideration." American Sociological Review 49: 526-540.

Rushton, J., D. Fulker, M. Neale, D. Nias, and H. Eysenck (1986) "Altruism and aggression: the heritability of individual differences." Journal of Personality and Social Psychology 50: 1192-1198.

Saltzman, L., R. Paternoster, G. Waldo, and T. Chiricos (1982) "Deterrent and experiential effects: the problem of causal order in perceptual deterrence research." Journal of Research in Crime and Delinquency 19: 172-189.

Sampson, R., T. Castellano, and J. Laub (1981) Juvenile Criminal Behavior and Its Relation to Neighborhood Characteristics, Monograph 5. National Institute for Juvenile Justice and Delinquency Prevention. Washington, DC: Government Printing Office.

Simca-Fagan, O. and J. Schwartz (1986) "Neighborhood and delinquency: an assessment of contextual effects." Criminology 24: 667-703.

Simon, R. (1977) Women and Crime. Lexington, MA: D.C. Heath.

Smith, D. and C. Visher (1980) "Sex and involvement in deviance/crime: a quantitative review of the empirical literature." American Sociological Review 45: 691-701.

Snyder, J. (1986) "Determinants and consequences of associating with deviant peers during preadolescence and adolescence." Journal of Early Adolescence 6: 29-43.

Stafford, M. and S. Ekland-Olson (1982) "On social learning and deviant behavior: a reappraisal of the findings." American Sociological Review, pp. 167-169.

Stark, R. and M. McEvoy (1970) "Middle-class violence." Psychology Today 4: 52-54.

Stark, R., L. Kent, and D. Doyle (1982) "Religion and delinquency: the ecology of a 'lost' relationship." Journal of Research in Crime and Delinquency 19: 4-24.

Strickland, D. (1982) "Social learning and deviant behavior: a specific test of a general theory. A comment and critique." American Sociological Review 47: 162-167.

Thornberry, T. and R. Christenson (1984) "Unemployment and criminal involvement: an investigation of reciprocal causal structures." American Sociology Review 49: 398-411.

Thornberry, T. and M. Farnworth (1982) "Social correlates of criminal involvement: further evidence on the relationship between social status and criminal behavior." American Sociological Review 47: 505-518.

Tittle, C. (1977) "Sanction fear and the maintenance of social order." Social Forces 55: 579-596.

Tittle, C. (1980) Sanctions and Social Deviance: The Question of Deterrence. New York: Praeger.

Tittle, C., M. Burke, and E. Jackson (1986) "Modeling Sutherland's theory of differential association: toward an empirical clarification." Social Forces 65: 405-432.

Tittle, C. and W. Villemez (1977) "Social class and criminality." Social Forces 56: 474-501.

Tittle, C., W. Villemez, and D. Smith (1978) "The myth of social class and criminality: an empirical assessment of the empirical evidence." American Sociological Review 43: 643-656.

Tittle, C. and M. Welch (1983) "Religiosity and deviance: toward a contingency theory of constraining effects." Social Forces 61: 653-682.

Weis, J. (1976) "Liberation and crime: the invention of the new female criminal." Crime and Social Justice 6: 17-27.

Weis, J. (1987) "The elusive correlation: social class and crime." Positive Criminology: papers in honor of Michael J. Hindelang.

Wiatrowski, M., D. Griswold, and M. Roberts (1981) "Social control theory and delinquency." American Sociological Review 46: 525-541.

Wilbanks, W. (1984) "The elderly offender: sex and race variations in frequency and pattern," pp. 41-52 in W. Wilbanks and P. Kim (eds.) Elderly Criminals. New York: University Press of America.

Wilson, J. and R. Herrnstein (1985) Crime and Human Nature. New York: Simon and Schuster.

18

MEDIA SYSTEMS
AND MASS COMMUNICATION

S. J. Ball-Rokeach

University of Southern California

The history of sociological inquiry into media and mass communications has been shaped by sociopolitical forces, the ebbs and flows of sociological theory and research, and by an incredibly diverse community of nonsociologists. That community includes the fields of communications, anthropology, cultural studies, political science, psychology, linguistics, information science, economics, law, and, more recently, systems engineering and technology policy analysis. Michael Schudson's (1986) scanning of the major lines of inquiry in and out of sociology leads him to conclude that much of this activity is rooted in three classical paradigms of sociological thought—those of Marx, Weber, and Durkheim. This mode of simplification rings true, particularly when applying it to comprehend the bases of heated theoretical and methodological conflicts so characteristic of scholarly inquiry into media systems and mass communications phenomena.

Historically, these conflicts have centered on paradigmatic differences concerning the nature and the degree of mass media power relative to audience power (e.g., mass versus gesellschaft social organization that generate passive susceptible or active "obstinate" audiences, respectively), the nature of media-state relations (e.g., media subservience versus interdependence), the culture-creating role of the media (primary versus secondary), the usefulness of quantitative methodologies for revealing "important" media effects (e.g., cumulative effects on symbolic and structural processes versus short-term effects on individuals' attitudes or behaviors), and the extent to which media researchers should stand in opposition to media systems in capitalist societies (e.g., "administrative" research that may wittingly or unwittingly benefit the media system versus critical research designed to demystify the media system). While debaters of these issues emanate from numerous scholarly disciplines, debate content is heavily rooted in sociological paradigms.

Sociological paradigms dominate inquiry, but few present-day American sociologists pursue media phenomena as their primary line of research. This situation is a departure from the historical dominance of American media sociology from the Chicago through the Columbia schools of the 1920s, 1930s, 1940s and 1950s—recall the work of the likes of Park, the Lynds, Ogburn, Lazarsfeld, Janowitz, or Mills. The last three decades of media sociology have been increasingly dominated by European sociologists, linguists, and political scientists. Among the most visible and prolific of these European communities have been the British Marxists and the French semioticians representing both Weberian and Marxian thought. Durkheimian modes of analysis are most evident in Scandinavian media sociology, particularly in the culture and society emphases of Swedish sociologists.

If the "crisis" in sociology is said to be due to the absence of paradigm consensus, then contemporary media study in American sociology is prototypical. Whereas Durkheimian thought dominated American media inquiry in the 1950s and 1960s, as evidenced in micro- and macrofunctional analyses of media systems and effects (e.g., Katz and Lazarsfeld, 1955; Breed, 1955; Riley and Riley, 1959; Wright, 1959), no one paradigm has dominated since. Marxian, Weberian, and Durkheimian paradigms and various hybrids thereof coexist, albeit in relative obscurity from the larger sociological enterprise. Such heterogeneity and obscurity makes the forecasting of media inquiry in American Sociology difficult. Complicating matters further is a related sociology of knowledge issue: Why, when American sociologists are or should be among the most alert to the sociostructural determinants and consequences of "the information age," should we find less attention today to one of the most significant information/communication systems—the mass media—than is evident in the 1950s prior to widespread recognition of the transition to an information or "post-industrial" society? We must briefly address this question, because the future of American media sociology probably rests more on whether the scarcity of attention paid to media phenomena will continue than on which paradigm of thought dominates.

AMERICAN MEDIA INQUIRY
OF THE LAST QUARTER-CENTURY:
A PATTERN OF DECLINE

Present-day inattention to media systems and mass communications in American sociology stands in stark contrast to international sociology. In the developing and the developed worlds alike, media theory and research are generally considered central to the many questions sociologists seek to answer about the conditions that facilitate or retard transition to new socioeconomic orders—those basic questions of integration, conflict, adaptation, change, and control.

Among the features of American sociology that might account for the pattern of declining attention of the last quarter-century (Ball-Rokeach, 1986) is *premature closure concerning the power of the media system.* Sociology graduate students were and are still being taught the overgeneralized and outdated "weak media-powerful audience" position articulated by Klapper (1960) more than a quarter-century ago. It is rarely noted that most of the research that produced this view (i.e., that spearheaded by Lazarsfeld) was conducted at the social psychological level of analysis with a limited range of questions about media effects on individuals. This position lazily hangs on, despite its strangeness in an age when information and communication systems have become dominant in economic, political, and other spheres of social life (Porat, 1977; Bell, 1979; Machlup, 1980). The weak-media position logically suggests to the talented and ambitious student that it would be unwise to invest in the study of media systems when mentors and gatekeepers regard them as relatively unimportant social forces.

The peripheral nature of the structural position of media studies within American sociology exacerbates the situation further. Few (approximately 12) Ph.D.-granting sociology departments offer a media speciality. Few accomplished "media" sociologists reside in departments of sociology, having left for more fertile departmental settings not easily accessible to the sociology student. In those departments in which media study is available, the practice of classifying it as a subspeciality of social psychology places it outside training and discourse in macrosociology.

The inherent difficulties of creating theory and research methodologies for explanation of such ubiquitous phenomena as the mass media is another consideration. Scholars must dedicate themselves to sustained inquiry over many years, an unlikely prospect unless the phenomenon under investigation is regarded as critical to the field's progress by those who control material and nonmaterial resources. Finally, *funding priorities that affect most social science research, have undermined the sociological relevance of the most visible media research.* In his elucidation of the historical role of media theory and research within American sociology, Charles Wright (1986a) notes that the psychological level of analysis has dominated funded media research of recent decades, leaving little in its wake that resonates to contemporary sociologists. Concerns for the media as forces affecting the structure and process of integration, conflict, change, and control so prominent in the work of Park, Ogburn, the Lynds, and other founders of American sociology, have not been among the priorities of funding agencies and thus have not received the financial resources necessary to keep these issues prominent in American sociology.

AMERICAN MEDIA STUDIES
IN THE NEXT QUARTER-CENTURY:
A PATTERN OF RESURGENCE

The obvious hope of those concerned about the future of media inquiry is that American sociology will lose its distinctive disinterest in media theory and research. The question is whether there is a critical mass of American sociologists who are doing sufficiently sound sociological analyses of media systems and mass communications to bring about this change. The fact that many trained as sociologists are not located solely or at all in departments of sociology (e.g., Katz, Kurt Lang, Gladys Engel Lang, Wright, Mendelsohn, Gerbner, Hirsch, Altheide, Schudson, Beniger, Tichenor, and now, myself) often masks, if not their visibility, the visibility of their media work in the sociological community. To demonstrate the presence of a critical mass, citations made in the following discussion are largely to American sociologists. The discussion is organized around the theoretical questions that seem most likely to dominate their future inquiry.

What Is Mass Communication?

It is not as strange as it may seem to begin with the primitive question of the nature and form of mass communication. The mass media, being information/communication technologies as well as social systems, have evolved rapidly in the century and a half of their existence. Until recently, their communication form has changed largely in the direction of becoming more technologically authentic, appealing with more and more fidelity to the primary human senses of sight and sound (e.g., going from newspapers to television). We are in the midst of a more revolutionary change of form, from the monological or one-way conventional mass communications to dialogical forms. Perhaps the best examples today are *interactive* media, such as interactive video discs. They permit a kind of dialogue in which partners to the communication have more equality of control over the communication act than is evident in conventional mass media. The strict separation of communicator and audience roles found in monological media will give way when dialogical media forms take hold on a mass basis. Established distinctions between mass and interpersonal communication will also give way.

On the down side of such developments is the prospect of communication and information inequalities that challenge the idea that mass communications are, by definition, accessible to the masses. To the extent that new media technologies require computer literacy—a likely prospect—and to the extent that computer literacy is delivered in a stratified manner to the upper strata of the social structure—a present reality—we are looking at new media that are semi-mass media. Concerns about "knowledge gaps" created by unequal access to conventional mass media pale in comparison to the gap that is already being created by unequal access to computer-based media.

What Is a Mass Media Audience?

The classical meaning of "mass" audience as an aggregate of anonymous individuals focused on the same communication was revised long ago (Katz and Lazarsfeld, 1955) to add the idea that audience members are embedded in stable, diverse, and influential interpersonal networks. Further revisions have been made. Audiences have been conceptualized as fluid constellations of specialized audiences that share discernible and heterogeneous preferences for certain types of cultural content (e.g., Gans, 1974; Cantor and Cantor, 1986). Specialized audiences may also be discerned in terms of a typology of media system dependencies or the personal understanding, orientation, and play goals that people seek to attain via consumption of media products (Ball-Rokeach et al., 1984). Contemporary advertisers have their own way of breaking the audience into subparts—demographically and even psychodynamically defined "target" audiences.

Following the lead of Cantor and Cantor (1986) and others, we are likely to see more research designed to demonstrate direct and indirect interactions between media organizations and audiences. The most common forms of direct interaction occur when interest groups attempt to affect media entertainment content and media organizations attempt to negotiate content with them (Lewels, 1974; Gitlin, 1981; Lewis, 1984; Montgomery, 1981, 1986). Indirect interaction is evident in the content consequences of the assumptions that those in control of the production process make about the tastes, values, or lifestyles of their audiences (Cantor and Pingree, 1983; Gitlin, 1983). With some notable exceptions (e.g., Johnstone et al., 1976; Gans, 1979; Gitlin, 1980; Lang and Lang, 1983), the negotiation (as opposed to the construction) of news content has been left to analysts outside American sociology (e.g., the imaginative work of Gandy, 1982) and of non-social scientists (e.g., Halberstam, 1979). The degree of media-audience interaction and negotiation of content should increase greatly as more dialogical media forms develop. Research on the consequences of such "new audiences" should increase accordingly.

What Is the Media System and Does It Have Consequences for Important Social Processes?

Thelma McCormack (1986) correctly laments the sparse attention given to issues of social change that had generated much of the media theory and research of early American sociology. With few exceptions (e.g., Katz and Szecsko, 1981; Ball-Rokeach and Tallman, 1979; Lang and Lang, 1984), change is addressed more in terms of mechanisms of change prevention than change facilitation (e.g., Tuchman, 1974, 1978; Sallach, 1974; Coser, 1975; Gitlin, 1979, 1980; Griswold, 1983). In contrast, there has been a return to classical sociological concerns for the macro-level consequences of the media system on processes of control, integration, adaptation, and conflict. This return has been stimulated, in large part, by the work of European scholars, a general disenchantment with the nature of the questions posed in experimental psychology, and by the works of a small number of American sociologists who pursued such lines of inquiry during the "famine" years.

The return also required a move away from psychological conceptions of the media system dominant in American sociology of the last quarter-century—a message-creating persuasion system designed to affect individuals on a mass basis. The kind of reconceptualization likely to relaunch valid inquiry into change and related social processes is now taking hold in

American sociology. Reconceptualizations include adoption and revision of the dominant British view of the media as a system in control of a major means of mental production (e.g., Ewen, 1976); extensions of the Frankfurt School's conception of media as meaning and culture-creating systems (e.g., Gerbner et al., 1980a); and elaborations of Innis's communication technology arguments to conceive of the media as a culture-destroying system (e.g., Postman, 1979). Other more Weberian and Durkheimian reconceptualizations treat the media system as an information system central to the structure and the process of societal, community, group, and individual life (e.g., Ball-Rokeach and DeFleur, 1976; Bell, 1979; Ball-Rokeach et al., 1984, de Sola Pool et al., 1984; Ball-Rokeach, 1985; Wright, 1986b; Beniger, 1986).

These reconceptualizations have already spawned a number of theory and research efforts directed at one or more social processes. Lines of contemporary inquiry that are likely to be pursued further include: (1) the news construction process and its social control consequences (e.g., Epstein, 1973; Roshco, 1975; Johnstone et al., 1976; Tuchman, 1974, 1978; Gans, 1979; Altheide, 1985; Gitlin, 1980); (2) the control and conflict processes entailed in the production of culture and its control, integration, and conflict consequences (e.g., Mills, 1963; Cantor, 1971, 1979, 1980; Hirsch, 1972, 1978; Gans, 1974; DiMaggio, 1982; Gitlin, 1979, 1983; Best, 1981; Coser et al., 1981; Becker, 1982; Newcomb and Hirsch, 1983; Cantor and Pingree, 1983); (3) Beniger's (1986) analysis of the media system as part and parcel of the control apparatus of information societies; (4) "media events" research focused on the capacities of the media system to transform audiences into temporary communities, but in so doing enhancing societal integration by the reaffirmation of norms, myths, and other modes of engendering solidarity (Katz et al., 1981; Dayan et al., 1984); (5) a renewed concern for the role of mass communications in community adaptation processes (e.g., Tichenor et al., 1980; Goltz, 1984; Turner and Paz, 1986; Hirschburg et al., 1986); (6) questions of adaptation (e.g., avoidance of information overload) generated out of the work of the late Ithiel de Sola Pool in collaboration with W. Russell Neuman (Neuman and de Sola Pool, 1986); (7) efforts spearheaded by Gladys Engel Lang and Kurt Lang (1983, 1984, 1986) to articulate the cumulative effects of media information-gathering and information-processing practices upon political processes; (8) applications of the "spiral of silence" thesis to instances of public opinion formation and conditions of its expression in context of community conflict (e.g., Taylor, 1986); (9) the nature of macro dependency relations between the media system and the political, economic, and other systems and their consequences for social processes within and between organizations and societies (Ball-Rokeach, 1985); and (10) the effects of dominance of the mass communication form upon community integration and the conduct of civic life (e.g., Sennett, 1974).

How Are Media Systems Affected by Social Processes?

How societal changes, conflicts, and adaptations affect the nature and the conduct of the media system are questions that have gone almost unexamined in American sociology. Two illustrative questions that follow from media system dependency theory and that may be answered in future historical and comparative research are: (1) Under what societal conditions (e.g., rapid social change and widespread social conflict) do media systems become more or less central to the operation of society? and (2) What do social processes (e.g., adaptation, integration, conflict, technological change) have to do with the scope and nature of media dependencies that groups and individuals can develop? There are a host of other issues being examined by legal scholars, economists, and communications scholars that should be of interest to sociologists. Among these are: (1) social movement, interest group, and state use of the legal system and regulatory agencies to exert social control on media content and ownership structure, and (2) the effects of technological development on the structure of the media system and the kinds of products it produces.

Does the Media System Have Consequences upon Social Structure and Vice Versa?

Far and away the central concern among Marxist media scholars has been to articulate the mechanisms by which "capitalists media" act to maintain stratified social structures domestically and to export such structures internationally. In recent decades, impetus has come from Great Britain (e.g., Williams, 1975; Glasgow University Media Group, 1976; Hall, 1977, 1980), Europe (e.g., Habermas, 1975; Mattelart, 1979), Canada (e.g., Smythe, 1981), and also American macroeconomics (e.g., Schiller, 1976, 1981). Among the specific concerns that American sociologists have addressed and are likely to continue to examine in the future are embedding of class structure and capitalist ideology on the national and international scene via (a) information and knowledge inequality owing to the failure of the media to speak meaningfully or saliently to the working and underclasses (e.g., Gouldner, 1976), (b) commodification or the reduction of cultural forms to commodities (e.g., Sewart, 1986), (c) containment of alternative media (e.g., Gray, 1986), (d) mystification (e.g., Tuchman, 1978), and (e) information control in the service of the state (e.g., Griswold, 1983).

Examination of other effects of media systems on social structure are likely to expand and flourish as American sociologists better articulate the social transformation to "information society." Such articulation should spawn reexaminations that locate media information systems in structurally central positions in all aspects of the social fabric. Of the many questions likely to be of interest are the effects of "new" information and communication technologies upon the structure of (a) economic organization, (b) residential ecology; (c) work, (d) political decision making, (e) family relations, (f) interinstitutional relations, and (g) international relations.

The more traditional concern among American sociologists for the effects of social structure on patterns of media consumption persists in the work of such scholars as Blumler and Katz (1974), Wright (1975), DiMaggio (1982) and Robinson and Fink (1986). Thinking has, however, gone beyond demographic analyses and descriptive analyses of class differences in media use. The previously noted move to a conception of the audience as active in its selection and use of media has generated a more substantive approach wherein research questions are grounded in larger theoretical issues. Consumption patterns, for example, may be viewed as products of not only socioeconomic factors, but also of variable environmental conditions, such as the rate of social change and conflict, and, ultimately of the structure of the media system's relations with other social systems (e.g., in interdependence, dominance, or subordinance). The rise of new forms of mass communication should also alter the nature of the questions posed about the effect of social structure on the media system and its "audiences." Alleged class differences in use of electronic and print media, for example, may become moot as it becomes harder and harder to distinguish between electronic and print media. More important may be research to discover the effects of sociostructural variables on the degree and ease of access to media information required to attain personal, community, interest group, subcultural, organizational, and societal goals.

What Is the Content and Structure of Media Messages?

Conventional quantitative content analyses addressing "social problems" or political issues (e.g., drugs, violence, racism, sexism, and gay rights) are usually designed to speak to issues of audience effects. These studies traditionally have been criticized for their failure to demonstrate effects or to even demonstrate that the messages sent are the messages received. Despite these criticisms, conventional content analyses are likely to continue to be part of the scene, because they provide descriptive enumerations essential to more explanatory projects in the production of culture, news construction, effects, and other lines of research (e.g., Singer and Endreny, 1986). Few (e.g., Gerbner et al., 1980a, 1980b) have been able to mount the resources necessary to link this descriptive enterprise with explanatory research, but such linkage will remain a desirable goal.

The rise of semiotic and hermeneutic modes of analyses have lead to an even more basic challenge of conventional content analysis; namely, that quantitative methods may tap relatively superficial aspects of media content, but cannot tap "deep" symbolic meaning and cultural content. Semiotic, hermeneutic, and other forms of qualitative content analysis are usually based on the assumption that the media system is a, if not the, most important culture-creating system. Analysis is thus designed to peel off levels of symbolic and cultural meaning contained in media messages. In most cases, it is assumed that such messages are in the service of the status quo and are thus more likely to produce behavioral continuity than behavioral change—for example, mystification, myth creation or perpetuation, ideological hegemony—macro effects not easily demonstrated by quantitative techniques (e.g., Sallach, 1974; Gitlin, 1979; Dayan et al., 1984; Parker, 1986; Press, 1986). Quantitative examination of similar effects has not, however, been abandoned as the work of Gerbner and his colleagues attests (Gerbner et al., 1980a, 1980b). A related line of research likely to gain in visibility is the study of the structure of media products, their form and format (Schudson, 1982; Newcomb and Hirsch, 1983; Swidler, 1986; Alexander, 1986; Press, 1986). The concern is not so much with explicit content, but with how that content is structured and the effects of different structural forms upon the nature of the cultural product and the social reality it helps to create among audience members.

Do the Media Have Social Effects on Audiences After All?

For more than a decade, "effects research" has been a target of media scholars who, for a variety of reasons, became disenchanted with experimental psychological research. One of the benefits of such disenchantment has been the resurgence of the many kinds of sociological inquiry that have been discussed heretofore. One of the negative consequences has been a certain dogmatic rejection of anything that came under the label of audience effects research, particularly if that research employed quantitative methodology. It has been rare to find "catholic" media scholars who argued that quantitative research might be well-suited to the study of some phenomena, while qualitative research strategies might be more appropriate for the study of other phenomena. Also rare are scholars openly rejecting the assertion that all quantitative research is necessarily "administrative" research in the sense that it serves the interests of the media system and the state. A curious blindness to instances in which quantitative research has been employed by interests groups against the interest of the media system, as in the case of research on television violence (see Rowland, 1983), serves to mask internal contradictions of argument. On the other side of the ideological fence, is the equally disturbing, previously discussed assertion that the mass media are unimportant forces in the creation and change of audience beliefs and behaviors. Proponents of this position also seemed blind to internal contradictions of argument, such as that posed by common sense (DeFleur and Ball-Rokeach, 1982). So, on the one hand, we have those who argue that the media are all powerful, but quantitative research can never reveal their power; on the other hand, we have those who argue that quantitative research shows that the media are relatively powerless, despite their centrality to everyday life of people and modern societies.

There is, nonetheless, a growing community of scholars conducting research on media effects upon their audiences' beliefs and behaviors. Much of this activity goes under the label of "media intervention" research (see Solomon, 1982 for a review) and is designed (1) to increase audience members' levels of knowledge about health matters (e.g., cardiovascular disease prevention or smoking and other drug addiction prevention or cessation techniques) in the hope of (2) altering beliefs and behaviors of specialized audiences (e.g., high health risk groups, unsafe drivers, alcoholics, or patient groups). This is a likely area for resurgence of participation by American sociologists, particularly with the coming of "dialogical media" that may be employed to effect change in organizational as well as public behavior.

In addition to the breaking of new effects research ground, there is also some sign of resurgence of activity in a classical concern of American media sociology—media effects on audiences' political beliefs and behaviors. We have previously referred to the Langs's leadership in building a theory and research effort designed to address the cumulative effects of the media upon political process. Their effort is indicative of a larger move away from experimental laboratory research designed to study short-term attitude change effects. Others researchers, for example, have directed their attention to relatively long-term effects of TV programming upon audiences' socially important political values, attitudes, and behavior, such as egalitarianism and environmentalism (Ball-Rokeach et al., 1984), and have conducted their research outside the laboratory with quasi-experimental field methods that are capable of handling threats to external as well as internal validity. For the future remains a challenge that ultimately all media and mass communication researchers will have to solve, that is to construct the conceptual mechanisms that will logically and convincingly link macro structural and process phenomena to micro processes of belief and behavior stability and change.

CONCLUSION

The ethnocentrism of this chapter is intentional. It is with a certain sociology of knowledge curiosity that I have pursued the questions of why a once lively and preeminent concern of American sociology became peripheral, and what intradisciplinary and external forces might create a return to its former centrality to the discipline of sociology. Both themes have been outlined in context of the past and present as prologue to future lines of inquiry. Resurgence of media inquiry is predicated on three major observations: (1) sociological paradigms are central to the media theory and research activity of other disciplines; (2) there is a critical mass of media sociologists who have gone beyond the limits of past inquiry and are likely to continue to do so in the future (see Ball-Rokeach and Cantor, 1986); and (3) there is an ongoing social transformation to an information society that in and of itself should stimulate renewed inquiry. To these, it is necessary to add a fourth; namely, the wonderfully diverse theoretical and empirical work that is being conducted in the many fields that "media sociologists" must encounter in the conduct of their work.

REFERENCES

Alexander, J. (1986) "The 'form' of substance: the Senate Watergate hearings," in S. J. Ball-Rokeach and M. G. Cantor (eds.) Media, Audience, and Social Structure. Beverly Hills, CA: Sage.
Altheide, D. L. (1985) Media Power. Beverly Hills, CA: Sage.
Ball-Rokeach, S. J. (1985) "The origins of individual media system dependency: a sociological framework." Communication Research 12: 485-510.

Ball-Rokeach, S. J. (1986) "The media and the social fabric," in J. F. Short, Jr. (ed.) The Social Fabric: Dimensions and Issues. Beverly Hills, CA: Sage.

Ball-Rokeach, S. J. and M. G. Cantor [eds.] (1986) Media, Audience, and Social Structure. Beverly Hills, CA: Sage.

Ball-Rokeach, S. J. and M. L. DeFleur (1976) "A dependency model of mass media effects." Communication Research 3: 3-21.

Ball-Rokeach, S. J., M. Rokeach, and J. W. Grube (1984) The Great American Values Test: Influencing Behavior and Belief Through Television. New York: Free Press.

Ball-Rokeach, S. J. and I. Tallman (1979) "Social movements as moral confrontations: the case of the Southern Christian Leadership Conference," in M. Rokeach (ed.) Understanding Human Values: Individual and Societal. New York: Free Press.

Becker, H. (1982) Art Worlds. Berkeley, CA: University of California Press.

Bell, D. (1979) "The social framework of the information society," pp. 163-211 in M. L. Dertouzos and J. Moses (eds.) The Computer Age: A Twenty Year View. Cambridge: MIT Press.

Beniger, J. (1986) "Technological and economic origins of the information society," in S. J. Ball-Rokeach and M. G. Cantor (eds.) Media, Audience, and Social Structure. Beverly Hills, CA: Sage.

Best, J. (1981) "The social control of media content." Journal of Popular Culture 14: 611-617.

Blumler, J. G. and E. Katz (1974) The Uses of Mass Communications: Current Perspectives on Gratifications Research. Beverly Hills, CA: Sage.

Breed, W. (1955) "Social control in the news room: a functional analysis." Social Forces 33: 326-335.

Cantor, M. G. (1971) The Hollywood TV Producer: His Work and His Audience. New York: Basic Books.

Cantor, M. G. (1979) "The politics of popular drama." Communication Research 6: 387-406.

Cantor, M. G. (1980) Prime-Time Television: Content and Control. Beverly Hills, CA: Sage.

Cantor, M. G. and J. M. Cantor (1986) "Audience composition and television content: the mass audience revisited," in S. J. Ball-Rokeach and M. G. Cantor (eds.) Media, Audience, and Social Structure. Beverly Hills, CA: Sage.

Cantor, M. G. and S. Pingree (1983) The Soap Opera. Beverly Hills, CA: Sage.

Coser, L. (1975) "Publishers as gatekeepers of ideas." Annals 42: 14-22.

Coser, L., C. Kadushin, and W. Powell (1981) Books: The Culture and Commerce of Publishing. New York: Basic Books.

Dayan, D., E. Katz, and P. Kerns (1984) "Armchair pilgrimages: the trips of Pope John Paul II and their television public." Presented at the Annual Meetings of the American Sociological Association, San Antonio.

de Sola Pool, I., H. Inose, N. Takasaki, and R. Hurwitz (1984) Communications Flows: Census in the United States and Japan. Amsterdam: North Holland Press, and Tokyo: Tokyo University Press.

DeFleur, L. and S. Ball-Rokeach (1982) Theories of Mass Communication (4th ed.). New York: Longman.

DiMaggio, P. (1982) "Cultural capital and school success: the impact of status culture participation on the grades of U.S. high school students." American Sociological Review 47: 189-201.

Epstein, E. J. (1973) News from Nowhere: Television and the News. New York: Random House.

Ewen, S. (1976) Captains of Consciousness. New York: McGraw Hill.

Gandy, O. H., Jr. (1982) Beyond Agenda Setting: Information Subsidies and Public Policy. Norwood, NJ: Ablex.

Gans, H. J. (1974) Popular Culture and High Culture: An Analysis and Evaluation of Taste. New York: Basic Books.

Gans, H. J. (1979) Deciding What's News: A Study of CBS Evening News, NBC Nightly News, Newsweek and Time. New York: Pantheon.

Gerbner, G., L. Gross, M. Morgan, and N. Signiorielli (1980a) "The mainstreaming of America: violence profile No. 11." Journal of Communication 30: 10-29.

Gerbner, G., L. Gross, N. Signiorielli, and M. Morgan (1980b) "Aging with television: images of television drama, and conceptions of social reality." Journal of Communication 30: 137-148.

Gitlin, T. (1979) "Prime time ideology: The hegemonic process in television entertainment." Social Problems 26: 251-266.

Gitlin, T. (1980) The Whole World is Watching: Mass Media in the Making and Unmaking of the New Left. Berkeley, CA: University of California Press.

Gitlin, T. (1981) "The new crusades: how the fundamentalists tied up the networks." American Film 7: 60-64 and 80-81.

Gitlin, T. (1983) Inside Prime-Time. New York: Pantheon.

Glasgow University Media Group (1976) Bad News. London: Routledge and Kegan Paul.

Goltz, J. D. (1984) "Are the news media responsible for disaster myths? A content analysis of emergency response imagery." Mass Emergencies and Disasters 2: 345-368.

Gouldner, A. (1976) The Dialectic of Ideology and Technology. New York: Seabury.

Gray, H. (1986) "Social constraints on the production of an alternative medium: the case of community radio," in S. J. Ball-Rokeach and M. G. Cantor (eds.) Media, Audience, and Social Structure. Beverly Hills, CA: Sage.

Griswold, W. (1983) "The devil's techniques: cultural legitimation and social change." American Sociological Review 48: 668-680.

Habermas, J. (1975) Legitimation Crisis. Boston, MA: Beacon.

Halberstam, D. (1979) The Powers That Be. New York: Dell.

Hall, S. (1977) "Culture, the media and the 'ideological effect,'" pp. 315-348 in J. Curran, M. Gurevitch, and J. Woollacott (eds.) Mass Communication and Society. London: Edward Arnold.

Hall, S. (1980) "Encoding/decoding," pp. 128-138 in S. Hall, D. Hobson, A. Lowe, and P. Willis (eds.) Culture, Media, Language. London: Hutchinson.

Hirsch, P. M. (1972) "Processing fads and fashions: an organization-set analysis of cultural industry systems." American Journal of Sociology 77: 639-659.

Hirsch, P. M. (1978) "Occupational, organizational and institutional models in mass media research," in P. Hirsch, P. Miller, and F. G. Kline (eds.) Strategies for Mass Media Research. Beverly Hills, CA: Sage.

Hirschburg, P. L., D. A. Dillman, and S. J. Ball-Rokeach (1986) "A test of media system dependency theory: response to the eruption of Mount St. Helens," in S. J. Ball-Rokeach and M. G. Cantor (eds.) Media, Audience, and Social Structure. Beverly Hills, CA: Sage.

Johnstone, J.W.C., E. J. Slawski, and W. W. Bowman (1976) The News People: A Sociological Portrait of American Journalists and Their Work. Urbana: University of Illinois Press.

Katz, E., D. Dayan, and P. Motyl (1981) "In defense of media events," in Communications in the Twenty-First Century. New York: John Wiley.

Katz, E. and P. F. Lazarsfeld (1955) Personal Influence: The Part Played by People in the Flow of Mass Communications. Glencoe, IL: Free Press.

Katz, E. and T. Szecsko [eds.] (1981) Mass Media and Social Change. Beverly Hills, CA: Sage.

Klapper, J. T. (1960) The Effects of Mass Communication. Glencoe, IL: Free Press.

Lang, G. E. and K. Lang (1983) The Battle for Public Opinion: The President, the Press, and the Polls During Watergate. New York: Columbia University Press.

Lang, G. E. and K. Lang (1984) Politics and Television Revisited. Beverly Hills, CA: Sage.

Lang, G. E. and K. Lang (1986) "Some observations on the long-range effects of television," in S. J. Ball-Rokeach and M. G. Cantor (eds.) Media, Audience, and Social Structure. Beverly Hills, CA: Sage.

Lewels, F. J. (1974) The Uses of the Media by the Chicano Movement: A Study in Minority Access. New York: Praeger.

Lewis, C. (1984) "Television license renewal challenges by women's groups." (unpublished, University of Minnesota)

Machlup, F. (1980) Knowledge: Its Creation, Distribution, and Economic Significance, Vol. 1. Princeton, NJ: Princeton University Press.

Mattelart, A. (1979) Communication and Class Struggle, Vol. 1: Capitalism, Imperialism. New York: International General.

McCormack, T. (1986) "Reflections on the lost vision of communication theory," in S. J. Ball-Rokeach and M. G. Cantor (eds.) Media, Audience, and Social Structure. Beverly Hills: CA: Sage.

Mills, C. W. (1963) "The cultural apparatus," pp. 405-422 in I. L. Horowitz (ed.) Power Politics and People: The Collected Essays of C. W. Mills. New York: Oxford University Press.

Montgomery, K. (1981) "Gay activists and the networks." Journal of Communication 31: 49-57.

Montgomery, K. (1986) "The political struggle for prime time," in S. J. Ball-Rokeach and M. G. Cantor (eds.) Media, Audience, and Social Structure. Beverly Hills, CA: Sage.

Neuman, W. R. and I. de Sola Pool (1986) "The flow of communication into the home," in S. J. Ball-Rokeach and M. G. Cantor (eds.) Media, Audience, and Social Structure. Beverly Hills, CA: Sage.

Newcomb, H. and P. M. Hirsch (1983) "Television as a cultural forum: implications for research." Quarterly Review of Film Studies 8: 45-55.

Parker, James J. (1986) "The organizational environment of the motion picture sector," in S. J. Ball-Rokeach and M. G. Cantor (eds.) Media, Audience, and Social Structure. Beverly Hills, CA: Sage.

Porat, M. U. (1977) The Information Economy: Definition and Measurement. Washington DC: Office of Telecommunications, U.S. Department of Commerce.

Postman, N. (1979) Teaching as a Conserving Activity. New York: Delacorte.

Press, A. (1986) "Historical development in the 'hegemonic female fantasy' in postwar Hollywood films," in S. J. Ball-Rokeach and M. G. Cantor (eds.) Media, Audience, and Social Structure. Beverly Hills, CA: Sage.

Riley, J. W. and M. W. Riley (1959) "Mass communication and the social system," pp. 537-578 in R. K. Merton, L. Broom, and L. S. Cottrell (eds.) Sociology Today: Problems and Prospects. New York: Basic Books.

Robinson, J. P. and E. Fink (1986) "Beyond mass culture and class culture: subcultural differences in the structure of music preferences," in S. J. Ball-Rokeach and M. G. Cantor (eds.) Media, Audience, and Social Structure. Beverly Hills, CA: Sage.

Roshco, B. (1975) Newsmaking. Chicago: University of Chicago Press.

Rowland, W. (1983) The Politics of TV Violence: Policy Uses of Communication Research. Beverly Hills, CA: Sage.

Sallach, D. L. (1974) "Class domination and ideological hegemony," pp. 161-173 in G. Tuchman (ed.) The TV Establishment. Englewood Cliffs, NJ: Prentice-Hall.

Schiller, H. I. (1976) Communication and Cultural Domination. White Plains, NY: Communications Arts and Sciences.

Schiller, H. I. (1979) Who Knows Information in the Age of the Fortune 500? Norwood, NJ: Ablex.

Schudson, M. (1982) "The politics of narrative form: the emergence of news conventions in print and television." Daedalus 111: 97-112.

Schudson, M. (1986) "The menu of media research," in S. J. Ball-Rokeach and M. G. Cantor (eds.) Media, Audience, and Social Structure. Beverly Hills: CA: Sage.

Sennett, R. (1974) The Fall of Public Man. New York: Vintage.

Sewart, J. L. (1986) "The commodification of sport," in S. J. Ball-Rokeach and M. G. Cantor (eds.) Media, Audience, and Social Structure. Beverly Hills, CA: Sage.

Singer, E. and P. Endreny (1986) "The reporting of social science research in the media," in S. J. Ball-Rokeach and M. G. Cantor (eds.) Media, Audience, and Social Structure. Beverly Hills, CA: Sage.

Smythe, D. W. (1981) Dependency Road: Communications, Capitalism, Consciousness and Canada. Norwood, NJ: Ablex.

Solomon, D. S. (1982) "Health campaigns on television," in D. Pearl, L. Bouthilet, and J. Lazar (eds.) Television and Behavior: Ten Years of Scientific Progress. Rockville, MD: U.S. Department of Health and Human Services.

Swidler, A. (1986) "Format and formula in prime-time TV," in S. J. Ball-Rokeach and M. G. Cantor (eds.) Media, Audience, and Social Structure. Beverly Hills, CA: Sage.

Taylor, D. Garth (1986) "Awareness of public opinion and school desegregation protest," in S. J. Ball-Rokeach and M. G. Cantor (eds.) Media, Audience, and Social Structure. Beverly Hills, CA: Sage.

Tichenor, P. J., G. A. Donohue, and C. N. Olien (1980) Community Conflict and the Press. Beverly Hills, CA: Sage.

Tuchman, G. [ed.] (1974) The TV Establishment. Englewood Cliffs, NJ: Prentice.

Tuchman, G. (1978) Making News: A Study in the Construction of Reality. New York: Free Press.

Turner, R. H. and D. H. Paz (1986) "The media in earthquake warning: research in Southern California," in S. J. Ball-Rokeach and M. G. Cantor (eds.) Media, Audience, and Social Structure. Beverly Hills, CA: Sage.

Williams, R. (1975) Television: Technology and Cultural Form. New York: Schocken.

Wright, C. R. (1959) Mass Communication: A Sociological Perspective (1st ed.). New York: Random House.

Wright, C. R. (1975) "Social structure and mass communication behavior," in L. Coser (ed.) The Idea of Social Structure: Papers in Honor of Robert K. Merton. New York: Harcourt Brace Jovanovich.

Wright, C. R. (1986a) "Mass communication rediscovered: its past and future in American sociology," in S. J. Ball-Rokeach and M. G. Cantor (eds.) Media, Audience, and Social Structure. Beverly Hills, CA: Sage.

Wright, C. R. (1986b) Mass Communication: A Sociological Perspective (3rd ed.). New York: Random House.

19

SOCIAL CHANGE

Wilbert E. Moore

University of Denver

It might be supposed that sociologists primarily interested in the analysis of social change should have special tools and talents in forecasting the probable directions of theory and research in their chosen subject matter. After thoughtful and at least partially informed consideration, I find the specialty about as confused and directionless as most other fields in the discipline. Part of that diversity is intrinsic to the range of subject matter. Social change is a way of looking at the whole range of social phenomena as compared with somewhat more readily bounded topics, such as the family, polity, or religion, or such problem areas as white-collar crime or ethnic conflict. The concept of social change may be applied to socialization, attitude and opinion change, small group dynamics, immanent and adaptive change in complex organizations, the dynamic ecology of urban areas, national policies, international interdependence, or the world as a singular system, or such general processes as may fit the metaphor of social evolution or such undeniable trends as the spread of structural rationalization.

In the first edition (1963) of my small but ambitious book, *Social Change* I urged, I think persuasively, the impossibility of a single, encompassing theory of social change. In the intervening nearly quarter-century I have seen no basis for changing that judgment, which could, of course, be taken simply as an enduring or increasing incapacity to learn. It is scant comfort that Tilly (1984: 33-40) agrees, for, as I shall discuss later, he is uncomfortable with my generalization. My own primary, though not exclusive, attention over those years has been given to the comparative dynamics of societies in the contemporary era, focusing on what may be rather inadequately characterized as "modernization." If more properly identified as "structural rationalization," the components (*and limits*) of that general process appear to me to encompass more of the world's places and cultures and more aspects of social behavior than any other (see Moore, 1979). Yet that global process will not encompass much of small-scale and some medium-scale change. Nor will rationalization "sweep all before it" or lead to a convergent, uniform, "look-alike" world. To these matters I shall return.

My focus here will be on the large-scale and long-term, with such associated medium-scale and middle-term dynamics as space and my wits permit. Also, I shall attempt such predictions of sociological developments in this sphere as appear to be warranted and especially to indulge the temptation to assert what I believe should be done, trying not to confuse the two. Thus some enduring and some more recent trends in dealing with large processes will, I fear, continue to engage their current adherents and even attract their students or others, despite the sterility or even the fundamental errors of the theoretical framework used.

ON SOCIAL EVOLUTION

A few paragraphs ago I used the phrase, "the metaphor of social evolution," and I did so advisedly. Darwinian evolution has had a persistent appeal to anthropologists and sociologists, especially when the evidence seems to fit some part of the model. The progression from simple to complex may be the one most commonly used. But that rule is true in biological evolution only if the entire biosphere is the unit of analysis. By the fossil evidence, species of simple organisms may endure through many geological eras to the present day, and complex organisms become extinct after a relatively brief appearance in geological time. Indeed, a substantial majority of the plant and animal species that have existed are extinct, mainly without naughty human intervention. That fact casts a dark cloud over "selective adaptation" or "adaptive selection" as the master process of evolutionary change. Seeming improvements of coping with the environment, perhaps over considerable time, may prove insufficient or even lethal with even slight changes in relevant conditions. There are other problems that I shall pass over here, but the most fundamental one is that biological evolution is mindless and mechanical. Some biologists are careless; they capitalize Nature and attribute to that pseudodeity, teleological intent: "Nature so intended" this or that morphological feature or symbiotic relationship. That of course is rubbish. It is precisely human purpose that makes the concept of social evolution metaphorical at best. Over the history of the human species there has been cumulative knowledge and understanding of many matters of human interest, and a growing propensity to use observationally based understanding for prediction and control. To call that social evolution probably does little harm, but it has no explanatory power at all.

There is some probability that a demonstrably "better way" for achieving this-worldly human goals will be accepted, given favorable conditions. Such favorable conditions would include the institutionalization of instrumental rationality as a normatively sanctioned expectation. That condition is met in much of the contemporary world and over a fairly broad spectrum of human desires. However, social values and behavioral principles held to be sacred may provide strong resistance from true believers: witness the resistance to rational control of human fertility. And in any complex social system, and perhaps even in less internally differentiated ones, any social change (in technology, in rules of conduct, in beliefs and values) will affect some interests adversely. If those interests are those of persons respected or even merely powerful, the probability of successful change may be eliminated, attenuated, or delayed: witness the poor prospect for genuinely representative government in a vast majority of the world's actually or nominally sovereign countries. (Appeals to the indefinite long-run future may leave us with some faint optimism but also with some justifiable impatience.)

Increasing differentiation, a presumably invariable trend much favored by neoevolutionists and even some "neofunctionalists," cannot be safely taken as a given. Increasing size of social units makes differentiation possible. The "cumulative growth of useful knowledge, especially to the point that the collective store of such knowledge is beyond the capacity of each (or any) individual to command all of it" makes differentiation certain (Moore, 1979: 47). As Edward Tiryakian's (1985) discussion of dedifferentiation calls to our attention recurrent attempts to emphasize unity and commonality within complex systems makes the assumption of ever-increasing differentiation presumptuous.

Human intentionality figures prominently in the limits both on technical innovation and on increasing differentiation, two processes that fit the metaphor of evolution.

WORLD SYSTEMS

Another approach to large units and processes has emerged more recently under the rubric of "world system theory." At a plenary session of the American Sociological Association in 1965 I presented a paper titled "Global Sociology: The World as a Singular System" (Moore, 1966). There I argued that increasingly there is a world pool not only of technology (useful knowledge) but also of political ideologies, subject to eclectic selection and adaptation. Since nationalism is also a nearly universal element of political ideology and intrinsically divisive on a global basis, uniformity is not to be expected. However, interdependence is undeniable, and we must convert the sociologists' societies and the anthropologists' cultures as self-subsistent units into a conceptual model having analytical utility, but without an exact empirical referent. A part of this "globalization" I should now identify as the growth and spread of structural rationalization of economic orders but also of legal systems, the administrative structure of the state, secularized formal education, control of mortality and, haltingly, fertility.

Early starters in economic development and other forms of rationalization have substantial, and enduring, advantages over those who, for whatever reasons, have only recently joined in the quest for modernity (Levy, 1972). Immanuel Wallerstein (1979) and other self-identified "world system" theorists, including adherents of a conspiratorial view of the "dependency" of poor countries on rich countries (for example, Frank 1975), have attempted to depict this situation from a neo-Marxist perspective. It is even argued that the "class struggle" has gone beyond single capitalist countries (as anticipated by Lenin 70 years ago), and that we may expect increasing polarization between "bourgeois" states and "proletarian" states not anticipated by Lenin. Aside from neglecting the substantial social inequalities within highly rationalized states (now including the Soviet Union and Eastern Europe), increasing polarization among nations along "class" lines seems no more likely to be the future course of international relations than it has been for the original capitalist countries, all of which have become "welfare states" with "mixed economies" in various forms and degrees.

An interesting comparison is afforded by two books by David Chirot: *Social Change in the Twentieth Century* (1977) and *Social Change in the Modern Era* (1986). In the earlier book, Chirot, a former student of Wallerstein, refers (p. 8) to the poor countries as an "international lower class," kept in that condition not necessarily by a "plot" but by "interconnected forces within rich countries and within the entire world system" (p. 9), whatever that may mean. The political, economic, and perhaps "cultural" exploitation of colonial and other backward areas has been real but commonly exaggerated. Enduring capital improvements (for example, the Indian railway system), the education of a native civil service, diversification of economic production, public health improvements are often neglected by critics. Chirot's later book (1986) covers not only a longer time period but also a more comprehensive view of world changes with less emphasis on the quasi conspiracy of capitalist countries to keep most of the world poor and exploited.

It is all very well to identify the "center" and the "periphery," but the division becomes simplistic if actual measures or indicators of current conditions and temporal trends show the necessity of recognizing such intermediate categories as "near-center" and "semi-periphery." Surely there is room for sociologists whose field of vision encompasses the world to analyze the dynamics of all sorts of interdependencies (which are not necessarily inhibitors of conflict), the formation of unstable coalitions, the possibilities of peaceful conflict resolution. We do not in fact have a realistic, quantitatively informed typology of "developmental careers" of countries across the broad spectrum of cultures and historical paths to the present. I do not underestimate the difficulties in getting credible information or in dealing with the complexity of a multiplicity of variables. But we do not now know enough of the relative success or failure of various courses of "induced development" to support our natural cautions against trusting only economists and engineers as advisors to decision makers. We know that "culture," social structure, and political ideologies and interests "make a difference," but it will help if one can specify more precisely the probable resistances and reinforcements these factors will provide to a planned course of change. I should like to think that the future will bring some increase in research on the "world system" that does not start with discredited simplification.

SOCIAL INEQUALITY

While it comes handy, I should like to comment briefly on future studies of trends in social inequality. For most of the highly rationalized Western societies, and particularly for those without a feudal past, the term *class* has a diminishing or virtually no applicability to social reality. Frequently it represents an arbitrary line drawn across continuous distributions, the number and placement being at the discretion of the analyst. Chirot (1986: 233-244) is too good an objective sociologist to treat "class relations" in mature capitalist societies as marked by ever-increasing polarization, but still confuses "interest conflicts," some of which have little to do with measures of social inequality, as clashes between "classes."

Increased diversification—especially of education and occupation—will almost certainly lead to forms and degrees of inequality that will more nearly approximate the bell-shaped curve than the expectation of increased polarization. (Incidentally, an array of countries in terms of income per capita shows a similar pattern.) Within countries, whether there are observationally verifiable discontinuities in the distribution (for example, between the managers and the managed, a variant on Marx's conception of class, or almost no intergenerational or career mobility) is subject to inquiry, not to be assumed in order to fit our conceptual apparatus or theoretical preconceptions.

The ubiquity of social inequality has too often been neglected by the concern of Western sociologists with the "class" inequality in capitalist regimes. Several years ago Treiman (1977) developed an international occupational prestige scale that included "socialist" regimes. Two "country" studies have come to my attention: Reszke (1984) on "social" (including occupational) prestige in Poland, and Yanowitch (1977) on social and economic inequality in the Soviet Union. "Classes" in the Marxist sense have been abolished in these countries by state ownership of the means of production, but of course patterns of inequality remarkably similar to those in capitalist countries are to be found. In the present context we should like to know the extent and direction of change, and on that we know relatively little. Western neo-Marxists concerned with capitalist "deskilling" of the labor force without attention to the rising minimum and median skill levels will of course be of no help.

LARGE TRENDS

There are signs that at least a few people are concerned with the large scale depicted with a broad brush. Although the authors are not certified in our craft, Alvin Toffler's popular *Future Shock* (1970) and *The Third Wave* (1980) come to mind, along with John Naisbitt's also popular *Megatrends* (1982). Toffler emphasizes such trends as consumerism, the volatility of fashion and fad, diversity of life styles, the flattening of authority structures, the threatened psychological insecurity of those coping with rapid change and its uncertainties. For those unfamiliar with *The Third Wave*, it represents Toffler's large-scale periodization of history: the invention of agriculture, the industrial revolution, and postindustrial society.

Naisbitt notes the shift from goods to services (the "information society"), increasing world economic interdependence—his one concession to "globalism," though he does (pp. 221-229) compare American business managerial styles with the Japanese and Swedish patterns. Like Toffler, Naisbitt emphasizes growing diversity of life styles, and the decentralization of economic and political controls.

Richard D. Lamm (1985), Colorado's governor at the time of this writing, produced a more gloomily challenging image of the future. His *Megatraumas* is chiefly concerned with such national problems as health care, pensions, immigration, crime, and the "litigation explosion." Lamm, a generalist and a rationalist in a society rife with special interests and emotional attachment to ideologies, sacred and profane, seeks to secure attention to problems that afford possibilities of rational palliation if not complete solution. His aim, in other words, is self-defeating prophecy. As a prophet of "gloom and doom," in characterizations by the public press, Lamm provokes much controversy, with emotional reactions from opponents who display that they are part of the problem.

Toffler, Naisbitt, and Lamm—respectively a journalist, a business consultant and supplier of trend information to subscribers, and an intellectual (former academic) state governor address principally American trends and problems for an American audience. Although the United States is a large and multiply diversified country, concentrating attention only on America has a strong taint of parochialism. It is a criticism that American sociologists as a disciplinary body cannot in good grace make against outsiders, as it applies equally to a very large proportion of our own scholarly work.

Any ambitious generalizations such as those just briefly noted will be subject to criticism, not altogether carping. For the social scientist, the absence of quantitative information, such as trend data, leave the reader at the mercy of the writer's impressions, buttressed by a few examples. Yet have we become so intimidated by our methodologists, who tend to analyze small, not to say trivial subjects, that we leave the large units and trends to laypersons, though admittedly talented and articulate? Well, not entirely. A recent small volume by one of our own, Charles Tilly, bears the modest title: *Big Structures, Large Processes, and Huge Comparisons* (1984). Not surprisingly, Tilly continues to emphasize the uses of history, not only to broaden our comparative cases but also, and necessarily, to derive or test theories of change. Tilly (1984: 20-26) is critical of the assumption of the autonomy of societies, critical to the point that he is indifferent to the fact that nominally sovereign states do have empirical reality, including the function of assembling statistical materials that provide some measures of social performance. But, then, Tilly (pp. 76-79) also does not like numbers. He is suitably cautionary about increasing differentiation as a "progressive master process" (pp. 43-50), but in the course of that discussion he expresses displeasure at theories of "modernization" (pp. 45-46), failing to note Weber's (1946, 1968; also Collins, 1986: 61-79) work on rationalization, which is unforgivable, as well as my own (Moore, 1979), which is at least indicative of a highly selective literature review.

Despite Tilly's promise of the large scale (and perhaps the long run) in his book's title, he persistently shows a preference for less sweeping concerns and for the details that appeal to the historian. The best example he can find of "universals" is the three-country comparison of the role of the peasantry in revolutions in the commendable work on *States and Social Revolutions* by Skocpol (1979). Even so, the author is scolded by Tilly (1984: 109-115) for neglect of details. True, in his final two pages (pp. 146-147) he suggests that it is possible that "the tendency of populations to spend smaller shares of their income on food and shelter as income rises . . . will prove to be quite general" (p. 146). Known as "Engel's law" (see Zimmerman, 1936: 22-41) and not so identified by Tilly, this generalization can probably be extended to all physical goods, as services figure increasingly in household budgets (Moore, 1965: 71-72). Finally, in the next-to-last sentence (p. 147) we learn of "the two interdependent master processes of the era: the creation of a system of national states [but not societies?] and the formation of a worldwide capitalist system." The latter trend is not self-evidently true, in view of the substantial number of avowedly socialist (mainly Leninist) countries. All are affected by international trade and capital flows, however. Yet to suggest that political regimes are inconsequential is the sort of over-simplification that Tilly dislikes.

Tilly, with relatives and associates, will no doubt continue to do exemplary historical work, informed by sociological theory. It is doubtful that many other sociologists will share their enthusiasm for fine-grained "microhistorical" research.

COMMENTS ON METHODOLOGY

Again, while it is handy, I shall make some comments on methodology. With the notable exception of the measurement tools of sociological demographers, almost all of our innovations and refinements in statistical analysis are correlational and thus synchronic. Relatively little attention is given to time series. Time-lagged correlations keep us in familiar territory, and are useful in determining whether a deliberate intervention in a pattern of action has a measurable or statistically significant effect. Enthusiasm for misnamed "general systems theory" appears to me to have waned. (It is misnamed because it is not a theory at all, but a conceptual or analytical model.) Most of the applications have been devoted to optimizing some goal or limited set of goals through tracing the consequences of some induced change in a rather sharply bounded system. Yet not only do the concepts associated with cybernetics have broader applications, as Talcott Parsons (1975: 374-383) attempted, in late work, but the whole approach also has an even broader methodological lesson: Consequences have consequences. The fact that the general systems approach seems to fit best the consequences of deliberate change does not necessarily relegate it to the status of a "management tool." Much of contemporary change is made up of the consequences, positive or negative, intended or unanticipated, of deliberate and even planned change. The challenge will be that of developing predictive measures of consequences for situations that are more complex, less discrete or bounded, and thus marked with greater uncertainties. For years I have realized—and done nothing about except infrequent hortatory admonitions on occasions like this—that the measurement methodology needed must fit linked sequences of probability distributions: that is, stochastic processes. A recent collection of essays provides a good array of procedures and applications (Diekmann and Ritter, 1984). Perhaps the most familiar illustration would be predicting the probable outcomes of games of chance, such as various board games relying on the throw of dice or the spinning of roulette-type wheels for each successive move. An even better illustration in its closer approximation to the world of serious affairs would be games characterized by differences in resources (including skills) as well as chance, such as baseball. Any ambitious social planning project will provide a "real life" opportunity for such analyses. Courses of planned action will have intermediate outcomes that change the parameters and probabilities of ensuing intermediate and "ultimate" outcomes.

DIALECTICAL RELATIONS

Finally, for this occasion, I revert to my revisit to Max Weber's (1968) concern with the spread of structural rationalization in the contemporary world. In my book on world modernization (Moore, 1979: 136-149) I concluded that common processes of rationalization—such as bureaucratization or the partial secularization of formal education—will not lead to common results as long as the ultimate goals or values of such instrumental action differ, as they do among, and not infrequently within, more or less independent states. Whether those goals or values are largely consensual or more or less effectively imposed has small relevance in this context. The comfort or boredom offered by a look-alike world cannot be expected. It may, however, be necessary to reinvent Auguste Comte's "Religion of Humanity" to find a superordinate value in order to avoid planetary life-destroying conflict among such discordant political units. I have also argued that "total rationalization" is inhibited by the reality of human emotion and sentiment, and thus the resistance to rationalization of all social structures strongly or even crucially characterized by affective ties among the members. As the precarious state of the traditional family in the Western world illustrates, this "affective shield" can be pierced. Still, a life sterilized of human emotional ties and behaviors is both uninviting and improbable. The proliferation of structural alternatives to conventional forms of affectivity and their relative durability may deserve more attention than now received.

In a book I am writing jointly with Joyce Sterling (Sterling and Moore, forthcoming), we have come to realize that structural rationalization will often not lead to a steady state. The limit now perceived is apart from changes in goals or relevant conditions, changes in instrumentally useful knowledge, or even the probably ineradicable propensity for irrational action. Our study is on the comparative dynamics of legal systems, and the extent to which they are subject to progressive formal or instrumental rationalization. In the course of our analysis we have come to recognize, and at least partially identify, what we have come to call "unsolvable social problems." I shall note a few very briefly, with particular but not exclusive applicability to legal systems. We call these antinomies "dialectical relations" despite the caution that all dichotomies are false. They generally prove to be "false" in practice, as the typical pattern is one of oscillation between conflicting principles and policies, all attempts at balanced compromises proving to be unstable.

Uniform rule versus discretionary justice. Each has its own persuasive justification: Justice as "blind" to the character or social position of the accused, but also blind to possible mitigating circumstances of the actual offense, or justice tempered by circumstances but at the risk of favoritism and lack of predictability.

Centralization versus decentralization. In complex, hierarchical adminis-trative organizations centralization seemingly assures firmness of executive control but at the probable cost of delays in problem solving and neglect of genuine difference in the actual situation of various nominally comparable parts of the system. Decentralization attends to those problems, at the risk of setting precedents or adapting to unusual situations that threaten the integrity of the whole organization. In a multicommunal state (multiethnic, multilingual, multireligious) enforced uniformity risks conscientious disobedience or, more likely, subterfuge and evasion, and the legitimacy of authority impaired or withheld. Tolerated diversity avoids those problems at the risk of impaired uniformity of public policy or mobilization for collective goals.

There are other dilemmas in the political and legal spheres, such as the public interest versus special or private interests. When pure cases cannot be found in nature, one may safely assume a dialectical situation. This is true of Parsons's (1951: 58-67, 101-112) "pattern variables," for example. Parsons (p. 59) does refer to a couple of his paired alternatives as "dilemmas" but does not pursue the uncertainty and thus instability implicit in that designation.

The implications of these and other dialectical relations are, first, cautionary, the hazard of projecting a long-term trend from what is in fact a short-term oscillation; second, challenging, the development of measures and indicators of such oscillations, and the determination of whether there is a predictable periodicity in what, over the longer term, is essentially a cyclical pattern; and, finally, humbling, to all of us who assumed that adequate knowledge and instrumental technique, fostered by good will, could eventually find solutions to any problem.

REFERENCES

Chirot, Daniel (1977) Social Change in the Twentieth Century. New York: Harcourt Brace Jovanovich.

Chirot, Daniel (1986) Social Change in the Modern Era. New York: Harcourt Brace Jovanovich.

Collins, Randall (1986) Max Weber: A Skeleton Key. Beverly Hills, CA: Sage.

Diekmann, Andreas and Peter Mitter [eds.] (1984) Stochastic Modelling of Social Processes. Orlando, FL: Academic Press.

Frank, Andre Gunder (1975) On Capitalist Underdevelopment. New York: Oxford University Press.

Lamm, Richard D. (1985) Megatraumas: The World at the Year 2000. Boston: Houghton Mifflin.

Levy, Marion J., Jr. (1972) Modernization: Latecomers and Survivors. New York: Basic Books.

Moore, Wilbert E. (1963) Social Change. Englewood Cliffs, NJ: Prentice-Hall.

Moore, Wilbert E. (1965) The Impact of Industry. Englewood Cliffs, NJ: Prentice-Hall.

Moore, Wilbert E. (1966) "Global sociology: the world as a singular system." American Journal of Sociology 71: 475-82.

Moore, Wilbert E. (1979) World Modernization: The Limits of Convergence. New York: Elsevier.

Naisbitt, John (1982) Megatrends. New York: Warner.

Parsons, Talcott (1951) The Social System. Glencoe, IL: Free Press.

Parsons, Talcott (1975) Action Theory and the Human Condition. New York: Free Press.

Reszke, Irena (1984) Social Prestige and Gender: Criteria of Occupational and Personal Prestige. Warsaw: Polish Academy of Sciences.

Skocpol, Theda (1979) States and Social Revolutions: A Comparative Analysis of France, Russia, and China. Cambridge: Cambridge University Press.

Sterling, Joyce S. and Wilbert E. Moore (forthcoming) The Rationalization of Law: A Comparative Analysis.

Tilly, Charles (1984) Big Structures, Large Processes, Huge Comparisons. New York: Russell Sage.

Tiryakian, Edward A. (1985) "On the significance of de-differentiation," pp. 118-134 in S. N. Eisenstadt and H. J. Helle (eds.) Macro-Sociological Theory. Beverly Hills, CA: Sage.

Toffler, Alvin (1970) Future Shock. New York: Random House.

Toffler, Alvin (1980) The Third Wave. New York: Morrow.

Treiman, Donald J. (1977) Occupational Prestige in Comparative Perspective. New York: Academic Press.

Wallerstein, Immanuel (1979) The Capitalist World-Economy. Cambridge: Cambridge University Press.

Weber, Max (1946) From Max Weber (H. H. Gerth and C. W. Mills, trans. and eds.). New York: Oxford University Press.

Weber, Max (1968) Economy and Society (G. Roth and K. Wittich, trans. and eds.; German edition, 1922).

Yanowitch, Murray (1977) Social and Economic Inequality in the Soviet Union. White Plains, NY: M. E. Sharpe.

Zimmerman, Carle C. (1936) Consumption and Standards of Living. Princeton, NJ: Van Nostrand.

PART V

SOCIAL STRATIFICATION

The field of social stratification can be viewed inclusively, or in terms of the many types of stratification that occur. Traditionally, concepts of class and caste have been of central importance to the description of societies, but with the rise of modern industrial society, stratification has come to have different emphases from the categorical ascribed status systems. Much attention in the study of social stratification focuses on the vestiges of ascribed statuses in social systems that are nominally presumed to emphasize individual achievement of status. The chapter by Borgatta and Hatch gives particular attention to the focus of social stratification as it existed in the Post World War II period, and then notes some of the shifts that have occurred in the interim, including the civil rights movement, the development of concern with sex roles, and the emphasis on studies of intergenerational social mobility. The issue of the values involved in the interpretation of law by the U.S. Supreme Court is noted, particularly pointing to the question of whether rights of individuals are universalistically at issue or equalization of status by categorically defined groups.

The study of race relations is reviewed by Bonacich, placing emphasis on a perspective of examining who the creators of the knowledge in the sociology of race have been. She sees the 1980s as a period in which "gains made by minorities, the working class, and other disadvantaged segments of society" have diminished. The role of academics and of sociologists in particular is examined, and emphasis is placed on the notion that the institution in which "[we] are embedded in deeply affects the way we think about race and ethnic relations." Bonacich then addresses issues of a socially responsible sociology of race and ethnic relations.

The sociology of gender is not new, but it has grown rapidly in the last two decades. Marini briefly reviews the manifest differences between men and women, giving attention to differences that are demonstrated and differences that are reflections of stereotypes. The question of why men and women differ is addressed, examining sources of influence, both at the macro and the micro levels. Marini sees a need in the future of monitoring changes in the status of women, with the development and testing of rigorously formulated theory as the biggest challenge facing sociologists.

The demographic changes in the population have been accompanied with a growing interest in age, aging, and the aged. Treas and Passuth indicate how the interest in these three perspectives on research have developed as areas of knowledge, and raise the question of whether they can be unified into a single specialization in sociology. They suggest reasons for optimism and see the inclusive area as one of vital research with the potential for integration.

The essays in this part reflect different perspectives, but they all reflect what may be seen as areas of vital research attention. The issues involved in each can be seen in a developmental perspective as having similar bases, although the content may differ. A reasonable conclusion is that the study of stratification may well produce some more general theory than is commonly experienced in studies on specific foci.

20

SOCIAL STRATIFICATION

Edgar F. Borgatta

University of Washington

Laurie Russell Hatch

University of Kentucky

Among the concepts that are important to sociology, possibly social stratification has been easiest to identify as central to the discipline and to justify as a distinct subdiscipline. If sociology is the scientific study of society, what better to study than the existence of social structures and how they are ordered? If there are differences between categories of people, why do they exist, and how do the differences come about? And if there are differences between positions or statuses in society, how are they maintained, how does the structure operate, and who fills the different positions? These are the kinds of questions that can be made meaningful to nonsociologists, and indeed these are the kinds of questions that predate any of the social sciences. So, to pick an anchorage to suggest where the study of social stratification began is a matter of options, and no one would be surprised to find references to Plato and Aristotle, to the Old Testament, or to other ancient sources. For our purposes, however, we will avoid this temptation and try to pick a few more recent reference points that are basic to current sociology.

In this chapter, we review developments in the study of social stratification from the 1950s to the present. Social changes and upheavals have been great during this period, possibly corresponding most directly to changes in communications and the media, which permit the quick spread of knowledge and ideas. Such changes have altered structures of stratification in many societies. For example, during the last half-century, Africa has changed from a colonial continent to one of nations, India and Pakistan became independent, and other areas have become detached from empires. Internally rigid caste and class controls, including slavery, have been nominally rejected. While the Union of South Africa is a contrary example (and there are others, particularly the theocratically restrictive nations), much of the world has moved away from rigid legal status classifications in the last half-century. These classifications persist, however, as custom-based residues that often are as strong as the legal ones.

Differences among nations in material development and wealth also obviously continue, with radical contrasts between highly developed and underdeveloped nations. Recent famines in the north African nations demonstrate the marginal existence of large segments of these populations. Comparison of these populations to the poor in the developed nations makes the latter look like privileged persons. National borders establish legal differences among people and can have massive consequences. Thus issues of social stratification can be examined more broadly than within the immediate political concerns of a single nation.

Distinctions among people persist in all societies. Although there have been nations associated with Marxist and related philosophies who have called themselves socialist and communist, they have not eliminated many of the social status distinctions that might be expected to disappear. But in general, the thrust in the more developed nations has been at least to attenuate abject poverty.

These brief notes on recent history are both incomplete and intuitively global. With tolerance on the part of the reader, they may set the stage for us to consider some aspects of the area of social stratification during the past four decades.

THE STUDY OF SOCIAL STRATIFICATION AT MIDCENTURY

In 1953 a rather durable reader in social stratification was published under the title *Class, Status and Power*. Edited by Reinhard Bendix and Seymour Martin Lipset, this volume is representative of sociology's expansive period following the Second World War. In the first section, "Theories of Class Structure," the contributions range from Aristotle to Talcott Parsons, with intervening contributions from Adam Smith, Karl Marx, Max Weber, and other notables. A broad variety of perspectives is represented, but the older contributions share a belief in the reality of classes. That is, writers assumed that class boundaries, although permeable, could be identified and that class entities are a critical way of conceptualizing stratification. In temporally more proximate contributions to the reader the focus moves from defining classes to identifying "major classes" in western society. In his essay, "What Is a Social Class?" Sorokin identifies the following categories: "(a) the industrial-labor, or proletarian, class; (b) the peasant-farmer class; (c) the dwindling class of large landowners; (d) the capitalist class, now being transformed into the managerial class" (Bendix and Lipset, 1953: 90). These categories are descriptive at a macro level, but as Sorokin acknowledges, they are historically bounded and difficult to use effectively.

Parsons' chapter in the Bendix and Lipset reader probably is of greater importance in the historical analysis of social stratification. His essay, "A Revised Analytical Approach to the Theory of Social Stratification," can be considered a cornerstone in the transition to modern social structural analysis. It represents in large part the system analytic orientation of Parsons' subsequent work. In this essay Parsons states that the units of systems must be subject to evaluation, and "Stratification, *in its valuation aspect*, then, is the ranking of units in a social system in accordance with the standards of the common value system" (Bendix and Lipset, 1953: 93). This broad beginning point permits a general analysis of Parsons' approach, the flavor of which cannot be communicated in just a few paragraphs. Here it is of interest primarily because of the shift in focus from the concept of classes to dealing directly with the units of society. Parson's analysis focuses on the major areas in which distinctions are made in a society, including occupations, families and kinship, sex and gender, race and ethnicity. These bases of differentiation are placed in a systems context in which both maintenance and change are key concepts. In retrospect, this analysis is a natural precursor to the recent focus on social mobility.

In 1957 two notable books on social stratification appeared, one by Bernard Barber and one by Joseph A. Kahl. These may be taken to identify further where the subdiscipline of social stratification was moving. Barber wanted to fill a gap he identified as follows: "There is no book which comprehensively examines the several parts of this growing body of knowledge [on social stratification] and systematically relates them to one another and to more general sociological theory" (Barber, 1957: vii). In many ways Barber accomplished his objective, and his presentation tends to be systematic and well-grounded. His bibliographic notes are instructive about the theoretical issues of the times. Barber credits Talcott Parsons for much of his own orientation, as in the following: "Having concluded that some system of stratification is a functional requirement of societies as they are in fact constituted, we now have to inquire more deeply into the different bases on which positions within a system of stratification are determined" (Barber, 1957: 19). In addition to Parsons, Barber notes other major thrusts, such as Marxian theory, which he characterizes as saying less about social stratification than one might expect. He discusses the theoretical contributions of Kingsley Davis and Wilbert E. Moore (1945) and the scholarly exchanges that followed. Barber also identifies the work associated with W. Lloyd Warner and his associates as an additional theoretical and methodological thrust.

It is instructive historically to examine not only the topics Barber covered in his review, but also to point out those not seen as central to the study of stratification. For example, Barber states: "Different age and sex roles, for instance, are always evaluated in society, but they do not, for important reasons we shall analyze later, become criteria of evaluation for the stratification system" (Barber, 1957: 20). Minority groups also tend to get brief treatment. Although group differences are acknowledged, these are not seen as focal for the study of social stratification:

> Comparative evidence from different societies seems to indicate that membership in ethnic, racial, or religious groups cannot be a primary criterion of evaluation for systems of social stratification because such affiliation is *not necessarily* a determinant of the way a member of a society performs in functionally essentially social roles. . . . Membership in ethnic, racial, or religious groups may be, like wealth, a secondary criterion, in the sense that it *may* determine functional role and therefore position in the system of social stratification [Barber, 1957: 59-65].

Some subsequent interests in the field are anticipated, however: A substantial part of Barber's book is devoted to issues of social mobility and social change.

The book by Kahl (1957) focused on American society, emphasized empirical studies, and focused more on the concept of classes rather than the emerging, more inclusive concept of stratification. Kahl gave some attention in one chapter to "ethnic and race barriers," but the coverage is not major, probably reflecting the interests and research of the period. The words *sex, gender,* and *women* are not listed in the index. In the recent revison of the book (Gilbert and Kahl, 1982), *women* does appear in the index, and there is a modest treatment of topics under this heading.

SOCIAL CHANGE AND THE 1960s

Many social changes took place in the U.S. during the 1960s, which led to the current period of sociology. The major social changes, of course, included the civil rights movement, the student movement, and the beginning of the feminist and women's movements. Shifts occurred in the theoretical orientations in sociology as well as in research technology. In this context, a major change in the study of social stratification took place, with greater attention paid to occupations and their prestige. In 1961 a book, *Occupations and Social Status* was published. Written by Albert J. Reiss, Jr., with collaborators Otis Dudley Duncan, Paul K. Hatt, and Cecil C. North, this book discussed North and Hatt's earlier work in the study of occupations and provided an overview of studies that had used North-Hatt occupational prestige scales. The study of occupational prestige and its relationship to other social and economic variables help set the stage for research on social mobility.

RESEARCH ON SOCIAL MOBILITY AND STATUS ATTAINMENT

Blau and Duncan's 1967 work, *The American Occupational Structure*, characterized the emerging focus on social mobility and the occupational structure. Blau and Duncan investigated factors that influence intergenerational occupational mobility. Using path analysis, a procedure becoming viable in sociology, they examined the direct and indirect effects of background variables (such as father's occupation) and a spectrum of other variables on occupational attainment. Restricted by the source of data, the study focused exclusively on men.

The concept of universalism underlies Blau and Duncan's investigation, by which objective criteria for evaluation of status are presumed to be critical. It is assumed that expanding universalism is associated with greater importance attached to achieved status and lesser importance attached to ascribed status. If universalistic values are in place, it is assumed that social status is not transmitted directly, although family background continues to influence career outcomes. Education is viewed as the medium through which intergenerational status is transmitted.

The status attainment literature has since been modified and extended. A recent review (Knotterus, 1987) suggests that Blau and Duncan's individualistic focus has been modified by researchers who have given greater weight to social structural or ascriptive variables, including race and sex. Researchers such as William A. Sewell, Robert M. Hauser and David L. Featherman have been able to specify more precisely the status attainment process.

Education has been reported frequently as an important predictor of occupational attainment. Equality of schooling has consequently received much attention, such as in Hauser and Featherman's 1976 article "Equality of Schooling: Trends and Prospects." In this study the dependent variable of education was regressed on a variety of background factors, by year of birth. Thus, for example, relationships between education and critical variables could be compared for persons born, say, between 1947-1951 and 1907-1911. Shifts in the importance of predictors of education could thus be noted for successive age groups. In these data, for example, it is possible to see shifts in the relationship between education and race, controlling for the effects of other variables. A strong negative relationship was found between nonwhite status and education for the older age groups, but this relationship was positive and nonsigificant for the most recent age group. These data were based on males only, and the authors suggest caution in interpreting their results. The study is important, however, in showing how processes of attainment can change over time.

SOME POTENTIAL NEXT STEPS IN THE STUDY OF SOCIAL STRATIFICATION

In our review, we have selected a few highlights in the not too distant past to suggest a few areas in which research on social stratification may go, or at least can go, to address some important questions. As has been suggested, issues of inequality with regard to minority groups and women have become more prominent in the last three decades, and a number of special problems for study have surfaced. Competing values are associated with many of these problems. Thus it is difficult to evaluate the consequences of proposed policies, even assuming that there are funds for research and good intentions about obtaining required knowledge.

One of the more fundamental areas requiring clarification and exploration is the apparent incompatibility of universalistic values and the maintenance of strong ethnic group identities. Universalistic values are commonly associated with a "melting pot" notion, in contrast to the idea of maintaining separate cultural or other identities. Strong identification with a group may provide the basis for pride in group membership, which may then assist occupational and other attainments. Is this in fact the case? Exploring this issue requires asking questions that can at minimum be described as delicate, as suggested by a recent review (Scarr, 1988). On this score, William J. Wilson's (1980) study of the changing status of blacks provided new insights, but may have provoked community questioning and some hostility because his approach did not conform to some preconceived notions.

Issues concerning minority groups and social stratification present intriguing questions for future exploration. Some of these questions reveal inconsistencies in societal values. For example, some immigrants to the United States achieve status comparable to or even better than the general population, while the status achieved by other groups is substantially lower. Explanations provided for status differences among immigrant groups are usually simplistic, often at the level of tautological naming, as in: Asians have those values that earn high status.

Questions concerning individuals' rights to equal treatment and what, exactly, constitutes equal opportunity are neither clear nor settled. Many of these questions were reviewed recently by the U.S. Commission on Civil Rights (1987) in response to a U.S. Supreme Court decision. Analyses conducted by the Commission and its staff indicate that there is less than full agreement, not only on the Supreme Court but also in the Commission, as to what the relevant facts are, the interpretation of the facts, and what the intentions of legislation were or are.

Issues associated with sex and gender have also been noted as a recent area of major sociological interest. The importance of this interest may be underestimated if it is not placed in the broader context of social stratification. Issues often thought of solely as "women's issues" have broad ramifications and suggest the need for a broader exploration of social values. For example, if there is concern with the question of equal treatment in labor force participation, questions arise concerning alternative meanings of equal treatment. This requires not only finding out the values held by subsegments of the population, but also exploring models of structural arrangements that may be more acceptable and efficient in the future. Addressing this concern requires involvement in policy-oriented research, a thrust from which sociologists have often shied away.

In addition to more direct involvement in policy-oriented research, and particularly the prospective testing of models, sociologists may appropriately become more directly involved in studying values. More specifically, to what degree and under what conditions should the larger society intervene in family life? Emphasis on equality of opportunity has suggested that external institutions, and particularly the school, should provide resources to children of less advantaged families. Another example derives from concerns about "child abuse," a concept that is not well defined except in extreme cases. These issues are not new, and have been visible in court and other interventions to provide children with medical care when parents, on a basis of religious belief, have rejected such care for their children. These issues are often defined in terms of children's rights, but they also arise as a result of changing societal contexts. Social concerns about children's rights obviously compete with some traditional values concerning ideal family forms and relationships.

An apparent emphasis in the study of social stratification has been that macro-level forces operate to keep a system in place. This assumption has not been well demonstrated. We are suggesting that values held at the family level may have greater collective impact than is usually recognized. With regard to equality of opportunity, values involved in micro-level decision making may cumulatively create conditions that policymakers may wish to change. For example, in the case of the 13-year-old unmarried girl who has a baby, what values apply if there is a concern for "equal opportunity"? The rights of the girl to "motherhood" are often advanced, but what does this do to the rights of the child to have equal opportunity? The answers to such questions are not advanced here, obviously. Rather, sociologists should explore these questions to understand more fully how the social stratification system operates. Further, sociologists should address societal values more directly by providing alternate models of potential changes and exploring the consequences these changes may produce if identified values are implemented.

REFERENCES

Barber, Bernard (1957) Social Stratification. New York: Harcourt, Brace and Company.

Bendix, Reinhard and Seymour Martin Lipset [eds.] (1953) Class, Status and Power. Glencoe, IL: Free Press.

Blau, Peter M. and Otis Dudley Duncan (1967) The American Occupational Structure. New York: John Wiley.

Davis, Kingsley and Wilbert E. Moore (1945) "Some principals of stratification." American Sociological Review 7: 242-249.

Gilbert, Dennis, and Joseph A. Kahl (1982) The American Class Structure. Homewood, IL: Dorsey.

Hauser, Robert M. and David L. Featherman (1976) "Equality of schooling: trends and prospects." Sociology of Education 49 (April): 99-120.

Kahl, Joseph A. (1957) The American Class Structure. New York: Rinehart.

Knotterus, J. David (1987) "Status attainment research and its image of society." American Sociological Review 52 (February): 113-121.

Parsons, Talcott (1953) "A revised analytical approach to the theory of social stratification," in R. Bendix and S. M. Lipset (eds.) Class, Status and Power. Glencoe, IL: Free Press.

Reiss, Albert J., Jr., with Otis Dudley Duncan, Paul K. Hatt, and Cecil C. North (1961) Occupations and Social Status. New York: Free Press.

Scarr, Sandra (1988) "Race and gender as psychological variables: social and ethical issues." American Psychologist 43 (January): 56-59.

Sorokin, Pitirim A. (1953) "What is social class?" in R. Bendix and S. M. Lipset (eds.) Class, Status and Power. Glencoe, IL: Free Press.

U.S. Commission on Civil Rights (1987) Toward an Understanding of Johnson. Clearinghouse Publication 94, U.S. Commission on Civil Rights, Washington, DC: Government Printing Office.

Wilson, William J. (1980) The Declining Significance of Race: Blacks and Changing American Institutions (2nd ed.). Chicago: University of Chicago Press.

21

SOCIOLOGY OF RACE RELATIONS IN THE UNITED STATES

Edna Bonacich

University of California, Riverside

In this chapter, I plan to analyze the sociology of race relations from outside of itself. That is, I want to examine its evolution holistically, considering the material roots of our thought as it has evolved through history. Rather than treating the sociology of race as a body of knowledge independent of its creators, I start with the assumption that knowing who its creators are and why they are doing what they are doing is a vital aspect of social science knowledge and probably all human knowledge.

Analyzing the material roots of knowledge stands in opposition to the dominant approach to knowledge in the western university. We usually treat knowledge as if it is disembodied, as if it exists "out there," in purity, uninvolved in the motivations of human beings. We believe that the best knowledge is disengaged, impartial, and therefore unbiased. But it seems to me that the opposite is true. First, all knowledge is motivated, whether we like it or not. It is communication from someone to some audience. We may pretend that there is no particular audience being addressed or that our audience does not affect what we say, but we are only fooling ourselves. To ignore who is talking to whom and why is to put blinders on reality, to fragment it, to hide from ourselves an important part of what is going on, and thus to see only a partial truth.

Second, I believe that motivated knowledge is superior knowledge because the knower is not alienated from the knowledge. Alienated knowledge, knowledge purposely alienated from the self, tends to be irresponsible knowledge. If you do not care, if you have no real need to

Author's Note: I would like to thank Celestino Fernandez, T. R. Young, and the participants in our session at the 1986 PSA meetings in Denver for their very helpful feedback on the first draft of this chapter.

know, then you can be careless with the results. Secondary motivations take over, like careerism—impressing your peers, making a name for yourself—and these do not necessarily promote the pursuit of the truth. On the other hand, when the knowledge is of vital importance to you, you cannot afford to be sloppy or inaccurate. Lives hinge on your research. You had better do a good job.

Thus I am going beyond the idea that we need to acknowledge our biases in order to transcend them. I am standing that idea on its head and suggesting that the only true objectivity is derived through pursuing our needs and motives, by rooting our pursuit of knowledge in our material reality.[1]

For most of this chapter, I will focus on the social and material forces that are currently shaping the way sociologists think and write about race relations. I want to consider the serious limitations on that body of work, and propose ways that we might move beyond those limitations. Before I begin that task, however, I shall briefly trace the evolution of the field to this point, attempting to show how certain social and historical developments have shaped our thought.

HISTORY OF THE FIELD

For the purpose of this chapter, I will confine myself to the American experience of race and ethnic relations and its accompanying sociology. Europe has had a long history of dealing with the problems posed by ethnic and national minorities and the intellectual constructs developed there had some influence on sociological thought in the United States. However, the American experience grew out of very different historical circumstances. The basic reality of the United States is that it began and developed as a white settler colony, an offshoot of Europe. This reality "required" the conquest of indigenous peoples. It was also associated with the importation of a slave labor force to produce raw materials for Europe's developing industries. And it brought forth a massive immigration of Southern and Eastern European peasants to work in the developing industrial northeast, as well as a small, controlled immigration from Asia. The forces that created race and ethnic relations in the United States were thus very different from those that created the national minorities question in Europe though, of course, there are some overlapping themes. Overall, however, the United States has most in common with other white settler colonies, such as Canada, Australia, New Zealand, and South Africa (to cite the most prominent products of British colonialism). The white settler colonies that arose as a consequence of European imperialism all produced complex mixes of indigenous-immigrant-imported labor types of race and ethnic relations.

The sociology of race and ethnic relations, as is probably true of the sociology of most topics, grew up in response to the social problems created by these new population mixes. Generally speaking, racial minorities and immigrants were impoverished workers, and impoverished workers have a way of causing all sorts of problems for their exploiters. They refuse to work as hard as their employers would like. They engage in "self-destructive" behaviors, such as beating each other up or drinking too much alcohol, which interfere with their capacity to work hard. And they sometimes raise dangerous threats to the social order by challenging its legitimacy. The study of race and ethnic relations was thus, at heart, a study of how to control these groups with a minimum disruption to the dominant social order.

Social policy with respect to ethnic and racial minorities has varied over time, and the sociology of the subject has varied along with it. During the 1930s and early 1940s, when radical movements flourished in the United States, and the government was forced to make major concessions to progressive elements, including minority groups, the sociology of race and ethnic relations took a sweeping perspective of world evolution. Books were written about "race and culture contacts" and "when peoples meet"[2] showing the global forces that created immigration and the importation of labor.[3]

But in the 1950s, when conservative forces reestablished their dominance, the field of ethnic and race relations shrank to a narrow concern with prejudice and discrimination.[4] Problems of racial disadvantage were reduced to interpersonal problems of faulty overgeneralization, or the individual rationalities or irrationalities of hiring minorities or selling them houses. Lost was a sense that the social system as a whole needed to be examined critically. Nothing was wrong with the system, it seemed. Only individual actors gummed up the works with their foolish attitudes and choices. If only we could educate them to see the errors of their ways, racial and ethnic minorities would be gradually assimilated.

The 1960s and early 1970s brought a new wave of attack on the dominant order and with it came a more critical approach in the sociology of race and ethnic relations. Concepts like internal colonialism and institutional racism burgeoned in this period,[5] reflecting the frustration felt by racial minorities, in contrast to the European immigrants, at being locked out of the system. Once again large-scale social forces were brought into view as necessary to study.

The 1960s were different from the 1930s in that the distinction between racial and ethnic minorities had sharpened. Racial minorities were demanding access to institutions of higher learning where they could participate in the evolving academic definitions of their own experience. Whereas 1930s race relations sociologists, or at least the progressives among them, may have tried to empathize with the "plight" of minorities, the activity of developing a sociology of ethnicity remained almost exclusively in white hands, inevitably paternalistic. There were important exceptions, like Oliver Cox, but their work was grossly ignored.[6] The absorption of white ethnics into the dominant power structure was mirrored in their absorption into the field, with names like Znaniecki and Lewin becoming prominent. (For this reason the remainder of my chapter will focus on racial minorities as distinct from white ethnics.)

In contrast to the 1930s, in the 1960s and 1970s racial minorities were more able to impress on the authorities their fundamental right to speak for themselves, both in the formation of social policy and in sociology. Ideas like community control and self-determination flourished in this era. Many white sociologists of race and ethnic relations fled the field in guilt or anger. And Ethnic Studies programs with minority personnel grew up all over.[7]

THE 1980s

Now we turn to our own era. What is going on today in the larger society, and how is that related to the ideas that are developing in the sociology of race relations? The social policy of the 1980s is, in large measure, a reaction to the developments of the 1960s and 1970s. The United States is in a period of retrenchment and even dissolution of the gains made by minorities, the working class, and other disadvantaged segments of society. The welfare state is being dismantled, and along with it, those provisions that guaranteed continued efforts to overcome the systematic oppression racial minorities had faced throughout this country's history. The claims of minorities are being terminated. We are being declared a society in which equal opportunity of individuals is the sole legitimate goal.[8]

The sociology of race relations follows more or less dutifully in tandem. A dominant theme in racial studies concerns upward social mobility within the current social order. Many studies concentrate on measuring the "progress" of minority groups by their occupational, income or educational distribution.[9] The goal is to see whether or not members of the groups are being absorbed into the society at a proper rate.

The social philosophy of assimilationism has regained hegemony. Gone are the ideas of the 1960s and 1970s which suggested that racial minorities could and should hold a radically different blueprint for society based on their special experiences of the oppressiveness of the system. The idea of "self-determination" has been cleverly twisted by the Reaganites to mean "termination of government support." Independence is lauded, welfare dependency is deplored, and the only alternative that is offered is absorption into the capitalist system as individuals.

This development is reflected in the ethnic studies programs on our campuses. Once centers of radical debate and community-oriented activism, many have been transformed into respectable (or should I say semirespectable?) units of the bourgeois university. They are indistinguishable in form from other departments and research units, held to the same criteria of productivity and performance that the white-male-dominated university sets for itself. Ethnic studies has frequently been domesticated and made into an avenue of career mobility for a few members of racial minorities.

In sum, there are two major models of the "solution" to the problems of racial minorities, each associated with different visions of the way our society works. One view is that minorities are victims of individual prejudice and discrimination, and have thus been cut out of opportunities to participate equally in the American dream. These barriers need to be overcome so that we can create a colorblind society, with opportunities to advance and make a fortune for anyone of ambition and ability.

Advocates of the other point of view contend that American society (or capitalism) depends on exploitation, poverty, and racial oppression. Wealth and "opportunity" feed upon an impoverished stratum both here and abroad. While individual minority members may be able to climb into the exploiting class, the oppression of people of color shows no signs of disappearing. To "solve" the problem of racial oppression, it is necessary to alter the fundamental structures of our society. So long as we have a society based on the principle of private ownership of productive property for profit, those with power will take advantage of the powerless.

The latter point of view has never gained hegemony within American sociology, but it has had periods of entering the arena as a serious contender. Today it is against the ropes, struggling to keep on its feet in a society in which conservative ideas dominate the political order. Clearly there is a relationship between the politics of the day and sociology.

RELATIONSHIP OF FORCES

So far, I have presented a diachronic overview. Now let us turn to a synchronic approach and, by focusing on the current period, consider the forces at work that shape race relations as a field. The central issue I want to address is: What is the class position of academics, including those in race relations, and how does this shape the ideas they develop?

I would characterize academic sociologists (along with other academics) as members of the petite bourgeoisie. They are part of a stratum of society that is neither strictly a part of the working class nor of the capitalist class, but something in between. Along with other professionals (and perhaps managers) they are employed by the capitalist class to perform certain invaluable functions for that class, and they are paid fairly handsomely to do so.

What functions do we perform? These are well described by Barbara and John Ehrenreich (1979) in an analysis of what they call the professional-managerial class.[10] Academics are ideological workers. We concentrate in the reproduction of the social order. Our function is essentially one of control of the working class, both at the level of production and at the ideological level. Engineers, for example, plan production in such a way as to strip workers of their intellectual participation in it and make their labor easier to control for purposes of profit making. Social scientists help to provide ideological justifications for capitalist institutions or help to reform them so they will work more smoothly.

As teachers, academics are also engaged in reproducing the petite bourgeoisie. We prepare students to become the next generation of managers and professionals, and inculcate in them the ideology of their social class.

Now, right away, I expect people will become angry and defensive. Am I not horribly distorting the social functions and activities of academics? Are we not more liberal and progressive than almost any other element in American society today? I will not deny that there is a liberal aspect to academia that leads it sometimes to be critical of the dominant order. Yet I still contend that the basic reality of servitude to capital remains, and that this servitude sets distinct limits on the freedom of academics to criticize. Liberals we may sometimes be, but when we are, we tend to be liberal reformers. We work to get the system to work more smoothly and efficiently. We help get rid of the social problems that threaten the current order. We seldom work to challenge it.

The Ehrenreichs characterize our class as follows: On the one hand, we experience some antagonisms with the capitalist class because that class attempts to control our expertise. Professionals are very concerned with the issue of autonomy. This issue can be an important basis for the development of professional unionism. We want to set our own "standards" based on our exclusive and special knowledge.

On the other hand, we experience antagonisms with the working class, which sees us as the middleman for capital and the state. This may be clearer in the case of such professionals as social workers, probation officers, and the like, but, as the problems of inner-city schools demonstrate, teachers also face antagonisms with working-class and minority communities.

Now it is true that academics in elite universities rarely front directly with the working class. Our students are mainly middle-class youngsters, and in the rare cases when they have working-class origins, their current class aspirations clearly point them toward the petite bourgeoisie. Thus we are once removed from the middleman role. Our students will be the real middlemen as they become teachers, probation officers, social workers, and the like. We ourselves, however, can keep our hands clean by not engaging directly in the controlling function.

Figure 21.1 presents a very rough sketch of the class position of sociologists of race relations. As employees of the university (arrow 1) we have certain designated responsibilities to fulfill with respect to the teaching (arrow 2) and research and service (arrow 3) functions. Much as we may claim autonomy in both these areas, our freedom of thought and action is really quite restricted. I will return to this point in a moment but first let me review the sources of the restriction.

Universities are run either by the state or as private enterprises (arrows 4 and 5), but even as private operations they are heavily subsidized by the state and when state run they depend on private funds. The difference between public and private thus becomes quite blurred in reality. Furthermore, the state itself is obviously not free from the tremendous penetration of, and influence by, private capital (arrow 6). This is not the place for a lengthy discussion of theories of the state. Suffice it to say that there is plenty of evidence that private corporations are able to exercise inordinate influence over the state. And this influence trickles down to state-run institutions of higher learning. The state-appointed regents of the University of California, for instance, are heavily skewed toward wealthy businessmen (e.g., Smith, 1974). Finally, private capital comes directly to the university and to individual researchers through various private granting agencies and donors (arrows 5 and 7). These funding sources are, naturally, heavily slanted toward the wealthy because that is where funds can be raised.

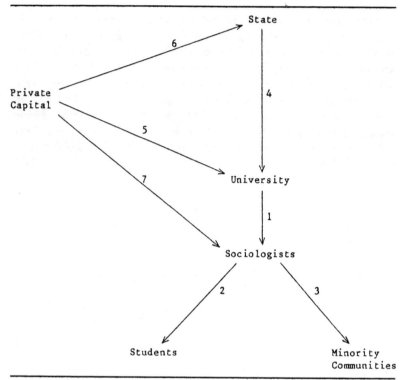

Figure 21.1 Class Position of Sociologists of Race Relations in America

I do not think anyone can deny this basic picture of the structure of power and resources, but one could still claim that this has little influence on what we actually do. We are, after all, protected by the principles of academic freedom and professional ethics. A granting agency cannot simply buy the research results it might like to see.

This is certainly true on the surface. And yet there are subtle ways in which we are nevertheless limited and controlled. Often this control is exercised by our peers rather than by the "authorities," much as women have often historically been the direct oppressors of other women in patriarchal systems. When we do our own policing for the power structure we develop the illusion of autonomy, even if we do not possess its substance.

Let me give one example of this control. In teaching we are compelled to follow elitist, meritocratic principles in the allocation of social rewards. If I, as a teacher, disagree with these principles, I will run into serious trouble.

To be more explicit: I do not believe in the social principle that all rewards should go to the most able and advanced. On the contrary, I believe that more energy and resources should be put into those who, for a variety of reasons, suffer disadvantages. I believe we should foster equality, not just equality of opportunity. But everything in my teaching situation forces me to play the meritocratic game. I must grade on a meritocratic principle which, in turn, feeds my students into other rewards marked with a meritocratic tag. Neither am I allowed to democratize my classroom. I try to do it anyway but know if I am caught that I will be rebuked. The school administration does not care *what* I teach, but they do care whether I evaluate students and make distinctions among them so that they can fit into different levels of the system. And, of course, I teach in an institution that participates in this system on a grander scale by having preselected students. At the University of California, I already teach only the most privileged, and there they get far more in the way of resources than do the poor, less advantaged students who go to the community colleges. Whether I like it or not, I am participating in reproducing the class system and, significantly, the racial system.

In sum, the petite bourgeoisie has two dynamics. On the one hand it is subservient to the capitalist class; on the other, it attempts to be autonomous from capital by claiming independent expertise. The claim to autonomy, to "academic freedom" in the case of academics is, I am contending, circumscribed. The range of freedom may feel limitless to those who dutifully stay within its boundaries. But when these boundaries are challenged, the power that lies behind them will be unambiguously felt.

RELATIONS WITH MINORITY COMMUNITIES

The university—and academic sociologists within it—has developed a particular kind of relationship with minority communities. I want to examine four aspects of that relationship: that it is based on the principle of laissez faire, that it fosters individualism, that it is essentially assimilationist, and that it is elitist. Each of these characteristics reflects capitalist ideology and social practice. Thus in pursuing their normal activities within the university, sociologists of race relations are helping to reproduce capitalism and the ways in which capitalism perpetuates racial oppression.

Laissez faire. There is a widespread belief that each sociologist should do his or her "own thing" in terms of research and teaching and that, somehow, the benefits will "trickle down" to the minorities in question. In the research area, for example, academic sociologists pursue whatever tickles their fancy. Some will be interested in minority questions and the hope is that their research will eventually work its way down to benefit those being studied. However, no one actually ever checks to see whether this happens. Researchers are not held accountable for the effects of their research. And thus it is really a matter of faith that any good effects result.

The social philosophy of laissez faire works about as well in academia as it does in the economy. In the economy, basic social necessities are overlooked in favor of unnecessary but profitable luxuries. High-priced condominiums, for example, bump out low-cost public housing because more money can be made on the former. And the result is widespread homelessness. The belief that the competitive free market will lead to the social benefit without having to look after it directly is a farce. The examples of the ways in which a capitalist free market ends up poisoning, polluting, and maiming the public are too many to enumerate here.

Part of the problem is that free competition does not remain free for long. Those with an advantage are able to gain an edge in the competition and swamp their competitors. Power and wealth become concentrated in the hands of a few and they can stack the game in their favor. In the research world, the model of freedom to pursue any topic is distorted by the fact that the big buyers, including the large corporations, private foundations, and the capitalist state, can pay for, and get their research needs met, while the poor cannot purchase research on their behalf. Agricultural research, for instance, is much more likely to be conducted on behalf of agribusiness interests than on behalf of farm workers, many of whom are minorities.

But even if the model of free competition were not distorted by the concentration of wealth and power, the problem would remain: Competition does not automatically produce social welfare. The invisible hand of classical economic theory does not work. If that is evident anywhere, it is evident in the condition of racial minorities in this country. Yet we go on acting as if the theory were true.

Individualism. The one area in which the university appears to take some responsibility, under pressure from the state that was ultimately under pressure from minority communities, is in the bringing in of students for training. Their mission is one of education and this they offer to fulfill for minority youngsters, provided, of course that they meet the qualifications.

The education that is offered, however, follows a particular model. Individuals are encouraged to come to the university in order to pursue their upward mobility on an individualistic basis. The emphasis is on achievement within a competitive environment. The individual is supposed to leave his or her community behind and try to "make it." Indeed, focusing on one's community's needs is considered a mistake, a diversion from what is really important—self-advancement. If a person (student or faculty) focuses too much on community welfare he or she will not survive long.

Again the idea of "trickle down" prevails here. It is assumed that advancing the social position of a few individuals will somehow benefit the whole community. But will it? Will the creation of a few more Black executives and professionals alleviate the problems of unemployment and teenage pregnancies in the ghetto? If anything, those professionals and executives will be used by the capitalist establishment to help control, manipulate, and exploit ghetto residents. For example, most of the American Indian students who come through UCR end up being employed by the Bureau of Indian Affairs—that gargantuan state bureaucracy that controls all aspects of Indian life with few good effects for Indian peoples (Talbot, 1981).

Let me make it clear that I am not singling out minority members for special responsibility for "their" communities. All of us, regardless of ethnicity, bear responsibility for the continuation of racial oppression in this society and in the world. Minority members have no extra responsibility. I am thus not saying that minority members should be excluded from the university so that they will assume responsibility for their communities. Rather, I am saying that white and minority alike are bombarded with individualistic values such that none of us take responsibility for the social whole. The absorption of minorities into the university on an individualistic basis only underscores the hegemony of this ideology.

Assimilationism. The implicit model of the university is assimilationist. Even as lip-service may be paid to cultural pluralism, the deep structure of the institution recognizes only one way of doing things. Multiculturalism treats culture as the most superficial veneer of human life. It recognizes differences in customs or symbolisms, but it fails to treat culture at the level of how things are done, how life is lived.

Thus universities feel they have done their duty to the principle of multiculturalism if they celebrate Martin Luther King's birthday as a holiday and recognize Black History Month and give it some resources. Meanwhile, the actual operation of the university is based strictly and narrowly on a white middle-class value system of individualism and meritocracy. If the Black community wants to represent a different idea— an idea of humanism, collectivism, and social responsibility—that idea has no chance of survival in the university's actual practice.

There is a tension in the university between the theories generated therein and the social practice of the institution. Ethnic studies programs generate models of internal colonialism and systematic racial oppression, but the university operates as if only one model exists, namely, that minorities are handicapped individuals who need to be upgraded and improved so they will fit better into the system.

This style of thought is, of course, a general feature of United States' capitalism. Instead of creating institutions to meet the needs of people, we invert this and treat people as having to meet the needs of institutions. We reify our institutions and feed people into them like pizzas into an oven. The prime example of such reification is the economy. We treat the economy as an end in itself, an altar on which human lives should be sacrificed.

Thus there is no room in the university for an alternative, a minority-generated model. Racial minorities are not permitted to come forward with another blueprint of how the university might operate so as truly to represent the needs of their communities. All they can do is push for the extremely limited program of affirmative action, that is, get more of their members in the system, and hope that somehow, some day, this will produce social change.

Assimilationism does not only pervade the practices of the university. As we have said before, practice gets translated into thought. Instead of thought creating practice, too frequently the relationship is reversed and thought trails behind practice like a lost puppy. Thus the obsessive concern with mobility studies, with examining the distribution of minorities along a given and unquestioned social hierarchy, reflects an assimilationist bias in sociology. Minorities will have "made it" when their distribution looks like the white distribution. No questions are raised about the structure of the dominant society that might be a little less than the ideal of human happiness. Obviously, it goes without saying, that all minorities want is to become like the "white man," fit neatly into his world and never raise another peep.

Elitism. As I said before, the petite bourgeoisie has a class interest in protecting its monopoly over expertise. This is the basis of its claim to the privileges of status and high salaries. The development of a special stratum of experts has a detrimental impact on minority communities for it strips them of the power to define their own needs and determine their own future.

Academic social scientists often treat minority communities as objects about which they have expertise. A couple of years ago I attended a meeting on bilingual-bicultural education organized by a branch of the California State Board of Education. It was attended solely by a group of experts who were deciding the fate of minority communities in the schools. Never were those communities consulted about what they wanted for their children.

Of course, sometimes token community representation is encouraged. For instance, in Riverside there is a federally run boarding school for American Indians called Sherman Indian High School. This school is supposedly run by an Indian school board, with representatives elected by the various tribes. Self-determination, it is called. But the truth is, the rules of election and the actual power of the board are so limiting that nothing can be accomplished. The experts retain control of the school, and one can seriously question how much they have the interests of the youngsters at heart.

Imagine yourself as a working class member of a minority community. How would you feel if you knew there was a group of experts meeting in universities and deciding your fate behind closed doors? And what if it occurred to you that those experts may, in fact, be your class enemies—the very people who want to maintain you in a state of passivity because their jobs depend on it?

What I am trying to say is that the very institution in which we, as sociologists, are embedded deeply affects the way we think about race and ethnic relations. And the product of this influence is of questionable benefit to minority communities.

We need to ask ourselves: What does our discipline do on behalf of minorities? Have oppressed racial groups been helped or hindered by our activities? This question is the ultimate criterion by which we must judge our work because, however elegant our models, if they don't bring about betterment in the lives of people, of what earthly use are they?

Now a fair amount of sociological research is aimed at showing that the condition of racial minorities has indeed improved in the post-World War II period (e.g., Farley, 1984). Efforts are made to demonstrate that minorities have experienced upward mobility, more minorities are professionals and that the income gap between (for example) blacks and whites has narrowed.

But what is the purpose of such research? Does it serve the interests of minority communities, or does it serve the interests of the establishment which can feel self-satisfied that it is accomplishing social justice? "Yes, American capitalism works," this research tells us. "When our system decides it is going to rid itself of racism, it succeeds. There is no need for profound social change."

Ignored in this model are the masses of unemployed, embittered people in the ghetto and barrio who know they are locked out of the system. For those people the system does not work at all. They are the 7% acceptable level of unemployment, whose lives are shattered by the need of capitalism to keep wages low. They do not look with hope at a school system that picks out only the "best and brightest" and discards them as worthless, claiming that the fault lies with them because they are stupid or lazy or have broken families or take too many drugs.

Among Asian Americans there is a literature on the "model minority." Asians are often touted as examples of how racial minorities can "make it" in America if only they are ambitious and work hard. Praise is heaped on the Asians for their success. But as many Asian activists have pointed out, this laudatory treatment is using Asians for some other end. They are being used by the power structure as a club against other minorities. They are being held up as a demonstration model to prove that racism doesn't really exist in America, and that those who claim they are oppressed by racism are just using it as an excuse. Meanwhile, the Asians know there is racism from their own experience, and consider this very praise of their adaptation by others for their own manipulative ends as one manifestation of it (e.g. Suzuki, 1980).

Let me give an example of the failure of American capitalism, and its academic handmaidens, to address the real problems of racial minorities. The atmosphere at Sherman Indian High School is one of sullenness and self-destruction. Many of the youngsters who go there are already alcoholics. The school is plagued by an excessively high drop-out rate and sporadic violence. How does our system deal with this condition? It takes the tiny minority of children who have a chance of "making it" in college and gives them every support and encouragement. The rest, the vast majority, are left to fester, to become the failures, the derelicts of society.

By fostering the few who are "college material," our public statistics look better. Now we have more Indian professionals. Isn't that great? Things are getting better for the Indians. Meanwhile, in the reservations surrounding UCR the average individual does not go to school beyond eighth grade. And whatever potential new leadership that might have developed has been siphoned off, wooed by the lure of a good, well-paid job, so that those individuals will never go back and lead in any meaningful way.

THE FUTURE: DEVELOPING A SOCIALLY RESPONSIBLE SOCIOLOGY OF RACE

What is to be done? First, it seems to me that we must decide which side we are on. Are we working on behalf of the oppressed or the oppressors? As

I have suggested, most of us do not want to address this question. It is too uncomfortable. So we would rather ignore it and hope it will take care of itself. We see ourselves as well-meaning people. Surely our good intentions will be manifested in the results of our actions? We do not really need to trace them out to see what happens to them, do we? The answer is: Yes we do. We cannot ignore our own activities within the social system. Willy nilly, we are social actors and our actions have consequences.

A socially responsible sociology of race relations will thus look directly at the question: What effects does the sociology of race have on racial minorities? What effects do sociologists have? And what are the effects of the universities that employ us? Are these effects benign, indifferent, or negative?

My hypothesis is that they range between indifferent and negative. When I look at the impact of UCR on the local American Indian population, for example, I am struck by how little has been done and how, generally, what is done feeds into systems of domination. UCR plucks potential Indian leadership out of the community and teaches those people to be opportunistic. It encourages them to pursue careers competitively and does nothing to foster any responsibility to their communities. It sets an example of opportunism in its own practices by cynically using statistics of increased Indian enrollment to justify more funding from the state.

Meanwhile those Indians who do graduate are likely to become government employees of one sort or another who help to maintain the same system of domination and control. They work for the university or the BIA or some other agency to manipulate and control the poorer Indians and thus maintain the stability of the system. The majority of the community is left to fester in impotence and rage. Thus the reservations are riddled with juvenile gang warfare, substance abuse, and social decay.

When we asked the chancellor of UCR what he is doing about this condition, his only response was: "It isn't our responsibility. Our charge is to reach out to those who are UC eligible, to make sure they are prepared to come to the campus, and to help them to survive academically." Thus the intellectual leadership of our nation, the so-called experts, have no answers for the immense social problems of our day. They are hamstrung by their own institutional practice.

In the future we need to tear this reality apart. We need to request accountability from our employer. We need to develop the expectation, indeed the demand, that they not ignore the implications of their own actions on the social development of our nation and its minorities.

This brings me to my second point. A socially responsible sociology of race and ethnic relations cannot be developed in isolation from the people whose lives it affects. A group of experts cannot sit in the hallowed halls of academia and issue pronouncements about other people's lives. Or rather, they can, but only as adjuncts to an oppressive system. It is inherently oppressive to deny people a voice in their own affairs. It is inherently oppressive not to allow them to participate in the definition of their own reality. Bringing in a few individuals from a particular social category does not negate this problem. In bringing people into the university you automatically change them, at least to some extent. If they do not change, they will not survive. Thus they can never be adequate representatives of their "people" unless an effort is made to engage in a continual dialogue with the people.

As a start for thinking about this question, I would recommend that we all read Paulo Freire's *Pedagogy of the Oppressed*. The basic idea of this wonderful book is that knowledge created and imposed by an elite dehumanizes people and robs them of their ability to speak their own word. Educators and researchers who want to align themselves with the oppressed must engage in continual dialogue with oppressed peoples. We can't come to them with predigested assumptions, but can only offer to help people study their own reality with a view to helping to change it.

For example, sociologists have certain research skills. We could teach people to use these skills as a means of gaining important knowledge in their struggles for liberation. Instead of making these skills widely available to oppressed peoples who need them, we either sell them to the highest bidder, or we keep them as esoteric as possible so as to keep control over them and enhance our market value. If we worked to negate our own specialized role and, instead, shared our skills as broadly as possible, imagine the resulting empowerment. Instead of sullen minority students feeling that learning was their enemy, imposed upon them by an overwhelmingly powerful, domineering, callous, alien white society, there would be a reason to learn: One learns in order to struggle to enhance life for oneself and others; one learns in order to humanize one's life.

It is not easy for academic sociologists to go out and engage in dialogue with poor minority people. The class gulf is enormous. There is a vast chasm of distrust and hatred that separates us. Few of us have any notion of the intensity of that hatred toward us. We live in a bitterly divided society that continuously threatens to break into open warfare. We are kept from civil race war only by the armed might of the state, and even then it breaks out in sporadic explosions of so-called crime, violence, and passion.

Just attempting to open the dialogue would be a tremendous learning experience for us. We would be forced to see the hatred in the other's eyes. We would have to become the students rather than the teachers. We would have to learn of the reality of our nation's oppressed from their point of view. Instead of being bookish experts, safely holed up behind ivy-covered walls, we would have to confront what it means to live the life of oppression in our society. It would be a transforming experience just to try to open a dialogue even if we failed.

A third imperative is that we do battle against oppressive institutions alongside the oppressed minorities of our nation. This includes fighting against our own institution and its oppressive, antidemocratic practices. Too often we see this necessity clearly for other people in other situations. We think South Africans should stand up against their government. Or workers should strike against exploiting employers. But when it comes to our own lives we don't think they bear closer scrutiny. We are reasonably comfortable so we see no need to move. Besides, we are afraid that, if we do speak out, we will lose our comfortable position in society.

For example, we need to do battle against university administrations that treat minorities as numbers that advance their own careerism. We need to fight against the cordoning off of racial issues into safely segregated ethnic studies programs so that the vast majority of the increasingly technocratic university can ignore them with what it feels to be a clear conscience. We need to fight for the idea of access to institutions of higher learning by minority communities—not just for the "qualified" middle class, not just for the sake of appearance, or as a means of domestication, but to open the university to the potentially "dangerous" and revolutionary ideas of this sector of our nation.

Finally, we need to commit ourselves to the idea of praxis, the idea that knowledge is gained through efforts to create a better world. We need to rid ourselves of the dualism between thought and action. We need to recognize the idleness of sitting in offices and spinning out models while remaining uninvolved in efforts to change the world. We need to see its self-serving character. As you sit in your office writing articles for professional journals, you are not merely a neutral social force. That very act is part of a gigantic bureaucratic leviathan that sits on the heads of oppressed Third World peoples both here and abroad.

Let me end by saying that, for me, the future of the sociology of race and ethnic relations depends on the negation of an elitist, professional role in a social structure of class and racial domination. I believe that in the long-run we will be overthrown no matter what we do. But we have a choice right now about how we conduct ourselves. We can hold on to our elitist position, dig our heels in, arm ourselves, and be prepared to defend our positions in bloody battle to the last man. Or we can try to participate as midwives to change. We can use our positions of relative prestige and social influence to help our nation start down the long, hard road to racial justice. Which side are you on? That is a question that will inevitably be asked of you whether you pay attention to it or not. Your life, your work, speaks your answer.

NOTES

1. These concepts derive heavily from the philosophical writings of Ortega y Gasset (see references). I am sure other philosophers have expanded on these themes though perhaps none with as much eloquence and poetic expression. I am also forever indebted to Ralph Cuaron, a Chicano worker without a formal education, who taught me more about race relations than I could ever learn in school.

2. *Race and Culture Contacts* was edited by Reuter in 1934; Locke and Stern edited *When Peoples Meet* in 1942.

3. Robert Ezra Park's work is a good example of the attempt to look at race relations globally (e.g., *Race and Culture*). For a review of Park and his followers, see Geschwender (1978: 19-32). Some of them, such as E. Franklin Frazier, continued writing with this scope into the 1950s (e.g., Frazier, 1957).

4. Typical texts of this epoch include Simpson and Yinger's *Racial and Cultural Minorities: An Analysis of Prejudice and Discrimination* (1953) and Gordon Allport's *The Nature of Prejudice* (1954). The psychological reductionism of the period perhaps began with the publication of *The Authoritarian Personality* (Adorno et al., 1950), a profound study in itself but one that, as often happens, was simplified and misused to dominate a decade with the F-scale.

5. See, for example, Allen (1970), Blauner (1972) and Tabb (1970).

6. See Cox (1948). Another good example is Williams (1944).

7. For examples of the new perspectives developed by these minority scholars, in the case of Asian Americans, see Tachiki et al. (1971) and Gee (1976).

8. The historical progression of liberal-paternalism, conservative-assimilationism, and minority self-determination, in the 1930s to the 1940s, the 1950s, and 1960s to the 1970s, is clearly shown in the shifting policies toward American Indian education (see Szasz, 1979).

9. This was clearly shown in a conference on "Ethnicity and Race in the Last Quarter of the Twentieth Century" held at SUNY Albany in April, 1984. The conference topic was not confined to racial minorities and included papers on white ethnics. With rare exceptions most of the papers dealt with upward mobility conceived as a process of the movement of individuals to produce aggregate "group" measures of social change.

10. See Walker (1979) for a full debate about the definition and class character of this stratum.

REFERENCES

Adorno, T. W., E. Frenkel-Brunswik, D. J. Levinson, and R. N. Sanford (1950) The Authoritarian Personality. New York: Harper & Row.

Allen, R. L. (1970) Black Awakening in Capitalist America. Garden City: Doubleday/Anchor.

Allport, G. W. (1954) The Nature of Prejudice. New York: Addison-Wesley.

Blauner, R. (1972) Racial Oppression in America. New York: Harper and Row.

Cox, O. C. (1948) Caste, Class and Race. New York: Doubleday.

Ehrenreich, B. and J. Ehrenreich (1979) "The professional-managerial class," pp. 5-45 in P. Walker (ed.) Between Labor and Capital. Boston: South End Press.

Farley, R. (1984) Blacks and Whites: Narrowing the Gap? Cambridge: Harvard University Press.

Frazier, E. F. (1957) Race and Culture Contacts in the Modern World. Boston: Knopf.

Freire, P. (1981) Pedagogy of the Oppressed. New York: Continuum.

Gee, E. (1976) Counterpoint: Perspectives on Asian America. Los Angeles: UCLA, Asian American Studies Center.

Geschwender, J. A. (1978) Racial Stratification in America. Dubuque: William C. Brown.

Locke, A. and B. T. Stern [eds.] (1942) When Peoples Meet: A Study in Race and Culture Contacts. New York: Hinds, Hayden and Eldredge.

Ortega y Gasset, J. (1957) Man and People. New York: Norton.

Ortega y Gasset, J. (1961) History as a System. New York: Norton.

Ortega y Gasset, J. (1969) Some Lessons in Metaphysics. New York: Norton.

Reuter, E. B. [ed.] (1934) Race and Culture Contacts. New York: McGraw-Hill.

Simpson, G. E. and J. M. Yinger (1953) Racial and Cultural Minorities: An Analysis of Prejudice and Discrimination. New York: Harper & Row.

Smith, D. N. (1974) Who Rules the Universities? New York: Monthly Review Press.

Suzuki, B. H. (1980) "Education and the socialization of Asian Americans: a revisionist analysis of the 'model minority' thesis," pp. 155-175 in R. Endo, S. Sue, and N. N. Wagner (eds.) Asian Americans: Social and Psychological Perspectives, Vol. II. New York: Science and Behavior.

Szasz, M. C. (1979) Education and the American Indian. Albuquerque: University of New Mexico Press.

Tabb, W. K. (1970) The Political Economy of the Black Ghetto. New York: Norton.

Tachiki, A., et al. [eds.] (1971) Roots: An Asian American Reader. Los Angeles: UCLA, Asian American Studies Center.

Talbot, S. (1981) The Roots of Oppression: The American Indian Question. New York: International.

Walker, P. [ed.] (1979) Between Labor and Capital. Boston: South End Press.

Williams, E. (1944) Capitalism and Slavery. New York: Capricorn.

22

SOCIOLOGY OF GENDER

Margaret Mooney Marini

University of Minnesota

Within the past 15 years, the study of gender has emerged as a major research area in sociology. The purpose of this chapter is to review the current state of knowledge and suggest directions for future work. The discussion is necessarily selective due to strict limitations on the length of the chapter.

THE CURRENT STATE OF KNOWLEDGE

How Do Women and Men Differ?

Social roles. The social roles and behavior of males and females have differed in all known human societies. Research on tribal societies indicates that men tended to be the warriors, hunters, and processors of hard raw materials used for weaponry and tools, whereas women tended to do the cooking and preparation of vegetal foods (Sanday, 1981). Women have sometimes been full-time warriors and hunters, but instances of their performing these roles are rare and have occurred under special circumstances. As a result of this gender differentiation in the division of labor, men have been in a better position to acquire and control the valuable resources of the society. Power, privilege, and status have rarely, if ever, been shared on a equal basis by women and men.

Author's Note: This chapter was written while the author was supported by Grants K04-AG00296 and R01-AG05715 from the National Institute on Aging. The assistance of William Chan, Pamela Navatta, and Laurie J. Alioto is gratefully acknowledged. I am also indebted to Joan Huber and Barbara Reskin for helpful comments.

Despite claims about the existence of matriarchal societies, there is no sound anthropological evidence that such societies existed (Blumberg, 1984). Debate continues even about the existence of societies in which there was a rough equality between women and men. A number of anthropologists now argue that egalitarian hunting-gathering and horticultural societies existed prior to colonial contact (e.g., Sanday, 1981; Sacks, 1982). Anthropologists agree that more complex forms of social organization brought intensified gender stratification and that agricultural, pastoral, and industrial societies have all been male-dominated.

To the extent that women have had relatively high status in a society, it has largely been as a result of their role in economic production and distribution (Friedl, 1975; Blumberg, 1984). There are a surprising number of societies in which women controlled as much or more property than did men. However, among stratified, state-level societies, there is no example of a society in which women have held even half of the economic power above the level of the local group. There is also no concrete evidence of any society in which women have held half of the political power or more than a tiny percentage of the power of force. No society has ever had an ideology of female supremacy, although there are a few that posit that women and men are equal (e.g., the Israeli kibbutz, the U.S.S.R.).

In modern industrial societies, work has largely become an activity performed away from home for monetary return. Men have specialized in work in the market, earning wages to support the family. Women have specialized in work in the home, becoming economically dependent with primary responsibility for child rearing. Although there are signs of change in this division of labor as women enter the labor market in increasing numbers, the predominant world-wide pattern is one of gender-role differentiation.

The participation of adult women in the nonagricultural labor force is today generally highest in the Soviet socialist bloc, the Scandinavian countries, the countries of Northwestern Europe, Canada, the United States, and Japan. In these countries over 40% of women aged 15 and over are working in nonagricultural jobs. In no country, however, is the proportion of women in the nonagricultural labor force greater than 60%. In the Southern European countries, between 30% and 40% of adult women tend to be in the nonagricultural labor force, although in Spain and Greece the figure is less than 20%. In Latin America, less than 30% of adult women are employed in nonagricultural jobs, and less than 15% in some Latin American countries. In the African and Middle Eastern Islamic countries, less than 10% of adult women hold nonagricultural jobs (United Nations, 1986: tables 26 and 28). In all countries women are highly underrepresented in positions of power, authority, and prestige; their average earnings are considerably below those of men (Youssef and Hartly, 1979; Epstein and Coser, 1981; Treiman and Roos, 1983). Since women workers are disproportionately found in low-level, unskilled jobs, women's labor force participation represents only a first step toward improvement of the status of women.

In the United States, the most dramatic improvements in the status of women have occurred in the wake of the resurgence of the women's movement. Women are earning a higher percentage of degrees and are more highly represented at the entry levels of high status occupations than they have been in the past, although they still earn far less than half of the highest degrees awarded, and their overall representation in high status occupations is low.[1] Women remain to a large extent in traditionally female occupations (Beller, 1984). The median annual earnings of women working full-time, year-round continue to be only about 65% of those of men. Women are running for and winning elective offices and being appointed to administrative posts and major boards of directors in greater numbers than ever before, but they continue to be only a small minority of those occupying positions of power (U.S. Bureau of the Census, 1986).

Abilities and traits. Gender-role differentiation is associated with gender differences in behavior, attitudes, and dispositional traits. It also leads to gender stereotyping, or the formation of consensual beliefs about differences between the sexes. In keeping with similarities in the pattern of gender-role differentiation across societies, there is a considerable degree of similarity in gender stereotypes (Williams and Best, 1982). Instrumental traits tend to be associated with males and expressive traits with females. Evidence from the United States indicates that people commonly believe sex differences to be far greater than they are (Broverman et al., 1972; Williams and Bennett, 1975). A high level of agreement exists among males and females with respect to traits that differentiate the sexes (Broverman et al., 1972; Williams and Bennett, 1975), and these consensual beliefs are independent of race, age, religion, education, and marital status (Broverman et al., 1972; Hershey, 1978).

Research on sex differences indicates that there is little basis for many gender stereotypes (Maccoby and Jacklin, 1974; Block, 1976; Tavris and Wade, 1984; Deaux, 1985; Fausto-Sterling, 1985). There is no consistent evidence, for example, that the sexes differ in cognitive style, creativity, independence, general self-esteem, emotionality, empathy, nurturance, sociability, or loquaciousness. Some evidence indicates the existence of sex differences favoring males in quantitative and spatial abilities and sex differences favoring females in verbal abilities, but these differences are small and do not appear in all studies. Their magnitude has also declined over time (Rosenthal and Rubin, 1982). Evidence pertaining to sex differences in dispositional traits is weaker. Among the most well documented differences is the tendency for males to be more aggressive. Again, this sex difference is small and may emerge in only some situations. Interpretations of the evidence on sex differences in other traits differ (see Block, 1976). Some research on conformity and susceptibility to influence suggests that females are more easily influenced than males and are more likely to conform to group pressure under surveillance (Eagley and Carli, 1981). Gender differences have also been found in nonverbal behaviors, such as touching, gaze, posture, and personal space, and there is evidence of female superiority in both encoding and decoding nonverbal cues (Hall, 1979). Recent and controversial work by Gilligan (1982) further suggests that women and men may have different images of themselves and how the world works, which are reflected in the way they resolve moral conflicts and arrive at moral standards.

Why Do Women and Men Differ?

A primary objective of the study of sex and gender is to determine why sex differences in social roles and behavior exist. Because there are biological differences between the sexes, there has been a tendency to assume that observed differences between women and men are biologically determined. In the limited space available it will not be possible to discuss research that has attempted to identify the degree to which differences observed between the sexes are cultural rather than biological in origin. Separating these influences is difficult, not only because there is widespread agreement that both biology and culture play a role in the development of sex differences, but also because that role is increasingly believed to be interactive. However, research suggests that male dominance in humans is not genetically inherited, that there is considerable variability in what constitutes female and male labor and dispositional traits across societies, and that the gender according to which a child is reared can override the influence of sex hormones in determining gender identity. These and other findings provide evidence that social influences play a major role in the development of differences between the sexes.

Macro-level social influences: Intersociety comparisons. Since there is evidence that socialization plays an important role in the development of sex-related differences but that the content of what is learned varies widely across societies, anthropologists and sociologists have sought to determine what gives rise to gender differentiation and why it takes the forms it does. As noted earlier, all known societies have been characterized by a division of labor by sex, and there are a few universal principles of task differentiation, which although not absolute, form probabilistic constraints on the division of labor. Current thinking about the basis of the sexual division of labor is that biological factors have constrained the division of labor and that economies of effort, or efficiency, operate within those constraints (Friedl, 1975; Burton et al., 1977).

The major biological factor constraining the division of labor is women's role in reproduction—specifically, childbearing and nursing. Because there are economies in having the same individuals perform adjacent tasks in production sequences and in assigning tasks in clusters based on physical location and temporal sequence, and because there are diseconomies in the exposure of females—the source of reproduction—to danger, women have tended to perform tasks involving less travel and danger which are consistent with childbearing and nursing. This is not to say that women's work activities have not had an effect on their childbearing and nursing but only that childbearing and nursing have posed some constraint. Although nonbiological factors can condition or override the constraint imposed by women's childbearing and nursing, throughout most of human history, restriction due to pregnancy and nursing has not been minimal (see Chafetz, 1984: 22).

Another biological factor believed to have a constraining effect on the sexual division of labor is men's greater physical strength, although its effect has been found to be highly probabilistic. There is great variation in the development of physical strength, which produces large cross-cultural variation in the extent to which males are stronger than females, and many tasks performed by males require little physical strength. Thus there has been a trend away from explanations emphasizing physical strength and other male characteristics to those emphasizing the compatibility of tasks with women's childbearing and nursing. This does not mean that men's greater physical strength is irrelevant to the sexual division of labor but that its effect is less important.

The division of labor by sex is affected not only by biological constraints but by societal characteristics. Among the most important of these is the technological base of the society. In foraging societies women tend to provide more than half of the food needed for subsistence. Women provide somewhat less of the food in horticultural societies, but a predominantly male labor force has been found in only about a fifth of such societies. In agrarian societies women play only a minor role in production. Although women's productive role is greater in industrial societies, it is still highly subordinate to the male role. In developing theories of gender stratification, Chafetz (1984) and Blumberg (1984) have sought to identify the factors responsible for differences in women's productive role in different types of societies.[2]

One of the reasons social scientists have focused attention on the division of labor by sex, and especially on women's productive role, is that the division of labor has been found to be related to the degree of gender inequality in a society. In analyzing preindustrial societies, Sanday (1973) found that where women did not contribute to production, their status was invariably low. But even in societies where women did most of the production, women's status could also be low. Participation in production was a necessary but not a sufficient condition for relatively high gender equality.

Development of a general understanding of why societies differ in degree of gender inequality has become an important area of both theoretical and empirical analysis (e.g., Sanday, 1981; Rosaldo, 1974; Friedl, 1975; Schlegel, 1977; Blumberg, 1984; Chafetz, 1984). The most recent and comprehensive theories of gender stratification are those of Blumberg (1984) and Chafetz (1984), and there is a high degree of convergence between them on major points. According to Blumberg and Chafetz, there is evidence to indicate that women's relative control of the means of production and the allocation of surplus or surplus value is an important determinant of the status of women in a society. In societies with subsistence economies, Friedl (1975) has argued that the degree to which women control the distribution of the products of their labor (usually food) will strongly influence their relative status because it creates nonkin networks of mutual obligations that establish a basis for power and prestige. Schlegel (1977) and Blumberg (1984), however, attach primary importance to control of the means of production rather than distribution, since control of the means of production tends to be associated with control of the allocation of surplus. In societies that produce a surplus, both Blumberg and Chafetz argue that those who profit will be the product owners or controllers, who choose the manner in which the surplus is distributed.

Blumberg and Chafetz consider factors that affect women's relative economic power and, therefore, the degree of gender inequality. Both identify factors that enhance what Blumberg calls the "strategic indispensability" of women's work. Characteristics of the family structure, such as lineality and locality, are also seen as affecting women's relative economic power. In addition, Chafetz views gender stereotypes and the degree to which dominant religions or secular ideologies explicitly support gender stereotyping and inequality as variables that buttress the gender stratification system.

Historical change within societies. In the agrarian societies that existed prior to industrialization, work and family structures were integrated (Oakley, 1974; Tilly and Scott, 1978; Hareven, 1982). The unit of production was the unit of kin relationships, and the location of work was not separate from family life. There was no distinction between economically productive work and domestic work. Because a large family was an economic asset, both the mother's reproductive role and her productive work were valued.

Even in preindustrial societies societal complexity affected the sexual division of labor. With urbanization and increased population density, female participation in many activities declined. For example, female participation in crafts declined when occupational specialization caused craft activity to move from the home to the workshop. The intensification of agriculture, associated with high population density, a short growing season, use of the plow, and high dependence on domesticated animals, also produced a decrease in female participation in farming and an increase in female participation in less economically visible activities in the home (Boserup, 1970; Ember, 1983; Burton and White, 1984).

With the coming of industrialization, the relationship between the family and the economy was altered dramatically by the establishment of institutions, separate from the family, to perform economic activities (Boserup, 1970; Oakley, 1974; Tilly and Scott, 1978; Hareven, 1982; Ryan, 1983). Work increasingly became an activity performed away from the home for monetary return. Although there was initially some tendency for whole families to be employed outside the home, technological change and protective labor legislation imposed restrictions on the employment of children, making them dependent on adults and creating a need to provide for their care. Children therefore became an economic liability rather than an asset. The need to care for children and the continuing constraints imposed by women's reproductive role, coupled with the absence of a demand for women's labor outside the home, led to a heightened differentiation of roles within the family.

The specialization of men in work in the labor market and women in work in the home had important consequences. It isolated housework and child care from other work, made women and children economically dependent on men, separated men from the daily routine of the household, and affected the value attached to the work of women in the home. Since industrialization made housework less burdensome, the nature of the work performed by women changed. Children came to occupy a more central place in the family, and standards and ideals of child care rose. Similarly, new standards of cleanliness emerged. Thus although housework was less difficult, it became no less time-consuming (Vanek, 1974; Robinson, 1980). Women also became society's primary consumers as the change to a market economy occurred.

During the twentieth century, industrial societies have experienced economic and social changes that are again altering the sexual division of labor. A major source of these changes has been the occurrence of structural changes in the economy that increased the need for large numbers of white-collar workers and thereby created a demand for female labor (Oppenheimer, 1970; Oakley, 1974). This change was accompanied by the development, acceptance, and use of effective methods of contraception, which made it possible for women to exert a large measure of control over their fertility and freed them from the constraints of their reproductive role. Labor-saving devices and other products for the home also became widely available, reducing the amount of work required for the physical maintenance of a household. Together, these changes produced a marked increase in the employment of women outside the home.[3]

Despite the increase in the employment of married women outside the home, relatively little change has occurred in the division of household labor. The last detailed United States surveys in 1976 and 1977 of the work performed by husbands and wives in the home indicate that wives continued to do most household work and child care (Berk and Berk, 1979; Robinson, 1980; Sanik, 1981; Pleck, 1985). Even employed wives spent, on average, almost three times as much time on household work as did their husbands (Walker and Woods, 1976; Robinson, 1977; Sanik, 1981; Pleck, 1985).

Between the 1920s and the 1960s studies of the amount of time spent on housework showed no significant changes, although new technology did result in the substitution of some routine, repetitive work for more managerial types of activity (Vanek, 1974; Robinson, 1980). Between the 1960s and the 1970s, Pleck (1985) suggests that there has been a decrease in the amount of time spent on family work by women in the United States, coupled by a small increase in the amount of time spent on family work by men. The decrease observed for women appears to be due in large part to changes in women's labor force participation and marital and fertility behavior over the decade (Robinson, 1980). Interestingly, the increase for men is evident among both wife-employed husbands and sole-breadwinning husbands (Pleck, 1985). This pattern of change suggests a general value shift toward somewhat greater family involvement by husbands rather than a response to the wife's employment in two-earner households. As a result of these changes, the average proportion of time spent on family work by husbands has increased, although even this increase is small.

When a broad range of child care and housework responsibilities is considered, the employed wife spends a greater total number of hours working either in or outside the home than does her husband or her nonemployed counterpart (Walker and Woods, 1976; Geerken and Gove, 1983; Pleck, 1985). In contrast, the husbands of employed wives actually spend less time working than the husbands of nonemployed wives because their wives' earnings enable them to reduce their hours of market work, and they spend little additional time on housework (Walker and Woods, 1976; Geerken and Gove, 1983). Employed wives, therefore, have less "free" time than do either their husbands or nonemployed wives (Robinson, 1977; Geerken and Gove, 1983). These findings indicate that the increased labor force participation of married women has produced an imbalance in the division of work and leisure between the sexes. As women's labor force participation has increased, there has not been a significant reallocation of household work. During the late 1970s and 1980s, however, there is some indication that change may be occurring. One study based on a small sample of married couples surveyed in 1981-82 showed that husbands now do an average of about 30% of the couple's total family work (Juster, 1985). There is also evidence of greater change among the young (Sanik, 1981).

Overall, the record of historical change in gender roles since the coming of industrialization provides strong evidence of the malleability of such roles and attitudes in response to social influences. Industrialization brought about major changes in the roles of women and men. As subsequent changes in technology increased the demand for female labor, changes in gender roles began to occur again. Since World War II, women have entered the labor market in ever-increasing numbers. This change initiated an important move toward reduction in gender-role differentiation, with women increasingly taking on work roles previously held only by men and men now beginning to do a larger share of the family work previously done by women.

Micro-level social processes: Socialization. Within a society at a particular point in time, individuals come to adopt gender-specific behavior, attitudes, and dispositional traits through processes of socialization and allocation that perpetuate gender-role differentiation. Social and developmental psychologists have advanced a number of theories of gender-role socialization that differ primarily in the mechanism by which sex-typed behavior is hypothesized to be learned (Huston, 1983). Although the process by which individuals learn behavior appropriate for their sex may occur in a variety of ways, the content of what is learned depends on the association of sex with particular types of behavior in the society in which a child is raised.

Much attention has been devoted by both psychologists and sociologists to studying the content of messages communicated to the two sexes by various socialization agents (Maccoby and Jacklin, 1980; Block, 1976; Huston, 1983; Marini and Brinton, 1984). Research has indicated that parents treat boys and girls differently and serve as models for gender-specific roles and behavior. Gender-role socialization also occurs within the schools via curricular materials, the availability of role models, differential treatment by teachers and counselors, and interaction with peers. The mass media, including films, television, books, newspapers, and magazines, are another source of gender-role socialization.

Through the process of socialization individuals internalize gender stereotypes that buttress existing gender differentiation and stratification (Hamilton, 1981; Deaux, 1985; Ashmore et al., 1986). Beliefs that the sexes are different have important implications for the overall evaluation of each sex, since the characteristics ascribed to each sex are not equally valued. There is evidence to suggest that both sexes view the characteristics ascribed to males as more desirable than the characteristics ascribed to females and, therefore, that the overall evaluation of males is higher than that of females (Broverman et al., 1972; but see Ashmore et al., 1986, for a discussion of the limitations of this evidence). Since the characteristics ascribed to males are also those important for gaining access to positions of power and privilege, gender stereotypes create expectations for performance that negatively affect evaluations of women's past and expected future performance in high-level jobs.

Allocation. Another process by which individuals come to adopt gender-specific behavior, attitudes, and traits is through the allocation of individuals to institutional positions on the basis of sex, often to sex-typed positions. Whereas socialization shapes the choices of individuals by conditioning their desires and expectations, allocation involves action by others, which channels individuals into positions on the basis of sex irrespective of their desires and expectations.

Allocation is pervasive in the workplace. Recent analysis of the degree of sex segregation in the U.S. labor force indicates that between 60% and 70% of the workers of one sex would have to change detailed occupational categories in order to make the occupational distributions of the two sexes equal (Beller, 1984). Within occupations workers are also segregated both within and between firms so that it has been estimated that 96% of workers of one sex would have to change job titles to equalize the distributions of the two sexes across jobs (Bielby and Baron, 1984). This high level of sex segregation arises in part from the allocation of workers to jobs by employers. Exactly what motivates these allocation decisions is unclear. Economists have argued that they are affected by a process of "statistical discrimination," whereby employers attempt to maximize efficiency based on perceptions that the marginal productivity of women and men differs on average for different lines of work. However, perceptions about the suitability of women and men for different types of work are based largely on gender stereotypes that are highly inaccurate (Kiesler, 1975). Moreover, given that women and men sometimes perform the same work under different job titles in different parts of the same organization (Bielby and Baron, 1986), even perceived aggregate differences between men and women in marginal productivity in a given type of work cannot explain all instances of job segregation within firms. It may be that both perceptions of gender differences and perceptions of employee preferences for same-sex work groups—in particular, male preferences for working with males— cause employers to discriminate by sex.

Evidence that women and men are evaluated differently comes from studies of selection situations and studies of performance outputs. Males have been found to be more likely to be selected or ranked highly for managerial, scientific, and semiskilled positions than are equally qualified females. When identical professional articles and paintings are attributed to a male or a female, there is some evidence that the work believed to be done by a man is rated more highly than the work believed to be done by a woman. Studies have also shown that males prefer to work and interact with competent males rather than competent females. Not all studies report these differences, but most do (see Nieva and Gutek, 1981; Wallston and O'Leary, 1981). Studies of explanations given for the success or failure of women and men performing the same task find differences in causal attributions of the performance of males and females as well (see Nieva and Gutek, 1981). In general, male success is more often attributed to ability, whereas female success tends to be attributed to luck, hard work, or an easy task. By comparison, male failure tends to be attributed to external factors such as luck or a difficult task, whereas female failure is more often attributed to lack of ability.

Gender bias in evaluation is not consistent across all situations. It is greater in the evaluation of qualifications and in causal attributions of performance than in the evaluation of past performance. Gender bias occurs less often when assessment is confined to a specific behavior or product exhibited because the level of inference required is lower. When the criteria on which an individual is judged are ambiguous or there is little information available about the individual's performance, gender stereotypes play a more important role. Generally speaking, reducing the ambiguity of an evaluation situation through the establishment of clear criteria for evaluation or the provision of information about performance reduces the likelihood that gender-biased inferences will be made (Nieva and Gutek, 1981; Wallston and O'Leary, 1981).

In recent years simple demonstrations of differential evaluation have given way to more sophisticated analyses of the structure and process of gender stereotyping (Hamilton, 1981; Deaux, 1985; Ashmore et al., 1986). This new research has been influenced by recent work on social cognition and views stereotypes as operating in the same way as other cognitive categories. These systematic efforts to place the stereotype concept within a broader framework are likely to provide a basis for understanding discrepancies in the findings of earlier studies of performance evaluation.

Emergent interaction. Gender differences are maintained in part through the effects of gender stereotypes on emergent interaction. Berger et al. (1980) have suggested that the effects of gender stereotypes are a manifestation of a more general status organizing process. Expectation states theory postulates that status characteristics provide a basis for the formation of performance expectations, which affect group interaction even if the status characteristic bears no relation to the goal or task of the group. In other words, group members assume that men are generally more capable than women are and therefore that men are probably more capable at the task the group is performing, even though sex is not known to be relevant to the task. This status generalizing process has been argued to explain research findings that males are given and take more opportunities to perform, are evaluated more highly for the same qualifications or performance, are more often rewarded for their performances, and have more influence than females (Berger et al., 1980). Meeker and Weitzel-O'Neill (1977) have also argued that because men have higher status than women have, competitive or dominating behavior is viewed as legitimate for men but not for women.

Since a status characteristic will be applied to new tasks and new situations as a matter of normal interaction, expectation states theory suggests that the "burden of proof" is on demonstrating that sex is irrelevant to task performance. In the absence of some intervention, females will tend to defer to the judgment of males, and males will refuse to be influenced by females. Pugh and Wahrman (1983) found that the effect of gender could be eliminated as a factor influencing judgment when women were shown to be more competent than their male partners at a task related to but distinct from the group's task. Wagner et al. (1986) showed that unambiguous demonstrations of ability at a task that disconfirmed gender stereotypes could actually invert gender-related performance expectations for the task. However, gender biases continued to hinder women and help men even after intervention.

LIMITATIONS TO KNOWLEDGE AND A
PRESCRIPTION FOR THE FUTURE

To date, sociologists have devoted considerable attention to documenting the existence of gender differences and describing the distinctive aspects of women's experience, particularly those aspects indicative of quality of life. Attempts to understand what produces these gender differences have been limited largely to descriptions of patterns of associations among variables. Even when research has been motivated by a model formulated on the basis of expected relationships among variables, the mechanisms producing those relationships have usually not been specified. Most recent progress has involved describing the pattern of associations among variables in ever greater detail by employing new variables, better measures, and more sophisticated statistical methods. Although this research informs us about the complex structure of relationships associated with gender at a particular time and place, failure to move beyond description of this type to the development and testing of theories is likely to impede cumulation of a general body of knowledge.

There are a number of specific problems with the descriptive research being carried out that are not unique to the study of gender but can be found in most areas of sociological investigation. One is that there is insufficient justification for many of the empirical analyses that are undertaken. In addition to documenting the existence of gender differences on particular variables, multivariate models are rather routinely estimated separately for each sex. There is nothing inherently wrong with this procedure, but nothing obviously right about it either. It is a procedure often employed with little justification other than vaguely stated hypotheses about expected gender differences in the effects of independent variables on some outcome. Why it is important to document these gender differences in "effects" is usually not discussed, often because the relationship of gender to each of the independent variables and to their interrelationships is not understood. Before estimating a model by gender, we should have a precise rationale for doing so, which includes arguments about the relationship of gender to each independent variable and to the structure of relationships among the independent variables, as well as arguments about gender differences in relationships of the independent variables to the dependent variable.

In analyses where multivariate models are estimated separately by sex, the goal of the analysis is frequently unclear. In some analyses the goal appears to be to explain gender differences in a particular outcome. However, documentation of gender differences in the effects of independent variables on a dependent variable may tell us little about what causes gender differences in the dependent variable unless information is available about gender differences in the independent variables as well. In analyses in which there is no gender difference in the dependent variable, the estimation of multivariate models by sex presumably is motivated by interest in gender differences in the process by which the dependent variable is determined. However, even this process cannot be understood without knowledge of gender differences in the independent variables and their interrelationships.

Another problem with much empirical research on gender is that the set of variables included in the multivariate models that are estimated by gender varies greatly from study to study, even among studies of the same dependent variable. This variation occurs because the inclusion of independent and control variables is justified largely on the basis of what is available in a particular data set and ad hoc hypotheses about expected effects. Because the variables included vary across studies, the findings of multivariate analyses are often inconsistent in ways that cannot be reconciled.

Even the procedure of estimating the effect of one variable with the effects of other variables held constant can be problematic. In attempting to simulate the controlled randomized experimentation that goes on in some branches of physical and biological science, social scientists have used "control variables" as surrogates for the actual controlling that goes on in an experiment. However, as Lieberson (1985) argues, it becomes practically impossible to deal with the operation of selective processes with full and appropriate controls in a typical sociological research problem. Many complex layers of selectivity are involved, only some of which may be known and fewer controlled. Moreover, when control variables are used, conclusions rest on the assumption that relevant variables are free to vary with one another and that every possible combination of the values of the variables can appear. If a control variable is inextricably tied to levels of the independent and dependent variables, a conclusion about the relationship between the independent and dependent variables net of the control variable will be based on assumptions about combinations of variables that cannot exist and therefore may have little applicability to the real world.

Problems of the type just mentioned arise in sociological research in part because the research is not designed to test rigorously formulated theories. To date, theoretical and empirical analyses in sociology have been largely disjoint. The vast majority of empirical studies have attempted to describe empirical regularities in the contemporary United States. These studies are usually motivated by hypotheses about expected relationships among variables, but the hypotheses are rarely derived from a general theory. On the contrary, the hypotheses are usually justified by reference to time-and-place-bound (historical) social conditions. For example, it might be hypothesized that the presence of children has a stronger effect on the socioeconomic attainments of women than of men because women have primary responsibility for child rearing. In this case a hypothesis about gender differences in an expected relationship is advanced on the basis of reference to the existing sexual division of labor. Thus the only explanation given for the hypothesis is an empirical regularity —that is, that women tend to have primary responsibility for child rearing.

Although most empirical research on gender has not been motivated by theory and most work on gender has been empirical, some theoretical development has occurred. Theory at the macro level has focused on the explanation of societal variation in the degree of gender inequality. Theory at the micro level has focused primarily on the explanation of sex-related differences emerging in interaction, viewing these as outcomes of gender stereotyping and a more general status organizing process. This theoretical work is an important beginning, but far more theoretical work is needed. The documentation of empirical regularities, in which major advances have been made, is an obvious starting point in the development of a new area of study. However, we have reached a point of diminishing returns from this type of work and now need to turn more of our attention to theory development and testing.

One factor hampering the development of theory related to gender is the limited amount of theory developed within sociology as a whole. This disciplinary condition is important because progress in the study of gender is likely to require theory development of two types: theory about basic social processes and theory about the relationship of gender to those processes. At present, we tend to think primarily of the unique aspects of gender differentiation and stratification, and the empirical research we undertake reinforces that particularistic orientation. However, it is likely that many observed gender differences are generated by general social processes that interact with gender.

The importance of understanding basic social processes and drawing a connection between those processes and gender is already evident in the theoretical work on gender done so far. For example, both Blumberg (1984) and Chafetz (1984) see the "strategic indispensability" of women's work as affecting women's relative economic power. In identifying factors that enhance the strategic indispensability of women's work, Blumberg (1984: 57) notes that these factors "bear strong relation to the variables that labor economists might consider in weighing the bargaining power of a given labor force." In her concluding statement she also notes, "all the 'strategic indispensability' factors were developed from the standpoint of general stratification. They are hypotheses about the factors that enhance the leverage and bargaining power of any subordinate group that functions as a labor force for a superordinate group" (Blumberg, 1984: 76). Similarly, Berger et al. (1980) and others have suggested that the sex-related differences in behavior that emerge in social interaction resemble differences in behavior associated with other status characteristics and that the effects of gender stereotypes are a manifestation of a more general status organizing process. Work on gender stereotyping within psychology also increasingly views stereotypes as operating in the same way as other cognitive categories. In short, theoretical work on gender is likely to be informed by work on basic social processes and is likely to develop along with general theoretical development in the field. However, theories that link gender to basic processes must also be developed if gender differentiation and stratification are to be understood.

Research on gender has been limited not only by an absence of theory but by an attempt to analyze macro-level questions at the micro, or individual, level. Many, if not most, of the sociological questions that bear on gender are macro-level questions, since the degree of gender differentiation in behavior and resources is a societal, or other macro-level, characteristic. Most sociological research on gender, however, has been carried out at the micro level, often examining within-sex variation among individuals. The problem with this approach is that it permits analysis of only the unfolding of individual action within a given social structure—that is, within a given system of gender differentiation and stratification. It does not tell us how that system of gender stratification came into being or what is likely to produce change in it.

Because social science research and the knowledge it produces serve a number of different and interrelated purposes, future developments in the study of gender-related issues will be needed on several fronts. There should be an ongoing attempt to describe more fully and monitor changes in the status of women in the United States and other contemporary societies. Applied research will also continue to be needed to evaluate programs and policies designed to assist women and raise the status of women relative to men. In addition, there should be a continued and intensified search for basic understanding of the determinants and consequences of gender differentiation and stratification. In seeking to develop basic knowledge of the processes of gender differentiation and stratification, the biggest challenge facing sociologists is the development and testing of rigorously formulated theory. Theoretical advances will necessarily involve the development of theories about basic social processes that have applicability across different areas of sociology, but it is the unique task of sociologists of gender to develop theories about the interface between gender and those basic processes.

NOTES

1. Between 1970 and 1984, the percentage of bachelor's degrees earned by women rose from 41.5 to 49.1, the percentage of master's degrees from 39.7 to 49.5, and the percentage of doctor's degrees from 13.4 to 33.3 (U.S. Bureau of the Census, 1986). However, although women earned 28% of the medical degrees and 37% of the law degrees awarded in 1984, only about 17% of all physicians and 18% of all lawyers in the United States were women in 1985 (U.S. Bureau of the Census, 1986). Similar patterns of change are occurring in other high status, "male" occupations, although the percentages of women currently in those occupations remain relatively low.

2. For example, the relative emphasis on sustenance versus surplus production, the relative importance of physical strength and mobility, the degree of separation between the work- and homesites, the degree of environmental harshness and threat, the level and type of technology, the attention span required for various production activities, and the relationship between the economic and family structures.

3. In 1900, 20% of U.S. women aged 18 to 64 were in the labor force (Wertheimer, 1977: 210). By 1980, this figure had risen to almost 60% (U.S. Bureau of the Census, 1986).

REFERENCES

Ashmore, Richard D., Frances K. Del Boca, and Arthur J. Wohlers (1986) "Gender stereotypes," pp. 69-119 in R. D. Ashmore and F. K. Del Boca (eds.) The Social Psychology of Female-Male Relations. New York: Academic Press.

Beller, Andrea (1984) "Trends in occupational segregation by sex and race, 1960-1981," pp. 11-26 in B. Reskin (ed.) Sex Segregation in the Workplace: Trends, Explanations, Remedies. Washington, DC: National Academy Press.

Berger, Joseph, Susan Rosenholtz, and Morris Zelditch, Jr. (1980) "Status organizing processes," pp. 479-508 in A. Inkeles, N. J. Smelser, and R. H. Turner (eds.) Annual Review of Sociology, Vol. 6. Palo Alto, CA: Annual Reviews.

Berk, Richard A. and Sarah Fenstermaker Berk (1979) Labor and Leisure at Home. Beverly Hills, CA: Sage.

Bielby, William T. and James N. Baron (1984) "A woman's place is with other women: sex segregation within organizations," pp. 27-55 in B. Reskin (ed.) Sex Segregation in the Workplace: Trends, Explanations, Remedies. Washington, DC: National Academy Press.

Bielby, William T. and James N. Baron (1986) "Men and women at work: sex segregation and statistical discrimination." American Journal of Sociology 91: 759-99.

Block, Jeanne H. (1976) "Issues, problems, and pitfalls in assessing sex differences: a critical review of 'The Psychology of Sex Differences.'" Merrill-Palmer Quarterly 22: 283-308.

Blumberg, Rae Lesser (1984) "A general theory of gender stratification," pp. 23-101 in Sociological Theory 1984. San Francisco: Jossey-Bass.

Boserup, Ester (1970) Women's Role in Economic Development. London: Allen and Unwin.

Broverman, Inge K., Susan Raymond Vogel, Donald L. Broverman, Frank E. Clarkson, and Paul S. Rosenkrantz (1972) "Sex-role stereotypes: a current appraisal." Journal of Social Issues 28: 59-78.

Burton, Michael L. and Douglas R. White (1984) "Sexual division of labor in agriculture." American Anthropologist 86: 568-83.

Burton, Michael L., Lilyan A. Brudner, and Douglas R. White (1977) "A model of the sexual division of labor." American Ethnologist 4: 227-51.

Chafetz, Janet Saltzman (1984) Sex and Advantage: A Comparative, Macro-Structural Theory of Sex Stratification. Totowa, NJ: Rowman and Allanheld.

Deaux, Kay (1985) "Sex and gender." Annual Review of Psychology 36: 49-81.

Eagley, Alice H. and Linda L. Carli (1981) "Sex of researchers and sex-typed communications as determinants of sex differences in influenceability: a meta-analysis of social influence studies." Psychological Bulletin 90: 1-20.

Ember, Carol R. (1983) "The relative decline in women's contribution to agriculture with intensification." American Anthropologist 85: 285-304.

Epstein, Cynthia Fuchs and Rose Laub Coser [eds.] (1981) Access to Power: Cross-National Studies of Women and Elites. London: Allen and Unwin.

Fausto-Sterling, Anne (1985) Myths of Gender: Biological Theories About Women and Men. New York: Basic Books.

Friedl, Ernestine (1975) Women and Men: An Anthropologist's View. Basic Anthropology Units. New York: Holt, Rinehart & Winston.

Geerken, Michael and Walter R. Gove (1983) At Home and at Work: The Family's Allocation of Labor. Beverly Hills, CA: Sage.

Gilligan, Carol (1982) In a Different Voice. Cambridge, MA: Harvard University Press.

Hall, Judith A. (1979) "Gender, gender roles, and nonverbal communication skills," pp. 32-67 in R. Rosenthal (ed.) Skill in Nonverbal Communication: Individual Differences. Cambridge, MA: Oelgeschlager, Gunn, and Hain.

Hamilton, David L. (1981) Cognitive Processes in Stereotyping and Intergroup Behavior. Hillsdale, NJ: Lawrence Erlbaum.

Hareven, Tamara K. (1982) "American families in transition: historical perspectives on change," pp. 446-66 in F. Walsh (ed.) Normal Family Processes. New York: Guilford Press.

Hershey, Marjorie R. (1978) "Racial differences in sex-role identifies and sex stereotyping: evidence against a common assumption." Social Science Quarterly 58: 583-96.

Huston, Aletha C. (1983) "Sex-typing," pp. 387-467 in P. H. Mussen (ed.) Carmichael's Manual of Child Psychology (4th ed.). New York: John Wiley.

Juster, F. Thomas (1985) "A note on recent changes in time use," pp. 313-32 in F. T. Juster and F. P. Stafford (eds.) Time, Goods, and Well-Being. Ann Arbor: Institute for Social Research, University of Michigan.

Kiesler, Sara B. (1975) "Actuarial prejudice toward women and its implications." Journal of Applied Social Psychology 5: 201-16.

Lieberson, Stanley (1985) Making It Count: The Improvement of Social Research and Theory. Berkeley: University of California Press.

Maccoby, Eleanor Emmons and Carol Nagy Jacklin (1980) "Sex differences in aggression: a rejoinder and reprise." Child Development 51: 964-80.

Marini, Margaret Mooney, and Mary C. Brinton (1984) "Sex typing in occupational socialization," pp. 192-232 in B. Reskin (ed.) Sex Segregation in the Workplace: Trends, Explanations, Remedies. Washington, DC: National Academy Press.

Meeker, Barbara F. and P. A. Weitzel-O'Neill (1977) "Sex roles and interpersonal behavior in task-oriented groups." American Sociological Review 42: 91-105.

Nieva, Veronica F. and Barbara A. Gutek (1981) Women and Work. New York: Praeger.

Oakley, Ann (1974) Women's Work. New York: Vintage.

Oppenheimer, Valarie Kinkade (1970) The Female Labor Force in the United States: Demographic and Economic Factors Determining Its Growth and Changing Composition. Population Monograph Series, No. 5. Berkeley: Institute of International Studies, University of California.

Pleck, Joseph H. (1985) Working Wives/Working Husbands. Beverly Hills, CA: Sage.

Pugh, Meredith D. and Ralph Wahrman (1983) "Neutralizing sexism in mixed-sex groups: do women have to be better than men? American Journal of Sociology 88: 746-62.

Robinson, John P. (1977) How Americans Use Time. New York: Praeger.

Robinson, John P. (1980) "Housework technology and household work," pp. 53-67 in S. F. Berk (ed.) Women and Household Labor. Beverly Hills, CA: Sage.

Rosaldo, Michelle Zimbalist (1974) "Women, Culture, and Society: A Theoretical Overview," pp. 17-42 in M. Z. Rosaldo and L. Lamphere (eds.) Women, Culture, and Society. Stanford, CA: Stanford University Press.

Rosenthal, Robert and Donald B. Rubin (1982) "Further meta-analytic procedures for assessing cognitive gender differences." Journal of Educational Psychology 74: 708-12.

Ryan, Mary P. (1983) Womanhood in America. New York: Franklin Watts.

Sacks, Karen (1982) "The case against universal subordination," in Sisters and Wives: The Past and Future of Sexual Equality. Urbana: University of Illinois Press.

Sanday, Peggy Reeves (1973) "Toward a theory of the status of women." American Anthropologist 75: 1682-1700.

Sanday, Peggy Reeves (1981) Female Power and Male Dominance: On the Origins of Sexual Equality. Cambridge, MA: Cambridge University Press.

Sanik, Margaret Mietus (1981) "Division of household work: a decade comparison—1967-1977." Home Economics Research Journal 10: 175-80.

Schlegel, Alice (1977) Sexual Stratification: A Cross-Cultural View. New York: Columbia University Press.

Tavris, Carol and Carole Wade (1984) The Longest War: Sex Differences in Perspective (2nd ed.). San Diego, CA: Harcourt Brace Jovanovich.

Tilly, Louise A. and Joan W. Scott (1978) Women, Work, and Family. New York: Holt, Rinehart & Winston.

Treiman, Donald J. and Patricia A. Roos (1983) "Sex and earnings in industrial society: a nine-nation comparison." American Journal of Sociology 89: 612-50.

U.S. Bureau of the Census (1986) Statistical Abstract of the United States: 1987 (105th ed.). Washington, DC: Government Printing Office.

United Nations (1986) Demographic Yearbook: 1984. New York: Department of International Economic and Social Affairs, United Nations.

Vanek, Joann E. (1974) "Time spent in housework." Scientific American 231: 116-20.

Wagner, David G., Rebecca S. Ford, and Thomas W. Ford (1986) "Can gender inequalities be reduced?" American Sociological Review 51: 47-61.

Walker, Kathryn E. and Margaret E. Woods (1976) Time Use: A Measure of Household Production of Family Goods and Services. Washington, DC: American Home Economics Association.

Wallston, Barbara Strudler and Virginia E. O'Leary (1981) "Sex makes a difference: differential perceptions of women and men," pp. 9-41 in L. Wheeler (ed.) Review of Personality and Social Psychology, Vol. 2. Beverly Hills, CA: Sage.

Wertheimer, Barbara M. (1977) We Were There: The Story of Working Women in America. New York: Pantheon.

Williams, John E. and Susan M. Bennett (1975) "The definition of sex stereotypes via the adjective check list." Sex Roles 1: 327-37.

Williams, John E. and Deborah L. Best (1982) Measuring Sex Stereotypes: A Thirty-Nation Study. Beverly Hills, CA: Sage.

Youssef, Nadia H. and Shirley Foster Hartley (1979) "Demographic indicators of the status of women in various societies," pp. 83-112 in J. Lipman-Blumen and J. Bernard (eds.) Sex Roles and Social Policy. Beverly Hills, CA: Sage.

AGE, AGING, AND THE AGED

The Three Sociologies

Judith Treas

University of Southern California

Patricia M. Passuth

Drexel University

Sociological inquiries in aging have come of age in the last decade. Perhaps no other sociological specialty has seen its standing rise as sharply. It has attracted new converts, broadened its knowledge base, and achieved considerable sophistication in its paradigms and methodologies. Despite these advances, the field has yet to be unified by consensus on the research questions that fall most appropriately within its domain. Indeed, three very distinct research traditions are identified with the renaissance of aging studies. These traditions are the sociology of age, the sociology of aging, and the sociology of the aged (see Knipscheer, 1985, for a similar typology).

The sociology of age treats age as an organizing principle in society. This perspective is a macrostructural one, emphasizing social institutions within which age serves as one basis for the division of labor and the distribution of rewards. The sociology of age addresses institutional arrangements, socially constructed understandings, and cultural norms that give rise to socially acknowledged age-group differences. The age structure is singled out as an important characteristic of societies, institutions, and groups— one with implications for the social metabolism and functioning of the group. Age groups or cohorts themselves are recognized as potential sources of conflict, cohesion, and social change.

Authors' Note: The second author thanks Robert Lynott for helpful comments on an earlier draft. A longer version of this chapter, in which the issues are discussed in greater detail, is available from the authors upon request.

The sociology of aging represents a more microsocial perspective. Its concern is with continuity and change in the lives of individuals as they grow up and grow older. Research has focused on adaptation to life cycle transitions, historical events, or habituating experiences. Both the modal tendencies and the patterned diversity in age-related change suggest that some changes may be channeled (i.e., developmental). Both social and biological explanations have been posed for the myriad age-related changes in individuals, but the sociogenic and biogenic roots of development have only begun to be formally recognized and reconciled.

The sociology of the aged or social gerontology focuses on older people and later life. Grounded in a social problem perspective, it has been characterized by a preoccupation with the well-being of the aged. Studies have considered morale (Tallmer and Kutner, 1970), social supports (Krause, 1986), income (Liang et al., 1980), mortality (Crimmins, 1984), health (Wolinsky et al., 1984), retirement (Atchley, 1971), loneliness (Creecy et al., 1985), voluntary associations (Babchuk et al., 1979), and a host of other topics. In contrast to the sociologies of age and aging, the sociology of the aged has not manifested a particular commitment to either macrosociological or microsociological approaches. As a field, it has embraced research on roles, resources, and adaptations of the older individual (George, 1980) as readily as studies of retirement communities (Streib et al., 1985), old-age political movements (Pratt, 1976), and nursing homes (Gubrium, 1975). It has displayed a similar agnosticism with regard to social theory, drawing on structural functionalism (Cumming and Henry, 1961) in its heyday, and turning more recently to contemporary theories of the state (Myles, 1984; Olson, 1982).

In distinguishing between the three sociologies, we do not wish to leave the impression that they share no common ground. In practice, the sociologies of age, aging, and the aged have often adopted similar theoretical orientations (e.g., the life course perspective). They have grappled with similar methodological challenges, particularly in modeling change and its components. They have even converged on certain research problems such as the causes of retirement (contrast Myles, 1984; Pampel and Park, 1986; O'Rand and Henretta, 1982). Despite efforts to develop an omnibus sociology that would unite these three traditions (see, for example, Riley et al.'s 1972 model of age stratification), this compartmentalization remains very much with us. This chapter considers the origins of the three sociologies, assesses the contemporary course of each research tradition, and speculates on the prospects for attaining a unified sociological specialty embracing age, aging, and the aged.

THE ORIGINS OF THREE SOCIOLOGICAL TRADITIONS

Age has yet to unify sociologists into one research community, and the field remains balkanized into the sociologies of age, aging, and the aged. In tracing the historical development of these three traditions, two points may be made.

First, the recognition of childhood as a legitimate concern of the social and behavioral sciences was a significant stepping stone to the study of adulthood and later life. In the social welfare field, for example, the appreciation of the special needs of juveniles led to the recognition of the special needs of the old. Similarly, the human development school, which nurtured the sociology of aging, had its roots in the study of child development. For example, Erik Erikson's (1950) formulation of adult developmental stages grew out of the psychoanalytic tradition with its preoccupation with childhood. The study of childhood sensitized social scientists to the differentiation of the life course. Today, childhood provides a point of departure, a reference for comparison (Preston, 1984), and a straw man for demonstrations of life-long human adaptability (Levinson, 1978; Vaillant, 1977). Unfortunately, contemporary stage theories of adulthood tend to discourage explicit consideration of the relationship between childhood and adulthood (Passuth, 1984; Perlmutter, 1986).

Second, the differentiation of these traditions is due in good measure to the fact that each grew up at the interface of sociology and another discipline. At the junction of social work and sociology, the sociology of the aged emerged. The sociology of age was anticipated both by anthropology and by demography. The sociology of aging was shaped by developmental psychology, especially as interpreted by the eclectic human development school. Given the biological bases of human aging, the acceptance of multidisciplinary perspectives is understandable.

The sociology of age was informed by both demographic and anthropological insight. Stable population theory, for example, gave a formal predictability to the relative sizes of various age groups. In 1907 in *Science* magazine, Alfred J. Lotka demonstrated that a closed population (i.e., one without inward or outward migration) subjected to fixed schedules of age-specific fertility and mortality rates would eventually assume a fixed age structure.

Early anthropologists drew on observations of "primitive" societies to demonstrate the importance of age-grades. Writing on rites of passage, van Gennep (1960) focused on rituals that smoothed the transition from one age status to another. Anthropological work (e.g., Benedict, 1946) established age as a social phenomenon. Cross-cultural studies left no question that age-sex classifications and norms were not simple reflections of biological differences; they were social creations. As a leading sociologist (Linton, 1942: 592) put it, "such classificatory systems are sufficiently divorced from physiological considerations to make possible almost any amplification of formal categories and almost any choice of transition points."

The roots of the sociology of aging are found in the field of developmental psychology in which longitudinal studies of children documented age-related changes in physical and mental development. Longitudinal studies of children which began in the 1920s and 1930s included Terman's (1925) study of gifted children as well as the Oakland Growth Study and the Berkeley Guidance Study (see Elder, 1974, 1979). As their subjects moved into adulthood, researchers were challenged to rethink theories of development that ended in childhood or adolescence.

In sociology, an implicit interest in how individuals change over time was evident both in community studies such as *Middletown* (Lynd and Lynd, 1929, 1937) and in studies of the link between culture and personality such as *The Polish Peasant* (Thomas and Znaniecki, 1918). Sociological research on childhood *socialization* greatly influenced the sociology of aging. Although aging was conceived in terms of socialization, the term was defined in different ways. Linton (1942) saw it from a behaviorist perspective and pointed to animal studies in which changes in behavior depended on a system of rewards and punishments. The structural functionalist perspective emphasized the shaping of personality and expectations so as to fit a complex sequencing of preexisting social roles structured by the social system.

The sociology of the aged began to take shape in the United States in a bygone era of social reform. With the professionalization of social welfare, the misfortunes of the aged were noted by social workers and social reformers who argued for collective solutions to their woes (Epstein, 1922, 1928; Rubinow, 1931). In *The Challenge of the Aged,* Abraham Epstein (1928) debunked the notion that late-life poverty was a result of character flaws in the old. Instead, he pointed to superannuation (i.e., mandatory retirement), economic depressions, the high cost of living, chronic illness, and a lack of family supports. Coining the term *social security,* Epstein called for the establishment of a national old-age pension system. In defining personal troubles as a social problem, Epstein's analysis was distinctly sociological. Ironically, this structural perspective was largely abandoned by the 1950s when social gerontologists turned to individualistic explanations for the problems of old age.

Perhaps because old people were culturally devalued, the study of old people did not achieve a high status among sociological specialties. As sociology evolved as a discipline, sociologists signaled their increasing theoretical and methodological sophistication by distancing themselves from the practice orientation of social work—the very specialty on which the sociology of the aged was founded. The sociology of the aged languished, isolated from the developments within other sociological specialties, and rarely at the cutting edge of broader sociological debates. It was redeemed during the 1970s when an infusion of federal monies legitimated the study of later life.

In sum, the sociologies of age, aging, and the aged developed along parallel tracks, pursuing distinctive research questions and influenced by different intellectual traditions. Given their different origins, it is not surprising that they have bred three identifiable research literatures. In a brief chapter, we cannot adequately summarize the research that developed over decades; we can, however, point to characteristic research problems and significant results for each of the three specialties.

STATE OF THE ART: THE SOCIOLOGY OF AGE

Research on the sociology of age has been characterized by a concern with social processes and social structures transcending the individual. Central concepts are those of population and cohort, institution and organization, norms and understandings.

Stable population theory offers a jumping off point for demographic research informing our understanding of population aging and its social implications. Drawing on formal models of population, Preston (1982) clarifies the differential effects of changes in mortality and fertility on the prevalence of age-related characteristics (e.g., school enrollment or nursing home institutionalization) in the population and over the life cycle. Prevalence of a characteristic in a population is responsive to mortality change, whereas prevalence over the life cycle is influenced by shifts in fertility regimes. While failing to allow for social adaptation to demographic transitions, this approach offers a useful tool in predicting aggregate change on age-salient dimensions.

Particularly interesting applications of formal demography are to be found for organizational settings. Keyfitz (1973) observed that it took less time to reach the middle of a young, fast-growing population pyramid than an old, slow-growing one. The implication—age-specific promotion chances depend on growth—was confirmed by Rosenbaum (1979) in a study of a public utility in periods of rapid expansion and stability. Stewman and Konda (1983) demonstrate the importance to promotion chances of grade ratios, that is, the relative number of persons in various managerial levels within the organization. Age structures may affect more than the life chances of the individual. Pfeffer (1981) has hypothesized that rapidly-growing organizations with "young" work forces must rely on formal means of social control while organizations with long-tenured work forces can count on internalized organizational values to ensure adequate performance.

Research on the family has also exploited demographic calculus. Hammel et al. (1981) employ simulations to chart the expected number of surviving grandparents for persons of various ages in 1950 and 2000. Glick and Norton (1979) estimate the expected years of widowhood for women born in the 1880s and 1920s. Demographic calculations pinpoint population shifts that constrain kinship support capacities (Treas, 1977), opportunities for intergenerational socialization (Bengtson and Treas, 1980), and the distribution of advantage linked to birth order (Heer, 1985).

As these studies suggest, a major focus of research in the sociology of age has been at the level of the social institution, the organization, and the group. Given some rough biological constraints that are age-related, social institutions shape, exploit, and reward both competencies and needs over the life cycle. Age operates as an institutionalized means of matching people with roles. Thus the institutional processing and packaging of age as a diffuse status characteristic accounts for why age is important. It also offers concrete insights into general social processes of conflict, differentiation, and adaptation while accounting for the life course transitions of individuals.

Study after study has demonstrated that age group differences actually grow out of institutionalized responses to the perceived needs of an age group. The recognition of childhood has been linked to the development of formal education (Aries, 1962). The emergence of adolescence has been traced to the exclusion of teenagers from meaningful employment (Empey, 1982) and marked by the invention of special social arrangements ranging from the Boy Scouts (Gillis, 1974) to the juvenile justice system (Sutton, 1983). At the other end of the life cycle, political conflict gave rise to both mandatory retirement (Haber, 1978; Phillipson, 1982; Atchley, 1976) and old age pensions (Treas, 1986; Myles, 1984; Quadagno, 1984; Orloff and Skocpol, 1984)—social devices that translated chronological age into the assumption of decrepitude and the practice of exclusion.

That the differences between groups are socially constructed points to the normative and phenomenological bases of the sociology of age (Starr, 1982-1983). Gubrium and Buckholdt (1977), for example, argue that age-related concepts such as *maturity* and *development* are features of ongoing discourse as much as they are concrete realities of everyday life. From this perspective, the entire enterprise of aging studies comes into focus not so much as a "scientific" endeavor, but as an example of how reality about aging is generated. Lynott (1983) and Lyman-Viera (forthcoming) demonstrate how reactions to Alzheimer's patients are socially constructed (e.g., on the basis of medical typologies). Kohli et al. (1983) consider the "meaning structures" generated within an industrial firm where the retirement system organizes the life course of workers so as to further the enterprise's economic interests as defined by management.

Apart from Neugarten et al. (1965), sociologists have made little effort to study age norms directly. Replications (Passuth et al., 1984; Plath and Ikeda, 1975) generally support the notion of societal age constraints. Indeed, chronological age is invoked often in legal norms governing age relations, criminal culpability, civic obligations, and entitlement benefits (Cain, 1976). The general notion of age norms against which one's progress may be measured has been profitably exploited by organizational sociologists who have pointed to the (de)motivating aspects of age norms for job promotion (Kanter, 1977; Lawrence, 1984; Rosenbaum, 1979). By and large, sociologists have been content to infer cultural norms from statistical norms of behavior (Hogan, 1980). This is problematic, because behavior may be responsive to other influences, such as economic conditions (Marini, 1984). For instance, age is associated with an end to childbearing, because of normative considerations, but also because of declining fecundity, a lack of pronatalistic peer influences, the development of competing interests, and the fact that widely spaced births do not benefit from economies of scale (Rindfuss and Bumpass, 1978). Norms may lag, rather than lead, behavior, as seen with respect to married women's labor force participation (Oppenheimer, 1970) and age at marriage (Modell, 1980). At the very least, normative timetables depend on one's position within the social order based on, for example, gender, ethnicity, and socioeconomic status (Hagestad and Neugarten, 1985).

Cohort differences in life course have offered powerful evidence refuting notions that aging is biologically or psychologically determined. Surely the most influential statement on the experience and impact of recent American cohorts is by economist Richard Easterlin (1968, 1980). Although most cohort studies have been largely descriptive rather than theoretically driven, Easterlin draws on sociological reference group concepts and economic supply and demand principles. According to Easterlin, the relative size of successive cohorts has shaped their economic prospects and thus influenced behaviors as diverse as suicide, scholastic attainment, and marriage.

Although the sociology of age shares with the sociology of aging a concern with historically situated cohorts, their respective emphases are very different. In the sociology of age, cohorts are vehicles of social change. Confronting similar historical conditions, members of a cohort are apt to pursue similar courses of action. These common behavioral responses may strain existing institutional arrangements and thus become the impetus to social change. They may reverberate through time, too, since any behavioral choice may constrain subsequent behavior, even much later in the life cycle. As Ryder noted in his 1965 essay, social change is also brought about as a cohort with unique features passes from the scene, only to be replaced by a new and distinctive one.

In sum, the sociology of age is concerned with cohorts (and, indeed, age groups) not so much for what they imply for the lives of individuals as for what they mean for the structure, organization, and functioning of society and its institutions. From this perspective, the progression of interest need not be that of the individual life, but the sequencing of social roles or structural positions. For example, Spilerman (1977) has argued for considering "job trajectories" or "career lines" (i.e., work histories characteristic of a segment of the labor force). Oppenheimer (1981) has described life cycle adaptive "family strategies," adopted in response to particular external constraints, that permit families to maintain themselves from generation to generation.

STATE OF THE ART: THE SOCIOLOGY OF AGING

The sociology of aging focuses on continuity and change in the individual's life as he or she grows older. It has been influenced by developmental psychology, especially in human development programs where students are trained in both psychology and sociology. Developmental psychology theories began with a focus on children, especially their cognitive (Piaget, 1952), moral (Kohlberg, 1969), and ego development (Freud, 1962). From these emerged theories of adult development (e.g., Erikson, 1959), although both sociologists (Neugarten, 1979; Dannefer, 1984) and psychologists (Baltes, 1979) criticize stage theories as too deterministic.

Despite the influence of psychology, the disciplinary lines remain intact. Psychologists more often refer to the "life span" and focus on intrapsychic forces in aging; sociologists speak of a "life course" and study "age-related transitions that are socially created, socially recognized, and shared" (Hagestad and Neugarten, 1985: 35). Life-span developmental psychologists focus on age differences or age changes in personality, intelligence, and memory. Sociologists of aging investigate such issues as the timing of adult transitions and the effect of historical and situational factors on later life experiences.

Sociological theories of aging began with an emphasis on childhood socialization, which was defined by structural functionalists as the process by which individuals learn the norms and values of a group. Researchers who studied adult socialization adopted the functionalist perspective as well (Brim and Wheeler, 1966; Rosow, 1974).

In contrast to the functionalist stress on stable personality and learned values, symbolic interactionists conceived of adult development as a career or a set of interrelated roles and statuses forming a trajectory over time (Becker, 1964; Becker and Strauss, 1956). Becker explains continuity in adult behavior in terms of what he calls "side bets"—a series of decisions that keep an individual on one course of action rather than another. Although symbolic interactionists studied different aspects of aging (e.g., Lopata, 1972), only in the late 1970s did this perspective emerge as an explicit theory of aging (Karp and Yoels, 1982; Marshall, 1978-79).

Despite varied theoretical perspectives, one dominant view has emerged in the sociology of aging—the "life course perspective." Several conceptual developments contributed to this emergence. One was the recognition of the distinction between age changes and age differences. Schaie (1967) showed the fallacy of interpreting cross-sectional data on age *differences* (e.g., lower educational attainment of earlier cohorts) as age *changes* (e.g., declines in IQ with age). These concepts recast aging from a process largely of maturation to one including social and historical factors. We recognize these influences as age, period, and cohort effects.

A second source of the life course perspective is found in the age stratification framework (Riley et al., 1972) that pointed to cohort membership as the link between individual aging and social structure: "The life-course patterns of particular individuals are affected by the character of the cohort to which they belong and by those social, cultural, and environmental changes to which their cohort is exposed in moving through each of the successive age strata" (Riley, 1985: 374). Perhaps because it is so abstract (Hendricks and Hendricks, 1986) and encompasses so many processes (allocation, socialization, cohort flow, aging), age stratification has not been embraced in its entirety by researchers.

A major theme in life course research is the importance of historical events in shaping individual lives. Elder's *Children of the Great Depression* (1974) showed that relative economic loss, gender, and social class served to differentiate the experience of cohort members confronting a historical event. The effects of the Depression can still be seen with respect to values in adulthood (Elder, 1974) as well as health and well being in old age (Elder and Liker, 1982). Another strand of life course research has emphasized historical changes in the timing of adult transitions (Hogan, 1981; Modell et al., 1976; Winsborough, 1979). Studies consistently show that current male cohorts accomplish young-adult transitions (i.e., finishing school, completing military duty, marrying, and starting a career) in a shorter time span than did their counterparts at the turn of the century. The effect of timing and sequencing patterns for life outcomes is also of interest. Early marriage is associated with marital disruption (Weeks, 1976) as well as lower educational attainment (Marini, 1978). Hogan (1978, 1980) finds that men who did not achieve young adult transitions in the normative sequence (i.e., finishing school, getting a job, marrying) experienced more divorce and achieved lower job status and income. Although Marini (1984) criticizes this approach for assuming the existence of social norms, Hogan (1984) demonstrates that mothers' expectations do influence the timing of their children's young adult transitions.

Much life course research leaves out the individual in its focus on aggregates of people who share the same age or cohort (Hagestad and Neugarten, 1985). Exceptions include research on the meaning of transitions on individual lives, such as Plath's (1980) analysis of a Japanese novel in which family members' transitions affect one another. Micro-environments also get short shrift. Yet the situational nature of changes over the life course can be seen in the workplace. For example, Lorence and Mortimer (1985) find that worker autonomy has a greater effect on job involvement at the beginning of a career, but involvement changes over the life course, becoming more stable as one gets older. Kohn and Schooler (1983) demonstrate the impact on intellectual flexibility of the complexity of work.

In sum, the dominant perspective in the sociology of aging is the life course framework, growing out of the recognition of birth cohorts as important influences on individual aging. Although one tenet of the perspective is that "aging occurs from birth to death" (Riley, 1979), most of the research actually focuses on young adult transitions. There exists little life course research that examines the nature of transitions in childhood or old age.

STATE OF THE ART: THE SOCIOLOGY OF THE AGED

Because of its presumed association with ill health, poverty, and social isolation, old age has been viewed as a "problem" (Maddox and Wiley, 1976). The hallmark of this social problem orientation has been an interest in "adjustment" to old age. Early social reformers (Epstein, 1922) had seen the aged as victims of a social order that was in need of change. Research at midcentury, however, came to see the problem as resting not with society, but with the individual's response to society. Researchers were interested in how the elderly could best adapt to changes in their lives associated with getting older.

Cavan et al.'s (1949) *Personal Adjustment in Old Age* and Havighurst and Albrecht's (1953) *Older People* reflected these concerns. Although there was little formal theorizing, research and policy was informed by an implicit activity theory (Cumming and Henry, 1961) that assumed that adjustment in old age was tied to maintaining a wide variety of roles. Although Lemon et al. (1972) presented the first systematic statement of activity theory, their empirical data on new residents of a retirement community supported few activity theory hypotheses.

The 1961 publication of Cumming and Henry's book, *Growing Old,* introduced disengagement theory—the first formal sociological theory of old age. Applying structural functionalism to the condition of the elderly, disengagement referred to the universal, inevitable, and mutual withdrawal of older people from society. This process enabled society to make room for younger, more productive members while allowing older individuals time to prepare for death. Contrary to an activity perspective, these authors found high morale associated with less, not more, activity.

Disengagement theory was criticized on empirical (Maddox, 1964; Palmore, 1968), theoretical, and logical grounds (Hochschild, 1975). Little additional empirical evidence was presented despite the methodological inadequacies of the initial studies (i.e., the small, nonrandom samples of white, healthy, midwestern adults). The two important legacies of disengagement theory were the development of opposing theories of the aged (Hochschild, 1975) and an enduring interest in the "life satisfaction" of older people (e.g., Larson, 1978).

More recent theories examine older people's location within microinteractions and macrostructures. Exchange theory (Dowd, 1975) argues that elderly persons typically lack the resources to participate effectively in social relations. If interactions become too costly, older people decrease their participation in social encounters. Only those elderly who can maintain a balanced relationship with other age groups remain engaged. Focusing on macrostructural conditions, modernization theory (Cowgill, 1974; Cowgill and Holmes, 1972) argues that the status of the aged is inversely related to the level of societal modernization. In earlier preindustrial societies, the elderly held high status by virtue of their control of scarce resources and their knowledge of tradition. Changes associated with modernization—health technology, economic technology, urbanization, and mass education—resulted in lower status of the aged. Cowgill's (1974) formulation has served as a theoretical touchstone, inspiring research challenging its main propositions (Bengtson et al., 1975).

Fostering a historical-comparative perspective, the political economy of aging (Estes, 1979; Olson, 1982) has brought issues of power and conflict to the fore in understanding the condition of the elderly. Studies in this tradition call attention to the requirements of a capitalist economy, the role of the state, the competing interests of different social groups, and economic and political circumstances in the creation of the U.S. social security system (Myles, 1984), the British old-age pension (Quadagno, 1982), old-age policy in France (Guillemard, 1983), and the age-based benefit and eligibility structure of U.S. Civil War pensions (Treas, 1986). This approach is an important corrective to previous historical accounts of old age programs that implicitly emphasized the evolutionary, consensual aspects of political and economic changes.

Ironically, the major theories in social gerontology have been largely divorced from much empirical research. Research typically focuses on practical problems, such as social support (Krause, 1986), caregiving (Brody and Schoonover, 1986), housing (Lawton and Hoover, 1981), and long-term care (Mor et al., 1986). Given its highly descriptive emphasis, the sociology of the aged has been successful in dispelling popular beliefs about older people.

One persistent myth is the belief that older people are alienated from their families. Shanas's (1979a, 1979b) research consistently shows that (1) older people interact frequently with their grown children and other kin; (2) the family is the primary source of care for its older members; (3) siblings and other kin typically care for those elderly who do not have children; and (4) older people live alone because of economic affluence rather than social neglect.

Another popular myth about the elderly suggests that there once was a "golden age of aging" (Burgess, 1960) in which the elderly headed multigenerational households, controlled resources of the larger society, and were the source of tradition. Recent analyses in social history, however, call into question the notion of a simple, linear relationship between the degree of industrialization and status of the elderly (Stearns, 1982). The multigenerational household was never a dominant form in western European countries, if only because of demographic constraints on the availability of kin (Laslett, 1976). Current histories of old age emphasize variations in the experiences of the elderly depending on gender, race, ethnicity, social class, region, and historical period (Stearns, 1982).

The aged have never been a homogeneous group. Cain's (1967) classic article led to recognition of a new cohort of elderly who are healthier, more educated, and have greater income than did their predecessors. Neugarten (1974) characterizes this group as the "young old" as distinguished from the "old old." Indeed, some researchers point out that the aged are the most diverse age group (e.g., Neugarten, 1982), resulting from accumulated advantage (or disadvantage) over a lifetime (Dannefer, 1987).

In sum, the sociology of the aged began with an emphasis on adjustment to old age. Although the activity-disengagement debate has ended, most researchers in social gerontology continue to study the pragmatic problems affecting the lives of the aged.

PROSPECTS FOR THE SOCIOLOGIES OF AGE, AGING, AND THE AGED

To this point, we have selectively surveyed the historical origins of the three sociologies, their theories, and the body of research engendered by them. This review reinforces the contention that the developmental path of each sociology has been unique. Each sociology has had its own practitioners, its distinctive sources of inspiration, its guiding paradigms, its singular research focus. Although we can identify research areas poised for major development, their cumulative impact on the course of this balkanized field is less certain. Looking to the future, one question comes to mind. Can the sociologies of age, aging, and aged be unified into a single sociological field—that is, a disciplinary specialization integrating age as an organizing principle in society with age as a framework for individual lives?

The integration of *three* sociologies into *the* sociology is an appealing prospect. One might hope that a unification would promote theoretical cross-pollination, bring together a far flung knowledge base, diminish the wasteful duplication of research efforts between fields, and reduce intellectual dependence on other disciplines by distinguishing sociological approaches to age and aging. Recognizing the benefits to be reaped from an integration of the three sociologies, one might easily become sanguine about the practical barriers to a unified sociology of age, aging, and the aged.

The fate of the model of age stratification (Riley et al., 1972) is instructive. For nearly two decades, sociologists have had this framework at their disposal. This schema represents a valiant effort to link social institutions and individual lives in the context of historical time and chronological aging. As such, it stands as a powerful tool to span the macrosociological interests of the sociology of age, the micro-level concerns of the sociology of aging, and the focused research problems of the sociology of the aged. Despite the growing clarity of the model (Riley et al., 1972; Riley, 1985), one is hard put to identify empirical research that has been faithful to age stratification.

Indeed, sociologists seem to have thrown off the expansive age stratification "theory" with some relief, embracing instead its descendent— the less demanding life course "perspective." Even the most ambitious research in the life course tradition (Elder, 1974; Hogan, 1981) has studiously avoided the dialectical implications of the age stratification theory. This life course research has nested most comfortably within the sociology of aging. Its primary concern has been the impact of social structure and historical events on the lives of individuals. It has given little, if any, attention to the ways in which individuals have altered their environments, either through collective action or common behavioral responses. As such, the life course perspective falls short in informing the study of structural change (Hernes, 1976).

By contrast, the age stratification model wrestles with this broader dialectic. Its real strengths, however, are at the macrosociological level. It succeeds admirably in describing a societal metabolism driven by cohort flows, but is less successful in explaining the actions of individuals. Although it delineates macro-level changes that impinge on individual decision making, it fails to posit an explicit model of why individuals do what they do, at least apart from oversocialized conceptions of action. The age stratification model readily identifies contradictions in social structure that might serve as an impetus to behavioral change (e.g., a numerical imbalance between social roles and age-appropriate potential recruits). Without a formal statement of actors' goals, means, and motives, behavioral responses are hard to predict and explanations post hoc.

If it is not for want of an integrating framework, why have the three sociologies not merged? There are inherent difficulties in moving between levels of analysis—from individuals to primary groups to organizations to social institutions and ultimately society. This is further complicated by the need to incorporate a multidimensional concept of time with each analytic level running on different and multiple timetables. Aside from the conceptual difficulties, there is a dearth of empirical data meeting the demands of such an analysis. Despite a proliferation of panel studies, we still lack longitudinal studies of individual lives that permit aggregation into meaningful social units beyond the household.

To date, the sociologists of age, aging, and the aged have manifest only mild interest in one another's endeavors. The emergent debate between the sociogenic and ontogenic conceptualizations of human development (Dannefer, 1984; Baltes and Nesselroade, 1984; Featherman and Lerner, 1985), however, threatens to harden the lines between the three sociologies. Because the sociology of the aged has demonstrated a high degree of adaptability to prevailing theoretical currents, we would expect it to survive unscathed. The debate has greater implications for the sociologies of age and aging. At issue is whether development represents a natural (ontogenic) unfolding of programmed traits and behavior or whether development is channeled by the social structure. Obviously, both biological and environmental influences figure in development. All three sociologies acknowledge this, but the question is one of emphasis. At stake is the definition of the appropriate domain for sociological inquiry.

Should the ontogenic perspective triumph, sociologists may no longer be free merely to assume biological causes, but must instead incorporate them explicitly into their models of aging. One may be highly skeptical of the notion that biologically unschooled sociologists can advance our general understanding of aging by attending in any but the most superficial way to biological factors. With research funding increasingly tied to biomedical problems, however, the biological roots of development may hold greater appeal for sociologists. If biological factors are to be incorporated in sociological models, it is apt to be at the level of the individual, not that of the social institution. (Although human populations may evidence adaptation, this biological evolution is not likely to occur within a short enough time frame to interest most sociologists.) This stress on individual biological factors might lead to a marginalization of the sociology of age from the other two sociologies. Indeed, many practitioners of the sociology of age already identify more strongly with other substantive specializations in sociology (e.g., demography, organizations) than with the sociology of age.

The sociology of the aged merits particular comment. To the extent that the field maintains its applied mission, generating knowledge to improve the lives of older people, it will find relatively little common ground with the basic research orientations of the sociologies of age and aging. Beyond a general sensitivity to life course experiences of individuals, research on the practical concerns of the elderly are unlikely to be much advanced by the theoretical embellishments of these two sociologies. There is, however, room for considerable refinement and innovation in theories that might drive applied research.

To be sure, not all research in the sociology of the aged is or will be what we might think of as applied social gerontology. Later life might well emerge as the "strategic site" for life course research as Maddox (1979) has suggested. Given the enormous demographic changes, the rapid institutional development, and the rich concentration of life cycle transitions associated with old age, there is ample reason for old age to become the laboratory for developing and testing theory in the sociologies of age and aging. In fact, the social problem perspective that has driven the sociology of the aged (and which has inevitably narrowed the kinds of research questions asked) may be becoming less viable. There is, for example, a growing awareness that the aged are typically neither poor nor bereft of familial supports.

The task for the three sociologies, together and separately, will undoubtedly be the identification and application of theories that explain, predict, and make sense of the rich phenomena of age. Simplistic models of aging have been discredited. This is particularly true of the sociology of the aged in which one-variable models (e.g., retirement leads to dissatisfaction) have been largely swept aside by the weight of empirical evidence. In her critique of disengagement theory, Hochschild (1975) referred to this as the "omnibus variable" problem, in which a single variable such as age or disengagement refers to numerous processes. Theories that attempt to explain the process of aging in terms of one variable—whether it be disengagement, activity, or cohort membership—deny the complex ways that aging is experienced.

We caution against theories that go to the other extreme and attempt to take into account *every* aspect of aging, including biological, psychological, and sociological processes. The newly proposed biosocial life span perspective (Featherman and Lerner, 1985), for example, may run the risk of being overinclusive in its incorporation of select biological, psychological, and social structural factors. Moreover, the variables incorporated in a model of aging will vary with theoretical perspectives. Psychology and biology (like sociology) do not have a united paradigm so one needs to be explicit about the perspective informing the choice of factors in the analysis. The most useful research in aging, we suggest, is apt to be motivated by middle-range theory (much already available in the discipline) rather than by ambitious grand theories.

Although Featherman and Lerner (1985) call their integrating perspective "developmental contextualism," there is little attention to social context in research to date. By context we mean the situational, emergent features of social life, as opposed to individuals' location in a general social order. Future research will have to take context more seriously if there is to be an integrating, multidisciplinary framework. To their credit, Featherman and associates (Featherman and Lerner, 1985; Featherman and Peterson, 1986) have proposed a definition of development that could offer the three sociologies a common ground for discourse. They have argued for reconceptualizing development as a duration-dependent process, that is, dependent on time. This dynamic conceptualization has been associated with a methodological agenda focusing on event history models (Allison, 1984).

CONCLUSION

The study of aging is characterized by three distinct research traditions: the sociology of age, the sociology of aging, and the sociology of the aged. Each developed at the margin of sociology and another discipline. As a result, each has its distinctive historical origins and its own research questions; each favors particular theories and methodologies over others. At a time when the field is gaining in popularity and prestige within sociology, it is appropriate to examine the development of this research area. Although we see obstacles to the unification of the three sociologies, there is also reason to be optimistic about future research developments.

First, aging is a recent area of research within sociology. Age was such a taken-for-granted element of social life that sociologists virtually ignored it for decades. Only after race and gender were identified as critical elements of social differentiation did the field begin to recognize the social significance of age. In the past 15 years there has been an exponential increase in the number of studies focusing on age, aging, and the aged. During this relatively short period of time, the field has become much more sophisticated, both theoretically and methodologically.

Second, although the theoretical and methodological eclecticism of the field has led to a lack of consensus on a research agenda, it has also resulted in several positive developments. The field's multidisciplinary inspiration has challenged narrow sociological visions of human aging. Methodological variety has prevented mindless domination by the latest statistical advance. On the contrary, the field values both observational studies of old age environments and quantitative modeling of such processes as the decision to retire. The field has discouraged polemics through its firm tie to the practical issues associated with aging and growing old.

The study of aging is at a particularly promising point in its short history. It has transformed our taken-for-granted notions of age, demonstrating the myriad ways that age both structures and gives meaning to social life. There is promise of even greater insights in the field, as researchers begin to incorporate more contemporary theoretical perspectives using more appropriate research designs.

REFERENCES

Allison, Paul D. (1984) Event History Analysis: Regression for Longitudinal Event Data. Beverly Hills, CA: Sage.

Aries, Philippe (1962) Centuries of Childhood. New York: Alfred A. Knopf.

Atchley, Robert C. (1971) "Retirement and leisure participation: continuity or crisis?" Gerontologist 11: 13-17.

Atchley, Robert C. (1976) The Sociology of Retirement. New York: Halsted.

Babchuk, Nicholas, George R. Peters, Danny R. Hoyt, and Marvin A. Kaiser (1979) "The voluntary associations of the aged." Journal of Gerontology 34: 579-587.

Baltes, Paul B. (1979) "Life-span developmental psychology: some converging observations on history and theory," pp. 225-279 in P. Baltes and O. Brim (eds.) Life-Span Development and Behavior, Vol. 2. New York: Academic Press.

Baltes, Paul B. and John R. Nesselroade (1984) "Paradigm lost and paradigm regained: critique of Dannefer's portrayal of life span developmental psychology." American Sociological Review 49: 841-847.

Becker, Howard S. (1964) "Personal change in adult life." Sociometry 27: 40-53.

Becker, Howard S. and Anselm L. Strauss (1956) "Careers, personality, and adult socialization." American Journal of Sociology 62: 253-263.

Benedict, Ruth (1946) The Chrysanthemum and the Sword. Boston: Houghton.

Bengtson, Vern L., James J. Dowd, David H. Smith, and Alex Inkeles (1975) "Modernization, modernity, and perceptions of aging: a cross-cultural study." Journal of Gerontology 30: 688-695.

Bengtson, Vern L. and Judith Treas (1980) "The changing family context of mental health and aging," pp. 400-428 in J. Birren and B. Sloan (eds.) Handbook of Mental Health and Aging. .

Brim, Orville G., Jr. and Stanton Wheeler (1966) Socialization After Childhood: Two Essays. New York: Wiley.

Brody, Elaine M. and Claire B. Schoonover (1986) "Patterns of parent care when adult daughters work and when they do not." Gerontologist 26: 372-381.

Burgess, Ernest W. (1960) Aging in Western Societies. Chicago: University of Chicago Press.

Cain, Leonard D., Jr. (1967) "Age status and generational phenomena: the new old people in America." Gerontologist 7: 83-92.

Cain, Leonard D., Jr. (1976) "Aging and the law," pp. 342-368 in R. Binstock and E. Shanas (eds.) Handbook of Aging and the Social Sciences (2nd ed.). New York: Van Nostrand Reinhold.

Cavan, Ruth S., Ernest W. Burgess, Robert J. Havighurst, and Herbert Goldhammer (1949) Personal Adjustment in Old Age. Chicago: Science Research Associates.

Cowgill, Donald O. (1974) "Aging and modernization: a revision of the theory," pp. 123-146 in J. Gubrium (ed.) Late Life. Springfield, IL: Charles C Thomas.

Cowgill, Donald O. and Lowell D. Holmes [eds.] (1972) Aging and modernization. New York: Appleton-Century-Crofts.

Creecy, Robert F., William E. Berg, and Roosevelt Wright, Jr. (1985) "Loneliness among the aged: a causal approach." Journal of Gerontology 40: 487-494.

Crimmins, Eileen M. (1984) "Life expectancy and the older population." Research on Aging 6: 490-514.

Cumming, Elaine and William E. Henry (1961) Growing Old. New York: Basic Books.

Dannefer, Dale (1984) "Adult development and social theory: a paradigmatic reappraisal." American Sociological Review 49: 100-116.

Dannefer, Dale (1987) "Aging as intracohort differentiation: accentuation, the Matthew effect and the life course." Sociological Forum 1: 8-23.

Dowd, James J. (1975) "Aging as exchange: a preface to theory." Journal of Gerontology 30: 584-594.

Easterlin, Richard (1968) Population, Labor Force, and Long Swings in Economic Growth: The American Experience. New York: National Bureau of Economic Research.

Easterlin, Richard (1980) Birth and Fortune: The Impact of Numbers on Personal Welfare. New York: Basic Books.

Elder, Glen H., Jr. (1974) Children of the Great Depression. Chicago: University of Chicago Press.

Elder, Glen H., Jr. (1979) "Historical change in life patterns and personality," pp. 117-159 in P. Baltes and O. Brim (eds.) Life-Span Development and Behavior, Vol. 2. New York: Academic Press.

Elder, Glen H., Jr. and Jeffrey K. Liker (1982) "Hard times in women's lives: historical influences across forty years." American Journal of Sociology 88: 241-269.

Empey, Lamar (1982) American Delinquency: Its Meaning and Construction. Homewood, IL: Dorsey.

Epstein, Abraham (1922) Facing Old Age: A Study of Old Age Dependency in the United States and Old Age Pensions. New York: Alfred A. Knopf.

Epstein, Abraham (1928) The Challenge of the Aged. New York: Vanguard.

Erikson, Erik (1950) Childhood and Society. New York: Norton.

Erikson, Erik (1959) Identity and the Life Cycle. New York: International Universities Press.

Estes, Carroll L. (1979) The Aging Enterprise. San Francisco: Jossey-Bass.

Featherman, David L. and Richard M. Lerner (1985) "Ontogenesis and sociogenesis: problematics for theory and research about development and socialization across the lifespan." American Sociological Review 50: 659-676.

Featherman, David L. and Trond Petersen (1986) "Markers of aging: modeling the clocks that time us." Research on Aging 8: 339-365.

Freud, Sigmund (1962) The Ego and the Id. Standard Edition of the Complete Psychological Works of Sigmund Freud, Vol. 19 (1923). London: Hogarth.

George, Linda K. (1980) Role Transitions in Later Life. Belmont, CA: Brooks/Cole.

Gillis, John R. (1974) Youth and History. New York: Academic Press.

Glick, Paul C. and Arthur J. Norton (1979) "Marrying, divorcing and living together in the U.S. today." Population Bulletin 32: 1-41.

Gubrium, Jaber F. (1975) Living and Dying at Murray Manor. New York: St. Martin's.

Gubrium, Jaber F. and David R. Buckholdt (1977) Toward Maturity: The Social Processing of Human Development. San Francisco: Jossey-Bass.

Guillemard, Anne-Marie (1983) "The making of old age policy in France: points of debate, issues at stake, underlying social relations," pp. 75-99 in A. Guillemard (ed.) Old Age and the Welfare State. Beverly Hills, CA: Sage.

Haber, Carole (1978) "Mandatory retirement in nineteenth-century America: the conceptual basis for a new work cycle." Journal of Social History 12: 77-96.

Hagestad, Gunhild O. and Bernice L. Neugarten (1985) "Age and the life course," pp. 35-61 in R. Binstock and E. Shanas (eds.) Handbook of Aging and the Social Sciences (2nd ed.). New York: Van Nostrand Reinhold.

Hammel, E. A., K. W. Wachter, and C. K. McDaniel (1981) "The kin of the aged in A.D. 2000: the chickens come home to roost," pp. 11-39 in S. Kiesler, J. Morgan, and V. Oppenheimer (eds.) Aging: Social Change. New York: Academic Press.

Havighurst, Robert J. and Ruth Albrecht (1953) Older People. New York: Longman, Green.

Heer, David M. (1985) "Effects of sibling number on child outcome," pp. 27-47 in R. Turner and J. Short, Jr. (eds.) Annual Review of Sociology, Vol. 11. Palo Alto, CA: Annual Reviews.

Hendricks, Jon and C. Davis Hendricks (1986) Aging in Mass Society: Myths and Realities (3rd ed.). Boston: Little, Brown.

Hernes, Gudmund (1976) "Structural change in social processes." American Journal of Sociology 82: 513-547.

Hochschild, Arlie Russell (1975) "Disengagement theory: a critique and proposal." American Sociological Review 40: 553-569.

Hogan, Dennis P. (1978) "The variable order of events in the life course." American Sociological Review 43: 573-586.

Hogan, Dennis P. (1980) "The transition to adulthood as a career contingency." American Sociological Review 45: 261-276.

Hogan, Dennis P. (1981) Transitions and Social Change: The Early Lives of American Men. New York: Academic Press.

Hogan, Dennis P. (1984) "Maternal influences on adolescent family formation." Presented at the Midwest Sociological Society meetings, Chicago.

Kanter, Rosabeth Moss (1977) Men and Women of the Corporation. New York: Basic Books.

Karp, David A. and William C. Yoels (1982) Experiencing the Life Cycle. Springfield, IL: Charles C Thomas.

Keyfitz, Nathan (1973) "Individual mobility in a stationary population." Population Studies 27: 335-352.

Knipscheer, C.P.M. (1985) "Naar een Raamwerk voor een Sociologie van het Ouder Worden en van de Ouderdom" ("Towards a framework for a sociology of aging and the aged"), in C.P.M. Knipscheer (ed.) Sociologie van het Ouder Worden Sinds 1970: Onderzoek en Beleid (Sociology of Aging Since 1970: Research and Policy). The Netherlands: Nijmegen.

Kohlberg, Lawrence (1969) Stages in the Development of Moral Thought and Action. New York: Holt, Rinehart & Winston.

Kohli, Martin, Joachim Rosenow, and Jurgen Wolf (1983) "The social construction of ageing through work: economic structure and life-world." Ageing and Society 3: 23-42.

Kohn, Melvin L. and Carmi Schooler (1983) Work and Personality: An Inquiry into the Impact of Social Stratification. Norwood, NJ: Ablex.

Krause, Neal (1986) "Social support, stress, and well-being among older adults." Journal of Gerontology 41: 512-519.

Larson, Reed (1978) "Thirty years of research on the subjective well-being of elderly tenants in public housing." Journal of Gerontology 33: 109-129.

Laslett, Peter (1976) "Societal development and aging," pp. 187-216 in R. Binstock and E. Shanas (eds.) Handbook of Aging and the Social Sciences. New York: Van Nostrand Reinhold.

Lawrence, Barbara S. (1984) "Age grading: the implicit organizational timetable." Journal of Occupational Behavior 5: 23-35.

Lawton, M. Powell and Sally L. Hoover [eds.] (1981) Community Housing Choices for Older Americans. New York: Springer.

Lemon, Bruce W., Vern L. Bengtson, and James A. Peterson (1972) "An exploration of the activity theory of aging: activity types and life satisfaction among in-movers to a retirement community." Journal of Gerontology 27: 511-523.

Levinson, Daniel J. (1978) The Seasons of a Man's Life. New York: Alfred A. Knopf.

Liang, Jersey, Eva Kahana, and Edmund Doherty (1980) "Financial well-being among the aged: a further elaboration." Journal of Gerontology 35: 409-420.

Linton, Ralph (1942) "Age and sex categories." American Sociological Review 7: 589-603.

Lopata, Helena Znaniecki (1972) Widowhood in an American City. Cambridge, MA: Schenkman.

Lorence, Jon and Jeylon T. Mortimer (1985) "Job involvement through the life course: a panel study of three age groups." American Sociological Review 50: 618-638.

Lotka, Alfred J. (1907) "Relation between birth rates and death rates." Science XXVI: 21-22.

Lyman-Viera, Karen (forthcoming) "Infantilization of elders: day care for Alzheimer's disease victims." Research in the Sociology of Health Care, Vol. 7.

Lynd, Robert S. and Helen Merrell Lynd (1929) Middletown. New York: Harcourt Brace and World.

Lynd, Robert S. and Helen Merrell Lynd (1937) Middletown in Transition. New York: Harcourt Brace and World.

Lynott, Robert J. (1983) "Alzheimer's disease and institutionalization: the ongoing construction of a decision." Journal of Family Issues 4: 559-574.

Maddox, George L. (1964) "Disengagement theory: a critical evaluation." Gerontologist 4: 80-2.

Maddox, George L. (1979) "The sociology of later life," pp. 113-135 in A. Inkeles, J. Coleman, and R. Turner (eds.) Annual Review of Sociology, Vol. 5. Palo Alto, CA: Annual Reviews.

Maddox, George L. and James Wiley (1976) "Scope, concepts and methods in the study of aging," pp. 3-34 in R. Binstock and E. Shanas (eds.) Handbook of Aging and the Social Sciences. New York: Van Nostrand Reinhold.

Marini, Margaret Mooney (1978) "The transition to adulthood: sex differences in educational attainment and age at marriage." American Sociological Review 43: 483-507.

Marini, Margaret Mooney (1984) "Age and sequencing norms in the transition to adulthood." Social Forces 63: 229-244.

Marshall, Victor W. (1978-1979) "No exit: a symbolic interactionist perspective on aging." International Journal of Aging and Human Development 9: 345-358.

Modell, John (1980) "Normative aspects of marriage since World War II." Journal of Family History 5: 210-234.

Modell, John, Frank F. Furstenberg, Jr., and Theodore Hershberg (1976) "Social change and transitions to adulthood in historical perspective." Journal of Family History 1: 7-32.

Mor, Vincent, Sylvia Sherwood, and Claire Gutkin (1986) "A national study of residential care for the aged." Gerontologist 26: 405-417.

Myles, John (1984) Old Age in the Welfare State. Boston: Little Brown.

Neugarten, Bernice L. (1974) "Age groups in American society and the rise of the young-old." Annals of the American Academy of Political and Social Science 415: 187-198.

Neugarten, Bernice L. (1979) "Time, age, and the life cycle." American Journal of Psychiatry 136: 887-894.

Neugarten, Bernice L. (1982) Age or Need?: Public Policies and Older People. Beverly Hills, CA: Sage.

Neugarten, Bernice L., Joan W. Moore, and John C. Lowe (1965) "Age norms, age constraints, and adult socialization." American Journal of Sociology 70: 710-717.

O'Rand, Angela M. and John C. Henretta (1982) "Delayed career entry, industrial pension structure and early retirement in a cohort of unmarried women." American Sociological Review 47: 365-373.

Olson, Laura K. (1982) The Political Economy of Aging. New York: Columbia University Press.

Oppenheimer, Valerie K. (1970) The Female Labor Force in the United States: Demographic and Economic Factors Governing Its Growth and Changing Composition. Population Monograph Series No. 5. Berkeley, CA: University of California Press.

Oppenheimer, Valerie K. (1981) "The changing nature of life cycle squeezes: implications for the socioeconomic position of the elderly," pp. 47-81 in R. Fogel and J. March (eds.) Aging: Stability and Change in the Family. New York: Academic Press.

Orloff, Ann S. and Theda Skocpol (1984) "Why not equal protection? Explaining the politics of public social spending in Britain, 1900-1911, and the United States, 1880s-1920." American Sociological Review 49: 726-750.

Palmore, Erdman B. (1968) "The effects of aging on activities and attitudes." Gerontologist 8: 259-263.

Pampel, Fred C. and Sookja Park (1986) "Cross national patterns and determinants of female retirement." American Journal of Sociology 91: 932-955.

Passuth, Patricia M. (1984) Children's Socialization to Age Hierarchies within the Peer Group and Family. Northwestern University, Evanston, IL. (unpublished dissertation)

Passuth, Patricia M., David R. Maines, and Bernice L. Neugarten (1984) "Age norms and age constraints twenty years later." Presented at the Midwest Sociological Society meetings, Chicago.

Perlmutter, Marion (1986) "Cognitive development in life span perspective: from description to explanation." Presented at the Social Science Research Council Conference on Child Development in Life Span Perspective, Woods Hill, MA.

Pfeffer, Jeffrey (1981) "Some consequences of organizational demography: potential impacts of an aging work force on formal organizations," pp. 291-329 in S. Kiesler, J. Morgan, and V. Oppenheimer (eds.) Aging: Social Change. New York: Academic Press.

Phillipson, Chris (1982) Capitalism and the Construction of Old Age. London: Macmillan.

Piaget, Jean (1952) The Origins of Intelligence. New York: International Universities Press.

Plath, David W. (1980) "Contours of consociation: lessons from a Japanese narrative," pp. 287-305 in P. Baltes and O. Brim (eds.) Life-Span Development and Behavior, Vol. 3. New York: Academic Press.

Plath, David W. and Keiko Ikeda (1975) "After coming of age: adult awareness of age norms," pp. 107-124 in T. Williams (ed.) Socialization and Communication in Primary Groups. The Hague: Mouton.

Pratt, Henry J. (1976) The Gray Lobby. Chicago: University of Chicago Press.

Preston, Samuel H. (1982) "Relations between individual life cycles and population characteristics." American Sociological Review 47: 253-264.

Preston, Samuel H. (1984) "Children and the elderly in the U.S." Scientific American 251: 44-49.

Quadagno, Jill S. (1982) Aging in Early Industrial Society. New York: Academic Press.

Quadagno, Jill S. (1984) "Welfare capitalism and the Social Security Act of 1935." American Sociological Review 49: 632-647.

Riley, Matilda White (1979) Aging From Birth to Death: Interdisciplinary Perspectives. Boulder, CO: Westview.

Riley, Matilda White (1985) "Age strata in social systems," pp. 369-411 in R. Binstock and E. Shanas (eds.) Handbook of Aging and the Social Sciences (2nd ed.). New York: Van Nostrand Reinhold.

Riley, Matilda White, Marilyn Johnson, and Anne Foner [eds.] (1972) Aging and Society: Vol. 3. A Sociology of Age Stratification. New York: Russell Sage Foundation.

Rindfuss, Ronald R. and Larry L. Bumpass (1978) "Age and the sociology of fertility: how old is too old," pp. 43-56 in K. Taeuber, L. Bumpass, and J. Sweet (eds.) Social Demography. New York: Academic Press.

Rosenbaum, James E. (1979) "Organizational career mobility: promotion chances in a corporation during periods of growth and contraction." American Journal of Sociology 85: 21-48.

Rosow, Irving (1974) Socialization to Old Age. Berkeley, CA: University of California Press.

Rubinow, I. M. [ed.] (1931) The Care of the Aged. Chicago: University of Chicago Press.

Ryder, Norman B. (1965) "The cohort as a concept in the study of social change." American Sociological Review 30: 843-861.

Schaie, K. Warner (1967) "Age changes and age differences." Gerontologist 7: 128-132.

Shanas, Ethel (1979a) "Social myth as hypothesis: the case of the family relations of old people." Gerontologist 19: 3-9.

Shanas, Ethel (1979b) "The family as a social support in old age." Gerontologist 19: 169-174.

Spilerman, Seymour (1977) "Careers, labor markets, and socioeconomic achievement." American Journal of Sociology 83: 551-593.

Starr, Jerold M. (1982-1983) "Toward a social phenomenology of aging: studying the self-process in biographical work." International Journal of Aging and Human Development 16: 255-270.

Stearns, Peter N. (1982) "Introduction," pp. 1-18 in P. Stearns (ed.) Old Age in Preindustrial Society. New York: Holmes and Meier.

Stewman, Shelby and Suresh L. Konda (1983) "Careers and organizational labor markets: demographic models of organizational behavior." American Journal of Sociology 88: 637-685.

Streib, Gordon F., W. Edward Folts, and Anthony J. La Greca (1985) "Autonomy, power, and decision-making in thirty-six retirement communities." Gerontologist 25: 403-409.

Sutton, John R. (1983) "Social structure, institutions, and the legal status of children in the United States." American Journal of Sociology 88: 915-947.

Tallmer, Margot and Bernard Kutner (1970) "Disengagement and morale." Gerontologist 10: 317-320.

Terman, Lewis M. (1925) Genetic Studies of Genius: Vol. I. Mental and Physical Traits of a Thousand Gifted Children. Stanford, CA: Stanford University Press.

Thomas, W. I. and Florian Znaniecki (1918) The Polish Peasant in Europe and America. New York: Octagon.

Treas, Judith (1977) "Family support systems for the aged: some social and demographic considerations." Gerontologist 17: 486-491.

Treas, Judith (1986) "The historical decline in late life labor force participation in the U.S.," pp. 158-173 in J. Birren, P. Robinson, and J. Livingston (eds.) Age, Health, and Employment. Englewood Cliffs, NJ: Prentice-Hall.

Vaillant, George E. (1977) Adaptation to Life. Boston: Little, Brown.

van Gennep, Arnold (1960) Rites of Passage (1908). Chicago: University of Chicago Press.

Weeks, John (1976) Teenage Marriages. Westport, CT: Greenwood.

Winsborough, Halliman H. (1979) "Changes in the transition to adulthood," pp. 137-152 in M. W. Riley (ed.) Aging from Birth to Death: Interdisciplinary Perspectives. Boulder, CO: Westview.

Wolinsky, Frederick D., Rodney M. Coe, Douglas K. Miller (1984) "Measurement of the global and functional dimensions of health status in the elderly." Journal of Gerontology 39: 88-92.

About the Authors

S. J. Ball-Rokeach is Professor of Communications and Professor of Sociology at the Annenberg School of Communications, University of Southern California. She is involved in numerous research efforts to further develop her progam of research in media system dependency theory. She and her research team are assessing the validity of recent explications and expansions of this ecological theory of media systems in a variety of personal organizational and societal contexts. In concert with this work, she is continuing her belief-system research program taking it into such areas as value framing of public discourse and examination of the import of morality beliefs in effective problem solving. She is also exploring the theoretical and practical import of new communication forms with reference the opportunities they may or not afford for adaptive modifications in the organization of personal and social life.

Richard A. Berk is a Professor of Sociology at UCLA. His major interest for well over a decade has been applied sociological research. Major topics of current interest include criminal justice, environmental concerns, and AIDS.

Edna Bonacich is Professor of Sociology at the University of California at Riverside. She is conducting research on racial oppression in higher education and on Asian immigration to the United States.

Edgar F. Borgatta is Professor of Sociology at the University of Washington. He is working on a book on measurement that deals with issues specific to social sciences and is planning work in an area he has labeled "pro-active sociology," or the attempt to design alternatives to existing social structures that do not facilitate implementation of stated values (social engineering).

Paul Burstein is Assistant Professor of Sociology at the University of Washington. His major interests are political sociology, social stratification, and the sociology of law, and his book about equal employment opportunity is an attempt to show how politics and law may be used to redistribute income in democratic countries. His current work focuses on consequences of equal employment opportunity legislation for employment practices, intergroup relations, and American pluralism.

Lee Clarke is Assistant Professor of Sociology at Rutgers University. He is working on a project investigating organizational decision making regarding technological risks. He is the author of a forthcoming book about organizational processes involved in defining acceptable risk.

Karen S. Cook is Professor of Sociology and Director of the Social Psychology Laboratory at the University of Washington. She is also the Editor of *Social Psychology Quarterly*. Her current interests include social exchange networks, the structural determinants of power, and distributive justice. She is now engaged in collaborative research with Toshio Yamagishi and Mary Gillmore on generalized exchange systems.

Herbert L. Costner is Professor and Chair of the Department of Sociology at the University of Washington. A specialist in research methodology, his current work is concentrated on problems of measurement in social research, with emphasis on the impact of correlated measurement error on research conclusions.

Lois B. DeFleur is Provost and Professor of Sociology at the University of Missouri. She has completed a project focusing on the integration of women into previously all-male military units and has recently published an article in *Armed Forces in Society* that deals with the socialization experiences of male and female cadets at the U.S. Air Force Academy. Her current research project examines career ladders of academic women and how women move into administrative posts in higher education.

Howard E. Freeman is Professor of Sociology and Chair of the Sociology Department at the University of California at Los Angeles. He is completing analysis of a national study of the use of health services, funded by the Robert Wood Johnson Foundation, and has research in progress investigating institutional reactions to AIDS.

Leonard Gordon is Professor of Sociology and Chair of the Department of Sociology at Arizona State University. He recently completed a Rockefeller Foundation Bellagio Study Grant on cross-cultural racial and ethnic stereotyping analysis. His most recent writing includes articles on a half-century of stereotyping of blacks and Jews and on sociological expert witness in a case of collective interracial violence. He is cofounder of the Southwestern Urban Studies Research Group that plans to conduct omnibus state and metropolitan surveys.

Jeffrey K. Hadden is Professor of Sociology at the University of Virginia. He continues to conduct research in the role of televangelism and the New Christian Right as a political/social movement in the United States.

Gary G. Hamilton is Professor and Chair of Sociology at the University of California at Davis. His main interest is the study of East Asia. He has completed historical studies of Chinese commerce in the nineteenth century and is working on projects concerning the industrialization of East Asia.

Laurie Russell Hatch is Assistant Professor of Sociology at the University of Kentucky. Her research examines the influence of social status on attitudes and behaviors. She is conducting a longitudinal study of individuals' expectations and experiences in later life.

Kyle Kercher is Assistant Professor at Case Western Reserve University where he is doing research on subjective well-being as personality construct. He is also doing research on the relationship between age and criminal behavior.

Barrett A. Lee is Associate Professor at Vanderbilt University, specializing in Urban Sociology. He is conducting an NSF-sponsored study of neighborhood social networks with Karen Campbell. His other research interests include homelessness, community racial change, and residents' responses to urban growth.

Margaret Mooney Marini is Professor of Sociology at the University of Minnesota. She is researching gender differences in career processes and earnings and determinants of marital dissolution.

Robert F. Meier is Professor and Chair of the Department of Sociology at Washington State University. His research interests include processes of deviance and social control, criminology, and law. His recent writings include Crime and Society (forthcoming, Allyn and Bacon) and, with Marshall B. Clinard, *The Sociology of Deviant Behavior* (7th ed. forthcoming, Holt, Rinehart & Winston).

Rhonda J.V. Montgomery is Director of the Institute of Gerontology and Associate Professor of Sociology at Wayne State University. She has recently worked on research in health care, the family, and long-term health care issues. Planned research includes development of a model for decision making in nursing home placement.

Wilbert E. Moore was Professor Emeritus of Law and Sociology at the University of Denver. At the time of his death, he was working on a book with Joyce Sterling titled *The Rationalization of Law*. He passed away in December 1987.

Patricia M. Passuth is Assistant Professor of Sociology at Drexel University. Her research interests include aging and the life course, older women, and intergenerational relationships. Her current investigation is a longitudinal study of caregiving among members of three-generation families.

Kenneth C. Pike is a graduate student in the Department of Sociology at the University of Washington. His research interests include the impact of societal factors on attribution, distributive justice, and network analysis. He is currently investigating the impact of structural-cognitive factors on the legitimation of authority.

Thomas W. Pullum is Professor of Sociology and Research Associate of the Population Research Center at the University of Texas at Austin. His main interests and recent publications are in trends in fertility in developing countries and contextual effects on fertility in the United States. His current research concerns projecting the availability of kin for support of the elderly in the United States and Europe.

H. Laurence Ross is Professor of Sociology at the University of New Mexico. His current research is in prevention of alcohol-related problems, with a forthcoming publication examining policy alternatives in the area of drunk driving. He was recently a Fulbright lecturer in Finland and has written about the impact of policies there on alcohol and transportation.

Anson Shupe is Professor of Sociology and Chair of the Department of Sociology/Anthropology at Indiana University-Purdue University at Fort Wayne. His continuing research interest is sociology of social movements, especially religious movements. He has recently investigated televangelism, Mormonism, and new religions and is working on a publication about Mormonism and white-collar crime.

Lee E. Teitelbaum is Associate Dean and Professor of Law at the College of Law of the University of Utah. His current research concerns theory in family law and burdens of proof. Another major field of interest is careers of legal professionals.

Judith Treas is Professor of Sociology and Chair of the Department of Sociology at the University of Southern California. Her current research is in the demography of aging and international family relations with particular investigations of norms regarding public and family obligations for the young and the old in the changing family relationships of the aged in less developed countries. She is developing a transaction cost approach to family life.

Herman Turk is a Professor of Sociology at the University of Southern California. Seeking to improve the fit between selected general theory and quantitative methods, he is focusing on structural responsiveness and comparative social conflict in his research.

John Walton is currently Professor of Sociology at the University of California, Davis. His recent writings include an award-winning book, *Reluctant Rebel*. His current research includes a regional analysis of the Owens Valley dispute with the Los Angeles Water District.

NOTES

NOTES